BROKEN WINGS

BROKEN WINGS

The Hungarian Air Force, 1918-1945

Stephen Renner

INDIANA UNIVERSITY PRESS   *Bloomington & Indianapolis*

This book is a publication of

INDIANA UNIVERSITY PRESS
Office of Scholarly Publishing
Herman B Wells Library 350
1320 East 10th Street
Bloomington, Indiana 47405 USA

iupress.indiana.edu

The views expressed in this book are those
of the author and do not reflect the views
of the Department of Defense or any of its
components.

The paper used in this publication meets
the minimum requirements of the Ameri-
can National Standard for Information
Sciences—Permanence of Paper for
Printed Library Materials, ANSI
Z39.48-1992.

Manufactured in the United States of
America

Cataloging information is available from
the Library of Congress.

ISBN 978-0-253-02294-3 (cloth)
ISBN 978-0-253-02339-1 (ebook)

1   2   3   4   5   21   20   19   18   17   16

I will convince them of the tremendous importance of aviation to our country's reconstruction, and that without its development, a broken-winged Hungary will fall behind the other peoples of the world.

—COLONEL ISTVÁN PETRÓCZY, 1921

Contents

Acknowledgments

I must thank Professors Robert J. W. Evans and Sir Hew Strachan for their guidance, perceptive insights, and encouragement.

For his assistance on matters of style and grace, and for excising as many infelicities as possible, I shall always be grateful to my late friend Mr. Rodney Allan.

I could not have completed this book without the assistance of the archivists in Budapest: at the Defense Ministry Archives and Library, Mr. Balázs Kiss and Ms. Judit Hegedűs; at the National Archives, Ms. Ildikó Szerényi and Mr. Ádám Török; at the Transportation Museum and Archives, Mr. Sándor Krizsán. I am especially indebted to Professor Miklós M. Szabó (Lt. Gen., ret.), author of the best works on the Hungarian Air Force. Professor Szabó is a tireless correspondent and made time to meet me in Budapest. That meeting was facilitated by János Isaszegi, PhD (Maj. Gen., ret.), who also helped me with publications from Zrinyi Press. Colonel Greg Clawson and his wife Laura provided amazing hospitality during my trips to Hungary. Professor Eric Weaver of Debrecen University pointed me to critical sources and provided invaluable editorial assistance throughout the project. I thank my extraordinary friends, Szabolcs Takács and Andrea Szentendrei, whose calls and emails on my behalf are the least of their contributions.

The photographs are courtesy of Mr. Péter Zámbori (by way of Dr. Szabó), Mr. Dénes Bernád, various contributors to the Fortepan.hu online collection, and the Norsk Luftfahrtmuseum.

The faculty of the US Air Force School of Advanced Air and Space Studies have such enthusiasm for their work that I was inspired to join them. Professors Tom Hughes, Rich Muller, and Hal Winton have been particularly helpful with the thinking and writing; Professors Steve Chiabotti and Steve Wright and Ms. Sheila McKitt have been wonders of administrative support.

My parents, Gene and Ginny Renner, raised me with a love of reading, which has led indirectly to this project.

Finally, I thank my lovely wife, Jenny. For everything.

Note on Sources and Translation

Archival material for this book came primarily from the Hungarian Defense Ministry archives in Budapest. Most of the air force's own documents were destroyed in the Second World War, but sizable elements of the Defense Ministry and General Staff archives relate to aviation matters. The Defense Ministry archives also contain a number of unpublished manuscripts and memoirs. János Vesztényi's manuscript was extremely helpful, as was László Winkler's unpaginated scrapbook of documents, photographs, and press reports. In the Defense Ministry archives library can be found *Magyar Katonai Szemle*, the professional journal of the Honvédség, and the primary source for the discussion of air power theory in chapter 4. The Hungarian National Archives hold Admiral Horthy's papers, among which were his handwritten notes from the 1938 presentation on air force independence. The Hungarian Transportation Museum and Archives has valuable information on the Hungarian airlines and sport aviation. Other primary sources include various document collections of the Hungarian, German, and British Foreign Ministries, along with the printed confidential documents of Miklós Horthy. The destruction of the Royal Hungarian Air Force archives means that important operational details have been lost; in particular, those relating to logistics and intelligence, which would not have been addressed in General Staff or Defense Ministry records, and which might have seemed less important to memoirists or oral historians.

The most important secondary works on the Royal Hungarian Air Force have been authored by Dr. Miklós M. Szabó. His *Magyar Királyi Honvéd Légierő 1938–1945* is the best work on the subject, includes the major elements of his earlier work, and has extensive documentation. *Fejezetek a magyar katonai repülés történetéből*, coauthored by Szabó with S. Nagyváradi and L. Winkler, is the most useful guide to the early years of Hungarian military aviation; its reference notes are less complete than *Magyar Királyi Honvéd Légierő 1938–1945*, but it includes something rarely found in other Magyar books on the topic—an index. The journal *Hadtörténelmi Közlemények* carries the most relevant recent articles on military history. There are few English-language works on the Hungarian Air Force, and with the exception of the newly published *Baptism of Fire* by Csaba Stenge, those rely on personal reminiscences or German works. For the Habsburg aviation experience, the best work is the unwieldy but tremendously informative *Austro-Hungarian Army Aircraft of World War*, by Peter Grosz, George Haddow, and Peter Schiemer.

Memoirs play an important role in determining personal experiences and filling in crucial details, but due to the hyperpoliticization of Hungarian life in the twentieth century, they must be used with caution. Issues of motivation, both one's own and attribution to others, seem especially susceptible to post hoc revision. Works published in Hungary during the Communist period have the obligatory references to the "imperialists" and "counter-revolutionaries," but deeper biases exist as well. The Kassa bombing scarcely figures in pre-1990 journals in Hungary. Magyar-language works published by emigrants to the West have the same tendency toward self-justification, exacerbated by Cold War tensions.

For understanding Hungary's political situation in the period, C. A. Macartney's *October Fifteenth* and Gyula Juhász's *Hungarian Foreign Policy 1919–1945* were indispensable.

Unless otherwise noted, all translations from Hungarian are my own.

List of Abbreviations

AAA	antiaircraft artillery
AICC	Aeronautical Inter-Allied Commission of Control
BCR	Bombardement-Combat-Reconnaissance
CAM	Corpo Aeronautica Militare ([Italian] Military Air Corps)
DR.GY	Dunai Repülőgépgyár RT (Danubian Aircraft Factory)
DRT	Dél-olasz Repülő Tanfolyam (South Italy Flying Course)
FLIK	Fliegerkompagnie (Flying Company)
HFP	Hadsereg főparancsnokság (Army High Command)
HK	*Hadtörténelmi Közlemények* (*Military History Bulletin*)
HSR	Hungarian Soviet Republic
IMCC	Inter-Allied Military Commission of Control
JKRV	Jugoslovensko Kraljevsko Ratno Vazduhoplovstvo (Royal Yugoslav Air Force)
LA	Luftschifferabteilung (Airship Section)

Lepság	Légierő parancsnokság (Air Force Headquarters)
LF	Légügyi Főcsoportfőnökség (Air Chief Department)
LFT	Luftfahrtruppen (Aviation troops)
LHT	Legfelső Honvédelmi Tanács (Supreme Defense Council)
LÜH	Légügyi Hivatal (Aviation Bureau)
MAA	Militär Aeronautische Anstalt (Military Aeronautical Institution)
MAEFORT	Magyar Aeroforgalmi Részvénytársaság (Hungarian Air Traffic Company)
MÁG	Magyar Általános Gépgyár (Hungarian General Machine Factory)
MALERT	Magyar Légiforgalmi Részvénytársaság (Hungarian Air Transport Company)
MARE	Magyar Repülőgépgyár (Hungarian Aircraft Factory)
MASZ	Magyar Aero Szövetség (Hungarian Aero Club)
MÁVAG	Magyar Állami Vas-, Acél- és Gépgyárak (Hungarian State Iron, Steel, and Machine Factory)
MKHL	Magyar Királyi Honvéd Légierő (Royal Hungarian Air Force)
MKSZ	*Magyar Katonai Szemle* (*Hungarian Military Review*)
MLG	Motor-Luftfahrzeug-Gesellschaft (Aircraft Engine Company)
MWG	Magyar Waggon és Gépgyár (Hungarian Wagon and Machine Factory)

OLP	Országos Légvédelmi Parancsnokság (National Air Defense Headquarters)
RA	Regia Aeronautica ([Italian] Air Force)
RAF	Royal Air Force
RLM	Reichsluftfahrtministerium (German Aviation Ministry)
UFAG	Ungarische Flugzeugfabrik AG (Hungarian Aircraft Works Ltd)
VKF	Vezérkarfőnökség (Hungarian General Staff)
VR	Vörös Repülőcsapat ([Hungarian] Red Flying Corps)
WKF	Wiener Karosserie und Flugzeugfabrik (Vienna Chassis and Aircraft Factory)
WM	Manfréd Weiss

BROKEN WINGS

1

Legacy: 1811–1918

THE FIRST HUNGARIAN AVIATOR TOOK TO THE SKY ON June 3, 1811.[1] Dr. Károly Menner climbed into a basket suspended beneath a decorated fabric envelope on the outskirts of Pest, in a meadow that eighty-five years later would host the national millennial celebration.[2] By 1896, balloon flight had become sufficiently routine that, for the price of a single korona, a visitor to the Hungarian Millennium celebration in the Budapest city park could ride in a captive balloon to a height of 1,500 feet.[3] Franz Josef himself visited the exhibitions, and although he apparently did not chance a flight, some 7,000 of his subjects did.[4] Those Hungarians who took to the air with Monsieur Godard joined the growing number of aviation enthusiasts across Europe. Captive balloon rides were common at major expositions of the time: the 1893 Chicago World's Fair and Antwerp's 1894 Exposition featured them, as did the 1896 India and Ceylon Exhibition at Earls Court, and the Paris Exposition beginning in 1867.[5] Paris's precocity should be no surprise, since Frenchmen pioneered ballooning in 1783, and from the middle of the nineteenth century France "had total unsurpassed dominance in aviation."[6]

Despite Austria-Hungary's relatively late start (Italian, American, and Scottish aeronauts had flown as early as 1784), for the century following Dr. Menner's flight, Habsburg aviation kept pace with global advances and in some cases found itself on the leading edge.[7] As long as flight remained the province of visionaries and artisans, Austria-Hungary, blessed with superb technical universities and a small but highly skilled guild of craftsmen, held its own among the European powers. That ceased to be true in 1914, at the time when the world that awarded aviators cash prizes for feats of aerial navigation gave way to one in which airmen earned military honors for artillery observation. The advent of the First World War laid bare the monarchy's many structural problems that had been masked by the intellectual glitter of fin de siècle Vienna and Budapest. Austria-Hungary entered the Great War with an undersized air service that was starved of funds and plagued by inefficiency; supplied by an industrial base insufficient for mass production of aircraft; and directed by an acquisition policy that stifled competition and innovation. In the end, "the story of wartime Austro-Hungarian aviation is one of inadequacy and dependence upon Germany."[8]

Such judgments lay decades in the future, and indeed Germany did not yet exist as a united political entity when Austrian forces conducted the world's first aerial bombardment. Franz von Uchatius, a lieutenant in Marshal Radetzky's army besieging Venice in 1849, oversaw the construction and release of up to one hundred paper and linen balloons armed with fifty-pound bombs and delayed fuses.[9] The Austrians hoped the balloon-borne bombs "would devastate the city, and they also launched others from the deck of the side-wheel steamer *Vulcano*, the first use of offensive 'air power' from the sea." Unpredictable winds favored the Italians, however, and the balloons scattered, some of them falling among Austrian forces, who, fearing for their own safety, did not attempt further attacks.[10]

Although successful bombardment from aircraft would be delayed for half a century, the value of balloons as observation platforms was demonstrated during the American Civil War. The chief of the US Army Signal Corps lavished praise on an observer in a telegraph-equipped aerostat: "It may be safely claimed that the

Union army was saved from destruction . . . by the frequent and accurate reports." One year later, a similar Union observation balloon carried aloft on his first aviation experience a twenty-five-year-old Württemberg cavalry officer, Count Ferdinand von Zeppelin.[11] Zeppelin, whose airships later terrorized England on behalf of Imperial Germany, fought with the Habsburgs against Prussia in the 1866 Bruderkrieg (Brothers War). The Austrian army hastily formed an aviation unit when the Prussians approached Vienna, but the inexperienced ground crew lost the single balloon, putting an end to the experiment.[12] During the 1871 siege of Paris, balloons were pressed into service as transport, and successfully carried 1.5 million letters and 102 passengers out of the surrounded capital.[13] In the aftermath of its stunning defeat, the French army undertook serious reform. Among the initiatives was the establishment of a balloon section, the world's first permanent military aeronautics institution.[14] Great Britain followed the French example in 1882, as did Russia, Germany, Italy, and Spain two years later.

The first Austro-Hungarian balloon section was formed in 1893, although eight volunteer officers had received balloon training in 1890 from Viktor Silberer, a well-known Viennese civilian pilot.[15] The Militär Aeronautische Anstalt (MAA) was established at the Vienna Arsenal under the command of Lieutenant Josef Trieb, the first Habsburg military balloon pilot.[16] The section, initially composed of two officers and thirty men, was attached to the 1st Fortress Artillery Regiment and was considered an auxiliary to the garrison artillery.[17] The MAA acquired its first dedicated military balloon in 1896, a hydrogen-filled spheroid capable of tethered or free flight. Its next purchases would be the newly designed Parseval "sausage" balloons, whose streamlined shape was more stable and therefore could be operated in higher winds than the older round aerostats.[18] The Habsburg navy conducted annual exercises between 1902 and 1907 with one of the army's balloon sections, but after concluding that the practical problems of wind, storms, and corrosive salt water outweighed advantages in observation, discontinued the exercises and did not adopt balloons.[19] At the outbreak of the First World War, Austria-Hungary would have twelve balloon units in service: eight on the northern front and four in the south.[20]

That the balloon had some military utility was by the 1880s firmly established, but that utility was limited as long as the balloons remained at the mercy of the wind. During the 1871 siege, "though many balloons had flown *from* Paris, not a single attempt to fly a balloon *to* Paris had succeeded."[21] The first flight of a steerable airship took place in Paris in 1852, and experimentation continued with limited success for three decades before a true breakthrough occurred. In 1884, two French army officers piloted their 165-foot-long, streamlined, electrically powered airship, *La France*, on a twenty-three-minute flight and returned to the launch site, having completed the first powered flight in history. For a number of administrative and financial reasons, the men were unable to capitalize on their feat and produce a bigger, more capable airship.[22] In contrast to the semi-rigid, battery-powered *La France*, some inventors were pursuing rigid, petrol-engined designs. Among them was a Hungarian-born Croatian timber merchant turned self-taught airship designer named David Schwarz.

Schwarz envisioned a solid all-metal airship, which was a revolutionary departure from the fabric envelopes used by all other airship builders of the time. His critical contribution to the field was an enthusiasm for aluminum: his design used the new metal for both frame and skin. Aluminum had been discovered in 1827, and the first block fit for industrial use was offered at the 1855 Paris Exposition. Schwarz may have become familiar with its properties through a sawmill component, or perhaps only by reading available scientific literature; in any case he was convinced of aluminum's suitability for airship construction. Schwarz's proposal was rejected by Vienna, but the Russian attaché recommended him to St. Petersburg, where he eventually won a contract.[23] Although the resulting airship was not successful, his design brought him to the attention of the Prussian War Ministry, which granted him use of the Tempelhof balloon development facilities, to the chagrin of a competitor, Ferdinand von Zeppelin.[24] The fruit of Schwarz's collaboration with the German metallurgist Carl Berg finally flew in November 1897. Kaiser Wilhelm was present for the test flight, but Schwarz was not, having died earlier that year.[25] Due to the failure of a propeller belt, the airship crashed upon landing, and no further Schwarz models were built. Zeppelin, present at the demonstration and impressed by the aluminum frame, negotiated with Schwarz's widow for its rights, and thereafter incorporated the Schwarz-Berg aluminum body into his airships' designs.[26]

The growing capability of dirigible airships, particularly those of Zeppelin and the French brothers Paul and Pierre Lebaudy, led to increased interest on the part of military planners. By 1905, both the German and Italian armies were studying the airship's possibilities as a weapon; the French army had already acquired a Lebaudy dirigible and "had begun a variety of tests with the new airship, including its use for reconnaissance, for directing artillery fire, and for bomb dropping." There had been less enthusiasm for the airship in Britain, but French and German naval interest was contagious, and in 1909 the Royal Navy began to build its own dirigible.[27] The British aviation magazine *Flight* noted that 1908 German expenditures on aviation had amounted to nearly £400,000 (£265,000 of which came from private subscription). France had spent £48,000, while the United Kingdom allocated £5,270, slightly less than the £5,500 disbursed by Vienna.[28]

Some of the Dual Monarchy's aviation budget went to purchase the MAA's first airship, a Parseval-style blimp designated the Militärballoon Nr. 1, or M I.[29] The M I, 160 feet long and 30 feet in diameter, could carry six people at a maximum speed of 24 nautical miles per hour (knots).[30] During its acceptance trials, the M I made a seven-hour circuit from Vienna that included flight over Franz Josef's winter palace at Schönbrunn.[31] The monarchy's next airship purchase, a 230-foot Lebaudy (M II) with a semirigid keel, proved a disappointment and was retired after just two years. After cutting its teeth on German and French dirigibles, the MAA turned to domestic airships: first the Körting M III, similar in size to the Lebaudy but powered by two engines and 20 percent faster, and then the Bömches M IV, designed by an Austrian captain and presented to the air service as a gift. Though the M IV was smaller than its predecessors, its excessive operating costs soon drove it from active service.[32] As the Austro-Hungarian airship and balloon fleet grew, so did the command's conception of its possibilities, and organizational changes followed. In 1909 the MAA, at a strength of 14 officers, 28 noncommissioned officers, and 150 other ranks, was transferred from the Fortress Artillery Command to the Transport Troops Command, and two years later, in a move that reflected the emphasis on dirigibles, it was renamed the Airship Section (Luftschifferabteilung, LA).[33]

If the Lebaudy and Bömches airships failed to live up to the LA's expectations, the Körting M III exceeded them, logging more than 200 successful sorties in its first four years of flight.[34] Unfortunately, while on a photographic reconnaissance training mission near its base at Fischamend on June 20, 1914, the M III collided with a Farman biplane and was completely destroyed.[35] According to eyewitnesses cited in a contemporary press release, the Farman, piloted by an army lieutenant and with a naval officer on board, overtook the airship and flew around it several times before brushing the top of the M III's envelope. "The spilling gas burst into flame, a powerful explosion, after which both aircraft crashed." All seven men (four officers, two technicians and one engineer) on the Körting and both officers in the Farman were killed. Eyewitnesses described the airship descending slowly, wreathed in smoke, the remaining gas in the yet-unburned section of envelope restraining its fall, the crew's "horribly frightful death screams" (*iszonytatóan rémes halálordítása*) clearly audible. Although a 1907 balloon crash in Debrecen that killed thirteen (three officers—two French, one Habsburg—and ten peasants) took a larger toll in human lives, the very dramatic death of nine men of the air service, along with the destruction of the fleet's best dirigible, made this Austria-Hungary's worst aviation accident, and hastened the end of the empire's airship program.[36] The service had already mothballed the M IV due to its operating costs, and the realities of the tight LA budget could not be ignored. To one historian of Austro-Hungarian aviation, "it was soon apparent that the vast expense required to house and feed these unwieldy monsters would swallow the total funds allotted to military aviation."[37] In later years, the Germans would find that for the expense of a single Zeppelin they could have had thirty Albatros biplanes.[38] That was an opportunity cost the Habsburg air service simply could not afford. The Fischamend crash, although a human catastrophe, increased the LA's effectiveness in the long run by removing a substantial drain on the air service's resources and forcing it to focus on the heavier-than-air craft that would soon surpass airships in capability.

With Otto Lilienthal's death in an 1896 glider crash, European heavier-than-air aviation "had entered a steep decline nearly as precipitous as that which killed the German master."[39] In Lilienthal's homeland as well as in France, inventors turned "away from winged flight and towards the total embracing of lighter-than-air balloons, blimps and ultimately Zeppelins."[40] For a decade, nearly all substantial advances in airplane flight occurred in the United States. Not until 1906, three years after the Wright brothers' historic first flight at Kitty Hawk, did a European fly a heavier-than-air powered aircraft. Inspired by Alberto Santos-Dumont's success (he had previously been known for his small, highly maneuverable airships), Europeans took a renewed interest in airplanes, and over the next two years narrowed the gap opened by the Americans. Nonetheless, Wilbur Wright's 1908 aerial demonstrations in France amazed the public and silenced the doubters. Wright made a total of 113 flights without major incident, one of them lasting nearly two and half hours. American supremacy, while convincing, was fleeting: within a year of Wright's triumphant tour, Louis Blériot crossed the English Channel in a monoplane of his own design.[41] Perhaps

more impressive than the thirty-seven-minute flight is the degree
to which Blériot's craft, with its tractor engine, enclosed fuselage,
identifiable tail section with rudder, and wheeled undercarriage,
looks to the modern eye like a proper airplane.

Blériot's exploit mobilized air-minded Hungarians, and across
the country they began to build airplanes. Some were unwilling to
wait for a domestic industry to arise, and instead headed to France
to learn to fly. One of those early French-trained Magyar pilots, a
pharmacist named Ágoston Kutassy, returned home in his Farman
biplane and in 1910 earned the first Hungarian-issued pilot's license.
Blériot himself performed three aerial demonstrations in Budapest
in October 1909 that "dazzled" spectators and left a "tremendous
influence on the crowd."[42] On the former cavalry-training field at
Rákosmező where Blériot held his air show there soon appeared
numerous hangars. Among them could be found Dr. Kutassy's
Farman as well as János Adorján's homebuilt plane, which in January 1910 made the first flight of an aircraft designed and manufactured entirely within Hungary. Adorján's flight marks the birth
of the Hungarian aircraft industry, and Rákosmező airfield earned
the title "cradle of Hungarian aviation."[43] The birth may have been
met with joy by most of the family, but some members clearly
thought it overdue. After the incredible success of the 1909 Rheims
Aviation Week (some half a million visitors), in which seven of the
top eight prize winners were French (earning 137,000 francs),[44] one
Magyar wag displayed a characteristic combination of wit and
pique, as well as extensive knowledge of international aviators:

Repül a fecske, repül a gólya,	The stork flies, and the swallow,
Repül a franciák Blériotja.	So flies the Frenchman Blériot.
Repül a Paulhan, repül a Latham,	Paulhan flies, and so does Latham,
Warchalowski is repül már tán.	Warchalowski already can.
Repül a gólya, repül a fecske,	The swallow flies, and the stork,
A német sas, az olasz kecske,	The German eagle, Italian goat.
Csak a szegény magyar turul—	Only the poor Hungarian hawk—
gurul.[45]	walks.[46]

Hungarian patriots were not alone in their dismay at the French prowess on display at Rheims. Commenting on the "established fact" of the airplane's possibilities, David Lloyd George, the future prime minister, felt "as a Britisher, rather ashamed that we are so completely out of it." The German attaché reported to Berlin that "the French have made in a relatively short time enormous progress in the field of aviation technology."[47] Taken together, these three reactions reveal two important aspects of aviation in the first half of the twentieth century: first, the intensely nationalist feeling that flight engendered, and second, the rapid swings of ascendancy brought on by the speed of technological innovation. Airmen were already aware of the importance of aviation as an instrument of national prestige (and had a growing appreciation for its role in defense), but often that was tempered by a sense of kinship with other fliers regardless of citizenship. Aviation boosters who were not themselves pilots tended to emphasize the importance of national competition. The pace of innovation in the early years of heavier-than-air flight exacerbated these feelings. From the Wright brothers' flight until near the end of the Second World War, the lead in aviation technology changed hands frequently. Neither despair nor dominance lasted. In the first decade alone, leadership had swung dramatically from France to the United States and back. During the First World War, Germany, France, and Britain would each have periods of unmistakable technical mastery. The rate of technological change slowed immediately after the war, but no single country achieved sustained technological superiority until the United States did so in 1944.

Austria-Hungary entered a brief period of prewar prominence just as the nameless Magyar poet was lamenting its backwardness. The source of the prominence was the widespread acclaim met by the Taube, a "remarkably birdlike and attractive" monoplane designed by Igo Etrich, who began work on the craft as early as 1904 before achieving satisfactory flight control in 1910.[48] Etrich was an

Austrian student of Friedrich Ahlborn, a German professor who had made extensive studies of the *Zanonia macrocarpa* seed, the influence of which was clearly visible in the shape of the Taube's wings. More important than the Taube's provenance was its performance, which was exemplary in all regards, as it "coupled gentle flying characteristics with excellent stability and safety. Well-harmonized controls, a rugged structure, and a powerful Austro-Daimler . . . engine assured its success."[49] It could also be assembled in thirty minutes and taken apart in eight—a trait whose advantage now is hard to credit, but one that was critical in the days when the airplane was expected "to move with the Army train and reconnoiter in the manner of traditional cavalry employment."[50] The LA took delivery of twenty-nine Taubes between 1911 and 1913, and the aircraft was exported to Italy, Russia, Spain, England, China, and especially Germany, where Gotha and Rumpler built them in large numbers under license.[51] Both the German and Austro-Hungarian air services maintained Taubes in frontline units even in the early days of the First World War before relegating them to basic training service.[52] Germany had entered heavier-than-air flight late, and its initial attempts at aircraft development had been fraught with problems, which forced the government to consider both American and French machines before settling on the Austrian Taube for its earliest suitable military craft.[53] Thus at the very beginning of the military aviation relationship between Vienna-Budapest and Berlin, the technology transfer had gone from south to north. That would never again be the case.

Another important Austrian design went into production in the autumn of 1910. In contrast to the curvaceous single-wing Taube, the Pfeilflieger ("Arrow-Flier") was an angular biplane with distinctive sweptback wings. It was designed by an Austrian army officer and graduate engineer, Hans Umlauff von Frankwell, and was built in the Vienna factory of Jacob Lohner and Company, the same firm that produced the fuselages for Etrich's Taube. In June 1911, Umlauff won the Vienna-Budapest-Vienna racing prize in a

Pfeilflieger, and secured for Lohner a LA contract. Eventually 212 Pfeilfliegers of various versions were built, including six for export to Spain. Austro-Hungarian aviators soon began setting world speed and altitude records in their Lohner Taubes and Pfeilfliegers, such that in 1912 the Dual Monarchy, with eighteen world aviation records, trailed only France (45), and was ahead of Italy (11), the United States (8), Germany (5), and Britain and Belgium (1 each).[54] Too much could be made of this brief period in the forefront of aviation, but it does demonstrate a significant intellectual capacity for, and interest in, flight, and therefore points to material deficiencies to explain later failures and shortcomings.

The LA began procuring aircraft in 1909, a full year before Etrich introduced his Taube. Of the first five acquisitions, two were Farman-Voisin products, one a Wright Flyer, one a Blériot of the type demonstrated at Rákosmező, and one a domestic design by Hungarian engineer Sándor Svachulay. Three of the airplanes, like the Bömches M IV airship, were gifts from wealthy citizens.[55] Austrian officers Miescislaus Miller and Hans Umlauff, the first two Habsburg military pilots, had taken instruction on the Farman-Voisin. The Dual Monarchy's third army pilot (and first Magyar), Captain István Petróczy, learned to fly the Wright machine, and established the army's first flying school two years later at Wiener-Neustadt.[56] Conrad von Hötzendorf, the chief of the General Staff, became convinced of the advantages of aerial observation after a September 1910 flight with Adolf Warchalowski (becoming on that occasion perhaps the first army chief of staff of any nation to fly).[57] Conrad issued a staff directive the following month that called for an air force of 200 planes and 400 pilots. This force was to be distributed in pairs of aircraft to the General Staff, army, and corps headquarters, as well as to the forty-eight infantry regiments, while the four primary fortresses (Cracow, Przemysl, Pola, and Cattaro) would receive three planes each.[58] Conrad's "clear appreciation of the importance of aviation in a future war was influential in counteracting the conservatism of the War Ministry."[59] In addition to increasing the LA's funding he also initiated the domestic airplane competition in which the Taube made such an impression. Such full-throated support of aviation was unusual among contemporary chiefs of staff, but it should be remembered that Conrad was an avowed social Darwinist who campaigned ceaselessly for a preventive war against Serbia.[60] His embrace of air power might therefore have owed more to a general enthusiasm for war than to his shrewd perception of the efficacy of a new arm. Whatever his motivation, Conrad's 1910 directive was not realized. Four years later the Dual Monarchy entered the First World War with fewer than one hundred aircraft of all types.[61]

In France, meanwhile, the situation was very nearly reversed: even as some military intellectuals dismissed the airplane's potential, the army began to purchase them in large numbers. In 1910, Brigadier General Ferdinand Foch, then the commandant of the French staff college and later the supreme commander of Allied forces, observed an aerial display and was not impressed: "L'aviation pour l'armée, c'est zéro."[62] Nevertheless, the French army ordered more than 200 airplanes in 1910–1911, with plans to add 100 machines in the years 1913–1914 and 600 in 1915.[63] British producers continued to rely on French designs for inspiration and translated French aviation documents to keep abreast of current aeronautical trends. The degree to which French technology dominated British thinking is demonstrated by the Royal Aircraft Factory's type designations of B.E., F.E., and S.E., which stand for Blériot, Farman, or Santos Experimental.[64] Germany, whose early struggles with airplane design and fascination with dirigible airships stymied domestic production, started to make up lost ground, spending twice as much as Britain on military aviation in 1911–1912.[65] Italy established an aviation service in 1910 and appropriated 10 million liras (approximately £400,000) for its equipping. The tsar's brother-in-law founded the Committee for Strengthening the Air Fleet and organized Russian air forces along French and German lines, with an initial outlay of 900,000 rubles (£10,000).[66]

Public enthusiasm for flying grew faster even than government interest. It was estimated at the end of 1910 that there were 500 licensed pilots in the world. Of those licenses, the Aéro-Club de France had issued 345 (of which 272 were to French nationals, 27 to Russians, 19 to Britons, and the remaining 36 to citizens of 18 other countries).[67] The Deutschen Luftschiffer Verbandes, a distant second in pilot production, had certified sixty-three pilots by that time, and the Royal Aero Club forty-seven pilots.[68] Austria-Hungary had eighteen certified pilots, all of whom earned their licenses within the Dual Monarchy. Russia could boast of more licensed pilots, but had no domestic training establishment—all of its fliers were foreign-trained.[69] Two years later, nearly 2,500 certificates had been granted around the world, and although Austria-Hungary's share remained the same (91 pilots for 3.6 percent), Russia had also maintained its position (162 pilots, 6 percent), and Italy had grown its pilot corps from three in 1910 to 186 in 1912. The 1912 world records show a qualitative Habsburg edge over its future adversaries in both men and machines, but the large disparity in numbers of trained pilots should have alarmed the General Staff in Vienna.

During this time aircraft first participated in large-scale military maneuvers. In the September 1910 French army exercises, airships were grounded due to high winds, while airplanes managed to get airborne and were praised as "indispensable to armies as the cannons and the rifles."[70] British pilots flew in Indian maneuvers in 1911 and in the United Kingdom in 1912, in each case providing important intelligence about opposing units' dispositions. The Italians followed a similar scheme in their 1911 war games, each side having five airplanes, with a dirigible at the disposal of the general directing the exercise.[71] The Austro-Hungarian army first experienced airplane reconnaissance in its V Corps' 1911 autumn maneuvers, during which both military and civilian pilots took part, flying Etrich and Pischof machines. Despite the mountainous terrain and river fog in the Pilis hills north of Budapest, the "red" pilots were able to track the progress of "blue" forces attacking from Komárom. Their written observations, dropped into a meadow near the red force headquarters, proved crucial to the successful defense of a key Danube bridge. In the course of the exercises, the aircraft flew hundred-nautical-mile missions, and the M I Parseval airship stayed aloft five hours. These maneuvers demonstrated to the military leaders of Austria-Hungary the significance of the airplane and the necessity for attending to the further development of the air arm.[72] Implementation was not immediate, and X and XI Corps' exercises later in the month in the vicinity of Przemysl did not include an aviation component.[73]

Just weeks after the conclusion of the Habsburg maneuvers, Italy mobilized its embryonic air fleet for service against Ottoman forces in Libya. Nine aircraft (three Nieuport, two Taube, and two Blériot monoplanes, along with two Farman biplanes), eleven pilots and thirty enlisted men formed the initial cadre; three airships and additional aircraft and pilots arrived later (including a squadron of civilian fliers).[74] Italian aviators "immediately began to claim a number of 'firsts' in aerial warfare": the first combat reconnaissance missions, the first bombardment from an airplane (a Taube), as well as the first casualties from ground fire and the first captured airman.[75] The Italian General Staff was well aware that these were pioneering efforts. Its own summary report of the war praised the value of aerial reconnaissance and photography, and credited bombardment with "a wonderful moral effect," although it "did no material damage." "The value of this experiment," the report continued, "which Italy had the fortune to effect for the first time in history, will furnish a treasure for the future."[76] One officer who embraced that future was Giulio Douhet, a forty-year-old captain of artillery, who had predicted in 1909 that the air force would someday join the army and navy as an equal combatant.[77] In 1912 he was more emphatic: "A new weapon has come forth, the sky has become a new battlefield."[78] Italian leaders apparently agreed and began a rapid expansion of the air force. A national subscription

raised an additional three million liras (£130,000) for aircraft purchases, and by 1914 the Battaglione Aviatori had thirteen squadrons, two flying schools, and fourteen military airfields.[79]

Closer to the lands of the Dual Monarchy, the 1912–1913 Balkan
Wars provided additional, if somewhat less dramatic, examples of
the utility of air power. Neither side in the conflict had a substantial
air force, and most aircraft were French or German, as were many
of the pilots (joined by Britons, Russians, and Americans). Due to
technological constraints as well as moral scruple (the foreign pilots being in some cases unwilling to bomb), there was little offensive action or innovation. Nevertheless, the conflict gave "more
convincing evidence that aerial reconnaissance was of great benefit
in learning the enemy's dispositions and movements."[80]

The years 1911 to 1913 were a time of disruption in the senior
ranks of the Austro-Hungarian military establishment. In September 1911, Franz von Schönaich was replaced as minister of war by
Moritz von Auffenberg, and Conrad, chief of the General Staff
since 1906, was forced out in favor of Blasius von Schemua. The
proximate cause of Conrad's fall was his attempt to instigate a preventive war with Italy while Rome was preoccupied in Libya. Dismissed on December 2, 1911, Conrad was recalled by the emperor
only fifty-three weeks later.[81] In the midst of this turbulence, Major
Emil Uzelac, an engineer serving in the transport corps, was selected for promotion to lieutenant colonel and appointed head of
the LA. Uzelac, an "ideal choice to imbue the LA with substance
and character," was a bit of a character himself.[82] His own
origins—he was born in Komárom to an Orthodox smallholder
from Croatia—illustrate the ethnic variety of the Habsburg empire
as well as the opportunities available in its army to talented men of
any extraction. Uzelac learned to fly after taking command in April
1912, earning his pilot's certificate (Austria-Hungary's sixty-first)
in August of that year at the age of forty-five.[83] He became an accomplished and respected pilot and insisted on flying many of the
LA's new models himself before they reached operational units.

Table 1.1 Aviation spending, 1912–1914

	1912	1913	1914	3-year total	Population	Per million
Austria-Hungary	£13,400	£19,400	£67,700	£100,500	49.9	£2,000
Germany	£508,000	£2,011,200	£3,156,800	£5,676,000	67.0	£84,700
United Kingdom	£243,200	£551,300	£1,048,100	£1,842,600	46.4	£39,700
France	£1,359,800	£1,722,700	£1,953,500	£5,036,000	39.6	£127,200

Promoted to colonel in 1914 and brigadier general (*vezérőrnagy*) in 1918, he led the LA until being replaced in the closing weeks of the war.[84] The length of his tenure as Austria-Hungary's chief of the air service exceeded that of any other major combatants.

Although Uzelac was an energetic and capable leader, and Conrad a supportive chief of staff, Austria-Hungary's expenditures on military aviation in the years immediately preceding the First World War were dramatically lower than those of other major European powers.[85] As Table 1.1 shows, the population of the Dual Monarchy was 26 percent larger than that of France, but France spent fifty times more on military aviation than the Habsburgs (more than sixty times per person). The government in Vienna even declined to lend its support to the Austrian Air Fleet Fund, a civilian revenue-generating scheme copied from the successful German effort that raised 7 million marks (£340,000) for military aviation from 1912 to 1914.[86] German outlays brought the two future Central Powers nations to near parity with Great Britain and France, but the enormous discrepancy between spending in Vienna and Berlin was a precursor of future wartime dependency.

The Habsburg parsimony extended well beyond aviation to all areas of the armed forces, and "in the years before 1914 Austria-Hungary gradually dropped behind her competitors."[87] Russia, for example, had trebled its military expenditures from 1871 to 1914, while the Dual Monarchy's spending had only doubled. "Romania, with a population of seven and a half millions, most of whom lived in abject poverty, provided almost as much money for her armed forces as Hungary, with a population three times as great as that of Romania, did for the Common Austro-Hungarian Army."[88] The Hungarian parliament in fact refused to pass laws approving credits and increasing recruitment for the Common Army until Magyar became the language of command for regiments raised from Hungarian lands, and until the Honvéd was permitted its own artillery units. The pro-Habsburg orientation of Franz Josef's army is well established, and its role in holding together the fragmenting monarchy is not in doubt.[89] Among many Hungarians, however, the army was unpopular, a "remnant of royal absolutism [that] contradicted the spirit of dualism and the country's Hungarian character."[90] Parliamentary opposition to the increased military budget was overcome only in June 1912, when István Tisza, then speaker of the national assembly, "ordered the parliamentary guard to escort recalcitrant MPs from the debating chamber and got the government majority to vote through the program."[91] The new army bill would not take effect until 1915, which meant the Dual Monarchy went to war with a force whose size was constrained by an 1889 law. In terms of raw manpower, Austria-Hungary fielded 2.3 million men in 1914, while France, with 10 million fewer inhabitants, put nearly 4 million in uniform.[92] Nor could Vienna hope to make up with firepower what it lacked in soldiers: "the Austro-Hungarian army was the most under-gunned in relation to its (already inferior) strength of any army in Europe."[93] It was also the most "underplaned," with only fifty-three frontline aircraft in both the army and navy.[94] In contrast, Germany fielded 232 combat machines, and among the Allies, France had nearly 300, Russia 190, and Britain more than 90.[95]

An exceptionally well-managed acquisition process would have made the most of the few koronas available for aircraft purchases and, given the high standard of Austro-Hungarian aviation technology in 1912, might have made the numerical gap less significant than it seemed. Unfortunately for the Dual Monarchy, its aviation

procurement was marred by mistakes and inefficiencies at nearly
every turn. After the early success with the Taube and Pfeilflieger,
the War Ministry decided to order, at least temporarily, exclusively
from Lohner. This "grievous lack of judgment" put Lohner in a position of monopoly and forced smaller firms (such as Autobiplan
Werke, the builder of the Pischof planes that flew well in the 1911
maneuvers) out of business. The dwindling opportunities in
Austria-Hungary also caused a minor brain drain, as many engineer graduates of Vienna's Technische Hochschule sought work
abroad.[96] As long as peace prevailed and the Lohner airplanes continued to perform well, the effects of the monopoly remained hidden. An investigation that followed the crash of a new Pfeilflieger in
the spring of 1914 revealed that Lohner's wings were understrength,
and that the LA's entire fleet required retrofitting. Lieutenant Colonel Uzelac blamed complacency for Lohner's mistake and claimed
they employed "shoddy and primitive design practices" when compared to German and British firms he had visited. With its air force
grounded, "the war ministry had no choice but to reverse its policy
and permit the establishment of German-owned companies in
Austria-Hungary." Albatros and Aviatik quickly set up subsidiaries
in Vienna, and Deutsche Flugzeug Werke founded the Lloyd factory
outside Budapest. Austrian financier Camillo Castiglioni, a major
investor in Lohner, bought Igo Etrich's Brandenburg company, the
first of many acquisitions that would eventually give him enormous
power over Austro-Hungarian aircraft production.[97]

     While Uzelac's description of the "shoddy and primitive" work
on the Pfeilfliegers was undoubtedly accurate at the time, it was not
a fair characterization of all Habsburg aviation handiwork, the
quality of which was generally quite high.[98] That Austro-Hungarian
aviation industrial policy was a marvel of inefficiency, however, is
absolutely clear. Throughout the war Vienna consistently overestimated its ability to produce aircraft and underestimated the resources required to achieve its unrealistic goals. At the beginning
of the war, the LA's commander had estimated that domestic in-

dustry would need to produce forty-six aircraft per month by the end of the year. Even with the new factories, only sixty-four planes were built from August to December 1914. German imports added forty-eight machines to the inventory, but still the increase did not meet the LA's need. Uzelac then raised his estimate to sixty per month, but saw deliveries decline from twenty-four to seven aircraft per month due to the introduction of new types.[99] Austria-Hungary's aircraft industry expanded from 218 workers in August 1914 to 5,983 in January 1917, an increase of 2,600 percent, but demand continued to outstrip supply. After the Aviation Department successfully appealed to the War Ministry for exemptions from service for some critical workers, it still received less than 60 percent of the requirement, and many of those craftsmen were not suited to their tasks. Machinists capable of precise work found themselves assigned to mass production in munitions factories even as less-skilled lathe hands labored to build engines. "Skilled furniture makers and carpenters passed their time in frontline companies 'making ingenious war mementos to amuse themselves' while the aircraft industry had to utilize ordinary carpenters for extremely intricate work."[100] Production efficiency did increase over the course of the war as a result of greater standardization and experience, but through 1918 Austro-Hungarian firms required twice as many employees to build an aircraft as in German factories (thirty-nine versus nineteen).[101] With nearly one-fifth of its population—almost all the men aged eighteen to fifty-three—under arms, the Dual Monarchy could ill afford this level of inefficiency, but the relative lack of mechanization required skilled labor.[102]

Elements of Vienna's commercial policy exacerbated the existing problems of an underdeveloped industrial sector, increasing scarcity of natural resources, and deficiencies in labor. One of the most troubling aspects was the encouragement or tolerance of monopoly. After suffering the consequences of its decision to award an exclusive contract to Lohner in 1914, the War Ministry, by not acting to stop mergers and buyouts, was faced in 1916 with a cartel that was largely immune to government pressure. Domestic industry's inability to supply the Luftfahrtruppen (LFT, as the LA became known in July 1915) with sufficient aircraft forced Austria-Hungary to rely on German machines. The German government was naturally concerned with its own aircraft needs and permitted only a small number of companies to export planes to the Dual Monarchy, most notably Brandenburg, Fokker, Rumpler, Albatros, and Aviatik (the last two of which also had licensed production factories in Austria-Hungary).

Brandenburg was by far the biggest exporter, delivering more aircraft to Vienna in the war's first two years (243) than all other German firms combined.[103] After October 1915, it was in the hands of Camillo Castiglioni, whose involvement with Habsburg aviation dated back to 1909, when his trading company, Motor-Luftfahrzeug-Gesellschaft (MLG), brokered the LA's purchase of the M I and M II airships. MLG later bought the Austrian patent rights for Etrich's Taube and secured global sales rights for Lohner's products. Lohner and Castiglioni, along with a pair of Hungarian firms, Ganz and Manfréd Weiss (WM), also founded Ungarische Flugzeugfabrik AG (UFAG), the first aircraft factory in Hungary, which became the Dual Monarchy's second-largest aircraft producer. Austria-Hungary's most productive company was the local branch of Albatros, which, after its purchase by Castiglioni in early 1917, changed its name to Phönix. By March 1917, the Castiglioni conglomeration of Brandenburg, Phönix, and UFAG had produced half of all the Dual Monarchy's aircraft.[104] Brandenburg's importance to the LFT had already given Castiglioni leverage to "dictate comparatively high prices to the Austro-Hungarian Army, which had no choice but to pay them," and UFAG was able to squeeze a price increase of nearly 60 percent from the navy.[105] The navy staked its hopes in 1918 on new types from the Castiglioni concerns, but after the failure of a 350-horsepower flying boat, had no new aircraft models to meet the Italian threat in the Adriatic. Meanwhile, Castiglioni further strengthened his position early that year by acquiring Bayerische Motoren Werke. In the wake of a rumored consolidation of all Habsburg aviation industry under a single head, Uzelac requested that Castiglioni, then in possession of a navy deferment, give up control of his companies and "be immediately inducted and sent to a service post, for example, with the eastern corps in Palestine, that hinders any commercial transactions with the rear."[106] Nothing of the sort occurred, and the Castiglioni cartel did not prove fatal to the LFT. In fact its constituent firms produced some very fine products for the air service. The role of Brandenburg in keeping the Habsburg air troops aloft in 1915 cannot be denied. But the cost was high, not only in the actual prices the firms exacted from the ministry, but also in missed opportunities for promotion of other designs and developers, and in the damaging failure to deliver the navy's flying boat. The War Ministry awoke too late to the dangers of centralized ownership, and then directed an emotional and ineffective personal attack on Castiglioni.

Each of the major combatants approached the problem of aircraft production differently. France, befitting its position as the world's major aviation power, encouraged creativity among its designers and, as a result, had the greatest diversity of types. That approach sacrificed efficiency but gained ability to hedge against obsolescence. French engines—rotary, radial, and in-line—powered the Allies. Britain favored fewer designs and standardized production centered at Farnborough, an approach nearly the opposite of the French, but one that suited a relative latecomer with enormous experience in mass production. Germany also limited production types but did not insist on interchangeability between private companies and therefore did not reap the full benefits of standardization.[107] Austria-Hungary, after early attempts to choose single types for production proved problematic, was obliged to accept whatever designs could be manufactured and delivered in quantity, however insufficient.

Austria-Hungary's limited industrial base and small air service fleet magnified any acquisition errors, because it did not possess

the requisite reserves in either capacity or inventory to cushion
falls. After Italy entered the war in 1915, LFT requirements spiked.
At the same time, the rugged conditions on the Italian front exposed the inadequacies of earlier domestic designs, and forced the
Dual Monarchy to rely on Brandenburg imports. In an effort to
direct and improve Austro-Hungarian production, the LFT placed
orders for an untested biplane designed by Professor Richard Knoller
of the Vienna Technical University. Four domestic factories, Lohner,
Aviatik, Phönix, and Wiener Karosserie und Flugzeugfabrik (WKF),
were directed to build the Knoller craft. "Hamstrung from the start
by a conflicting chain of command, diffused responsibility, and
inept engineering, the Knoller program became a major scandal
and a vituperative political affair."[108] One hundred eighty-four aircraft were produced in the fiasco, few of which ever flew, at a tremendous cost in money, time, and diversion of resources. The incident tarnished Knoller's reputation and made it difficult for his
university research center to gather, analyze, and distribute technical reports.

The dynamics of a small fleet also made anticipating obsolescence and preparing aircraft replacements more critical and difficult. Existing contracts on operational aircraft would sometimes
be canceled to make way for more advanced designs, which often
failed to meet expectations. By the time production had been resumed on the proven craft, its technology was even farther behind.[109]
This phenomenon was by no means restricted to Austria-Hungary,
but without the depth of German production, the variety of France,
or the standardization of Britain, it was far more damaging to its
aviators. An anonymous letter to the war minister in 1916 illustrated
the destructive effects of these reactive procurement policies coupled with excessive fear of enemy bombers:

> The initial, mostly accurate reports concerning the superior qualities of
> enemy bombers were accepted as fact with no attempt at verification. This
> led to a precipitous rush to issue production orders—generally incapable
> of being fulfilled—to the detriment of normal supply. Priority contracts,

at unreasonably high cost, were awarded to many factories. The capture of
a Caproni had a sobering effect: further development was neglected and
interest waned. The bombers, rushed to completion are now stored at
Aspern (Brandenburg, Lloyd) or lie incomplete at factories (Aviatik,
Lohner, Öffag and Phönix). No one of authority cares a whit about them.
Frontline requests are passed off with excuses. Not a single test has been
performed to finally bring the bombers to the Front.[110]

The bombers in question never reached full operational capability,
although Gotha did supply thirty-nine twin-engined G.IVs for
bombing missions in 1918.[111]

The final production tallies show that Austria-Hungary's aircraft factories fell far short of those of the other major European
combatants. The incredible disparity manifested in prewar expenditures was reduced, but not nearly enough. Austro-Hungarian firms
built 5,181 airplanes during the war, while Germany produced
roughly 46,000. Great Britain led the Allies with 54,000 airframes,
France made 52,000 (but over twice the number of engines as Britain), and Italy contributed an additional 12,000 machines. Using
the population figures cited above, Austria-Hungary produced 101
aircraft per million people; Germany 676 per million. Italy constructed 3.5 times as many planes per capita as the Dual Monarchy,
and British and French fabrication rates were approximately twelve
times that of Austria-Hungary.[112] Habsburg production of other
weapons also trailed the other major powers, but by a smaller margin than its aircraft production. For instance, Austro-Hungarian
firms (primarily Škoda) made 225 artillery pieces per million
people, while Italy produced 338 per million (only 50 percent more,
or one-seventh the disparity in aircraft production). British and
French munitions plants created only twice as many cannon per
capita as did Austria-Hungary (one-sixth the difference in airplanes).[113] One could conclude from this disparity that the Habsburg
General Staff was more resistant to innovation and failed to embrace air power, but Conrad's 1910 expansion of the LA and the
appointment and subsequent support of the able Uzelac suggest

otherwise. A more plausible explanation can be found in the relative complexity and novelty of the weapons: artillery, although a critical component of modern warfare, was considerably less complicated to design and produce than aircraft; was a more stable technology; and the empire had a long history of manufacturing its own guns. Airplanes, on the other hand, were new, technologically volatile, and required nimble manufacturing processes to avoid obsolescence.

If Austro-Hungarian aircraft manufacturing and procurement were far behind the other combatants, the organization of its air service was on lines very similar to leading European powers. The French escadrille was the archetype, "built around six aircraft and their crews, a force that prewar maneuvers had seemed to indicate was adequate to supply the reconnaissance needs of an army corps."[114] German Feldflieger Abteilungen conformed to the French model, while the British doubled the number of aircraft in their squadrons because of a lack of experienced officers for command. Uzelac also settled on six airplanes (plus two in reserve) as the number for his Fliegerkompagnien (fliks), when in July 1914 the LA "converted the pre-war, static Flugparks into mobile combat units."[115] Within the first three months of the war, fifteen fliks had been created.[116] The six-aircraft flik remained the basic combat unit for the entire war, but units became increasingly specialized as air power matured. After the first fifty fliks were activated as reconnaissance units, flik 51 began its service in summer 1917 as a fighter unit. Bomber fliks soon followed, and after a 1918 reorganization, the LFT comprised seven types of Fliks: D-fliks, general purpose units that reported to army divisions; F-fliks, for long-range reconnaissance; G-fliks, equipped with multiengined bombers (Grossflugzeug); J-fliks, the fighter (Jagd) units; K-fliks, for corps-level reconnaissance (of which few were formed); P-fliks, for photo reconnaissance; and Rb-fliks, equipped with automatic cameras for strip photography (Reihenbild).[117] This reorganization amounted to an intellectual recognition of the distinct forms of air power, but came too late to have any real effect. Even in August 1918, most (fifty-one) fliks were D-fliks; ten were F-fliks, thirteen J-fliks, and five G-fliks.[118] By war's end however, all of the D-fliks had been converted into specialized companies (some had become Schlacht-Fliks executing rudimentary close air support). Reconnaissance remained the LFT's primary mission, with thirty-eight of the final seventy-seven fliks devoted to corps, photo, or long-range reconnaissance.[119]

In this development, the Habsburg air service followed the trend in the other combatants' air forces. In 1914, all operational military aircraft were devoted to reconnaissance. By the summer of 1915, 10 percent of the planes were fighters. The next year the percentage of reconnaissance craft had fallen to 51, fighters had climbed to 42 percent, and bombers accounted for the rest. In 1917, the proportion of reconnaissance units remained constant, while fighters dropped to 30 percent, with bombers and "battle planes" devoted to ground support, each making up approximately 10 percent of the forces. The war's final year saw a slight decrease in the number of reconnaissance craft and a commensurate rise in fighters, but no significant change in bombers or strike planes.[120]

When Austria-Hungary began mobilizing in July 1914, aviation units were first sent to the Serbian front, although the Russian front eventually received the preponderance of forces. Two fliks had departed from Austria for the south, and two were activated near the front itself (at Mostar and Újvidék) before any LA units headed east. As a result of Conrad's strategic indecision, Fliks 1 and 5 were redirected to the Russian front within days; in the case of Flik 1, without having flown a single operational sortie in the south. Flik 7, the first on the Russian front, was activated at Cracow on August 6, 1914. It was eventually joined by nine others, so that at the end of 1914 there were ten fliks serving in the east and four in the Balkans.[121]

It appears that LA aerial reconnaissance did not play a significant role in the early fighting against Serbia, but there were a few examples of successful air attacks. Habsburg aviators (it is unclear if they were LA or Seefliegerkorps crews) struck one of the war's first offensive aerial blows on August 15, 1914, against Montenegrin gun emplacements at Lovćen, a 5,800-foot-high mountain over-looking the Austro-Hungarian naval base at Cattaro.[122] No damage to the guns was recorded (they were eventually destroyed by naval gunfire), but the attempt shows an understanding of the potential of aerial bombardment and a spirit of innovation among Austro-Hungarian fliers. The Lovćen attacks were conducted with primitive bombs that had match-lit fuses, and one Austrian plane was nearly destroyed when the pilot dropped the bomb after lighting it and saw it roll under his seat. He was able to retrieve it and toss it overboard, where "it burst only a few hundred feet below him."[123] The pilot, Lieutenant Adolf Heyrowsky of Flik 2, was undeterred by this mishap. In September, he and his observer, flying in a German-built Aviatik B.I, destroyed a pontoon bridge at Kupinovo, "thereby cutting off a few thousand Serbian troops who were taken prisoner."[124] The Serbian campaign showed that the rigors of active operational flying were too much for the aged Taubes, and they were quickly removed from frontline service.[125] In the war's second year, observation crew performance improved, and their value to the army commanders increased. Aerial reconnaissance missions around Belgrade provided detailed sketches of Serb artillery positions, which enabled accurate counterbattery fire and contributed to the successful siege of the capital.[126]

The impact of aerial reconnaissance was mixed on the Russian front as well. There were, to be sure, instances of individual bravery and initiative. Fliers from Fliks 5 and 11 flew at extremely low altitudes in order to draw Russian fire that would reveal enemy positions and strength.[127] Unfortunately for Conrad and his army commanders, and in spite of such efforts by some Habsburg airmen, the LA failed to account for all the Russian forces in Galicia (the Austro-Hungarian cavalry fared no better). In late August 1914, Conrad's initial plan for a cautious movement to the Vistula had become instead an attempt at an envelopment of the tsar's forces in Poland.

His staff estimated fairly accurately the size of the Russian armies—about fifty divisions—but could not pin down their locations. A concentration to the north around Brest-Litovsk would make Conrad's pincer movement viable, so he trusted information that confirmed this wish. And when "aerial reconnaissance reported that there were no major Russian formations on the roads between the line Proskurov-Tarnopol to the north and the River Dniester to the south," Conrad's course was set.[128] Undetected, however, were the Russian and Third and Eighth Armies, "advancing from the east, marching by night but protected by the woods from overhead observation by day."[129] Those armies proved critical to blunting the Austro-Hungarian offensive in Galicia, and later formed part of the Russian force that besieged Przemysl.

That the LA was not able to find the tsarist armies should not necessarily be attributed to incompetence. The Russians had learned the importance of concealment from aerial observation in the first days of the war, German aircraft having begun reconnaissance flights over Russia as early as August 2. Movement at night and exploitation of overhead cover were the first of many tactics employed by land forces to negate aerial observation. Those countermeasures notwithstanding, German airmen were able to follow the progress of the Russian and First and Second Armies, which kept their own aircraft in reserve. Even when Russian planes were aloft, Russian commanders rarely trusted their observations. This decided advantage in aerial reconnaissance certainly contributed to the tremendous German victory at Tannenberg. At this time, the Central Powers' air services were similarly organized, trained, and equipped. But the Russians' rapid adoption of deception tactics made for a significant difference in the effectiveness of German and Austro-Hungarian air power in the first battles in the east. The German experience resulted in the high command's fervent embrace of aerial observation, and led Hindenburg to declare, "Ohne Flieger kein Tannenberg!"[130] Conrad spread blame for the Austro-Hungarian defeat liberally (his allies, his staff, his intelligence services), so the LA did not suffer in relation to the other arms, but neither was it able to capitalize on the promise showed by aerial reconnaissance in the prewar maneuvers.[131]

The LA did deliver in other trying circumstances on the Russian front. In a development that called to mind 1871 Paris and presaged the airmail boom of the 1920s, the planes of Fliks 11 and 14 made fourteen mail-carrying flights from Przemysl in the course of its four-month siege (balloons from the fortress balloon section were also used, as were homemade balloons). All but one successfully reached Austro-Hungarian lines.[132] The flights transported military dispatches as well as postcards and letters. This liaison function was especially critical since all ground communication with the fortress had been severed since early November, and the defenders relied on wireless telegraphy for contact with higher headquarters. Allied press agencies noted this use of air power, although they overestimated the frequency of the flights. The *Daily Telegraph* reported that "communication between the fortress and the Austrian lines seems to have been maintained almost daily by means of aviators, who kept up a regular post, taking out letters and bringing back as much stores as their machines could carry."[133] In fact, the flights averaged only one per ten days of the siege. When Przemysl fell to Russian forces on March 22, 1915, over 130,000 Austro-Hungarians surrendered, including elements of Flik 11.[134] A contemporary Hungarian magazine included the number of cannon lost ("1,050 of all calibers, for the most part completely obsolete, 1865 and 1875 patterns, which in any case were blown up"), but did not mention captured aircraft.[135] Presumably the fliks destroyed their aircraft before they fell into Russian hands.

The air war on the Eastern Front progressed at a much slower pace than in the west. In the east, the forces committed were smaller, they were dispersed over a wider area, and technological improvements tended to originate in the west. The lower density of forces meant that aerial combat occurred much less frequently in the east. Thus the Luftstreitkräfte (German air force), the only air service to field major forces on both fronts, sustained only 189 of its 3,128 total aircraft losses in the east, and counted just 358 Eastern Front kills among the 7,425 credited to its fighter pilots.[136] Since air-to-air engagements largely drove the air services' requirements for higher performance aircraft, the relative lack of these engagements contributed to the slower rate of innovation. Obsolescence came more slowly in the east, and older aircraft remained viable weapons long after they had been abandoned in the west. This did not mean that flying was easier on the Eastern Front. The larger area and more dispersed formations required airmen routinely to operate farther away from their aerodromes, which placed a premium on both navigation skills and mechanical reliability. "A French pilot who flew with the Russians in the Carpathians said that he reacted with 'intense stupefaction' when he discovered that his airfield was 80 kilometers from the front lines. Each mission thus entailed a flight of 200 kilometers 'in a glacial cold' unknown in France."[137] Just as the Habsburg aviators were settling into difficult but somewhat stable air wars in Russia and the Balkans, Italy joined the war against the Central Powers. Aerial combat over the Dolomites promised to be a combination of fighting on the Eastern and Western Fronts: environmental conditions equal to the worst previously encountered—rugged mountains, harsh weather, airfields too few and too small—as well as the prospect of up-to-date Allied fighters.

Italy fielded in May 1915 a Corpo Aeronautica Militare (CAM) of 169 aircraft (including 19 seaplanes of the naval section), primarily prewar French designs. That put Italy, entering a one-front war, at rough numerical parity with the Dual Monarchy, whose "air service consequently faced opposition on three fronts with a production base inadequate for one."[138] Austria-Hungary's domestic production and German imports made good on operational losses, but were not sufficient for creating new fliks for the Italian front. The first unit active in the southwest was Flik 8, pulled from Galicia on May 13, 1915 and sent to defend the naval base at Pola in anticipation

Figure 1.1. A LFT Fokker B.I on the Italian front in 1915. Photo: Fortepan/ György Punka.

of hostilities in the Adriatic. Other fliks moved from the Serbian front (2 and 4) or were converted from training companies (12).[139] By the end of 1915 the LFT had seven fliks serving in operations against Italy, three against Serbia, and eight against Russia.[140]

Operations on the Italian front began, as in the east, as observation missions, and eventually grew to encompass the entire range of air warfare: offensive and defensive fighter sweeps, air interdiction, close air support, and strategic bombing. Austro-Hungarian airmen had conducted small-scale aerial attacks intermittently since the Lovćen raid in the war's earliest days, but had not yet attempted long-range, multiship attacks, lacking both rationale and equipment. By mid-1915, the Italians had both. Giulio Douhet, the Italian officer who was an early air power proponent, had been promoted to colonel and was convinced that aerial bombardment offered a path to victory that would avoid the human wastage he was witnessing in the bitter Alpine warfare. Through his interest in aviation he had come to know Giovanni Caproni, a young airplane designer. Caproni had begun work in 1910 on large cargo aircraft before turning his hand to building bombers, and his aircraft equipped the Italian air service's first bomber squadron.[141] On August 20, 1915, the CAM launched its first raids against Austria-Hungary. Many more were to follow. The Douhet-Caproni partnership was responsible for the increasingly powerful three-engine bombers that attacked targets in Austria-Hungary in formations of up to thirty-six machines.[142] Italian forces with their superior airplanes ultimately bombed Habsburg cities on 254 occasions, while the LFT, flying less capable aircraft but aided by the geographical proximity of Italian cities to the front, managed 503 raids.[143]

The first of these targeted Venetian port facilities. A viable multiengined bomber was not available to the LFT until Gotha G.IVs arrived from Germany in 1918, so Austro-Hungarian bombing missions were generally conducted by the versatile two-seat B- or C-type reconnaissance planes. These single-engine craft ranged as far as the west coast of Italy, striking Spezia, Genoa, and, most dramatically, Milan. On February 14, 1916, a force of ten Lohner and Lloyds from Fliks 7, 16, and 17 launched from airfields around Trento for the 240-mile flight over the mountains and Lombard plain. In spite of Italian antiaircraft artillery (AAA) and attempts at fighter interception, all the LFT planes dropped their 150-pound bomb loads and returned safely to their bases.[144] This attack, fifteen months before the first raid on Britain by German airplanes, may have been the first strategic bombardment carried out by heavier-than-air craft.[145] One of the observer/bombardiers, a Magyar lieutenant from Transylvania, recounted the raid for *Csíki Lapok*, his hometown newspaper. During the approach to the city, a sudden change in the wind ruined his aim and forced the flight to turn around for another attempt at bomb release: "Once more here is the target. I wave: a little left, a little back to the right; I aim—now! Away with all five [bombs]. One spot is already covered in smoke. Something burns. I see four explosions from mine. They are in a good place."[146]

A *Daily Telegraph* reporter described the reaction of the Milanese to their first aerial attack:

> Firemen galloped through the town warning the inhabitants, most of whom, however, even after the anti-aircraft guns had begun sending shells into the sky, failed to realize the danger. The appearance of a number of Italian airplanes, which were gradually circling to the height of the assailants, gave the impression to the vast majority of the spectators in the streets that only aerial defense practice was in progress. Soon, however, the bombs dropped by the Austrian machines . . . revealed the real nature of their attack, but this hardly prevented the crowds satisfying their curiosity and standing in the streets and public squares to watch the progress of the aerial battle, which at a certain moment was of thrilling intensity.[147]

Twelve people, including two children, were killed in the attack. There was no damage reported to military installations, nor was there widespread panic among the population. The CAM retaliated four days later with a raid on Ljubljana by seven Capronis, one of which was seriously damaged by a LFT fighter.[148] Subsequent Austro-Hungarian bombing missions had some tactical success (one raid sank a British submarine in port at Venice), but most of the damage was to noncombatants, including ninety-three killed in a casemate in Padua—"the worst incident involving civilians taking shelter from an air raid during the entire course of the First World War."[149]

After months of reciprocal city bombing (more than 400 Italians died in Austro-Hungarian air raids on towns), the new Habsburg emperor Charles I prohibited bombardment that could endanger civilians or cultural landmarks.[150] Italian authorities did not extend the same consideration to Austrian landmarks, but they were concerned about civilian casualties—as long as the civilians were ethnic kin. "The *Italianità* of Venezia Giulia, Istria, Dalmazia and the Trentino prevented us from making the cities our targets and limited the objectives to those of strictly military nature," in the words of one Italian general.[151] Despite this restraint, the CAM bombed Trieste, Ljubljana, and Innsbruck. To defend against in-

creasing Italian attacks on lines of communication, the Dual Monarchy fielded AAA and a rudimentary air raid warning system that
also covered major cities far behind the front.[152]

The shortcomings of the early-warning system were made evident on August 9, 1918, when an air defense supervisor in the Graz
district took more than two hours to inform his superiors of a
squadron heading northeast. Defensive pursuit planes took off
from Wiener-Neustadt too late to intercept the intruders: Italy's
87th Squadron was already bombarding Vienna with half a million
propaganda leaflets. This raid was the brainchild of Gabriele
D'Annunzio, a "legendary poet-adventurer" who flew on the mission in a two-seater and personally composed one of the propaganda messages.[153] The mission over Vienna "electrified the
world," but it was only the most audacious element of a robust Italian airborne propaganda campaign against Austria-Hungary.[154] In
July 1918, the Habsburg Tenth Army reported that "plane propaganda has become even more intensive than earlier. Almost every
day planes appear and shower not only the front but also the rear
areas with a host of leaflets." By September, the CAM was dropping
90,000 leaflets per day on Austro-Hungarian formations. The LFT
initially resisted participation in propaganda flights due to fear that
captured pilots would be executed, but it was Allied air superiority
that ultimately prohibited effective Austro-Hungarian aerial
propaganda.[155]

Deep penetrations of the enemy's homeland were spectacular
feats and were therefore the focus of many news accounts of the
time. Perhaps even more fascinating to the warring publics were
the fighter aces who joined in individual combat above the clouds
and died gloriously and young. The Dual Monarchy was no less
susceptible to this romanticization of dogfighting than any other
European nation. The LFT produced its own aces: fourteen pilots
were credited with the required ten victories; another thirty-five
scored five or more kills, the number that made one an ace in the
French and American air services.[156]

Measured in weight of effort, however, most of Austria-Hungary's air power was used in direct support of the ground forces. Even the fighter and bomber units flew most of their missions near the front, either as escort for reconnaissance or doing battlefield interdiction. The LFT flew over 700 sorties during the Tenth Battle of Isonzo (May 1917), only 210 of which involved encounters with Italian airplanes. For Caporetto (Twelfth Isonzo), Uzelac was able to mass air power for the first time. His 150 Austro-Hungarian aircraft were joined by 90 German planes. He sent them "in formations of up to fifty machines, attacking Italian positions, lines of communications and reinforcements, and harried the retreating enemy to the Piave."[157] Attrition through the winter of 1917/1918 outpaced production, however, and for the June Piave offensive, Uzelac could only scrape together 170 planes including the German contribution. These airmen faced an Italian force augmented by British, French, and American pilots, and the Allies took control of the air. LFT losses increased dramatically. Only ten Habsburg planes and crews had been shot down in the first two weeks of June, but on the opening day of the summer offensive, they lost twenty-one aircraft. July brought no relief, with thirty-two LFT planes confirmed destroyed.[158] Allied aircraft attacked Austro-Hungarian lines with increasing impunity, the superiority of design evident to those watching from below. One Bosnian battalion commander, blessed with insight many airmen lack, observed, "In aviation, too, morale is very important, but technology is even more so."[159]

By September 1918, the LFT could no longer muster large formations, and on October 24, it made its last major contribution to the Dual Monarchy, attacking Allied columns advancing toward the Piave.[160] This last effort, against an Allied army fifty-five divisions strong, came one week after Charles I had declared the establishment of federalism within Austria, and one week before he released his officers to serve in the newly created national armies.

Thus the LFT, like the Austro-Hungarian army itself, "outlived the empire and dynasty it had been meant to defend."[161]

How well did the LFT serve the empire? And what legacy did it leave to the Hungarian national air service that followed it? That Austria-Hungary's grand strategy failed is indisputable. Franz Josef and his ministers fundamentally misunderstood the nature of modern warfare, and in particular its dependence on mass production of arms and materiel. They were certainly not alone in this error, but the combination of late national industrialization and decades of economizing on military spending left the Habsburg armed forces at a disadvantage that they could not overcome. This problem was especially acute in military aviation, where the situation called for strong leadership from the War Ministry or strong support from its coffers for innovative manufacturers. A directed war economy or a truly free market economy would have served the Dual Monarchy best, but it arranged itself instead as near monopoly with indecisive ministerial guidance and little financial incentive to producers. This was the worst possible, but most predictable, approach to aircraft acquisition, and it did nothing to mitigate Austria-Hungary's structural weaknesses.

At the operational level and below, however, the LFT was an effective fighting force. After the early reconnaissance mistakes in Galicia, Habsburg airmen provided solid intelligence, liaison, attack, and aerial defense to the imperial army and navy. The air services adapted well to improvements in aircraft technology, even when those improvements came to them later than to their opponents, and they recognized that increased specialization of air power required reorganization for maximum effect. First World War air-to-air victory claims are unreliable as a sole means of measuring air services' effectiveness due to irregularities in national rules and problems of confirmation, but loss rates and unit histories confirm that the LFT gave as good as it got. Its pilots were not easy prey for Allied fighters, even when outnumbered and outgunned.

That reflects well on the quality of LFT pilot training and leadership from the fliks up to Brigadier General Uzelac.

The national Hungarian air force that grew out of the LFT therefore had a mixed inheritance. The men who would build and lead the flying corps had experienced aerial combat, and in some cases had excelled at it. Yet the Habsburg air service had struggled from a lack of domestic industrial capacity that forced excessive reliance on a demanding ally, and had proved unable to avert a disastrous national defeat. Could a national Hungarian air force, formed in secret following its prohibition by the Great War victors, avoid the same fate?

NOTES

1. Bödők, *Magyar feltalálók*, p. 21.

2. Holló, *A Galambtól a Griffmadárig*, p. 8.

3. Price and height: see "Ballon Captif Godard" poster. One korona was approximately 1 shilling (the 1896 exchange rate was 1 GBP to 24 Kr). See Denzel, *Handbook of World Exchange Rates, 1590–1914*.

4. Franz Josef's attendance: Holló, *A Galambtól a Griffmadárig*, p. 12; number of balloon flights: see text accompanying "Ballon Captif Godard" poster.

5. Chicago: see "Balloon Park" poster; Antwerp: see "Chateau Aerien" broadside advertisement; Earls Court: see "India and Ceylon Exhibition of 1896" advertisement, *The Times*, Apr. 18, 1896; Paris: see "Ascension Captive" broadsheet advertisement.

6. Hallion, *Taking Flight*, p. 123.

7. In this chapter I include in Hungary's aviation heritage those developments within the Dual Monarchy that may have been achieved outside the borders of St. Stephen's realm. While one should expect that innovation by ethnic Magyars would have had special resonance for the Hungarian public, there is every reason to think that for Habsburg aviators themselves proximity and access to the results of technical advances would have counted far more than the nationality of the innovators. In particular, I treat the experience of the Dual Monarchy's Common Army and its air service as a legacy shared by all the successor states.

8. Morrow, *German Air Power in World War I*, p. 267.

9. Uchatius: Grosz et al., *Austro-Hungarian Army Aircraft*, p. 2; up to 100 balloons: Hallion, *Taking Flight*, p. 66; Rothenberg, "Military Aviation," p. 77; 25-kilogram bombs: Nagyváradi et al., *Fejezetek a repülés történetéből*, p. 11.

10. Hallion, *Taking Flight*, p. 66.

11. Ibid., pp. 68, 94.
12. Rothenberg, "Military Aviation," p. 77.
13. Hallion, *Taking Flight*, p. 72.
14. Kennett, *First Air War, 1914–1918*, p. 3.
15. Grosz et al., *Austro-Hungarian Army Aircraft*, p. 2.
16. Holló, *A Galambtól a Griffmadárig*, p. 12.
17. Rothenberg, "Military Aviation," p. 77.
18. Nagyváradi et al., *Fejezetek a repülés történetéből*, p. 11.
19. Csonkaréti and Sárhidai, *Az Osztrák-Magyar Monarchia tengerészeti repülői*, p. 21.
20. Holló, *A Galambtól a Griffmadárig*, p. 12; Nagyváradi et al., *Fejezetek a repülés történetéből*, p. 11.
21. Hallion, *Taking Flight*, pp. 81–83, 87. Airborne messages went into Paris via carrier pigeon.
22. Ibid., p. 87.
23. Bödők, *Magyar feltalálók*, p. 27.
24. Hallion, *Taking Flight*, p. 97.
25. Ibid.; Berg: Bödők, *Magyar feltalálók*, p. 28.
26. Botting, *Giant Airships*, p. 31.
27. Kennett, *First Air War*, pp. 5–7.
28. "The Great Powers and Aviation," *Flight*, Apr. 24, 1909, p. 232. All *Flight* articles cited in the notes can be accessed online from the Flightglobal Archive at https://www.flightglobal.com/pdfarchive.
29. Holló, *A Galambtól a Griffmadárig*, p. 13.
30. Nagyváradi et al., *Fejezetek a repülés történetéből*, p. 14. One nautical mile = 1.15 statute miles = 1.85 kilometers.
31. "Austrian Military Dirigible," *Flight*, Dec. 11, 1909, p. 801.
32. Holló, *A Galambtól a Griffmadárig*, p. 14.
33. Ibid.; MAA name change: Grosz et al., *Austro-Hungarian Army Aircraft*, p. 2.
34. Holló, *A Galambtól a Griffmadárig*, p. 14.
35. Nagyváradi et al., *Fejezetek a repülés történetéből*, p. 15.
36. Debrecen crash: "Forty-Seven Lives Lost in Airship Accidents," *New York Times*, July 14, 1910; airship program end: Nagyváradi et al., *Fejezetek a repülés történetéből*, p. 16.
37. Grosz et al., *Austro-Hungarian Army Aircraft*, p. 2.
38. Hallion, *Taking Flight*, p. 278.
39. Lilienthal, Wrights, and Santos-Dumont: Hallion, *Taking Flight*, pp. 165–166, 221, 231–232.
40. Kennett, *First Air War*, p. 7.
41. Ibid.
42. Blériot, Kutassy, and Adorján: Holló, *A Galambtól a Griffmadárig*, pp. 9–10.
43. Adorján: Bödők, *Magyar feltalálók*, p. 55; cradle: Holló, *A Galambtól a Griffmadárig*, p. 10.

44. Hallion, *Taking Flight*, p. 264.

45. Bödők, *Magyar feltalálók*, p. 54. Paulhan (French) and Latham (English) figured prominently at the Rheims meet, and Latham attempted a Channel crossing a week before Blériot's success.

46. "Stork" (*gólya*) and "swallow" (*fecske*) are transposed in each line, to retain in English some sense of the rhyme. Likewise, "hawk" doesn't do justice to the mythic Hungarian *turul*, which is usually rendered "eagle." The *turul* played a large role in the *Honfoglalas*, the foundational story of Magyar history in which the Árpád clan occupied the Danubian basin in the ninth century. It was the totem for Árpád's army and remained a powerful image of Hungarian military pride. See Dienes, *A honfoglaló Magyarok*, p. 55.

47. Lloyd George and attaché: Hallion, *Taking Flight*, p. 265.

48. Ibid., pp. 279–281.

49. Ibid.

50. Grosz et al., *Austro-Hungarian Army Aircraft*, p. 2.

51. Ibid.; Gotha, Rumpler: Nagyváradi et al., *Fejezetek a repülés történetéből*, p. 21.

52. Morrow, *German Air Power*, p. 10.

53. Hallion, *Taking Flight*, p. 279.

54. Grosz et al., *Austro-Hungarian Army Aircraft*, pp. 11, 4.

55. Holló, *A Galambtól a Griffmadárig*, p. 14. This was not an uncommon practice at the time. Zeppelin's airship program was rescued from financial ruin by a massive public subscription scheme, and in the United Kingdom a National Aviation Fund was established in 1912 with a goal of 1 million shillings to be used for aviation prizes.

56. Third army pilot: Holló, *A Galambtól a Griffmadárig*, p. 14; school: Grosz et al., *Austro-Hungarian Army Aircraft*, p. 2. Petróczy was the ninth person in Austria-Hungary to earn a pilot's license.

57. Nagyváradi et al., *Fejezetek a repülés történetéből*, p. 17; first chief to fly: Hallion, in *Taking Flight*, p. 286, gives that distinction to Prince Chakrabongse, the Siamese chief of staff, but Conrad's flight took place three months earlier. Warchalowski also took the grand duke and duchess for flights at the 1910 Budapest flight meeting. (*Flight*, July 9, 1910.)

58. Nagyváradi et al., *Fejezetek a repülés történetéből*, p. 17.

59. Grosz et al., *Austro-Hungarian Army Aircraft*, p. 2.

60. Strachan, *First World War*, 1:54–55.

61. Morrow, *German Air Power*, p. 167.

62. Quoted in Hallion, *Taking Flight*, p. 310.

63. 200 in 1910–1911: Morrow, "Defeat of the German and Austro-Hungarian Air Forces," pp. 102; 100 in 1913–1914 and 600 in 1915: Kennett, *First Air War*, p. 20.

64. Hallion, *Taking Flight*, pp. 272–276.

65. Grosz et al., *Austro-Hungarian Army Aircraft*, p. 3.

66. Hallion, *Taking Flight*, 280, 283; 900,000 rubles: Palmer, *Dictatorship of the Air*, p. 18. The exchange rate in mid-1910 was 25 Italian liras and 94 Russian rubles to the pound sterling ("City Intelligence," *The Times*, July 1, 1910, p. 19, col. 2).

67. 500 pilots: "Accidents to Flyers," *Flight*, Dec. 3, 1910, p. 997; "354 Aero Club de France Pilot Aviators," *Flight*, Feb. 4, 1910, p. 88.

68. "German Pilot Aviators," *Flight*, Mar. 18, 1911, p. 230; "Aviators" Certificates," *Flight*, Jan. 7, 1911, p. 11.

69. "More Continental Aviators," *Flight*, May 6, 1911, p. 402; "Federation Aeronautique Internationale," *Flight*, Apr. 5, 1913, p. 387.

70. French general Pierre-Auguste Roques, who soon became inspector of military aeronautics. Quoted in Hallion, *Taking Flight*, p. 310.

71. Kennett, *First Air War*, p. 17.

72. Nagyváradi et al., *Fejezetek a repülés történetéből*, pp. 17–18.

73. Imperial and Royal General Staff, *Die Armeemanöver in Nordungarn*.

74. Kerr, "Against All Comers," p. 293.

75. Kennett, *First Air War*, p.18; captured airman: Hallion, *Taking Flight*, p. 314.

76. Italian General Staff, *Italo-Turkish War (1911–12)*, p. 100.

77. Hallion, *Taking Flight*, p. 314.

78. Kennett, *First Air War*, p. 18.

79. Kerr, "Against All Comers," p. 293.

80. Kennett, *First Air War*, p. 19.

81. Sondhaus, *Franz Conrad von Hötzendorf*, pp. 104–107.

82. Grosz et al., *Austro-Hungarian Army Aircraft*, p. 3.

83. Kerr, "Against All Comers," p. 292.

84. Grosz et al., *Austro-Hungarian Army Aircraft*, p. 3.

85. Expenditures from *Die Militärluftfahrt bis zum Beginn des Weltkrieges 1914* (Berlin, 1941) quoted in Grosz et al., *Austro-Hungarian Army Aircraft*, p. 3. Sums were converted from 1914 US dollars using an exchange rate of 4.7 USD to 1 GBP. Population in millions of inhabitants, excluding colonies, from Ellis and Cox, *World War I Databook*, p. 245.

86. Morrow, *German Air Power*, p. 10.

87. Stone, "Army and Society in the Habsburg Monarchy, 1900–1914," p. 96.

88. Ibid.

89. See ibid.; Deák, *Beyond Nationalism*; and Rothenberg, *Army of Francis Joseph*.

90. Jeszenszky, "Hungary through World War I," p. 278.

91. Romsics, *Hungary in the Twentieth Century*, p. 56. The next day an enraged opposition minister of parliament tried to kill Tisza but managed only to wound himself.

92. Stone, "Army and Society," pp. 104, 107.

93. Strachan, *To Arms*, p. 285.

94. Morrow, *German Air Power*, p. 167.

95. Kennett, *First Air War*, p. 21.

96. Grosz et al., *Austro-Hungarian Army Aircraft*, p. 4.

97. Ibid., pp. 13, 4.

98. Ibid. Lohner's own seaplanes were finely crafted, robust, and effective; UFAG's quality of work was praised by the War Ministry even as its organization was criticized, and many licensed-produced versions of German aircraft were built to higher standards than in Germany.

99. Morrow, *German Air Power*, p. 167.

100. Ibid., pp. 171–174.

101. Grosz et al., *Austro-Hungarian Army Aircraft*, p. 4. In many cases due to license agreements, the aircraft would have been of the same model. In some cases (e.g., the German multiengine G and R planes), those built in Germany would have been substantially more complicated.

102. Romsics, *Hungary in the 20th Century*, p. 85.

103. Grosz et al., *Austro-Hungarian Army Aircraft*, p. 5.

104. Ibid., pp. 65, 264, 511; Holló, *A Galambtól a Griffmadárig*, p. 43.

105. Morrow, *German Air Power*, pp. 169, 173.

106. Ibid., p. 179; Grosz et al., *Austro-Hungarian Army Aircraft*, p. 66.

107. Morrow, *German Air Power*, p. 12.

108. Grosz et al., *Austro-Hungarian Army Aircraft*, p. 5.

109. Morrow, *German Air Power*, pp. 176, 180.

110. Grosz et al., *Austro-Hungarian Army Aircraft*, pp. 6–7.

111. Ibid., p. 448.

112. Austria-Hungary's figure of 5,181 from total acceptance tables in Grosz et al., *Austro-Hungarian Army Aircraft*, p. 511. Nagyváradi et al. give a total production number of 5,431 (*Fejezetek a repülés történetéből*, p. 38). The other combatants' numbers and Italian population figures are from Ellis and Cox, *World War I Databook*, pp. 245, 287. Ellis and Cox put A-H production at 4,338. Russian numbers are incomplete, and the United States entered the war too late for valid comparison.

113. Ellis and Cox, *World War I Databook*, p. 287.

114. Kennett, *First Air War*, p. 85.

115. Grosz et al., *Austro-Hungarian Army Aircraft*, p. 541.

116. Ibid.; and Kerr, "Against All Comers," p. 295.

117. Grosz et al., *Austro-Hungarian Army Aircraft*, p. 541.

118. Nagyváradi et al., *Fejezetek a repülés történetéből*, p. 34.

119. Ellis and Cox, *World War I Databook*, p. 253. The final LFT order of battle: 20 J-, 18 P-, 17 K- , 14 S-, 5 G-, 2 Rb-, and 1 F-flik.

120. Holló, *A Galambtól a Griffmadárig*, pp. 23–24.

121. Grosz et al., *Austro-Hungarian Army Aircraft*, p. 542. On Conrad and mobilization see Strachan, *To Arms*, pp. 281–296.

122. Csonkaréti and Sárhidai, *Az Osztrák-Magyar tengerészeti repülői*, p. 26.

123. Kerr, "Against All Comers," p. 295.

124. Grosz et al., *Austro-Hungarian Army Aircraft*, pp. 388, 536.

125. Holló, *A Galambtól a Griffmadárig*, p. 22.

126. Nagy, "A 3. Hadsereg átkelés a Dunán és Belgrád elfoglalása 1915 október 6–10," pp. 314–315.

127. Kerr, "Against All Comers," p. 295.

128. Strachan, *To Arms*, p. 348.

129. Ibid., p. 349.

130. Hallion, *Taking Flight*, pp. 340–341.

131. Conrad: Strachan, *To Arms*, p. 348.

132. Kupiec-Weglinski, "Siege of Przemysl, 1914–1915," pp. 544–555.

133. Quoted in "Aircraft and the War" *Flight*, March 26, 1915, p. 298.

134. Kupiec-Weglinski, "Siege of Przemysl," p. 545.

135. "Przemysl leltára," *Huszadik Század*, Apr. 1915.

136. Kennett, *First Air War*, pp. 175, 179.

137. Ibid., p. 178.

138. Morrow, *German Air Power*, p. 170.

139. Grosz et al., *Austro-Hungarian Army Aircraft*, pp. 542–543.

140. Ellis and Cox, *World War I Databook*, p. 253.

141. Kennett, *First Air War*, p. 46.

142. Hallion, *Taking Flight*, p. 359.

143. Czirók, "Az első légi háború Magyarország felett-1919," p. 335.

144. Kerr, "Against All Comers," pp. 306–308. The strike force composition is given as twelve Lohner B-VIIs in Holló, *A Galambtól a Griffmadárig*, p. 25.

145. Harvey, "Bombing and the Air War on the Italian Front," p. 37.

146. Quoted in Nagyváradi et al., *Fejezetek a repülés történetéből*, p. 95.

147. Quoted in "Aircraft and the War," *Flight*, Feb. 17, 1916, p. 144.

148. Kerr, "Against All Comers," p. 309.

149. Harvey, "Bombing and the Air War on the Italian Front," p. 38.

150. 400 killed: ibid.; Charles's restriction: Rothenberg, "Military Aviation," p. 81.

151. Kennett, *First Air War*, p. 56.

152. Rothenberg, "Military Aviation," p. 82.

153. Cornwall, *Undermining of Austria-Hungary*, p. 370.

154. Woodhouse, *Gabriele D'Annunzio*, p. 310.

155. Cornwall, *Undermining Austria-Hungary*, pp. 372, 85–86.

156. Chant, *Austro-Hungarian Aces*, p. 90.

157. Rothenberg, "Military Aviation," p. 82.

158. Kerr, "Against All Comers," pp. 343–345.

159. Quoted in Thompson, *White War*, p. 345.

160. Rothenberg, "Military Aviation," p. 82.

161. Rothenberg, *Army of Francis Joseph*, pp. 217, 221.

2

Upheaval: 1918–1919

HUNGARY EXPERIENCED TREMENDOUS TURMOIL IN THE months that followed the end of the First World War. The disruptions were pervasive and profound: no element of public life was left untouched. Military defeat led to the dissolution of the Habsburg Empire and was followed by successive revolutions and the eventual reimposition of a monarchy, albeit without a monarch. Entente forces initially held border regions under armistice terms, but eventually the armies of their allied successor states invaded and seized territory that had for centuries been united under the crown of St. Stephen. Budapest itself was occupied. Hungary's populace, having persevered through four years of war, was rewarded with expanded suffrage and some land reform, but continued to face severe material shortages and hardship. Hungarians also suffered the consequences of fighting in their own towns and villages, something they had largely avoided in the war just ended, and they were subjected to the ravages of both Red and White Terrors.

Against this backdrop of turbulence and radicalism, Hungarian airmen of the recently disbanded LFT established a national flying corps that emphasized continuity in personnel, organization, and operations. The alacrity with which the air force began operations in unfavorable conditions reveals the professionalism of those early Hungarian airmen, and the loyalty of their service under five governments in the course of a year suggests patriotism as a motivation.[1] With the parlous state of the domestic Hungarian aircraft industry, the continued shortages of raw materials, and the disruptions to production caused by political crises, it is no surprise that the flying corps was not the decisive arm in the battles of 1919. The air service did, however, make important contributions to the state's political and military security by performing a range of aerial missions. While the four years of combat in the First World War would have remained the defining experience of air warfare for the individuals involved, the relatively short period of consolidation and conflict was crucial in shaping the corporate self-image of the nascent Hungarian air force. Hungarian airmen became accustomed to operating at a disadvantage, but remained committed advocates for the efficacy of air power in defense of the nation. This commitment was sustained even in the years after the proscription of a Hungarian air force by the Treaty of Trianon (1920).

The idea of a national Hungarian air service first arose during the First World War within those Austro-Hungarian flying squadrons that had strong Magyar contingents. The air arm was too new to have been part of the traditional Habsburg regimental system, and there were no Honvédség or Landwehr flying units.[2] Nevertheless, Magyar pilots, some of them perhaps fleeing the "oppressive attitude of the ruling Austrians" (*az osztrák elnyomás uralkodo szelleme*), gravitated to those fliks commanded by Hungarian officers such as László Háry, Sándor Hartzer, Géza Csenkey, and István Wollemann.[3] This tendency toward voluntary segregation among fliers hints at the complicated relationship between Hungarian officers and the Habsburg state. The Common Army "was the most important all-monarchical institution in the realm"; its officers were its "nerve center and spiritual essence" and they felt a particular duty to Franz Josef, to whom they swore a personal oath of loyalty.[4] It was therefore a key centripetal force in the Dual Monarchy, resisting the centrifugal pull of nationalism, any manifestation of which was openly deplored.[5] Regular officers, whatever their origins, were expected to be above nationalism. Magyars, however, were underrepresented in the regular army officer corps, since a large proportion of the martially minded chose instead to serve in the reserves or, better, in the Honvéd.[6] This choice expressed a nationalist sentiment, and it was recognized as such by some non-Magyars in the officer corps, who resented Hungarian obstructionism and the concessions carved out for Hungarian officers after the 1867 Compromise.[7] Such resentment could account for the "oppressive attitude" described above. In any case, Hungarian airmen were drawn to the vision of a national independent air force, free from both Austrian oversight and Common Army supervision.

That vision was realized sooner perhaps than they anticipated. On November 6, 1918, the Hungarian Defense Ministry (Hadügyminisztérium) established its 37th Section, the Aviation Department (Légügyi osztály), and charged it with the direction of all aviation activity.[8] This clear line of control lasted just a few days. The government formed another body on November 12, the Aviation Commission (Légügyi Kormánybiztosság), subordinate to both the War and Commerce Ministries, to coordinate national aeronautics. The Aviation Commission included an executive branch along with three others (research and development, engineering, and accounting), and had directly under it another department confusingly given the same designation (Légügyi osztály) as the Defense Ministry's 37th Section. The commission's Aviation Department was separate from the Defense Ministry's, and it comprised four groups: traffic, personnel, engineering, and finance. Subordinate elements included the Air Corps Headquarters (Légi Csapatparancsnokság), the float-plane section, and aviation stores warehouses. There were also two departments based in Vienna that represented Hungarian interests in the liquidation of indivisible LFT assets.[9] That this was a complicated organizational structure is beyond doubt, but it was not without heritage and purpose. It remained somewhat simpler than the Habsburg military aviation organization, under which the Flight Arsenal at Fischamend had also been subordinate to two masters (in this case the Army High Command and Defense

Ministry Aviation Department 5/L) and was composed of five departments, each of which was further divided into between eight and twenty-two subdepartments.[10] It was hoped that the labyrinthine lines of authority and subordination to the Commerce Ministry would protect Hungarian aviation from future Allied inspectors, and the proliferation of bureaus provided billets for experienced officers whose expertise might otherwise have been lost.[11] As for the perplexing arrangement, circumstances and personalities clarified institutional relationships in a way that lines on a chart never could.

In spite of the republic's official policy of pacifism and an interest in developing the aerial post, military aviation crowded out commercial flight in 1918–1919, and the Commerce Ministry effectively ceded control of the Aviation Commission to the Defense Ministry. In January 1919, Lieutenant Colonel István Petróczy, the first Magyar military pilot and one of the most distinguished Hungarian aviators of the First World War, was selected to head the 37th Section. This made him the de facto chief of the air staff and gave him operational command of the Hungarian Flying Corps (Repülőcsapat) through the Air HQ.[12] The situation would be exactly reversed after Trianon, when the center of Hungarian air power would necessarily shift to the Commerce Ministry.

Commissioner Sándor Hangay, Petróczy's predecessor at the 37th Section, called senior air service leaders to Budapest immediately after his appointment in November. When their conference at the Nádasdy barracks broke up, critical personnel and organizational questions had been settled. By order of the war minister, airmen were exempted from forced demobilization.[13] The new national flying corps initially consisted of three air companies (repülőosztály): the 1st Air Guard Company, commanded by Captain József Gergye; the 2nd Airmail Company, commanded by Captain Ernő Szalay; and the 3rd Operational Training Company, commanded by Captain Sándor Hartzer. The flying corps would soon grow to eight companies, with a further five companies planned but never activated. Hartzer's training unit was assigned to Rákosmező airfield, the center of Hungarian pilot training since 1910. The 1st and 2nd Companies shared the airfields at Mátyásföld and Albertfalva with the country's two largest aircraft manufacturing plants. Albertfalva was the home of UFAG, a Castiglioni firm whose 1,700 employees at peak wartime production rolled out 40 aircraft per month. The factory, which changed its name to Magyar Repülőgépgyár (MARE) in reflection of the times, built Brandenburg designs, primarily the C.I, a capable two-seat multipurpose machine, and the fine W.29 float-plane. Magyar Általános Gépgyár (MÁG) had its plant at Mátyásföld (1,100 employees, 24 aircraft per month peak production), and was the main Hungarian supplier for single-seat fighter craft, especially the Aviatik D.I and state-of-the-art Fokker D.VII.[14] Production was already below peak levels by the end of the war, due to the dearth of men and materials, and an Aviation Commission decision further reduced output. Having declared on November 8 "the time of peace had set in," the Commission demanded a cut in aviation industry employment of 75 percent, beginning with workers of foreign origin (including those Austrians and Czechs who were fellow Habsburg subjects weeks earlier).[15]

That this policy went against the instincts of the Hungarian airmen can be inferred from their subsequent actions to preserve and consolidate as much aviation materiel as possible in front of the advancing Allied armies. It was, however, entirely consonant with the outlook of the new government headed by Mihály Károlyi, a long-standing opponent of the war and "friend to democracy and peace." [16] Károlyi's National Council had come to power in a near-bloodless revolution on October 31, carried along by an uprising of the newly established Soldiers' Council, and its first priority was terminating the war. Béla Linder, the new minister of war, ordered Hungarian forces to disarm on November 1.[17] Hostilities on the Italian front ended on November 4, but reports of Allied incursions from the south made it clear that the Padua Armistice did not constrain the Entente's Armée d'Orient. On the same day that the Defense Ministry established its 37th Section, Károlyi led a delegation to Belgrade to negotiate a ceasefire agreement with French general Louis Franchet d'Espèrey. Franchet d'Espèrey was cordial to Károlyi personally, but treated the delegation with disdain, reacting especially to the presence of Baron Hatvany, a Jew, and to the representative of the Soldiers' Council.[18] The armistice terms were harsh: Hungarian forces were to be withdrawn from most of Transylvania as well as from large portions of southern Hungary; Allied forces were to have the right of passage throughout the country; and Hungary's army was to be restricted to eight divisions.[19] In an apparent oversight that perhaps reflected a lack of knowledge or interest in aviation on the part of Franchet d'Espèrey or his staff, the armistice did not specifically address aircraft, although it did require Hungary to disarm the remnants of its navy and deliver to Belgrade six armored riverboats. (The Italians, having suffered much at the hands of Habsburg pilots in Brandenburg float-planes, insisted at Padua that "all naval aircraft are to be concentrated and immobilized.")[20] After receiving reassurance from Clemenceau that the agreement was strictly a military one—which Károlyi understood to mean that permanent lines of demarcation would be negotiated at the future peace conference—the National Council authorized Linder to sign the armistice. Allied troops, including Serbs and Romanians, contrary to Károlyi's specific request, immediately occupied the zones vacated by Hungarian forces. Meanwhile, the Czecho-Slovak National Council, dissatisfied with Article 17 of the Belgrade Armistice, the clause that permitted Hungarian administration of historically Hungarian lands, began to intervene militarily to bring disputed areas under Czechoslovak control. Károlyi momentarily abandoned the policy of passive resistance and used force to eject the Czechoslovak troops from Pozsony. Eduard Beneš, the Czechoslovak foreign minister, appealed to the French for assistance, which was promptly supplied in the form of a directive from the Allied Supreme Command for Hungarian evacuation of the contested land. With Article 17 thus rendered inoperative, Hungary's neighbors no longer felt constrained by the Big Four, and increased pressure on the Hungarian Republic's frontiers.[21] Disarmament continued nonetheless. These actions did not diminish Károlyi's belief that Hungary would receive justice from the Allies at the peace conference in accordance with Wilsonian ideals of self-determination.

Flying operations continued throughout this time. On November 6, the 1st Air Guard Company's Lieutenant Viktor Stohrer led a three-ship formation on an "air police" (*karhatalmi*) mission in the capital area to stop possible looting and agitation, and to drop leaflets encouraging support of the new government. Stohrer was dispatched again on November 8 on reports of civil disturbances, but he found the area calm. Later that day, two other fighters along with one of Szalay's 2nd Airmail Company planes were sent to Örkény at the request of the Pest County high sheriff (*főispán*) for reconnaissance and leaflet drops. One aircraft failed to return from the afternoon missions, but no casualties were reported. The 2nd Company also flew four air police missions on November 10 in Brandenburg C.Is. The situation was somewhat different in Transylvania, where the remnants of two reconnaissance fliks were still flying combat sorties in support of the Székely detachment. On November 7, these planes attacked a meeting of the Romanian National Council in Tusnád, inflicting, by the observers' accounts, 150 casualties.[22] Though the damage report from the Tusnád raid was almost certainly inflated, consideration of the missions flown in the second week of November shows that in the midst of national confusion, the essential components of an air force were present and operable: aircraft were serviced, fueled, and armed; pilots were available for flight; and a command-and-control system functioned sufficiently for requests from proper authorities to be fulfilled. Furthermore, the capital-area air police sorties demonstrated a sophisticated and restrained use of air power, while the operations of the Székely company exhibited initiative and aggressiveness.

Hungarian airmen attempted, sometimes in vain, to keep their
aviation stores out of the hands of the Entente. The Defense Ministry's Aviation Department was active on this front from its incep-
tion: on November 6 it sent a lieutenant to Csány airfield with orders
to ship the hangars' contents to Budapest. The following days saw
other officers assigned to the same task at Zalaegerszeg, Pándor-
falu, and Kolozsvár. These first missions succeeded in salvaging
crucial aircraft and parts, but a similar endeavor just days later at
Újvidék failed. After being advised that the terms of the Belgrade
Armistice would place that airfield, one of the Dual Monarchy's
primary training bases, under Yugoslav control, the Aviation Department planned a large-scale evacuation of its aircraft to Szeged.
Serb forces advanced more quickly than expected, however, and
occupied Újvidék on November 10, capturing every aircraft on the
field with the exception of a 2nd Airmail Company plane that took
off minutes before the Serbs arrived. Ninety miles east of Újvidék,
Habsburg soldiers of Romanian extraction seized the airfield at
Lugos in the name of the Romanian National Council. The station
commander, who could muster just eighteen armed Magyars, was
unable to offer effective resistance. An episode at Arad proved the
air service was not immune from the confusion afflicting the dis-
integrating Common Army. A second Air Group (Csoportparanc-
snokság) was to be established there, and the Aviation Department
requested the airfield's current strength. The initial report on November 8 from Major Frigyes Medvey, Arad's commander, counted
twenty-one flyable planes. A more detailed and distressing report
came two days later, explaining that, of the seventy machines possessed by the two squadrons at Arad, only seven were serviceable.
With the Újvidék debacle in mind, Medvey was ordered to keep a
section of aircraft on alert and prepare the rest for shipment by
wagon to Szeged.[23] In the event, the flying corps did not desert
Arad after all, maintaining a presence there until it was occupied
by French troops in early January 1919 as part of the buffer zone
between Hungarian and Romanian forces.[24]

After the intense activity in the first weeks of November, the air service settled in to a period of relative calm that lasted until the declaration of the Hungarian Soviet Republic (HSR) in March 1919. In these months the staff continued to oversee flight operations while they also inventoried, refurbished, and distributed equipment, and attended to bureaucratic matters. Since Károlyi remained convinced that diplomacy would eventually reverse the territorial encroachment by Hungary's neighbors, the flying corps devoted most of its energy to performing reconnaissance, transport, and liaison missions. Szalay's Airmail Company was especially helpful in the liaison role, as its ability to fly couriers around the country provided the new government with a method of communication that was fast, secure, and fairly reliable. In contrast to the LFT, the air service embraced propaganda operations, dropping leaflets proclaiming the formation of the Hungarian Republic, and even on occasion delivering copies of the socialist daily *Népszava* to workers in the countryside.[25] As technicians made planes airworthy, small detachments stood up at airfields across the country. Units at Arad, Szeged, Szombathely, Kaposvár, Beregszász, Pozsony, and Kecskemét reported ready, although not all were tasked with missions. When the realities of equipment shortages and the shifting demarcation line set in, the Aviation Department gave up on its thirteen-company plan, and instead accepted an eight-company structure, with some companies having detachments at other locations. A streamlined version of this organization, approved in January 1919 and updated in February, formed the basis for the HSR's flying corps.[26] With the border situation deteriorating, Petróczy directed in late February an intermediate organization consisting of six flying squadrons, one assigned to each of the six divisions. The 4th and 5th Squadrons were to be reconstituted with eight aircraft each and were to proceed to the headquarters of the 4th and 5th Divisions in Győr and Miskolc.[27]

The same material deficiencies that constrained the corps' size also affected personnel compensation. Pay for airmen was set at 500 koronas for pilots, 400 for observers and technical officers, 300 for engineers, and 100 for unskilled enlisted men. Fliers received monthly bonuses based on the distance of their flights, and pilots and engineers could earn additional pay for keeping the aircraft in good order.[28] In prewar terms those were extravagant figures, since Hungary's per capita gross domestic product in 1913 totaled 435 koronas annually, but inflation had eroded much of the korona's purchasing power.[29] The cost of living was twenty-four times higher in 1919 than in 1913, and the 1919 korona held only 1 percent of its prewar value.[30] Nevertheless, the monthly outlay of nearly 1.5 million koronas to pay the flying corps' 300 officers and 1,000 enlisted men was "a serious burden on the Defense Ministry's wallet."[31] The ministry's commitment to a dependable wage when the rest of the force was under mandatory demobilization indicates a high level of governmental support for the air service. It does not, however, suggest that the flying corps was a mercenary force—the pay was not generous enough for that. As a comparison, the Red Army, not known for extravagant compensation, had to offer common soldiers 450 koronas per month (the pay of a lieutenant colonel in 1907) plus a family supplement in order to increase enlistments in March 1919.[32]

If money was not the primary motivation, what was? What encouraged men to stay in the air service in spite of danger and deprivation? A feeling of esprit de corps and adventure would surely have been part of the motivation. The reality of aerial combat strips away military aviation's romantic appeal, but not its fundamental challenge, and it offers a satisfaction and sense of camaraderie that few other activities can match. Prospects for promotion and advancement may also have played a role. Demobilization forced the retirement of all general officers, and the Common Army's General Staff was dissolved; these vacancies provided opportunities for ambitious airmen to make rank and to enhance the standing of air power within the new Hungarian security establishment.[33] But the evidence suggests that the Hungarian airmen were chiefly animated by patriotism.

Although patriotism and nationalism are easily conflated, they can be distinguished. "The former seems to spring from love of home and the desire to protect it, while the latter is inspired by opposition or aversion to persons and things which are strange and unintelligible."[34] And even if some have attributed the birth of modern nationalism to the Magyars' opposition to Joseph II, and nationalism's role in Hungarian history in the period 1920–1945 cannot be overstated, the response of Hungarian airmen to the crises of 1919 is better explained by the desire to protect their homeland than by opposition to any other nationalities. They voiced no objection to Oszkár Jászi's plan for a Danubian Confederation or to Béla Kun's internationalist vision. Indeed, the best testimony of the airmen's patriotism is the constancy of their service under widely divergent governments. The same men who joined the Habsburg LFT flew under the flag of the bourgeois Hungarian Republic, the HSR, and finally the Kingdom of Hungary. There were no purges or large-scale defections. With the single exception of Ernő Szalay, who was killed in a crash on March 13, the air companies' commanders in the first order of battle issued by the Aviation Department of the People's Committee for War (Hadügyi Népbiztosság Légügyi Osztálya) matched exactly the last one published by Károlyi's Defense Ministry. The only apparent concession to communist ideals was the substitution of *proletárkatona* (proletarian soldier) for *százados* (captain) and *főhadnagy* (lieutenant).[35] Perhaps more striking is that nearly all of those leaders retained their positions under Admiral Miklós Horthy's counterrevolutionary government.[36]

This was true to some lesser degree for the land force as well, as Red Army officers "merged almost completely into the National Army," though in some cases their careers were monitored more closely as a result of their Red Army service.[37] Not all Red Army officers were accepted by the National Army; some were imprisoned and others were forced to retire or accept demotion.[38] For most, however, service with the Red Army did not stunt career progression in the regent's armed forces, and some reached the highest levels of leadership: of the thirty-five lieutenant generals (*tábornok*) in the 1938–1945 Hungarian Army, fifteen had served in the Red Army.[39] Reconciliation of that degree argues strongly for the officer corps' dedication to national defense. The majority of officers who left the Red Army for the Szeged Whites did so only after Béla Kun ordered the army to withdraw from Upper Hungary, a "fatal strategic and tactical mistake" that led to widespread desertions.[40] While common soldiers might have fought "to defend the new society, and not the old frontiers," officers felt much the opposite, questioning the need to defend a Soviet republic that would sacrifice Hungarian territory.[41] In the aftermath of the retreat, both War Minister Vilmos Böhm and Chief of Staff Aurél Stromfeld resigned in protest.[42] Stromfeld revealed the strength of his conviction in a diary entry addressed to his recently deceased sister: "You, a fanatical lover of the Hungarian fatherland, you now lie in foreign soil [Czechoslovakia]. Was I not right to have tried to prevent this?"[43] The resignations and desertions were not caused by disillusionment with communist ideology or even battlefield losses (although those were soon coming), but rather because many soldiers no longer believed that the Kun regime was willing or able to defend the country's borders. This realization was felt as a betrayal by a pair of officers who joined the Red Army for explicitly patriotic reasons, which they later related to a historian: "Even if we start into battle under red flags, by the time we reach the Carpathians our colors will be red-white-green!"[44] A former Red Army political commissar acknowledged in a posthumous article decades later that "the Red Army was in essence a Hungarian army: it was defending against foreign attacks."[45]

If the airmen of the Hungarian Red Flying Corps (Vörös Repülőcsapat, VR) and Red Army officers were motivated largely by patriotism and not revolutionary fervor, what was the nature of their obligation to the successive administrations in Budapest? It seems that the Hungarian officer corps exhibited conditional loyalty to the governments of the revolutionary period. A regime earned the officer corps' support and service to the extent that it defended Hungary, and that support was liable to be withdrawn. It can be argued that conditional loyalty is no loyalty at all—a government that must take into account the desires of its armed forces in formulating security policy is the servant, not the master. But that view reduces a nation to nothing more than its government. Such an idea would have been foreign to Habsburg officers, who pledged fealty to the emperor, and not to a particular combination of ministers, and its Hungarian successors carried on the concept, with the integrity of historic Hungary standing in place of the monarch. In Western democracies the situation is little different: British and American officers, then as now, swear allegiance not to governments but to the Crown and Constitution respectively. The HSR benefited from officer corps' willingness to transfer allegiance from one government to another in March 1919, just as it suffered in June and July when the retreat from Felvidék undermined its legitimacy. The Hungarian officer corps was professional, but that did not mean it was apolitical. Habsburg officers had seemed so only because of their close identification with the person of Franz Josef. Once the empire dissolved and revolution ensued, the officer corps' conservatism stood out in stark contrast, being no longer part of the background, but having a shape and color of its own. Nevertheless, most of the officers suppressed any personal dissatisfaction about the particularities of their new governments' domestic agendas, and when permitted, served faithfully and bravely. A minority of restorationist and committed anticommunist officers began plotting against the revolutions, first in Vienna and later in French-controlled Szeged.

The HSR came into being on March 21, 1919, following the crisis brought about by the Allies' demand that Hungarian forces in the east withdraw some 60 miles further west, thereby ceding several thousand square miles to Romania.[46] The Entente, anticipating a large-scale invasion of Soviet Russia, wanted to secure eastern Hungary as a base of its operations.[47] Károlyi believed the new lines to be final political decisions, and concluded that the Allies had finally and completely abrogated the terms of the Belgrade Armistice.[48] His government, whose legitimacy rested in large part on the assumption that it could garner goodwill and fair treatment from the Entente, was paralyzed. Nationalist members of the cabinet "could not accept the responsibility of giving up such extensive territories before the Peace Treaty was signed," but the party was too weak to command the country in resistance to the ultimatum.[49] The government therefore rejected the Allied demand as relayed by French lieutenant colonel Vix and immediately resigned. Károlyi remained head of state, and he asked the Social Democrats, who had the support of the trade unions (the best organized and functioning segment of Hungarian life at the time), to form a government that would seek help from the Soviet Union. They agreed, but entered without Károlyi's knowledge into power-sharing negotiations with the communists, whose leader, a journalist and former prisoner of war named Béla Kun, was still in jail for his role in a communist-inspired mob attack on the Social Democrat paper *Népszava*.[50] Later that evening, believing it was still in his power to do so, Károlyi appointed the centrist socialist Zsigmond Kunfi prime minister. In fact, the Workers' Council had already effectively seized power. Károlyi was notified of this when his secretary asked him to sign a prepared document in which he resigned and turned power over to the Hungarian workers. He refused, but was informed that the morning papers had already printed his resignation, and that posters proclaiming a dictatorship of the proletariat were appearing all over the capital. Feeling that clinging to power would incite a civil war, Károlyi retired to the Buda hills.[51]

On the morning of March 22, 1919, thirty-three "people's commissars" convened the first Revolutionary Governing Council (Forradalmi Kormányzótanács) of the new state—the Magyarországi Szocialista Szövetséges Tanácsköztársaság (HSR).[52] The Social Democrat Sándor Garbai was elected president of the council, but Kun, as the people's commissariat of foreign affairs, was wholly in control of it.[53] Although the March 21 manifesto had declared "complete ideological unity with the Soviet government" and offered "the proletariat of Russia a military alliance," Kun immediately sent Károlyi on a mission to Vienna to open negotiations with the Entente. Károlyi was to pledge that the Hungarian Soviet forces would not join with the Russian Red Army and would not spread revolution abroad. In return, the Allies should hold plebiscites in the disputed territories and provide Hungary with food aid.[54] Nothing came of the Károlyi mission, but the Entente, now keenly interested in Hungarian matters but deluged with conflicting reports, did send a mission of its own to Budapest, led by the South African lieutenant general Jan Smuts. Smuts offered Kun some concessions, namely an adjustment to the Vix lines in Hungary's favor, and acknowledgment that further changes could be possible. Kun submitted a counteroffer, demanding a conference of Hungary's neighbors to discuss territorial and economic matters. Smuts, who had been charged with presenting the Entente's position and who was not authorized to negotiate further, left Budapest the next day. In his report to the Entente, Smuts supported Kun's idea of a regional conference and suggested that the economic blockade be lifted once the Hungarians accepted the new demarcation lines. "Paris was not too interested in his propositions but paid close attention to his conclusion: Hungary truly had an essentially Bolshevik government."[55] With this established, the French army command continued its preparations for a military intervention. Czechoslovak and Yugoslav units were not ready for action, so the invasion was left to the Romanians.[56]

The March 24, 1919, order from the Aviation Department of the People's Committee for War was the foundational document for the VR. After a brief summary of the events that led to the establishment of the HSR, the order declared "the entire flying formation stands in the service of the new Red Army, and is placed in a state of war."[57] It accepted as the VR's current order of battle the earlier flying corps organization, with eight operational flying companies at eight airfields. This order established capital air defense procedures and instructions for maintaining telephonic contact with Air HQ. The Aviation Department warned that Budapest's industrial areas could come under air attack at any time, and it therefore instituted an aerial observation zone extending in a semi-circle from the capital 60 miles south. The order also detailed air raid alarm procedures. The entire force was directed to respond to unknown inbound aircraft; the Aviation Department specified a dedicated telephone line for the signal; and it instructed observers to note the intruders' type, number, flight direction, location, and estimated time over Budapest. Finally, it set expectations for air alert postures. Each company and detachment was to have one aircraft and crew on thirty-minute alert status from 07:00 until twilight. Companies in Budapest, Szeged, and Debrecen were re-quired to have an additional plane and crew ready to take off within ninety minutes daily from 08:00 until 17:00.[58]

Eventually the air defense system around the capital incorpo-rated AAA. The first emplacements, sited on hills overlooking Bu-dapest and near the Rákosmező airfield, comprised discarded Model 75 90-millimeter cannon. Air defense efforts intensified after hostilities began in April. The formation of the Budapest Air Defense Artillery Command in May 1919 brought order to the ground-based defense and extended the AAA coverage to a few batteries guarding the Csepel Island arms manufacturing plants. The Csepel batteries were armed with the more modern 76-millimeter guns capable of firing 10–15 rounds per minute with a maximum range of 12,000 feet.[59] By early summer 1919, the 43rd Artillery Regiment was established as an antiaircraft unit with five batteries, the fifth and newest protecting the western industrial city of Győr. In July, concern about night bombardment led to seven searchlight sections being deployed on strategic hills and rail lines around Budapest. Concentration of the few medium-caliber AAA pieces meant that ground-based air defense in the field consisted primarily of rifles and machine guns.[60]

The HSR had a three-week respite from the time of its founding until war began. While Kun met with Smuts, the Red Army tried to fill its ranks with proletarian soldiers. An air staff order on April 8 changed the VR's structure. The flying companies were redesignated as squadrons and given new numbers. Squadrons 1 through 7 (now at Kaposvár, Albertfalva, Rákosmező, Győr, Kecskemét, Békéscsaba, and Debrecen) took operational orders from the 1st through 6th Infantry Divisions and the Székely detachment.[61] Air HQ retained responsibility for training, supplying, and staffing these units. Control of the 8th Squadron (László Háry's fighter unit based at Mátyásföld) remained with Air HQ, but the 9th Squadron at Csepel Island (István Wollemann's float-plane fighters) was placed under the Warship HQ.[62] This reorganization was in part a reversion to the early days of military aviation, and stood in contrast to the general trend in the West toward centralized control of air power. A return to a field aviation model was not, however, an unreasonable response to conditions. Since the VR's primary mission was conducting reconnaissance in support of land forces, physical proximity and organizational subordination to those forces maximized effectiveness. Consolidation of aircraft in a single area under Air HQ control would have eased the VR's supply problem and might have put more planes in the air, but this advantage would have been offset to some degree by the increase in flight time to the front, and the coordination required between air and ground units that were no longer colocated. The relative merits of centralized versus distributed air power would be debated for years to come in professional journals and defense committees around the world, including in Hungary, but there is no evidence that this particular solution to the problem was controversial. The Aviation Commission's arrangement gave control of the capital defense force (8th Squadron's single-seat fighters) to Air HQ, while ensuring that army formations around the country could count on aerial reconnaissance assets that were available and responsive, if limited in number.

Figure 2.1. VR Aviatik Berg D.I fighter in 1919. Photo: Fortepan/Tibor Erky-Nagy.

When the Romanian army attacked across the broad eastern front on April 16, the nine squadrons of the VR had a programmed strength of seventy-eight aircraft. The exact number of aircraft available on that day is unclear, but since only the Békéscsaba and Debrecen squadrons were engaged (the others being kept on defensive duty around the rest of the country), the figure could not have exceeded fourteen, and based on later, more exact tallies, was probably closer to the six that the 5th and 7th Squadrons reported as serviceable on April 19. Pilots and observers of all ranks, including those in command and staff billets, numbered 317. Romanian air support came from the three squadrons of Grupul 5, which should have fielded thirty aircraft, but had in actuality only a dozen, primarily Sopwith and Nieuport machines.[63] The roughly two-to-one advantage enjoyed by Grupul 5 extended to the infantry, which fielded sixty-four regiments against thirty-five Hungarian battalions, and the Romanian edge in artillery and cavalry was even greater.[64] Benefits that normally accrue to the defenders, including prepared positions, shorter interior lines, and the incentive of fighting for one's own land, seem to have accounted for little in this case, and the Hungarians were defeated across the front. Their army had been deliberately neglected under Károlyi, communist political agitation had caused dissension in the ranks, and discipline was lax. The Red Army's recruitment drive had added 20,000 soldiers in ten days, and communist volunteers arrived from other countries (1,200 from Austria), but the reinforcements could not be fielded in time to stop the Romanian advance.[65]

Due to the chaotic retreat of the Hungarian forces, the VR contributed very little in this first round of fighting. Its crews conducted reconnaissance missions, but the information proved of small value to forces that were already under constant pressure. The Romanians' rapid advance forced the Debrecen squadron to flee to Mátyásföld on April 23. At first only a single UFAG/MARE C.I escaped, but the following morning a second machine made it out, getting airborne just as Romanian cavalry fired on the field.

Grupul 5 airmen, like their Hungarian counterparts, had before the invasion mostly flown reconnaissance and propaganda missions—in this case, scattering leaflets to encourage ethnic Romanians to rise up against the Magyar authorities. After hostilities commenced, Romanian airmen continued reconnaissance activities, but also intervened directly in the ground war, conducting low-level attacks on retreating Hungarian columns and bombing the airfield at Nagyszalonta. Due to the small numbers of planes involved on both sides, opposing airmen rarely encountered each other and there are no reports of air-to-air combat. One VR two-seater did make a forced landing behind Romanian lines, after which the crew was captured and the aircraft was repaired and pressed into service by the Romanians.[66] Red Army troops fell back throughout the last week of April, and by May 1 Romanian forces were established along the entire eastern bank of the Tisza River. The next day Kun sought a ceasefire, and under pressure from the Entente, Romania agreed.

Even in the midst of battlefield setbacks the HSR observed official communist May Day celebrations, and the VR had a role. One

VR pilot recalled flying low over the Danube, around the Vár, and above the Vérmező, where he saw thousands of people. He and his flight mates buzzed the crowd: "We arrived unexpectedly, which surprised the celebrating masses, and we flew so low that at the same time everybody stood looking in fascination at our airplanes."[67]

The republic's leaders were shocked at the ease with which the Romanians had defeated their army. Vilmos Böhm, the Social Democrat leader of the five-member People's Committee for War, had earlier recalled to active service Colonel Aurél Stromfeld, and now Böhm appointed him chief of staff and charged him with revitalizing the Red Army. Stromfeld, also a Social Democrat, was a gifted former Habsburg General Staff officer who had resigned his post in February 1919 after a five-week army recruiting campaign that was expected to return 70,000 soldiers yielded only 5,000.[68] Fortunately, the reality of the April 16 invasion had encouraged enlistment in a way that the mere threat of it in February had not, so Stromfeld's immediate problem was not a lack of soldiers, but rather poor leadership. Recruiting materials began to address directly former Habsburg officers, appealing openly to nationalist sentiment. Leaflets that weeks earlier cried out to "Proletariat soldiers! Comrades!" now implored "Commanders! Former officers! . . . We trust you!" Claims that workers who did not "rush enthusiastically and resolutely" to the recruiting office were not real communists or socialists were replaced by references to "thieving Romanian boyar occupying forces" (román bojárok rabló csapatai tartanak megszállva).[69] No longer barred from service because of class distinctions, former officers, over half of whom came from territories presently occupied by the Entente, joined the Red Army by the hundreds.[70] Their combat experience, planning expertise, and steady leadership were crucial to the Red Army's success in the northern campaign. With professional officers in charge, the fifty battalions of Jenő Landler's III Corps regained over 1,100 square miles of Upper Hungary in three weeks.[71] Stromfeld also introduced measures to streamline unity of command and effort, including the creation of an army high command (Hadsereg főparancsnokság [HFP]) to exercise operational control of all Red forces.[72]

As the chief of staff exerted more influence over the Red Army as a whole, the General Staff started to task the VR squadrons more directly, and the division-based system weakened. On May 8, the HFP issued detailed reconnaissance mission orders that allocated the 1st, 4th, and 5th Squadrons to I and II Corps, left the 3rd Squadron assigned to its division, and kept the 2nd, 6th, 7th, and 8th Squadrons to itself for tasking. The next day, the HFP created an air group from the last four squadrons. This arrangement did not affect the other units, and on May 16, the 8th Squadron was assigned to III Corps. The movement of squadron alignment from division to corps was formalized in a May 28 order from the People's War Committee. In the last major structural change in the VR, control of the flying units (all now honored with "Red" in their names, and the single-seat units designated as fighter squadrons) was returned to the Air HQ, with operational command delegated to the army corps.[73] The exact rationale for this series of decisions is unclear, but it fits the trend of increased centralization across the HSR armed forces as the competence of commanders and staffs grew and the disorder of the retreat subsided. Acquisition authority still resided with the Aviation Department, and on May 24 it proposed production targets to aircraft manufacturers. The suggested output was twenty aircraft per month: ten from MARE, six from MÁG, and four from Lloyd. That rate of production, it calculated, would allow complete replacement of five ten-plane squadrons per quarter, after accounting for the diversion of ten aircraft to training schools.[74] The next quarter's production figures are not available, but from November 1918 to August 1919 Hungarian factories turned out 123 aircraft.[75]

On the evening of May 19, the Red Army launched an offensive against Czechoslovakia. The regime judged the Czechoslovak army to be the weakest of the occupying forces; the Felvidék counties of Nógrád and Borsod were rich in manufacturing capacity; and the industrialized Czech lands appeared ripe for a proletarian revolution.[76] If successful, the invasion would reclaim part of Upper Hungary, establish a Slovak Soviet Republic, and overthrow the imperialist regime in Prague. Kun timed the operation to coincide with a planned uprising in Vienna, and he hoped that HSR troops would link up with the Russian Red Army attacking across Bessarabia. The Austrian rising fizzled and the Russian cavalry never arrived. Landler's III Corps acquitted itself well, however, and captured Miskolc on the morning of May 21.[77] This victory energized his soldiers and in less than three weeks they routed the Czech army.

Hungarian airmen played a bigger role in the northern campaign than they had in the April fighting against Romania. They conducted reconnaissance sorties before and during the invasion, attacked Czechoslovak ground forces, and served in the liaison role. One event brings to mind the 1911 autumn maneuvers in the Pilis mountains. On the first day of the advance, counterattacking Czechoslovak forces had cut off the 3rd Division's 80th International Brigade in Salgótarján. The division immediately dispatched a crew from the 3rd Squadron, who dropped instructions to the brigade to turn south to envelop the Czechoslovaks.[78] Some aerial attacks were made in close support of infantry (the method of coordination between air and ground is not recorded), but most targets seem to have been on fixed sites or along lines of communications. Armored trains fit in the last category, and they were perhaps the best-defended asset on the battlefield. Two 8th Squadron airmen were killed and Mátyás Bernárd, the new commander of the 7th Squadron, was seriously wounded during an attack on an armored train on May 29. Even the float-planes of the 9th Squadron saw action, supporting the river monitor operations and bombing an artillery battery in Komárom.[79] Counterrevolutionary river monitors became the targets of the VR on at least one occasion, when on June 24 the 8th Squadron was ordered to bomb gunships manned by anti-Kun forces that had attacked targets along the capital's riverbanks.[80]

The Czechoslovak air force was manned, like the VR, by pilots from the LFT. Unlike Hungary, Czechoslovakia did not have its own defense establishment under the Dual Monarchy. There were, of course, regiments raised from the Czech and Slovak lands, but they did not match the number of Magyars in the Common Army, and there was no home guard or staff equivalent of the Honvéd-ség.[81] On the other hand, Czechoslovakia enjoyed substantial support from the Entente, including eventually the direct intervention of a French squadron. Although Czechoslovakian airmen planned for an eighty-two-plane force of six squadrons, in December 1918 they had only eighteen serviceable machines in two squadrons. In early February the number was down to seven, but they added four fly-able reconnaissance planes later that month with the capture of the Hungarian airfield at Kassa. Czechoslovak forces flew fifty-nine combat sorties during the northern campaign. The French unit attached to them, a mixed squadron of Breguet and Salmson recon-naissance bombers and SPAD fighters, flew more than a hundred missions and provided excellent support to the ground forces, but did not change the outcome of the campaign.[82]

The Hungarian attack on Czechoslovakia was a tactical and operational success, but a strategic failure. The Red Army deci-sively defeated the enemy forces, reclaimed a thousand square miles of territory, and established a friendly revolutionary govern-ment in rump Slovakia. But Kun eventually gave in to Entente pres-sure to pull out of Slovakia, after securing a promise for a reciprocal Romanian retreat from the Tisza. Romania did not comply with the deal made in its name, and Hungary's voluntary withdrawal did irreparable harm to the Red Army. "The governing council's deci-sion fundamentally broke the morale of the troops ordered back to Hungary."[83] Its top leaders resigned, there was an unsuccessful coup attempt, and the counterrevolutionary National Army became a more hospitable place for noncommunist patriots. The chaos threatened the existence of the HSR, and for that reason the com-mitted internationalist Kun ordered the Red Army to prepare to eject the Romanian army. Universal conscription, made necessary by desertions and refused orders, was introduced on July 12. In some divisions the situation resembled the last weeks of the First World War. Nevertheless, Jenő Landler and Ferenc Julier, the new commander in chief and chief of staff, planned the offensive, which began on July 20. The Hungarians had some success early and managed a few bridgeheads on the east side of the Tisza, but the success was short-lived. On the fourth day Romanian reserves arrived. They pushed the Red Army back and eventually forced the river. From July 31, defeat turned to catastrophe. Julier reported that the troops "did not want to fight any more at any price."[84] That same day Kun received Lenin's response to his telegram for help. Lenin allowed that he would like to help his Magyar friends, but his own poverty of armed force precluded it.[85] Kun correctly apprehended the situation and the following day he addressed the Budapest Workers' Council, declared that the dictatorship of the proletariat had collapsed, and fled to Austria on a special train. On August 4, 1919, Romanian troops entered Budapest.

Air operations on the eastern front had intensified well before the ground offensive was launched in late July. Both sides conducted reconnaissance flights as well as defensive fighter sorties. On the morning of June 12, two 8th Fighter Squadron pilots recorded the first air-to-air victory for a national Hungarian air force. Géza Keisz and László Újváry were scrambled on reports of a Romanian observation plane in the vicinity of Miskolc. They caught the plane, a captured UFAG C.I in Romanian colors, headed toward the demarcation line southeast of Miskolc. Keisz and Újváry chased it to 300 feet before Újváry, an Italian front ace, shot it down. Both Grupul 5 airmen were killed. Three days later another 8th Fighter Squadron pilot, József Kretz, scored a victory on the northern front. Kretz, flying an Aviatik D.I, shot down a Breguet bomber that was attempting to bomb Győr.[86]

For the July offensive, four squadrons (2nd, 3rd, 6th, and 8th), comprising twenty-four aircraft, were available to the VR. Grupul 5 had three squadrons, and on July 20 could field seventeen airplanes—ten fighters and seven two-seaters, of which eight were

Hungarian machines captured on airfields or after forced landings. At the end of the fighting, only six Grupul 5 planes were serviceable. France tried to assist the Romanian air force by sending twenty Breguet bombers, but of the first eight deliveries, only two reached the front; the others crashed due to bad weather or the inexperience of their Romanian crews.[87] As in April, the length of the front (150 miles) divided by the number of aircraft engaged (perhaps twenty on both sides in a day) gave a very low aircraft density, and therefore few opportunities for dogfights. Reconnaissance was the primary mission of both forces. But some squadrons, including the VR's 5th at Kecskemét, which received in late June two new Brandenburg C. Is and three refurbished Anatra trainers, managed a number of ground attack sorties. They broke up a Romanian column near Szentes on July 21, and the following day three squadron aircraft supported the Red Army in the same area with bombs (most likely 25-pound devices) and strafing attacks.[88] On July 31, the last day of organized resistance, 2nd Squadron crews, also flying from Kecskemét, bombed bridges on the Tisza to slow the Romanian advance.[89]

The VR maintained its cohesion until the end, with no signs of the dissension that corrupted the ground component of the Red Army. Airplanes eventually have to land, however, and when the Red Army no longer could provide the VR secure airstrips, it ceased to be an effective combat force. In the aftermath of the Romanian occupation, it nearly ceased to be a force at all. When Romanian troops captured Kecskemét, all eight of the remaining 2nd and 5th Squadron aircraft were seized. The same fate befell the 6th Squadron, which had packed its equipment on rail cars and fled. The unit made it as far as Gödöllő before the being caught. The newly created 10th Squadron's eight Berg fighters never left the factory at Rákosmező. Ninth Squadron had only two W.29s remaining, but they too were captured. Elements of the 1st, 2nd, 4th, and 8th Squadrons managed to escape to Transdanubia, and these aircraft formed the basis for the brief pre-Trianon national air force.[90]

Figure 2.2. A VR Phönix C.I nosed over on the Mátyásföld airfield outside Budapest, June 1919. Courtesy of Dénes Bernád.

White forces in Szeged had created a paper squadron four months earlier and had offered 5,000 koronas for any pilot who defected with an airplane, but there were no takers. A later plan called for a five-squadron force that included an Austrian detachment to support the counterrevolutionary Lehár group. A party was dispatched to Vienna to secure thirty airplanes from the Liquidation Commission, but this attempt was blocked by the ruling Social Democrats' boycott on the transfer of arms to the Whites.[91] Therefore the flying corps prepared for the reoccupation of Budapest with the handful of aircraft saved from the Romanians.

The Defense Ministry reorganized the 37th Section on August 22, 1919, and officially established the National Army Flying Corps on October 12. Lieutenant Colonel István Petróczy was tasked to lead the thirteen officers of the 37th Section.[92] At the head of the Flying Corps was Major Artúr Bogyay, Hangay's deputy in the Károlyi-era service and later the commander of the 1st Air

Group. Subordinate units included squadrons at Szeged, Szombathely, and Budapest, with a detachment at Siófok. The Szeged squadrons had approximately fifteen officers and eighty enlisted men, and shared the three operable aircraft. Vince Martinek, commander of the 5th Squadron at Szeged in the VR, commanded the new training squadron there. At Szombathely, László Háry led the remains of the 8th Fighter Squadron: sixteen officers, thirteen noncommissioned officers, fifty-five men and five (later two) aircraft. József Steiner, also a VR Air Group commander, headed the Budapest squadron, which existed only in its hundred or so personnel—it had no aircraft at all. There were very few missions in those days. An airmail route between Siófok and Szeged was established, as was a standing flight from Szeged to Székesfehérvár.[93] In spite of the desultory pace of flying, losses still occurred. A medical report indicates that Hugó Matzenauer, then the commander of the 5th Squadron, had a hard landing on August 14 that completely destroyed the airplane and left Matzenauer sidelined for two months with broken ribs.[94] In mid-November there was a return to reconnaissance, air police, and propaganda sorties. A four-ship formation of fighters was dispatched to reconnoiter the city and its environs, monitor the Romanian army's withdrawal, and to stand ready to attack in support of the National Army if required. The Romanian pullout complete, the flying corps scattered White leaflets along the capital's main boulevards and accompanied the National Army's procession.[95]

The twenty months from the end of the First World War until the acceptance of the Treaty of Trianon helped shape the Hungarian air force for years to come. Magyar airmen learned that they could rely on their comrades to remain loyal and disciplined whatever the political orientation of their leaders. They grew in their appreciation for the contributions of air power, but understood its limitations and relationship to ground forces. And they expected that flight operations had to be conducted in spite of austere surroundings and minimal technical support. These lessons, first de-

UPHEAVAL

69

rived from their experiences in the Habsburg air service, were subsequently reinforced in the revolutionary period, and would inform operations in 1941–1945 as well.

NOTES

1. A few words about "patriotism" and "professionalism": I do not use these terms to express approval (that is, as synonyms for "good") but rather because the evidence shows that the overwhelming majority of airmen served Hungary regardless of the government's ideological orientation, and that they exhibited the traits of a professional armed force. Samuel Huntington, for example, listed expertise, responsibility, and corporateness as professional hallmarks in *The Soldier and the State* (pp. 8–10). The Hungarian air service, like the Habsburg force from which it descended, met these criteria. Huntington's analysis of what defines a modern officer corps is useful, although his later discussions of civil-military relations and objective control are not relevant.

2. The Austrian Landwehr and Hungarian Honvédség were the national land defense components of the Dual Monarchy's armed forces. Magyar was the language of command in the Honvédség.

3. Nagyváradi et al., *Fejezetek a repülés történetéből*, p. 109. The authors do not offer a reference for this claim.

4. Deák, *Beyond Nationalism*, p. 4.

5. Centripetal/centrifugal paradigm: Oszkár Jászi, cited in Cole and Unowsky, *Limits of Loyalty*, p. 2. Opposition to nationalism: Deák, *Beyond Nationalism*, p. 183.

6. In 1910, Hungarians made up 19.6% of the Imperial population, 23.1% of the Common Army's rank and file, 23.7% of reserve officers, but only 9.3% of career officers. See Stone, "Army and Society," p. 99; and Deák, *Beyond Nationalism*, pp. 179–183. Deák questions the accuracy of the ethnic calculations based on the accounting criteria, and thinks minorities among career officers may have identified as German due to their self-reported daily language.

7. Rothenberg, *Army of Francis Joseph*, pp. 127, 146. Deák found that Magyar officers born in Hungary advanced faster than any other nationality (including Germans), and eight Honvéd officers were admitted to each general staff school course without having to take the admission exam.

8. There seems to be no significance to the section's number: Section 36 was given to People's Uprising, and 38 was for Equine Affairs.

9. Gellért, "Adalékok a magyar történetéhez," p. 504.

10. Morrow, *German Air Power*, p. 182.

11. Gellért, "Adalékok a magyar történetéhez," p. 504.

12. Nagyváradi et al., *Fejezetek a repülés történetéből*, p. 122.

13. Gellért, "Adalékok a magyar történetéhez," p. 506.

14. Nagyváradi et al., *Fejezetek a repülés történetéből*, pp. 110–113.

15. Czirók, "A magyar repülőcsapatok," p. 614.

16. Károlyi, *Memoirs*, p. 102.

17. Farkas, "Military Collapse of the Austro-Hungarian Monarchy," p. 20.

18. Károlyi, *Memoirs*, p. 130.

19. Text of Belgrade Armistice in Krizman, "Belgrade Armistice of 13 November 1918," pp. 85–87.

20. See "Armistice Convention with Austria-Hungary . . . November 3, 1918."

21. Pastor, *Hungary between Wilson and Lenin*, pp. 65, 69. The Czechoslovak incursion on November 9 forced Linder to resign. He signed in Belgrade as minister without portfolio and ambassador at large.

22. Nagyváradi et al., *Fejezetek a repülés történetéből*, pp. 115–117.

23. Ibid.

24. Czirók, "A magyar repülőcsapatok," p. 607.

25. Nagyváradi et al., *Fejezetek a repülés történetéből*, p. 120.

26. Czirók, "A magyar repülőcsapatok," pp. 606, 619.

27. HL HM Eln. 5141/37.-1919.

28. Gellért, "Adalékok a magyar történetéhez," pp. 506–507.

29. Romsics, *Hungary in the Twentieth Century*, p. 29.

30. Nötel, "International Credit and Finance," 2:178, 193.

31. Gellért, "Adalékok a magyar történetéhez," p. 506.

32. 450 korona per month: Liptai, *A Magyar Vörös Hadsereg harcai*, p. 55. Lieutenant colonel's pay in 1907: Deák, *Beyond Nationalism*, p. 119.

33. Szakály, "Officer Corps of the Red Army," pp. 170–172.

34. Chadwick, *Nationalities of Europe and the Growth of National Ideologies*, p. 3.

35. "A Hadügyi Népbiztosság Légügyi Osztálya intézkedik a repülőalakulatok hadiállapotba helyezéséről és a legfontosabb feladatokról, 1919 március 24," in *A Magyar Vörös Hadsereg 1919*, pp. 85–86.

36. Nagyváradi et al., *Fejezetek a repülés történetéből*, pp. 128, 143.

37. Szakály, "Officer Corps of the Red Army," p. 175.

38. Ibid.

39. Romsics, "Social Basis of the Communist Revolution," p. 160.

40. Tőkés, *Béla Kun and the Hungarian Soviet Republic*, p. 200.

41. Hajdú, *Hungarian Soviet Republic*, p. 143.

42. Gosztony, "Collapse of the Hungarian Red Army," p. 70.

43. Balogh, "Nationality Problems," p. 114.

44. Quoted in Gosztony, "Collapse of the Hungarian Red Army," p. 76.

45. Ibid. The commissar in question was the Marxist philosopher György Lukács; the article was published in *Élet és Irodalom* in May 1975.

46. 60 miles west: Hajdu, "Revolution, Counterrevolution, Consolidation," p. 302; several thousand square miles: Károlyi, *Memoirs*, p. 152.

47. Romsics, *Hungary in 20th Century*, p. 98.

48. Károlyi, *Memoirs*, p. 152. Vix denied having stated that the boundaries represented a final decision. Bryan Cartledge in *Will to Survive* says the evidence that he did so is "compelling" (p. 307).

49. Károlyi, *Memoirs*, pp. 153–154.

50. Cartledge, *Will to Survive*, p. 306.

51. Károlyi, *Memoirs*, pp. 154–158; and Pastor, *Between Wilson and Lenin*, p. 143.

52. Tőkés, *Béla Kun and the Hungarian Soviet Republic*, p. 137.

53. Cartledge, *Will to Survive*, p. 309.

54. Pastor, *Between Wilson and Lenin*, p. 145.

55. Hajdu, "Revolution," p. 304. Károlyi wrote of Smuts's offer: "These amazingly favorable conditions should have been accepted without delay."

56. Romsics, *Hungary in 20th Century*, p. 105.

57. "A Népbiztosság Légügyi Osztálya intézkedik," pp. 85–87.

58. Ibid.

59. Deployment: Czirók, "Az első légiháború Magyarország fellett-1919," p. 338. 76-millimeter capability: Barczy and Sárhidai, *A Magyar Királyi Honvédség Légvédelme*, p. 10.

60. Czirók, "Első légiháború Magyarország felett," pp. 338–339.

61. Liptai, *Magyar Vörös Hadsereg harcai*, 73; and Csizmarik, "Magyar Tanácsköztársaság Légiereje," pp. 355–357.

62. Gellért, "Adalékok a magyar történetéhez," p. 510. Liptai places the float-planes also under Air HQ control, but Gellért's account accords with Nagyváradi et al.'s contention that 9th Squadron largely supported riverine operations (*Fejezetek a repülés történetéből*, p. 136).

63. Czirók, "A magyar repülőcsapatok," pp. 620–627.

64. Fogarassy, "Eastern Campaign of the Hungarian Red Army," pp. 36–37.

65. Liptai, *Magyar Vörös Hadsereg harcai*, pp. 64, 70.

66. Bernád, "A Román Királyi Légierő első magyarországi hadjárata," pp. 32–34.

67. Horváth, "Visszaemlékezés" (HL Tgy 3.643), pp. 17–18.

68. Vermes, "October Revolution in Hungary," p. 54.

69. *A Magyar Tanácsköztársaság Röplapjai*, pp. 35, 84, 163, 250.

70. Szakály, "Officer Corps of the Red Army," p. 172.

71. Gosztony, "Collapse of the Red Army," p. 69.

72. Csizmarik, "Magyar Tanácsköztársaság Légiereje," p. 355.

73. Ibid., pp. 361–362; Gellért, "Adalékok a magyar történetéhez," p. 511.

74. "A Hadügyi Népbiztosság Légügyi Osztályának előterjesztése a repülőgépgyártásról," in *A Magyar Vörös Hadsereg 1919*, pp. 265–266.

75. Czirók, "A magyar repülőcsapatok," p. 616.

76. Balogh, "Nationality Problems," p. 114.

77. Hetés, "Northern Campaign of the Hungarian Red Army," p. 56.

78. "A 3. Hadosztályparancsnokság repülőgépről ledobott parancsában

utasítja a salgótarjánnál bekerített csapatokat déli irányú támadásra," in
A Magyar Vörös Hadsereg 1919, p. 287.

79. Csizmarik, "Magyar Tanácsköztársaság Légiereje," p. 381; and Nagyváradi et al., *Fejezetek a repülés történetéből*, p. 135.

80. Horváth, "Visszaemlékezés," p. 27.

81. Of every 1,000 men in the Habsburg army, 223 were Magyars, 135 Czechs, and 38 Slovaks. Rothenberg, "Habsburg Army in the First World War," p. 74.

82. Czirók, "A magyar repülőcsapatok," pp. 624–625. The Société Pour L'Aviation et ses Dérivés (SPAD) was a successful French aircraft manufacturing consortium during the First World War.

83. Gosztony, "Collapse of the Red Army," p. 69.

84. Ibid., pp. 71–73.

85. "Lenin távirata Kun Bélához a kért katonai segítség ügyében," in *A Magyar Vörös Hadsereg 1919*, pp. 481–482.

86. Bernád, "A Román Királyi Légierő első magyarországi hadjárata," p. 37.

87. Czirók, "A magyar repülőcsapatok," pp. 625–626.

88. Kenyeres, *Kecskeméti katonai repülés története kezdetektől a Gripenig*, pp. 19–21.

89. Csizmarik, "Magyar Tanácsköztársaság Légiereje," pp. 385–386.

90. Bernád, "A Román Királyi Légierő első magyarországi hadjárata," pp. 40–41.

91. Nagyváradi et al., *Fejezetek a repülés történetéből*, p. 142.

92. Vesztényi, "A magyar katonai repülés" (HL Tgy 2.787), p. I/24.

93. Czirók, "A magyar repülőcsapatok," pp. 630–631.

94. HL HM Eln. 16385/37.-1919.

95. Nagyváradi et al., *Fejezetek a repülés történetéből*, pp. 142–143.

3

Evasion: 1920–1927

EVEN AS NATIONAL ARMY FLYING CORPS' AIRPLANES, each with a black-lettered "H" painted over the VR's red star, circled the parliament building during Admiral Horthy's triumphant parade on November 16, 1919, the Hungarian fliers knew the Corps' days were numbered. Germany had signed the Treaty of Versailles in June, Austria the Treaty of Saint-Germain-en-Laye in September, and both treaties required the vanquished countries to dismantle their air forces. Hungarian airmen expected to fare no better. Before the terms of the treaty were given the Aviation Department had declared its intention to preserve a national air service in spite of possible legal restrictions. For most of the next decade however, Hungary's military weakness, economic dependency, and diplomatic isolation prevented the airmen from defying the Allies directly. Instead they practiced subterfuge and obfuscation, attempting to disguise prohibited military activity as commercial or sport flight, while at the same time doing all they could to promote the growth of legitimate civilian aviation endeavors. This same pattern of resistance—protest the conditions, then pretend to accept them while working to prevent their implementation—was employed by the army as well as the Foreign and Finance Ministries to minimize the adverse effects of the Treaty of Trianon.

The foundation for resistance to the treaty by Hungarian airmen was laid in a memorandum circulated in late September 1919.

This memo contained both analysis and prescription, first describing the anticipated effects of the peace treaty and then offering a proposal to circumvent the air clauses:

> After assuming that the Hungarian peace treaty will agree in large measure with the Austrian, we have to count on the complete destruction of Hungarian military aviation (*a magyar aviatika teljes megsemmisítésével*). And this means an even greater loss for the Hungarian National Army being formed against the victor states' forces, since everywhere we see the enormous development of aviation as the armed forces' third branch, along with the land and naval forces. The explanation for this large-scale expansion of aviation in the modern armed force lies in the experience of the war, when the flying corps became the army's most important factor, without which not only will the army leaders be practically blind, but the infantry and artillery will also be incapable of accomplishing their missions.
>
> The 37th Section, as Hungarian military aviation's chief responsible directing organization, wants to fulfill its duty by calling its superiors' attention to the above, because it considers its duty to point out every possibility which could ensure that, if required, the national army would not be forced to do without a flying corps that is properly trained and possesses all appropriate equipment, even if by so doing we should have to account for the evasion of the peace treaty's relevant provisions (*ha ezáltal a békeszerződés idevágó rendelkezéseinek megkerülésével kellene számolnunk*).[1]

With the intention to skirt the treaty established, the author outlined the method. The Defense Ministry's 37th Section should be officially dissolved, along with the current Civilian Aviation Committee. The successor agency would combine their functions under the Commerce Ministry. The location in the Commerce Ministry was strictly for the Allies' benefit: the new Aviation Committee would in fact be "one of the Defense Ministry's organizations, which would be hidden under a civilian dressing gown due to the pressure of the peace treaty's conditions."[2] This plan was a clear signal that Hungarian airmen remained committed to air power despite the damage caused to the flying corps by the Romanian occupation, and that they rejected in advance the right of the Allies to strip the country of the means to exercise that power.[3]

The chief of staff accepted the proposal, and therefore the Aviation Department's first step to preserve the air service was to eliminate itself. On February 1, 1920, the 37th Section was abolished and its successor established under the auspices of the Commerce Ministry.[4] Section II Air Transport (Légiforgalmi szakosztály) had fifteen personnel, a budget of 1.4 million koronas, and worked from offices in the National Archives building.[5] István Petróczy remained in charge without his military rank.[6] This Air Transport Section functioned as the Hungarian air staff, and its establishing order left no doubt that commercial aviation personnel, materiel, and industry would be subordinated to the requirements of national defense.[7]

As if to illustrate that point, the first Hungarian national airline operated along clear military lines. MAEFORT (Magyar Aeroforgalmi Részvénytársaság) was created by decree in February 1920, equipped with the remains of the aviation materiel that survived the intervention. Count József Teleki led a survey of the existing stores and tallied their value at 20 million pengős. The government then "sold" the materiel (over 800 items, everything from hangars to unfinished fuselages to lubricants) to MAEFORT, which subsequently inflated its worth and publicized its operating capital at 50 million pengős.[8] The airline also received a 10-million-korona subvention from the government. MAEFORT was expected to provide two squadrons of fliers ninety minutes of flight time per month, to obtain and store spare parts sufficient for twenty-five aircraft, to support a training squadron, and to maintain airfields in working order.[9] Since MAEFORT's collection of one- and two-seat former LFT and VR aircraft was not suitable for passenger travel, the airline's first operation was a scheduled airmail service from Budapest to Szeged and Szombathely.[10] To celebrate the initiation of the service, MAEFORT hosted an exhibition at Rákosmező that featured stunt flying, an aerial combat demonstration, and parachute jumping. The air show drew the attention of the

Figure 3.1. The entrance to the Szombathely airfield. The MAEFORT sign hangs under the military crest. Photo: Fortepan/Dezső Szent-Istvány.

country's senior leaders, with Admiral Horthy, Count Pál Teleki, and the Archduke Joseph all in attendance.[11] This early attempt at deception ultimately failed. MAEFORT's transparently military organization and mission could not be hidden from Allied inspectors, who forced the company's dissolution in early December 1921.

The inspectors belonged to the Aeronautical Inter-Allied Commission of Control (AICC), the agency charged with verifying Hungarian compliance with the air clauses of the Treaty of Trianon. Those clauses were as bad as the airmen had feared. The national flying corps was prohibited, and all air service personnel were to be demobilized within two months of the treaty coming into force. All trade and manufacture of aircraft parts of any kind was forbidden for six months. The naval and military clauses were similarly severe. All warships were to be broken up, fleet auxiliary ships disarmed and reconverted to civilian use, and submarines were forbidden for any purpose. Command and control systems did not escape the Allies' notice. They demanded that the high-power wireless transmitter in Budapest was to be used only for commercial ends for a period of three months. Hungary's army was restricted to a volunteer force of 35,000 total personnel, of whom no more than one-twentieth could be officers. Because its mission was restricted to internal security and border control, the type and size of units and their armaments were specified.[12] These were vic-tors' terms, intended to ensure that the defeated belligerent would not have the capacity to threaten its neighbors.

Nearly identical provisions were included in the treaties with Austria, Bulgaria, and Turkey, whose armed forces also were drasti-cally reduced in size and scope. The treaties were unpopular in those countries, but they never became national obsessions as in Hungary. The difference, of course, was in Hungary's massive loss of territory and population to surrounding states. Historic Hun-gary covered nearly 109,000 square miles; post-Trianon Hungary was one-third that size. More land was ceded to Romania (40,000 square miles) than retained (36,000 square miles). Population changes were only slightly less drastic. From Hungary's 1910 popu-lation of 18.2 million people, just 7.6 million remained within its borders as drawn at Trianon. More than 3 million Magyars found themselves residents of neighboring, and generally hostile, coun-tries.[13] Budapest's reaction to the treaty was captured by *The Times* on January 19, 1919, the day after the conditions were published: "Although a hard peace had been foreseen, the severity of the actual terms has astonished not only the general public but also the Prime Minister himself and other public men. The whole city has gone into mourning. Black flags hang from the public buildings."[14] The signing of the treaty on June 4, 1920, brought a similar response. Hundreds of thousands protested in the streets, shouting, "Nem! Nem! Soha!" ("No! No! Never!"), the daily newspapers were printed with black borders, and the national colors were flown at half-mast, where they would remain until 1938.[15] Trianon was a "psychological shock . . . whose terms were unacceptable to all Hungarians regardless of social background or ideological orientation."[16] One recent study examined Hungarian irredentism through a sociological lens as a cult, and found that although government and right-wing social groups helped guide the response, "the spontaneous reactions of the population should not be underestimated since a great part of the society were personally affected by the loss of territory and of population."

> There were many whose birthplace, relatives, friends, forebears, assets or commercial interests were now on the far side of the new borders, others had treasured personal travel and literary experiences linking them to the lost areas and were embittered by the fate threatening their former compatriots. Some turned against the peace treaty simply because of their patriotism and there were also those who became severe critics of the treaty because of the sober realisation that there would be serious distortions in the world economy and world politics because of the new order. There were practically no Hungarians who approved of the changes. Those few, whose detestation of the counter-revolutionary system was so intense that they objected to any revision of the peace treaty for the benefit of 'Horthy's Hungary,' later and with a more thorough understanding of the situation became critics of the Treaty of Trianon and supporters of its revision.[17]

Revisionism became the animating impulse of the Horthy regime, the "fixed point to which every subsequent act of Hungarian international policy was directly related."[18]

The Horthy era officially began with the admiral's election to the regency on March 1, 1920, although as head of the National Army he had wielded considerable influence during the transitional Huszár government from November 1919. Law I of 1920, which established Hungary as a kingdom, also set out the means by which the regent (*kormányzó*) was to be elected and enumerated his powers, which corresponded roughly with those of the president of a republic. Though he was given a fairly free hand in matters of foreign affairs and defense policy, the regent's legislative mandate was rather constrained. He could not, for instance, veto legislation, being permitted instead only to send a bill back to the parliament for reconsideration, nor was his assent required for laws passed by the parliament to come into force. He retained, however, the once-royal prerogative of convoking or dissolving the assembly, and could appoint or dismiss the prime minister without consulting the legislature. Additionally, it was to the regent as supreme war lord (*legfelsőbb hadúr*) that the troops swore allegiance, and he had authority for the organizing, training, and equipping the armed forces within the budgetary limits approved by the parliament.[19]

Horthy's ability to rally the army to his flag proved crucial during Charles IV's second attempt to regain Hungary's crown. Charles's first foray into postwar Hungary had come in the spring of 1921, when he had arrived at Szombathely on Easter Saturday and proceeded to Budapest with an entourage of legitimists. Horthy knew well that the Allies would consider a Habsburg enthronement an act of war, and he managed to convince Charles to return to Switzerland.[20] Prime Minister Count Pál Teleki's ill-advised decision to publish Charles's manifesto caused Horthy to dismiss him and appoint in his place Count István Bethlen, who would hold the position for a decade. In October 1921, Charles sought to exploit the instability surrounding plebiscites in the Burgenland, and tried again to secure the throne. He avoided border controls by flying into Sopron in a German-piloted Junkers F.13 from the Swiss airline Ad Astra Aero.[21] After landing in a field outside the village of Dénesfa, Charles gathered a growing army of loyalists and marched on the capital, with Colonel Antal Lehár and Count Ostenburg at the head of his forces (Ostenburg's battalion had sworn the traditional Honvéd oath to Charles, apparently after being told that he was

responding to a communist uprising in Budapest).[22] Horthy declared martial law and persuaded Lieutenant General Pál Hegedűs,
the commander of the Sopron military region who had accepted
the leadership of the king's army, to withdraw his support from
Charles. With Hegedűs again on the side of the government, the
royalist force was substantially weakened, and following a brief
battle at Budaőrs, Charles agreed to an armistice.[23] Meanwhile,
Prague had ordered mobilization and demanded Hungary's immediate disarmament.[24] After being held under house arrest at the
Tihany monastery, Charles and his wife Princess Zita traveled by
boat, rail, and car through Hungary and Romania to the Black Sea,
whence they went into exile on Madeira.[25] With the possibility of
a Habsburg restoration now permanently foreclosed, Hungary's
position in the region was stabilized. Charles could no longer be
used as a bogeyman by Hungary's neighbors, and the legitimist-free
elector tensions within conservative Hungarian circles were resolved.
Horthy's personal authority was also enhanced by the failure of the
coup. For the 99 percent of the population who desired a king, the
regent was now the best and most authentic alternative.[26]

　　Charles's decision to initiate the royal putsch by air is revealing.
He clearly recognized the abundant advantages of air transport,
and he judged the risks of flight worth running. The incident also
points out the necessity and difficulty of controlling national airspace. The HSR had earlier come to a similar conclusion regarding
the efficacy of personal air travel. In May 1919, VR pilot István
Dobos carried Tibor Szamuely, one of Béla Kun's most trusted and
ruthless lieutenants, from Budapest to Kiev to lobby for Ukrainian
intervention against Romania. Szamuely's mission failed, but the
700-mile flight over the Carpathians in the Brandenburg C.I was
widely celebrated.[27]

　　Admiral Horthy, too, had experienced the power of arriving
personally by air. In the early days of the Szeged counterrevolution,
he flew to Siófok, not yet firmly under the control of his forces. "The
mere sight of the eagle feather on the cap of my aide-de-camp," he

wrote, "indicating his status as an officer in the National Army, sufficed to make the Bolsheviks turn their heels." Elsewhere in his memoirs, Horthy described how a leaflet drop from the White forces' only aircraft caused a "fully equipped squadron of hussars" to defect.[28] Naval aerial reconnaissance had also contributed to Horthy's signature victory over the Italians at Otranto in 1917.[29] The regent was slow to embrace new ideas, and so these examples of air power had not yet made their full impression. He would eventually emerge as an energetic supporter of the cause of Hungarian aviation, declaring, "We were a riding nation; we will become a flying nation" (*Lovas nemzet voltunk, repülőnemzet leszünk*). In the late 1930s his son István would be the country's most prominent airman.[30]

While the major political figures in Hungary and abroad were occupied with great affairs of state, Hungarian staff officers and Entente disarmament inspectors were engaged in a game of cat-and-mouse. The initial attempts to circumvent Trianon's air clauses have already been described: the Aviation Department went underground, a clandestine air staff was formed, and two squadrons were disguised as an airline. Hungary insisted that enforcement of the disarmament clauses could not begin until the treaty was ratified by parliament, which took place only on June 26, 1921. In the period from signing to ratification, the Magyar military establishment carried on business as usual whenever possible. The army increased its intake in the intervening months, squirreling away recruits against the coming winter.[31] The General Staff (Vezérkarfőnökség, VKF), dissolved under the Károlyi government and subsequently proscribed under Trianon, was briefly reestablished from August 1920, and its officers openly wore the distinctive branch badges.[32] In September, the VKF, noting that "aviation is becoming a factor of more considerable importance every day," added two airmen to the VKF, a military aviation representative and his executive deputy.[33] After the treaty came into force, Hungarian airmen initiated "Action E," a deliberate attempt to shuffle aircraft around the country to shield them from the Allies. Perhaps thirty-five machines were saved in this way. Nevertheless, AICC inspectors discovered and destroyed 119 airplanes, 77 aircraft motors, and some quantity of specialized production equipment not included in the peace treaty's terms. (In Austria, which had more aircraft to begin with and did not experience the wastage of an additional war and occupation, 1,333 aircraft and 3,289 motors were destroyed.)[34] Airplanes being difficult to hide, the AICC had good success in unearthing hardware; rooting out illicit organizations was substantially more challenging. Since the shadow air staff in the Commerce Ministry had so far gone unmolested, the government asked Colonel Petróczy to expand the small cadre into a covert air service. Designated Section XI Air Transport, Petróczy's organization consisted of nearly one hundred experienced pilots. The airmen were scattered to work in different government ministries, but ultimately reported to Section XI.

Petróczy had in July 1921 undertaken an intensive three-week research trip to Germany to study the Luftstreitkräfte's organizational reaction to defeat. His itinerary included the German Transportation Ministry, the Aviation Science Association, aero club headquarters, and major airline offices. He had also intended to participate in the Rhön gliding competition, but it was postponed due to inclement weather. The rapid German conversion from military to civilian aviation deeply impressed Petróczy, who reported that "German aviation, between the harsh current conditions and the pressures of the Versailles peace, has reached a degree of development which is exemplary even compared to the Entente."[35] In contrast, he thought Hungary's present situation matched that of prewar Austria, and that no time could be wasted in establishing domestic aviation: "Here is the last hour in which we can create those basic conditions without which aviation cannot develop. During the time of prohibition forced on us by the peace treaty in which we cannot fly, we have to create further opportunities, by increasing propaganda activities, establishing schools and courses, and organizing social and economic associations."[36] Petróczy consciously modeled aspects of his plan on the German experience, particularly the use of civilian flying as a vehicle for the preservation and future development of military aviation. That was the method employed by the pioneer aviator August Euler, who in 1919 was appointed to lead the Reich Aviation Office, an agency that maintained the "incestuous" ties between Luft Hansa and the Reichswehr.[37] Like his German counterpart, Petróczy believed air power was essential for national revival and that its cultivation was a multigenerational undertaking. "I turn to our youth," he wrote, "because Hungary's future greatness depends on them. I will awaken the interest in aviation in every beautiful and impressionable spirit. I will convince them of the tremendous importance of aviation to our country's reconstruction, and that without its development, a broken-winged Hungary will fall behind the other peoples of the world."[38]

Although Petróczy had taken close notice of Euler's bureaucratic initiatives, he apparently missed the operational analysis commissioned by General Hans von Seeckt. Von Seeckt, the commander in chief of the Weimar Reichswehr from 1920 until 1926, believed it "absolutely necessary to put the experience of the war in a broad light, and to collect this experience while the impressions won on the battlefield are still fresh."[39] To that end, in December 1919 he ordered a comprehensive study of the war, directing fifty-seven committees to consider how prewar expectations had borne out; how German forces had responded to unforeseen situations; how the fielding of new weapons had been managed; and which new problems that arose in the war remained unaddressed.[40] Nearly 500 officers ultimately contributed to the effort, out of which grew a new German army doctrine. In a related effort, the head of the Air Service led a study of the air war initially focused on organization, tactics, and technology. The project eventually involved 130 senior airmen, most of them combat commanders or general staff officers, and its scope broadened to include all aspects of aerial warfare. Their self-critical reports formed the basis for Army Regulation

487, *Leadership and Battle with Combined Arms*.[41] There was no Hungarian equivalent to this service-level debrief. Professional military historians published academic articles, and staff officers hustled to preserve men and materiel from Allied inspectors, but each tribe remained on its own reservation. There was no systematic evaluation of operational effectiveness conducted with the intent of incorporation into future doctrine. In the next decade, Hungarian airmen would engage in vigorous theoretical debates about the role and efficacy of air power, but a critical opportunity to improve the Honvéd's effectiveness in a manner not prohibited by Trianon had been missed. It must be mentioned that other countries did not follow Von Seeckt's example either. While most governments published official histories of the war and a few visionary strategists garnered enthusiastic reviews (Billy Mitchell, Basil Liddell Hart, Giulio Douhet), no force other than the Reichswehr subjected itself to such a rigorous examination.

The AICC reported in the spring of 1922 to the Ambassadors' Conference that Trianon's Article 132 requirements for turning over aviation materiel had been fulfilled. On April 5, the AICC was withdrawn.[42] The end of the commission did not mean the end of Entente oversight of Hungarian aviation, however. The Allies extended Article 131's six-month moratorium on the manufacture and import of aircraft and equipment for an additional six months, and in order to enforce the Article 128 prohibition on the establishment of military air forces they left behind an aeronautical inspector seconded to the Inter-Allied Military Commission of Control (IMCC).[43]

From the beginning of the IMCC's mission until its termination in 1927, Hungarian authorities worked diligently to undermine the commission and impede its progress. The Hungarian campaign was inventive and thorough, if not always effective, and the efforts to frustrate inspectors were not confined to warehouses, barracks, or airfields. The first line of attack was economic: the IMCC's expenses, including billeting and salaries, were borne by the defeated

country, and the Hungarian government pressed relentlessly for
reductions in the size of the inspector force.[44] The press was cooperative in this undertaking. *Pesti Hírlap* decried the "outrageous
wages paid to the members of the Commission which has long
terminated its work and remains on for its own convenience."[45]
Magyar protestations on this front eventually wore the Entente
down, and from 1924 the costs of operating the IMCC were deducted from the reparations account. Still, the papers ridiculed the
luxurious lifestyles the stipends afforded. Budapest's legation in
Rome pointed out that the IMCC's senior officer, an Italian general, was paid more than Admiral Horthy. When some wives of
French members were killed in a car crash, "the tragedy was used
to mock the high number of vehicles used by the French delegation."[46] Social isolation was another tool employed against the
monitors. The Hungarian representative to the IMCC, Colonel
Richárd Rapaich, learned the names of Hungarian officers likely to
be issued social invitations by the Allied members and quietly instructed them to shun the inspectors in public.[47]

From the moment the IMCC teams left their dwellings (first-
class hotels for the officers), interference was the order of the day.
Surprise inspections were permitted but rarely achieved. Convoys
were followed to the outskirts of Budapest by bicycle-mounted
scouts before having their destination confirmed by roadside observers. After the inspection location was ascertained, *csendőr*
(gendarme) checkpoints delayed officials' arrival until evidence of
illicit activity could be hidden. If the inspection were to take place
at an airfield, the gate guards would hold the inspectors outside the
field until the station commander approved their entry. The station
commander would invariably be hard to find at short notice; while
the guards were desperately searching for him, engineering staff
would make operable aircraft appear to be useless spares, and then
those personnel in excess of authorization would disappear. The
station commander could then turn up, make the appropriate apol-
ogies, and welcome the inspectors to his airfield. When a surprise

inspection did come off smoothly, IMCC personnel faced the possibility of angry crowds awaiting their departure. The mob always seemed to be better informed than the police, who tended to show up a bit late.[48] On at least one occasion, shots were fired at the French delegation, injuring the driver (almost certainly a Hungarian national). The government refused to apologize for the attack, a position the British Foreign Office thought "characteristic of their whole attitude towards military control."[49]

One series of incidents did lead to an apology from Count Bethlen, and to the sacking of a defense minister. In December 1922, Allied inspectors had been denied permission to search a hut on the premises of a barracks they believed held a stash of rifles. The confrontation occurred in full view of the public and was widely reported in the press as a defeat for the IMCC. The following month, "representatives of the commission discovered 300 carbines and 33,000 rounds of ammunition in the house of a retired colonel of the regular army in Budapest. The explanations furnished by the Hungarian Minister of Defense were described by the commission as puerile, and the tone of the two letters he has addressed to them on the subject have been defiant and truculent."[50] The situation nearly repeated itself in late March. Allied inspectors were searching a house in the garrison town of Kecskemét, and again they were denied access to a storage building. The inspectors could see long wooden crates in the shed through the door, and their interpreter overheard members of the crowd boast that they would not allow a single weapon to be seized. Nevertheless, the Hungarian army officer who showed up in mufti refused to open the gate without orders from his superiors. Meanwhile the local police declined to control the crowd, whose attitude "became more and more menacing." The Allied officers suspected the mob was largely composed of members of the irredentist group Ébredő Magyarok Egyesülete (Awakening Hungarians). When after nearly an hour the inspectors gave up and began to make their way "with great difficulty" back to their vehicles, the crowd pelted their cars with stones, breaking windows. The inspectors escaped unharmed but furious.[51] After the IMCC filed a formal complaint, the Hungarian government handed out "grossly inadequate punishments." The Foreign Office informed Budapest's chargé d'affaires that "His Majesty's Government were seriously displeased at the incident."[52] When this failed to bring about more than vague expressions of regret, the British minister in Budapest repeatedly addressed the issue with Bethlen, who promised to look into the matter further. Only when threatened with the loss of the loans he had secured in London did Bethlen take action. He asked for Sándor Belitska's resignation, and appointed in his place Count Károlyi Csáky. That Bethlen was willing to ignore the Allied demands for apology and redress until faced with losing the Western financial infusion demonstrates the contempt the IMCC engendered even at the top levels of government.

In spite of the constant obstruction, the IMCC did manage to limit Hungary's rearmament. Through its monitoring regime a number of illegal arms caches were discovered, most notably at the Kistétény and Hajmáskér weapons depots, and the Hungarian attempt to build an army reserve by shaving the minimum enlistment periods was slowed. A handful of secretly imported airplanes were seized, but some paramilitary flight schools survived.[53] And although the IMCC was hampered by its small size and a fluctuating degree of motivation (high when a French officer was in charge, less so when an Italian commanded), it at the very least imposed an opportunity cost on Hungarian rearmament. Magyar military officials spent considerable amounts of money and effort trying to evade Trianon's sanctions. Without the IMCC, those resources could have been poured directly into personnel, arms, and training.

Not all of the airmen's intellectual energy was expended in obstruction. The 1923 opening of the French-Romanian airline CIDNA was not an event expected to further the cause of Hungarian air power, but Magyar officers were able to use it to their advantage. The interest of air transport safety, they reasoned, demanded a high-altitude meteorological reconnaissance capability, and the best platform for that mission was the Bristol F.2B, a top-of-the-line British fighter. Somewhat surprisingly, the Entente agreed with this thinking and approved the purchase of two aircraft. The importer's request for "spare parts" was also approved, and under that name he was able to buy four additional machines, complete with state-of-the-art 300-horsepower Hispano-Suiza engines. These aircraft were maintained at the Székesfehérvár-Sóstó workshops, the best equipped maintenance facility in Hungary. The Székesfehérvár machinery had come from Szeged, where it had been quarantined under French occupation, and therefore had not been available for use by the revolutionary government. It was, however, protected from confiscation by Romanian troops, and the plant in its new location far from the frontiers was used for manufacturing and repair.[54]

Planning for a postinspection future carried on as well. In anticipation of the Entente lifting the aerial sanctions, Petróczy forwarded to Prime Minister Bethlen a proposal for the development of a twenty-eight-squadron air force under the cover of a commercial aviation agency. No action was taken until July 1923, when Sándor Belitska, still at that time the defense minister, raised the issue in a ministerial council meeting. Belitska reminded his colleagues that "according to accepted opinion, in a future war, aerial combat will have a large influence on the outcome. . . . Our neighbors, the successor states, have made extraordinary efforts in this direction, such that they have built their armed forces to the maximum extent possible. For us, there is only one path: under the guise of civil aviation, as much as circumstances permit, we must be ready, so that when the opportunity arises, we may move into military aviation quickly and without a hitch."[55]

Belitska's argument carried the day, and the council approved the creation of the Aviation Bureau (Légügyi Hivatal, LÜH), which opened for business in April 1924. Like Section XI, LÜH appeared to be an element of the Commerce Ministry, but was wholly directed by the Defense Ministry. Through such subterfuge Belitska

Figure 3.2. The Bristol F.2B "weather reconnaissance aircraft" was actually a top-of-the-line fighter. Photo: Fortepan/ Dezső Szent-Istvány.

was able to show to Allied inspectors an organization whose nominal strength was twenty, but which in reality numbered nearly 200 personnel, including seventy-four officers.[56] The defense minister's statement is a nearly perfect distillation of Hungarian (and German) air policy in the years of forced disarmament. It contains three of the essential components: certainty about the importance of air power in coming conflicts; concern about potential enemies' air forces; and the commitment to build an air service in spite of international agreements otherwise. The only missing piece was an exhortation to revanchism, support of which would have been assumed and therefore its open expression unnecessary.

Commercial aviation was important not only as a blind for the air force, but also as an engine of economic growth and as a link with the world outside the former Habsburg lands. After MAEFORT was shuttered by the AICC in December 1921, the establishment of a new national airline became a high priority for the government. Magyar Légiforgalmi Részvénytársaság (MALERT) was formed in November 1922, and began a daily service to Vienna in July 1923.[57] The end of the import ban meant that MALERT could purchase

new aircraft from abroad, and the Vienna flights were conducted
in Dutch Fokker F.IIIs, which could carry five passengers in a fully
enclosed cabin.[58] A German-financed competitor, Hungarian Aero
Express, sprang up in early 1923 and also flew the Budapest-Vienna
route. Aero Express pioneered river-based pleasure flights over the
capital, launching float-equipped Junker F.13s from the Danube and
flying to and from Lake Balaton.[59] In the years 1923–1925, the two
companies received equal subsidies from the LÜH (600 million
koronas each total), but the merger of Junkers Luftverkehr and
Deutscher Aero Lloyd into Luft Hansa caused the Bethlen government to worry about excessive German control of Hungarian aviation, and in 1926 the Aero Express subvention ended.[60] The company was dissolved that same year, which left MALERT alone in the
market and without competition for government support. The decision to favor MALERT over Aero Express was based on the prospects of future military necessity, not business efficiency. Aero Express had been more effective than MALERT, and had been a
member of the Trans-Europa Union, a consortium of German,
Swiss, and Austrian airlines that provided regular service along the
route Geneva-Zurich-Munich-Vienna-Budapest.[61]

Trans-Europa had been founded by the German aircraft giant
Junkers primarily as a means to develop markets for its airplanes,
which it hoped would be operated by subsidiary airlines around the
world. Negotiation of contracts with the southern European partners had been left to Erhard Milch, a former Luftstreitkräfte fighter
squadron commander turned Junkers executive, who would later
be named director of Luft Hansa and eventually a Luftwaffe field
marshal.[62] Milch's career trajectory, like the general development
of European aviation in the interwar period, was shaped to a large
degree by the First World War treaties.[63] The phenomenon, although unexpected, is in retrospect completely reasonable. The
victors, nearly as exhausted as the vanquished, were left with vast
stockpiles of military materiel, including aircraft and engines. After
securing peace in the palace halls, the people of the Allied nations

Figure 3.3. Aero Express operated float-equipped Junker F.13s from the Danube. Photo: Fortepan/Tibor Weygand.

lost interest in war and its implements, and aviation enthusiasts commenced beating swords into plowshares. Cheap surplus aircraft proved a windfall for individual pilots, spawning the age of barnstorming, but ultimately the ready availability of parts, especially 1918-vintage engines, retarded technological progress.[64] The situation in the defeated countries was quite different. The professional core of their armed forces chafed under forced disarmament, political leaders sought to restore national respect, and significant elements (in Hungary nearly the entire country) pressed relentlessly for revision. Destruction of the defeated powers' aviation stocks forced airmen in those countries to start with fresh designs rather than adapting older military airframes to civilian purposes. This was an unintended boon, especially to Germany, which retained its sources of raw materials and manufacturing centers in the postwar settlements. Germany also "benefited from the remarkable air-mindedness of the German people," who were willing to subsidize national aviation through subscriptions and donation drives, as they had demonstrated during the Zeppelin craze of the early 1900s.[65] With broad popular support, high levels of technological sophistication, and capable leadership, the German aviation industry was able to thrive despite Versailles' strictures, Weimar's chaos, and astronomical levels of inflation.[66]

Hungary lacked Germany's broad industrial base and deep financial pockets, and its aircraft-manufacturing sector was not able to capitalize on the opportunity of the clean slate. Separated from the Fischamend Arsenal and Škoda Works by imperial dissolution and the natural resources of Transylvania by treaty, the post-Trianon Hungarian aviation industry operated at a severe disadvantage. Nevertheless, domestic production resumed after the expiration of Article 131. In November 1922, Section XI solicited bids for a new training aircraft. The public tender stipulated that the new airplane must conform to the Ambassadors' Conference regulations, but the participating companies were informed secretly that the machine should be capable of being retrofitted with a more powerful engine for future military use.[67] Four designs were submitted and two prototypes requested, although it seems only the design from György Szebeny ever took flight. Szebeny was a former Fischamend engineer familiar with the metal construction techniques of Fokker and Junkers, and his plan was for a metal-skinned, high-wing monoplane with side-by-side seating. The development was plagued with problems. Appropriate metal sheeting could only be obtained from Germany, and in order to save money and reduce production time (Hungarian aircraft builders having very little experience with metal skin), Section XI decided on traditional wood and fabric construction.

The next major change involved the power plant. Jenő Fejes had promised a lightweight radial engine capable of 100 horsepower, but in tests at the end of January 1923 it was unable to lift the Szebeny machine (registration code H-MAAC) into the air. A Mercedes engine had to be fitted, and to reduce drag the fuselage was narrowed and seating changed to tandem.[68] Test flight reports showed that even with its increased output and reduced profile, the aircraft would barely climb above 200 feet. A new propeller improved performance, and the airplane made a series of short flights to airfields around Budapest in late February. After the fitting of a thinner wing in March 1923, H-MAAC managed to reach 1,000 feet.[69] It had in the meantime been presented to MALERT, its supposed purchaser, for inspection. In the middle of April, Szebeny's airplane climbed to 2,000 feet, but by that time Section XI had given up on it for military use. At the same time, a modified prototype of one of the rejected designs had been constructed. Test pilot Antal Fehér took Kocsárd Jánky, chief of the VKF, for a successful flight in H-MAAB, Béla Oravecz's parasol-winged adaptation of the UFAG C.I. With Jánky's enthusiastic support, and following a László Háry test flight, Section XI ordered the Oravecz model for the new flying school being established at Szombathely.[70]

Military flight training was conducted there using MALERT as a front, with expenses filed on fake invoices printed with the company letterhead.[71] Once the danger from Allied inspectors passed, the MALERT directors began to worry about the integrity of their accounts to creditors, prompting a letter to Defense Minister Csáky requesting written acknowledgment of the airline's relationship with the Defense Ministry. "In view of the fact that these secret instructions are only verbal," the letter ran, "major responsibility rests on the company's directors in the event that if for some reason the books are called into question. In light of this, we request that Your Excellency provide a secret transcript to our company for the accountants." Csáky provided the requested memorandum.[72]

The tribulations and ultimate failure of the Szebeny-Fejes design sapped the air service's confidence in domestic production and forced the resignation of Colonel Petróczy. He had insisted that the Hungarian aviation industry was capable of independent production, but he had underestimated both the extent of German and Austrian involvement in earlier Magyar manufacturing, and the effect of the three-year-long enforced suspension. Furthermore, it was suspected that his indiscretion about the tender had drawn the attention of the IMCC. Petróczy was replaced on May 18, 1923, by

Colonel Károly Vassel, a nonflying officer of the VKF. Vassel shared the concern of many of the service's pilots about the quality of the domestic aircraft, but he did not oppose the VKF chief's decision to order Oravecz's high-wing trainer.[73] By the end of 1924, Lieutenant Colonel Waldemár Kenese's flight school at Szombathely operated six Oravecz machines, along with the modified Szebeny prototype (even a poor design was too valuable to waste) and a Brandenburg B.I.[74] Nearly a hundred pilots learned to fly at Szombathely in the Oravecz airplanes, but after a pair of fatal crashes in September and October 1925 related to flight control and wing failures, the school withdrew the remainder from service and destroyed them. Thus ended the Hungarian experiment in aerial autarky. There would be further attempts to build indigenous designs, but never with the hope that domestic manufacture could fill the country's entire need.[75] The thirty-three grounded student pilots were sent to Budapest for a four-month academic course that included instruction in tactics, weapons, radio familiarity, aerial photography, air defense, meteorology, and aerial law.[76] The LÜH then dispatched officers to Austria, Britain, and Germany to search for suitable aircraft for import. Their efforts paid off: five Bristol School and five Udet 12a trainers were delivered to Szombathely by summer 1926. The WM factory on Csepel Island began producing the Udet aircraft under license in 1927.[77] Pilot training and flight time more than doubled after the arrival of the Bristols and Udets, with total hours increasing from fewer than 1,600 in 1925 to over 3,700 in 1927.[78]

The LÜH's turn to imported aircraft and licensed production might have created long-term problems for the Hungarian aviation industry, but it was a victory for Hungarian statecraft, which had sought since 1918 to reintegrate Hungary into European commercial and diplomatic life. Early isolation as a defeated power had been followed by quarantine behind the cordon sanitaire that protected the West from the contagion of communism. Still, the HSR's collapse did little to improve Hungary's international position. Anticipating the rise of treaty revisionism in Hungary, Czech foreign minister Eduard Beneš (Hungary's bête noire) had begun to form an alliance to hem in the Magyar state. In August 1920, Czechoslovakia and Yugoslavia signed a treaty of mutual defense against Hungary, and spurred by fears of Habsburg restoration, Bucharest joined the alliance through bilateral treaties with Prague and Belgrade in 1921. The Little Entente had the full backing of Paris, which had resumed its anti-Magyar orientation after an apparent thaw in Franco-Hungarian relations in 1920 proved illusory.[79] Relations with Austria remained strained after the Burgenland dispute, and Italian rapprochement with both Yugoslavia and Czechoslovakia had closed the door, at least momentarily, to Rome. Weimar Germany was hostile to the counterrevolutionary Horthy government, which itself was implacably opposed to the Soviet Union. Talks aimed at diplomatic recognition and trade agreements with the Soviets had begun in 1922 and recommenced in 1924, but they fell apart in 1925 after Admiral Horthy became aware of the previously secret negotiations. Hungary's only friend in the early 1920s was Poland, with whom it had shared monarchs in the past, and to whom it offered military support in the 1920 Russo-Polish War.[80] The economic situation was no less dire. Foreign investment had dried up, loans were hard to come by, inflation was on the rise, and Trianon had disrupted historic trading patterns and levied reparations.

Prime Minister Bethlen recognized the debilitating weakness of Hungary's international position, and he knew that financial assistance could only follow the breaking of the diplomatic impasse. In his first speech as prime minister, Bethlen declared that his government's primary goal was "the raising of the foreign policy horizon of the nation," and Foreign Minister Miklós Bánffy submitted Hungary's application to join the League of Nations soon after.[81] The Little Entente countries opposed Hungary's accession, as expected, but opposition also came from hard-line Trianon rejectionists within the country, who considered it an implicit endorsement of the hated treaty. The government pointed out that Trianon had already been signed once, and that by joining the League Hungary incurred no additional obligation. Moreover, the Covenant allowed for revisiting accords that threatened peace, and thus could pave the way for peaceful revision. Domestic objections were finally ignored, but international resistance proved harder. Czechoslovakia tried to attach specific reparations requirements to the admission, but after a motion by Poland, Hungary was admitted to the League. For a defeated power, admission to the League amounted to a "political rehabilitation" that allowed the new member to stand as an equal, at least formally under international law, with the victors.[82] Hungary planned to use that legal equality to address its reparations obligations, improve its financial situation, and loosen Allied military control.

The Finance Ministry attacked the reparations requirements in much the same way that the Defense Ministry had undermined the inspection regime. After having unsuccessfully objected to the institution of reparations, the Hungarian government allowed inflation to rise unchecked as a way of decreasing the value of its currency, and therefore reducing the burden of debt and reparations on Hungarian industry. Bethlen and Finance Minister Tibor Kállay then made the rounds of Western capitals, arguing that Hungary would be forced to default unless it received foreign loans.[83] They secured 307 million gold koronas, somewhat less than half what had been solicited, at a rate of 7.5 percent. The money, although intended strictly for reparations, was also used to fund the government's operating budget and to bring the deliberate inflation under control. This cash injection, along with reductions in government spending and increased tax revenues, allowed Hungary to end 1925 with its accounts in surplus. Hungarian financial stability fed international confidence, which led to dramatically increased private investment in the country, allowing strong growth through the rest of the decade until the onset of the Great Depression in 1929.[84]

Hungary wasted no time in confronting the issue of the IMCC. The day after joining the League of Nations, its representative petitioned to have League members assume responsibility for the inspection mission. The Ambassadors' Council prevailed on the League to decline the request, but Hungary had made its point regarding disparate treatment under international law and had served notice that it intended to use the League to further its own purposes.[85] Budapest opened a new front in its war against the IMCC: day-to-day tactical harassment of the inspectors was joined by a long-term strategic campaign to subvert the commission's authority. Hungarian emissaries worked to convert the standing permanent commissions into ad hoc bodies called by the League council to investigate possible treaty violations or threats to peace, and they strove to include the minor defeated powers and neutral countries as often as possible, while excluding the members of the Little Entente.[86] This diplomatic offensive was underway at the same time that military officials in Hungary were busy thwarting the IMCC's work at every turn. Petty persecution of inspectors has been described, but in one case an entire article of the military clauses was ignored. Article 115 required the consolidation of all munitions production in a single, government-owned factory, which was to be located at Csepel, an island in the Danube south of Budapest. After months of inaction, the IMCC brought the issue to the government's attention in December 1921. The government did not respond until October 1922, when it informed the commission that construction was beginning at the new site. Consolidation of the Diósgyőr cannon factory, the Frommer small arms works, and the Balatonfűzfő powder plant were to be completed by the end of 1923, but late that year Defense Minister Károly Csáky asked the IMCC to consider instead an organizational consolidation, since actual consolidation would be too expensive. Later, the Finance Ministry appealed to have the costs deducted from the reparations requirement.[87] The government continued to stall, and skillfully exploited the strength of its own public support and the weakening will of some members of the IMCC. The British minister to Budapest captured this dynamic in a cable to the foreign secretary in January 1925:

> I have received your dispatch ... in which you express concern at the attitude of calculated obstruction which the Hungarian Government are displaying towards the Inter-Allied Military Commission of Control in Hungary and request my views as to what possible measures of effective pressure might be taken to induce the Hungarian Government to adopt a more conciliatory attitude. I have had the question constantly in mind since my arrival here in July last and it has been evident to me from the first that the problem is not an easy one. On the one hand there is the stubborn obstinacy of the Hungarian Government, or rather Military Authorities, who have the weight of public opinion behind them, in non-compliance with the demands of the Conference of Ambassadors, and on the other the Allied Powers are under obligation to enforce the military Clauses of the Treaty of Trianon. The difficulty lies in the mode of enforcement of the will of the Powers. Military sanctions are out of the question, for the reason that they could only be applied by Hungary's neighbors, which would raise a storm here the consequences of which cannot be foreseen. And financial pressure, if too severe, might undo the good economic work already accomplished under the League of Nation's reconstruction scheme.[88]

Hungarian stonewalling finally succeeded and munitions production was never centralized. The League's final decisions on the IMCC accorded fairly well with Hungary's wishes, although the degree to which credit should be given to Hungarian diplomats is unclear. Interested states (including the defeated and their antagonistic neighbors) were not invited to participate in the League council's debates, which concluded that permanent military control ought to be phased out in favor of periodic inspections ordered by the council. In a turn disappointing to Budapest, it was determined that committee members would be drawn from all the League's states, and could include neighboring countries.[89] The Ambassadors' Conference officially ended the IMCC's mission in Hungary on March 31, 1927, and the last inspectors were withdrawn at the end of May.[90]

Admission to the League of Nations hardly improved Hungary's relations with the Little Entente. Budapest generally declined to deal with the other capitals, preferring instead to fuel discontent among the national minorities of the "artificial" states—Magyars in the first place, but also Slovaks, Ruthenes, and Croats. Bethlen and Beneš shared a deep distrust of each other's motives and had no desire for cooperation. The situation was similar in the southeast. "Hungary never seriously considered rapprochement with Romania: the mutual dislike between the two peoples was too acute, the numbers of Magyars in Transylvania too large, the possibilities of local revision too nearly non-existent."[91]

Since it was in Hungary's interest to chip away at the solidarity of the Little Entente, and no common ground could be found for negotiation with Czechoslovakia or Romania, Bethlen made overtures to Yugoslavia. The opening for negotiations came after the embarrassing disclosure of Hungarian support of Croat separatists emboldened Belgrade to press Budapest for arbitration of outstanding disputes. Despite being a member of the Little Entente and enjoying the patronage of the West, Yugoslavia had prickly relations with its neighbors and was jostling with Italy for ascendancy in the Adriatic. Easing tensions with Hungary over the Bánát and its inhabitants would strengthen Yugoslavia's hand in all its other disputes. Low-level consultations between the two countries proceeded through the summer of 1926, and in August the regent supported reconciliation during his speech commemorating the 400th anniversary of the Battle of Mohács.[92] He praised the "good friend" who had in the past joined Hungary in mutual defense, and bemoaned the recent and unfortunate adversarial relationship. "I believe and hope," Horthy said, "that soon we can reinstate the old friendship and understanding."[93] A deal seemed imminent, but the two sides could not agree on what sort of deal it would be. Hungary, whose primary goal was the disruption of the Little Entente, wanted a declaration of neutrality in conflicts with a third party, while Yugoslavia sought a treaty of nonaggression that would not violate its agreements with Czechoslovakia and Romania. Foreign Ministers Lajos Walkó and Momčilo Ninčić met in Geneva in September 1926 to begin high-level negotiations, but the bilateral talks ultimately went nowhere because Italy, which had earlier blessed the initiative, abruptly withdrew its support.[94]

Although Italy and Yugoslavia had signed the Rapallo Treaty in 1920 and a friendship and cooperation accord in 1924, the situation between them remained fractious. The tension increased as Benito Mussolini, in power since 1922, gained confidence and exercised more control over Italian foreign policy. In the years immediately following the war, the Italian orientation had been pro-Little Entente, and a pact with Czechoslovakia had followed the 1924 treaty with Yugoslavia. But Mussolini soon came to believe that the degree of French influence in central and southeastern Europe was incompatible with his vision of Italian supremacy in the region, and began to build a bloc to oppose the Little Entente. The new alliance was to be called the Quadruplice, and its members were to include Hungary, Romania, and Bulgaria—all, of course, under Italy's leadership. In the end Mussolini was not able to reconcile the differences between Romania and Hungary over Transylvania, and between Romania and Bulgaria over Dobruja, so the planned four-way pact was cut in half.[95] Bethlen met with Mussolini in Rome in the spring of 1927, and on April 5 they signed the Treaty of Friendship, Conciliation, and Arbitration. Perhaps the most interesting text of the short, five-article treaty is in the preamble, which notes "the concordance of numerous interests common to both nations."[96] Numerous they were: besides their common hostility toward the Little Entente and its French patron, both leaders were committed to treaty revision and shared an intense aversion to and suspicion of the Soviet Union.[97] Hungary and Italy also saw eye-to-eye on Germany. Both countries were concerned about its potential resurgence and the implications for their own freedom of maneuver, while at the same time recognizing the need to harness German industrial might to their revanchist schemes. The problem of gaining German assistance while avoiding German mastery would bedevil Hungarian and Italian leaders for most of the next decade.

In the early summer of 1927, however, things were turning up roses for Hungary's leaders. Thanks to foreign loans and investment accompanied by domestic austerity, the country's accounts were in the black. Allied military inspectors, whose work Magyar officials had tried to hobble at every turn, had ended their mission in March. The treaty with Rome was a double victory, as it both provided Hungary with an ally among the major Western powers and denied the same to the Little Entente. Finally, in late June the British press baron Lord Rothermere began a propaganda campaign on Hungary's behalf in his paper, the *Daily Mail*. Earlier in the year at Paris, the four Allied powers—France, Great Britain, Italy, and Japan—had rescinded the restrictions on Hungarian production of civilian aircraft, although manufacture of military airplanes still was forbidden.

Magyar military leaders welcomed this progress. Senior officers had protected some of their critical personnel and staff organizations from the control commissions, but recruiting had diminished, and the limitations of Hungarian aircraft industry had been made clear. There was hope, however. In a later classified protocol to the Friendship Treaty, Italy pledged 300 million pengős in weapons credits, which meant that Hungarian rearmament could now begin in earnest, if still in secret. The air service had survived treaty restrictions, Allied inspectors, reparative confiscation, and rampant inflation. Its next years would be no less challenging. Military aviation around the world had advanced very little since the end of the First World War, but that lull was over. The pace of innovation in doctrine and technology was beginning to accelerate, and it would not slow down until the end of the Second World War. Could Hungarian military aviation adapt in time to the changing conditions?

NOTES

1. HL HM Eln. 16059/37.-1919.
2. Ibid.
3. The Romanians captured nearly 400 aircraft of all types and conditions, along with hundreds of engines and various parts and armaments. The total cost of the aviation equipment lost by Hungary to Romania exceeded 95 million

koronas (1921 currency). Bernád, "A Román Királyi Légierő első magyarországi hadjárata," pp. 44–45.

4. HL HM Eln. 21.688/37.-1920.

5. Olasz, "Lépések a honi légvédelem kiépítésére," p. 643.

6. Vesztényi, "A magyar katonai repülés" (HL Tgy 2.787), p. I/28.

7. HL HM Eln. 16059/37.-1919.

8. HL HM Eln. 21626a/37.-1919' and Vesztényi, "A magyar katonai repülés" (HL Tgy 2.787), p. I/31.

9. *MKHL, 1938–1945*, pp. 8–9.

10. Niehorster, *Royal Hungarian Army*, p. 55.

11. Révész, *Repülőtér az Alpokalján*, p. 94.

12. See "Treaty of Peace between the Allied and Associated Powers and Hungary and Protocol and Declaration, Signed at Trianon June 4, 1920, Part V. Military, Naval and Air Clauses" (hereafter "Treaty of Trianon, Part V").

13. Data from *Magyar Statisztikai Zsebkönyv 1940* reported in Romsics, *Hungary in 20th Century*, p. 121; and Macartney, *October Fifteenth*, 1:4. Numbers exclude Croatia-Slavonia.

14. "How Hungary Received the Treaty," *The Times*, Jan. 19, 1920, p. 11. Viennese newspapers had reacted strongly against the terms of Saint-Germain-en-Laye seven months earlier, calling the terms "a crime against mankind" (*Neuer Tag*) and suggesting that Austria would become "a colony of the Entente" (*Mittagszeitung*), but "to the outward eye Vienna has taken her sentence quietly and with dignity." See "Austria Stunned," *The Times*, June 7, 1919, p. 11.

15. Romsics, *Hungary in 20th Century*, p. 124; and Cartledge, *Will to Survive*, p. 330.

16. Várdy, "Impact of Trianon," p. 28.

17. Zeidler, *Ideas on Territorial Revision in Hungary*, p. 186.

18. Macartney, *October Fifteenth*, 1:4.

19. Ibid., 1:49–50.

20. Secret correspondence with French prime minister Aristide Briand had given Charles reason to think otherwise. Romania had apparently declared itself neutral in the matter as well, as long as the terms of Trianon held. Vas, *Horthy*, p. 755. Horthy undoubtedly was correct.

21. *DBFP*, First Ser., Vol. 22, No. 460; Junkers type: Mulder, "Magyar Aeroforgalmi Részvény Tarsaság."

22. Sakmyster, *Hungary's Admiral on Horseback*, pp. 112–113.

23. The government's force at Budaőrs was led by Captain Gyula Gömbös, who in addition to his duties as an officer, was a member of parliament, and more importantly, the president of the Hungarian Association of National Defense (Magyaros Országos Véderő Egyesülete), one of the burgeoning far-right organizations. Lieutenant General Hegedűs was stripped of his rank and honors for his role in the uprising.

24. *DBFP*, Ser. 1, Vol. 22, Nos. 412, 473, 501, 506.

25. Ibid., Nos. 423, 473, 501, 506.

26. *DBFP*, Ser. 1, Vol. 12, No. 231. This was the assessment of a British diplomat, Wilfrid Athelstan-Johnson.

27. Csizmarik, "Magyar Tanácsköztársaság Légiereje," p. 379.

28. Horthy, *Memoirs*, pp. 100, 103.

29. Csonkaréti and Sárhidai, *Az Osztrák-Magyar tengerészeti repülői*, p. 54.

30. *MKHL, 1938–1945*, p. 2.

31. *DBFP*, Ser. 1, Vol. 12, Nos. 307–308.

32. Ibid., No. 260. After ratification, the VKF would be prohibited under Article 105: "All other organizations [than those permitted for divisions] for the command of troops or for preparation for war are forbidden."

33. *MKHL, 1938–1945*, p. 9.

34. Révész, *Repülőtér az Alpokalján*, p. 96.

35. Petróczy, "A legyőzött Németország aviatikája" (HIK 5271), p. I/3.

36. Ibid., pp. I/4–5.

37. Homze, *Arming the Luftwaffe*, pp. 11–12. Like Petróczy, Euler earned his country's first pilot license. See his obituary in *The Times*, July 3, 1957, p. 12.

38. Petróczy, "A legyőzött Németország aviatikája" (HIK 5271), p. V/20.

39. Quoted in Corum, *Luftwaffe*, p. 59.

40. Ibid.

41. Corum and Muller, *Luftwaffe's Way of War*, p. 72.

42. *DBFP*, Ser. 1, Vol. 24, No. 181.

43. Nagyváradi et al., *Fejezetek a repülés történetéből*, p. 146.

44. B. Juhász, "Inter-Allied Military Commission of Control," pp. 50–51, 59n.

45. *DBFP*, Ser. 1, Vol. 27, No. 13.

46. B. Juhász, "Military Control of Hungary," pp. 50–51, 59n.

47. Ibid., p. 57.

48. Ibid., p. 59.

49. *DBFP*, Ser. 1, Vol. 27, No. 13.

50. *DBFP*, Ser. 1, Vol. 24, No. 362.

51. Ibid.

52. Ibid.

53. B. Juhász, "Military Control of Hungary," pp. 55–64.

54. Nagyváradi et al., *Fejezetek a repülés történetéből*, pp. 159–164.

55. Quoted in *MKHL, 1938–1945*, pp. 9–10; and Nagyváradi et al., *Fejezetek a repülés történetéből*, p. 146. At the time the combined air forces of the Little Entente numbered over 400 aircraft; paltry by First World War standards, but a formidable threat against a country with no combat planes readily available. Olasz, "Lépések a honi légvédelem kiépítésére," p. 672.

56. M. M. Szabó, *A Magyar Királyi Honvéd Légierő a második világháborúban*, p. 15, and *MKHL, 1938–1945*, p. 10. Date for LÜH: Révész, *Repülőtér az Alpokalján*, p. 97.

57. Davies, *A History of the World's Airlines*, p. 26.

58. "The Fokker F III Commercial Monoplane," *Flight*, May 26, 1921, pp. 355–356.

59. Moys, "Légiforgalmi irányításunk története (1920–1945)," p. 2.

60. Subsides: HL HM Eln. 16606/6.k-1927.

61. Trans-Europa line: Davies, *History of the World's Airlines*, p. 26.

62. Irving, *Rise and Fall of the Luftwaffe*, p. 15.

63. Davies, *History of the World's Airlines*, p. 21.

64. Dick and Patterson, *Aviation Century*, p. 51.

65. Davies, *History of the World's Airlines*, p. 21.

66. Homze, *Arming the Luftwaffe*, p. 11.

67. Nagyváradi et al., *Fejezetek a repülés történetéből*, p. 152. Single-seat planes with engines producing more than 60 horsepower were considered military aircraft, as were "machines that can fly without a pilot," those with "any form or armor or protection or with fittings to take any form of armament," and those whose capabilities exceeded the following: maximum ceiling 13,000 feet; useful load 1,300 pounds, including crew; speed 105 miles per hour. *DBFP*, Ser. 1, Vol. 26, No. 901.

68. Nagyváradi et al., *Fejezetek a repülés történetéből*, pp. 152–155.

69. Fehér, "Berepülő pilóta naplója, 1915–1927" (MMKM 988).

70. Nagyváradi et al., *Fejezetek a repülés történetéből*, pp. 152–159.

71. Vesztényi, "A magyar katonai repülés" (HL Tgy 2.787), p. II/44.

72. HL HM Eln. 16606 6.k-1927.

73. Nagyváradi et al., *Fejezetek a repülés történetéből*, pp. 146–158.

74. Kenese, in 1920 a captain in the Vienna office charged with liquidating LFT assets, had been instrumental in arranging the delivery to Szombathely of eight Phönix C.Is purchased in Austria by István Bethlen. Révész, *Repülőtér az Alpokalján*, p. 93.

75. Nagyváradi et al., *Fejezetek a repülés történetéből*, pp. 146, 158.

76. Vesztényi, "A magyar katonai repülés" (HL Tgy 2.787), p. II/52.

77. Nagyváradi et al., *Fejezetek a repülés történetéből*, 160–162.

78. Vesztényi, "A magyar katonai repülés" (HL Tgy 2.787), p. II/53.

79. In the last months before the conclusion of the Trianon treaty, French negotiator Maurice Paléologue had offered hope for speedy border adjustments in Hungary's favor in exchange for sweeping economic concessions. Britain and Italy opposed the French initiative, which they contended would violate the treaty's terms, and they warned Budapest that Paléologue's promises would likely be repudiated by the French government in any case. As expected, the secret negotiations became public and amounted to nothing except public disappointment in Hungary. See Kertesz, *Diplomacy in a Whirlpool*, pp. 21–23.

80. Hungarian aid to Poland was opposed by the countries of the Little Entente, although some 60 million rifle cartridges made their way from Csepel munitions factories to Poland via Romania. Gy. Juhász, *Hungarian Foreign Policy 1919–1945*, pp. 55–57.

81. Quoted in ibid., p. 60.

82. Ibid.

83. Cartledge, *Will to Survive*, p. 341.

84. Romsics, *Hungary in 20th Century*, p. 132. Britain stood as guarantor for 50% of the loan.

85. B. Juhász, "Military Control of Hungary," p. 63.

86. Gy. Juhász, *Hungarian Foreign Policy*, p. 78.

87. B. Juhász, "Military Control of Hungary," p. 53.

88. *DBFP*, Ser. 1, Vol. 27, No. 29.

89. Gy. Juhász, *Hungarian Foreign Policy*, p. 78.

90. B. Juhász, "Military Control of Hungary," p. 67.

91. Macartney, *October Fifteenth*, 1:84.

92. On August 29, 1526, the Ottoman Turks under Suleiman the Great defeated the Hungarian army of King Louis II (who was himself killed in the battle). The defeat led to a century and a half of Turkish occupation and to the assumption of the Habsburgs to the Hungarian crown.

93. Quoted in Fülöp and Sipos, *Magyarország külpolitikája a XX. században*, p. 146.

94. Gy. Juhász, *Hungarian Foreign Policy*, pp. 77, 81.

95. Burgwyn, *Italian Foreign Policy*, pp. 37–40.

96. See "Treaty of Friendship, Conciliation and Arbitration between Hungary and Italy, signed at Rome, 5 April 1927."

97. Burgwyn, *Italian Foreign Policy*, pp. 37–40.

4

Theory: 1927–1937

THE TERMINATION OF THE IMCC MISSION IN MARCH 1927 meant that Hungarian rearmament was possible, though not formally permitted. Trianon's military restrictions remained in place, but the instrument for their implementation was removed, and the Allies' will for enforcement greatly diminished. By securing an Italian treaty and British loans, Hungarian diplomats and financiers had gained for its political and military leaders a narrow slice of maneuvering room in which to pursue Hungary's idée fixe, the nullification of the postwar settlement. Central to that pursuit was rebuilding Hungary's armed forces. There was broad agreement throughout the government that the possession of a credible military establishment was a necessary if insufficient condition for revision. A disarmed Hungary would never regain the territories lost at Trianon. A reconstituted Honvéd, however, would strengthen Hungary's hand in the region in the short term and provide the means for forced revision in the long run. Defense Minister Károly Csáky summarized this argument in a 1927 Crown Council meeting: "In foreign policy it is military strength above all that defines power. . . . The stronger our military forces, the more in demand will be our friendship. This is one reason why our forces cannot remain at their present standard."[1] A year earlier, in a resignation letter to Admiral Horthy (which the regent declined to accept),

Count Bethlen had given similar counsel. After offering his assessment that the "foundations of financial and political consolidation have been laid," Bethlen advised Horthy that "the next step should be to shake off military control and to build up armaments." He closed the letter on an optimistic note: "It is my feeling that in about four or five years Trianon might be liquidated. For this time all our forces will have to be kept ready, and every preparation must be made by then."[2] While Bethlen's predicted timeline of revision was off by nearly a decade, his call for rearmament was heeded as soon as conditions permitted.

There was no doubt that an air service would be an important part of Hungarian rearmament. Though the contribution of air power to the battles of 1919 had been limited by scarce resources, expectations for aviation's potential contribution to warfare had grown in the 1920s, and by the end of the decade there was support for (or fear of) air power at the highest levels of Hungarian government. Brigadier General Henrik Werth, then the commandant of the War College (Hadiakadémia) and later Honvéd chief of staff, considered the air arm "modern warfare's most powerful."[3] Retired Colonel Károly Mayer-Csejkovits, a well-known commentator on military affairs, sent to Admiral Horthy in March 1928 a memorandum titled "The strategical position of Hungary in the war of the future." This future war, according to the colonel, would be one of "panic, disorders, and mass movements" induced by gas and incendiary attacks on civilian populations from the air. Curiously, Mayer-Csejkovits did not recommend to the regent a multilayered air defense system, but rather outlined measures that could be taken to discipline and control the population. Although there is no record that Horthy took seriously his suggestion to form a national fire-fighting corps as a substitute for compulsory military service, it is clear that the regent shared both the colonel's appreciation for the airplane as a potent instrument of war and his dread of chemical attack. Horthy's notes on the memo included his observation that mobilization was impossible "when Yugoslavia and Czechoslovakia dispose over 1000 aircraft," and ended with an ominous refrain: "Aircraft, gas, aircraft, gas, aircraft, gas."[4]

The fear of massed formations of airplanes attacking with chemical weapons was common in Europe during the 1920s, stoked by popular depictions of future air war. Budapest had been spared aerial bombardment in the First World War, and Hungarian-language publications about air combat had to that time centered on personal accounts of wartime exploits. One Hungarian airman, László Madarász (né Hauser—"Madarász" means "birdcatcher") did expand his memoirs into a second volume that addressed broader themes of aerial warfare, but his conclusions in *Légi háború: A repülők harcászata (Air Warfare: Aviators' Tactics)* were quite conventional.[5] Madarász endorsed observation as an air service's first and most important role, contending that reconnaissance was "a war-preventing activity, though when it turns to action, it has a deciding influence."[6] He conceded that armed airplanes had become distinct instruments of war with their own characteristics that separated them from land or sea operations, but he did not advocate independent bombing campaigns.[7]

It is possible that the source of Horthy's apprehension could be found in Britain, where prominent politicians in and out of government discussed the most recent developments in aviation, and "the annual Commons debate on the defense budget served as a regular catalyst for dire proclamations about the menace of air warfare."[8] Among the most influential proclamations were those issued by J. F. C. Fuller and B. H. Liddell Hart. In his 1923 *Reformation of War*, Fuller envisioned repeated gas attacks against enemy cities, and Liddell Hart's 1925 *Paris, or the Future of War* suggested that urban populations, when subjected to sustained aerial bombardment, would rise in revolution.[9] Whether absorbed directly or at second hand, these fears are evident in the Mayer-Csejkovits memo and in Horthy's reaction. Their concerns were widely shared after

1931, when the works of Giulio Douhet, the Italian general and champion of air power, became available in Hungarian.

Douhet had begun writing about the utility of air power in 1910, and from the beginning he had preached the value of *domino dell'aria* (command of the air). In his early work, Douhet objected to targeting civilians on grounds of morality and effectiveness, calling it a "useless and savage act."[10] However, by the second year of the Great War, influenced by H. G. Wells' fiction and the reality of German planes ranging over France, Douhet began to embrace unrestricted air warfare.[11] In 1915 he advocated the formation of a force of 500 bombers to strike "the most vital, most vulnerable and least protected points of the enemy's territory."[12] After Italy entered the war, Douhet served at the front as the chief of staff of the 5th Infantry Division. There his observations turned to pointed criticism. With little concern for professional decorum, he repeatedly attacked Italian leaders for their inept employment of air power. Eventually his correspondence with members of the government came to the attention of the high command, and in September 1916 he was convicted of "issuing false news . . . divulging information differing from the official communiqués . . . diminishing the prestige and the faith in the country and of disturbing the public tranquility."[13] He served one year in prison and was released on the day the Battle of Caporetto began. After being recalled to active service in early 1918, he was named to head the Central Bureau of Aviation, which post he held until his retirement at the end of the war. The 1916 conviction was overturned in 1920, and in 1921 he was promoted to the rank of brigadier general.[14] That same year Douhet published *Il dominio dell'aria* (*The Command of the Air*) with War Ministry approval, and he later joined Mussolini's first cabinet as undersecretary for air.[15] Douhet's loud insistence that the air force grow at the expense of the other arms quickly alienated army and navy leaders, and they persuaded Mussolini to remove him from office.[16]

Command of the Air was Douhet's best-known work, and remains "the most eloquent, elaborate, and comprehensive theory of air power in the interwar period."[17] In the two editions of *Command* and in the pages of *Rivista Aeronautica*, Douhet laid out a complete theory of war. He argued that (1) modern warfare erased the distinction between combatants and noncombatants; (2) surface forces could no longer take the offensive; (3) successful defense against a determined aerial offensive was impossible; (4) nations must therefore launch massive bombing attacks against the enemy; and 5) this required an independent air force equipped with long-range bombers.[18] In his 1930 book *La Guerra del' 19__* (*The War of 19__*), Douhet further developed these themes, postulating a conflict between opposing sides having radically different views of air power. The German air force represented Douhetian purity; the Franco-Belgian alliance clung with outmoded allegiance to surface forces and relegated its air force to a supporting role. The folly of the old approach was apparent after the decisive three-hour air battle that left all of France and Belgium open to uncontested aerial bombardment. Long before the Franco-Belgian forces could mobilize their formidable armor divisions, the German air force had directly targeted their national wills, rendering irrelevant the massive allied advantage in ground troops. Nearly a decade before the Luftwaffe's defeat in the Battle of Britain proved otherwise, Douhet's contention that air attack had no effective defense was not unreasonable, and was indeed shared by many political leaders and professional airmen across Europe and America.

One of those professional airmen was Captain Ferenc Szentnémedy, who was in 1931 an instructor at the Hadiakadémia, the aviation editor of the military journal *Magyar Katonai Szemle* (*MKSz*), and his country's foremost "apostle of Douhetism."[19] Szentnémedy was of Swabian origin, born Ferenc Willwerth in 1896 in Orsova, a predominantly German town in the Bánát.[20] He entered the imperial army as a subaltern in the 5th Infantry Regiment on August 1, 1914, and remained with that unit until July 1917, when he joined the LFT's Flik 32 as an aerial observer. Szentném-edy finished the war with Flik 35, and like many of his comrades, he fought under the Kun government in the VR before serving in the new National Army's Flying Corps. From 1919 until 1923 Szent-némedy worked as an adjutant and earned his pilot's rating.[21] His duty performance must have been exemplary, because he was one of a dozen officers selected in 1923 to attend the Hadiakadémia, which was disguised at the time as the Budapest Regulation Re-view Course.[22] Among the regulations presumably not reviewed in the course was Trianon's Article 111, which prohibited military schools for purposes other than officer accession.[23] After graduating and earning the right to append *vezérkari szólgálatot* (General Staff officer) to his rank, Captain Szentnémedy, who had also been awarded the honorific *vitéz* (valiant), served a tour with an infantry brigade, followed by a year as a section director on the LÜH. In 1928 he returned to the Hadiakadémia as an instructor, and there began his career as a military intellectual and air power theorist.[24]

Szentnémedy's assignment coincided with a major curriculum revision at the Hadiakadémia. In the academic year beginning in the autumn of 1929, students began to study economics, law, and intelligence and espionage. They also were the first Hadiakadémia class to have a course on aviation, Aeronautics having replaced Naval Studies at the same time. Welcome as this change must have been for Hungarian airmen, there may have been some disappoint-ment in the restricted scope of the early air operations syllabus, which represented the "field aviation" point of view espoused by László Madarász. The course emphasized reconnaissance and local air defense at the expense of bombardment, and treated aviation as only a subordinate branch of the army. Academically, aerial opera-tion instruction was given the same weight as that covering artillery, army organization, and technological familiarization. Practical training in aeronautics was also introduced, although it too tended to reinforce a limited conception of air power: between the first and second years, each student attended a four-week aerial observer's course at Székesfehérvár.[25]

These innovations occurred under the leadership of Major General (Altábornagy) Henrik Werth. Werth had been sent to examine the German war college before his appointment as the Hadiakadémia commandant, and his changes reflected current German practice, so much so that one historian, himself a Hadiaka-démia graduate, considered the school under Werth "100 percent German." "Strategic education," he elaborated, "basically and essentially moved along a German line. Clausewitz's military philosophy formed the frame, his work *On War* was the Bible, and merely quoting from it made arguments and reasoning acceptable to the general staff."[26] In this deployment of Clausewitz to shut down discussion, the Hungarians joined the hordes of Western staff officers before and since who apparently cannot resist the temptation to pluck from the Prussian's voluminous writings a quote that seems to support precisely the position being advanced.

In any case, Hungarian exposure to *On War* long predated Werth's tenure at the Hadiakadémia. The first Magyar translation was printed at the Ludovika Military Academy in 1892 and was reissued in 1917. The translator, retired colonel Baron Samu Hazai, considered *On War* a work of "lasting value" (*örökbecsű*), and wanted to make it accessible to those Hungarians who did not read German. In the preface to the second edition, Hazai suggested that Clausewitz had continued relevance, and lamented that the lessons of *On War* had not been taken to heart: "I think that few people read it. That is unfortunate, because if they had studied it, it would have been possible to understand better the nature of the current great world war. Now I can say what I said in the preface to the first edition: that the trouble of translating this study will be useful, especially useful in these times when for many years we will be concerned with events and studies of the great world war."[27] Certainly Szentnémedy was influenced by his reading of Hazai's translation, and he on occasion appealed explicitly to the authority of the "great German soldier-philosopher."[28]

It was Douhet, however, who had the most profound impact on Szentnémedy, and it was through the popularization of Douhet's work that Szentnémedy himself became the most important figure in the development of Hungarian air power thought. From the first issue of *MKSz* in January 1931 until his last article a decade later, Szentnémedy set the terms of the discussion. That was partly due to his prolific output: through his final submission in May 1941, Szentnémedy had written more than a quarter of the 400 articles related to aviation that appeared in the journal. Because his pieces tended to be lengthy, his share of the total *MKSz* page count ran to nearly 40 percent. These numbers should not suggest that Szentnémedy avoided airing others' views. He appears to have relished argument, publishing with great regularity articles that took exception to his own entries. Instead of diminishing his importance, the running debate in *MKSz* between Szentnémedy and his critics only heightened authority. His status as the preeminent Hungarian aviation expert was furthered by the broad range of his reporting, the majority of which consisted of analysis of foreign aerial maneuvers and technological advances. With his ability to read German, English, Italian, and Romanian, he was able to keep *MKSz* readers (which should have included all serving officers, since subscription to the journal was mandatory) informed on the more mundane developments in international aviation.[29] His most impassioned articles, however, and the ones that generated controversy and stimulated dispute, invariably involved advocacy for the decisive role of air power in a future war.

That was the theme of his contribution to the inaugural edition of *MKSz*, "The Guiding Principles, Instruments, and Possibilities of Independent Air Warfare," which was followed two issues later by his translation of *The War of 19__*. From March to June 1931, *MKSz* featured Douhet's "hypothetical conflict among the great powers in the near future."[30] *The War of 19__* was originally published in the Italian Air Ministry's journal *Rivista Aeronautica* shortly after Douhet's death in February 1930, and was his last will and testament; his final vision of total war waged through the air with the aim of destroying the enemy's resolve. Szentnémedy found this vision quite compelling, calling it "an outstanding... work in which he demonstrates, from practical examples with undeniably convincing force, that it is the mass employment of air forces that led to the war's conclusion."[31]

This appears to be the first appearance of Douhet in the Hungarian language, although Szentnémedy assumed on the part of his reader some knowledge of the Italian general. He referred to Douhet as the "noted aviation expert" (*ismert nevü repülő-szakiró*) and to his having died suddenly, but he did not mention specifically any of Douhet's earlier works.[32] It is possible that Douhet had been discussed informally at the Hadiakadémia or in a presentation at the National Officers' Club, which periodically hosted events for professional development. Despite his knowledge of Italian, Szentnémedy translated *The War of 19___* from German, the source for his abridgement being a complete version published in the monthly aviation journal *Die Luftwacht*.[33] Szentnémedy abbreviated Douhet's 40,000-word monograph to roughly one-third, spreading approximately 13,000 words over four issues of *MKSz*, adding to the July issue his 5,000-word "Opinions and Thoughts." In keeping with his characterization of Douhet's work as "practical," Szentnémedy chose to retain in his articles the extensive lists of aircraft types and capabilities, along with detailed timings of the successive attack waves, at the expense of the rather lengthy excerpts of imaginary doctrine and staff memoranda. This decision, while understandable in context, is unfortunate, since it is through these literary devices that Douhet expressed most clearly the competing visions of air power's utility.

Although the fictional German air force clearly manifested Douhet's own vision, his description of the two camps remains compelling because he treated them, and therefore his reader, with intellectual honesty. The viewpoints might be exaggerated, but they did not descend into caricature. Douhet's Franco-Belgian prewar doctrine, portrayed as fatally flawed, was not depicted as ridiculous and indeed has internal logical consistency. It was, as one expert characterized the performance of the real Armée de l'air in World War II, "neither decadent, nor stupid, nor treasonous."[34] The fundamental assumptions were simply wrong:

> Because these two powers were victorious in the World War, they were led to perfect the armaments and systems of war which gave them the victory then, systems and armaments which experience had proved satisfactory. Consequently, the war doctrine they held to, which was reflected in the organization, instruction, and education of their armed forces, did not much differ from the one which had taken shape during the World War . . .
>
> This doctrine taught that the aim of war was the destruction of the enemy's land forces; and therefore gave to the army the position of greatest importance as the most suitable and reliable instrument for accomplishing this aim . . .
>
> All the experience of the World War had been brought to bear to give their land armed forces the maximum offensive power in order to destroy as quickly as possible the enemy's land forces by a war of movement.[35]

Douhet's German military planners had fought in the same war as their Franco-Belgian antagonists, but being possessed of different national goals, culture, and constraints, drew contrary conclusions. These conclusions were indeed those of Douhet himself, presented in the form of a memo from General Reuss, the fictitious Chief of the General Staff (not included in Szentnémedy's abridgement, although presumably present in the complete *Luftwacht* article):

> It is not in the armed forces of the enemy but in the nation itself that the will and capacity to make war is found. Warfare must therefore be waged against the people, to break their will and destroy their capacity to make war . . .
>
> The aerial arm makes it feasible to strike directly at the heart of the enemy, striking at all his interior activities without land and sea armed forces . . .
>
> For a decision in the air, it is only necessary to put the people themselves in an intolerable condition of life through aerial offensives . . .

By integrating the aerial arm with poison gas, it is possible today to employ very effective actions against the most vital and vulnerable spots of the enemy—that is, against his most important political, industrial, commercial, and other centers, in order to create among his population a lowering of moral resistance so deep as to destroy the determination of the people to continue the war.[36]

Szentnémedy approached the question of chemical warfare pragmatically. He translated without further discussion Douhet's passages concerning the development of the German chemical industry and the employment of poison gas bombs along with high explosives and incendiaries.[37] Given his obvious high regard for Douhet's ideas, one can assume Szentnémedy accepted without reservation the Italian's argument that "all nations will prepare for aero-chemical warfare, and in case of war all of them will be ready to wage aero-chemical war."[38] In the same way, Szentnémedy's lack of comment on Douhet's basic notion of direct aerial attack against the enemy's will should be seen as a validation of that position. Although Szentnémedy did not offer explicit endorsement of the efficacy of strategic bombing, his effusive praise for Douhet and his characterization of Douhet's contributions to air power offered proof of his allegiance. "It is undeniable," Szentnémedy wrote, "that his analysis in the first place influenced domestic aviation; however we can claim this too, that the organizational development of practically all the European powers' air forces bears the stamp of Douhet's thought."[39]

It was true that Douhet's ideas found fertile ground in air ministries around the world, but in no country, not even his own, was his conception of air warfare adopted completely. In Italy, the flamboyant air minister Italo Balbo was closely associated with the Fascist favorite Douhet, and routinely employed Douhetian language in public and in budget battles with the army and navy, but the Regia Aeronautica (RA) did not develop along strict Douhetian lines. Balbo was also influenced by the arguments of Amadeo

Mecozzi, Douhet's main Italian opponent and a serving RA officer. Mecozzi agreed with Douhet's insistence on aerial autonomy, but repudiated the bombing of civilian populations, calling it "war against the unarmed."[40] Instead, Mecozzi espoused a theory of three-service cooperation that he called *guerra aerea concomitante* (interconnected warfare).[41] Balbo and the RA vacillated between the ideas of Douhet, which suited both their ideological and bureaucratic prejudices, and those of Mecozzi, which were convincing but did little to advance the RA's agenda. The RA continued to hedge between the competing theories, and never trained or equipped itself to execute either concept sufficiently. Italian bomber aircraft did not attain the required payload, range, or armament to carry out Douhet's unrestricted air warfare, and the brief experiment with a heavy ground attack fighter was not sustained.[42]

The idea of strategic bombing found its most effective crusaders in the United States and Great Britain, though in neither country did its campaigners acknowledge a debt to Douhet. In the case of Britain, it is likely that Sir Hugh Trenchard was not aware of Douhet's work, and that Trenchard's zeal for long-range bombing was based on his own wartime experiences and postwar British studies. The earliest mention of Douhet in the English press appears to be an unsigned article in the April 1933 issue of *Royal Air Force Quarterly*, and this late appearance led one historian to conclude "it seems quite clear that Douhet had no influence in the forming of British air power theory."[43] Another researcher, however, noting marked similarities between the works of Douhet and J. F. C. Fuller, claimed an indirect Douhetian influence on Royal Air Force (RAF) doctrine.[44] The link between Douhet and Brigadier General Billy Mitchell, the public face of air power advocacy in America, was less ambiguous. The two men met in Europe in 1922, and that same year the Italian air attaché in Washington, DC, published an *Aviation* magazine article about *Command of the Air*. Furthermore, a translation of excerpts from *Command of the Air* appeared in the files of the US air service in 1923. A full translation of the work was not available until 1933.[45]

In Germany, Luftwaffe doctrine ultimately rejected Douhetism in spite of efforts by indigenous enthusiasts, such as Dr. Robert Knauss, to advance it. Knauss, a First World War pilot, director of Luft Hansa, and a future commandant of the Luftwaffe General Staff College, published pseudonymously a novel, *Luftkrieg 1936: Die Zertrümmerung von Paris* (*Air War 1936: The Destruction of Paris*), that echoed many of Douhet's themes.[46] In Knauss's fictional war, the RAF played the part of Douhet's German Air Force, and France reprised its role as France, surrendering after two weeks of RAF bombardment. As with *The War of 19__*, MKSz published a serialized Szentnémedy translation of the book. Knauss's polemic had little effect on the Luftwaffe, whose 1935 Regulation 16, *The Conduct of Aerial War*, after acknowledging its mission to "break down the will of the enemy," defined that will as "finding its greatest embodiment in its armed forces. Thus, [destruction of] the enemy armed forces is therefore the primary goal in war."[47] After dealing at some length with campaigns against "sources of power" that included military, transportation, and industrial targets, Regulation 16 declared "attacks against cities made for the purpose of inducing terror in the civilian population are to be avoided on principle." Such attacks should occur only in retaliation following enemy bombardment of "defenseless and open cities," and even then must be planned precisely because "selection of the wrong time, combined with a poor estimate of the desired effect upon the enemy, can in some circumstances result in an increase in the enemy's will to resist, rather than a reduction of the will." Finally, in stating "whether gas bombs can be used will be determined by international agreement and enemy behavior if he initiates a terror attack," the Luftwaffe contradicted Douhet's conviction that the employment of poison gas was inevitable.[48]

Douhet's doctrine was introduced to France in a 1927 issue of *Revue Maritime*, and it was well received by French airmen who "had begun to chafe in their subordinate role" to the army.[49] At the end of the First World War, the French air service had led the world, but a decade later the once formidable force had lost its position of preeminence. In addition to aging airplanes and an outdated concept of employment, there were deep institutional problems. Although France's air force comprised 260 squadrons of over 3,000 aircraft, there was no Air Ministry or Air Staff, and every officer and airplane was under the control of a French army unit.[50] By 1931, an Air Ministry had been established and the air force had gained some measure of autonomy, but the difficulties persisted. Szentnémedy, a keen and professional but distant observer, was able to point to "a succession of accidents, cancelation of aircraft types, repetitive financial crises in the aircraft industry and continuous reorganization manifested in the highest levels of the aviation ministry" as evidence that France's qualitative advantage was fading quickly.[51] Also recognizing this, and feeling constrained by "liberal disarmament ideals that characterized much of the Socialist agenda," French air power advocates were attracted to Douhet's prophetic vision both as a national strategy and a way to maintain the Armée de l'air's independence.[52] And although the doctrine of strategic bombing was never adopted in Paris, the French airplane industry came the closest in the interwar years to making Douhet's "battle-plane" a reality. Beginning in 1933, the air force took possession of a new class of multirole machines called Bombardement-Combat-Reconnaissance (BCR) aircraft. The BCR aircraft, endorsed if not inspired by Douhet's work, was a compromise between the requirements of the three services, and was meant to fulfill all of them. In fact, it failed to fulfill any: as a bomber it was too slow and carried too few bombs, as a fighter it was too heavy, and as a reconnaissance craft it was too vulnerable.[53] These shortcomings were readily apparent to some French military analysts, who disparaged the BCR concept as well as the doctrine of unrestricted aerial bombardment.

In his article that concluded the series, Szentnémedy quoted extensively two of those critics who had reviewed *The War of 19__* in

French aviation journals. In the August and September 1930 editions of *Les Ailes*, Jean Herbillon praised Douhet for his success in gaining recognition for the ascendancy of air forces, but doubted whether his work was revolutionary, pointing to the writings of three senior French officers whose work contained similar elements. Herbillon wrote with an acid pen, directing sarcasm not just at Douhet, whom he considered insufficiently imaginative for a futurist ("This wonderful writer shows us with clarity those probabilities which today are already afoot"), but also at the French services' cynicism (funds intended for a joint aerial effort would instead "go with these aims: to enrich the infantry, to increase security for the cavalry, and to build cruisers").[54] Herbillon also questioned Douhet's reliance on daylight bombing, postulating that future technological developments would "free fliers from the disadvantages of night aviation and give them back their eyes." In response, Szentnémedy recapitulated the challenges of night operations: the difficulties in navigating to and identifying the target, the danger of night landings, the near-certainty of aircraft damage in forced landings at night in unfamiliar terrain, and the risk of disorientation when flying into the enemy's searchlights. Szentnémedy also cited a French colonel's research that showed by month the paucity of suitable weather for night flying. Although he conceded that small countries might be forced to conduct night bombing operations in spite of the risks, and that night attacks could be important in maintaining "continuous effect" on the enemy, Szentnémedy reached a clear Douhetian conclusion: "There is no doubt that daylight bombing is the most effective."[55]

The more narrow and practical criticisms of another Frenchman, Camille Rougeron, received a fair airing, but no effective rebuttal. Rougeron, a naval engineer, presented objections based less on Douhet's theories and more on existing aeronautical technology and immutable geography. Implementation of the Italian's recommended single-aircraft fleet would require that the battle-plane be equal to the demands of territorial defense as well as offensive action. Rougeron examined the two giant aircraft that best embodied the battle-plane ideal, Caproni's PB 90 and Dornier's Do X, and found their performance in two critical areas inadequate. Neither of these airplanes could climb high enough and fast enough to intercept conventionally sized bombers; a problem in any case, Rougeron explained, but one exacerbated for countries whose critical centers of power were located near their frontiers, such as Britain and Italy.[56] Although Szentnémedy did not address this concern specifically, *MKSz*'s readers might well have added Hungary to that category.

In his closing paragraphs Szentnémedy added a pair of concerns of his own, of which the first was access to oil. "One of the largest problems, and one that cannot be undervalued, in the maintenance of a large combat air force, is the question of petroleum products, which would be a serious crisis for small landlocked and surrounded countries. This problem deserves a special study on its own." Then, in a phrasing that would have set on edge the teeth of his land forces readers, Szentnémedy characterized Douhet's fictional German Air Force as pursuing "the most extreme execution of the idea of the center of gravity (*súlypont*)," while the Franco-Belgian alliance "had a tendency toward frittering away, where the air forces are lost as the land forces' auxiliary service."[57] The passing reference to Clausewitz failed to mollify the critics, one of whom, Mihály Ibrányi, like Szentnémedy a captain of the VKF, argued in the August 1931 issue of *MKSz* that the most decisive use of the air force would be achieved in support of ground combat. Szentnémedy's answer revealed his devotion to the idea of air power as the ultimate arbiter in warfare: "The center of gravity is in the air, and to prevail in this regard will be to the detriment of all other equipment expenditures—everything must be devoted to the development of the air force. This will create an air force that if employed correctly in a future war, could surely, and above all quickly, bring the war to a decision."[58]

There was no European war to bring to a decision in 1931, and no Hungarian air fleet in being that could have taken part in such a war. But the *MKSz* articles provide clear evidence that Hungarian officers were aware of the currents of contemporary continental air power thought, and also debated their relevance and wrestled with their implications. Without regard to the ultimate outcome of Szentnémedy's enthusiasm for strategic bombing, this discourse reflects well on the officer corps' intellectual curiosity and *MKSz's* academic rigor. In penning these pieces, Captain Szentnémedy demonstrated broad knowledge and interest in European aviation developments: in a Magyar publication he promoted the ideas of an Italian general, about which he read in a German journal, and included trenchant criticism of leading French airmen. More than just a feat of linguistics and research, Szentnémedy's articles meant that in 1931 the Hungarian officers were better acquainted with Douhet (and his detractors) than were their counterparts in the United States or Britain, whose countries did not suffer from treaty provisions and diplomatic isolation.

By 1933 Szentnémedy had published *A repülés* (*Aviation*), a seventy-eight-page monograph that included history, theory and law, as well as an appreciation of Hungary's post-Trianon aeronautical situation. The fervor evidenced in Szentnémedy's *MKSz* articles was somewhat diminished, due perhaps to opposition from his colleagues (including then-captain Géza Vörös, who in 1941 became chief of the air staff), a lack of fresh Douhet writings, or simply his taking a more philosophical approach in this longer and broader work. In *Aviation* Szentnémedy acknowledged that the theory of independent air warfare remained untested, that its "finished or final form had not yet been shown," and that "many questions remain unclear."[59] Despite the less dogmatic trappings, Szentnémedy was in 1933 still a committed disciple of Douhet. The fifth chapter of *Aviation* contained a case for strategic bombing that began with a discussion of the nature of war. In this section Szentnémedy explicitly tied Clausewitz to Douhet: "According to Clausewitz, the great German soldier-philosopher, war, as policy's most energetic instrument, has as its final objective that the enemy be forced to our own will, with the use of every tool to overcome him. That would require the creation of such conditions that the enemy population would find unbearable, and which would force them to sue for peace."[60] Until the advent of the aircraft, Szentnémedy contended, land forces had to defeat directly the opposing army, or naval forces had to attack the enemy indirectly by blockade. In either case, the enemy populace, largely distant from the front lines, would not feel the full effects of war. The airplane "brought war of this nature to an end, because it allowed man to free himself from the earth." Thus freed, man could employ the aircraft as an instrument of war and attack the enemy at any place along his front, the effective range of this new weapon having "no practical limits." "It can hold at risk of death every citizen, without regard to sex, age, social position; the palaces, factories, industries, railways can be objects for attack just as well as military lines—perhaps even better. In short, air forces change completely the nature of war as it has been known and strengthen the notion that war will be a battle of peoples and not just a battle of armed forces."[61]

Szentnémedy also repeated Douhet's counterintuitive idea that unrestricted air warfare (*korlátlan légi háború*) would be more humane than previous wars.[62] Douhet considered it "the quickest and most economical way of ending the war, entailing the minimum loss of blood and wealth on both sides."[63] In his *MKSz* abridgement, Szentnémedy described General Reuss's plan as "the most simple, cheapest and quickest solution," and in the 1933 work he emphasized the importance of terror in undermining the enemy's will to resist: "Panics, which in dense populations can develop into mass hysteria and revolution, can bring about an end to the enemy nation's resistance, and quickly end the war. Therefore there will be fewer victims. The more terrible the air war, the more humane it will be."[64]

From the possible reactions of foreign peoples, Szentnémedy moved to consideration of the particular vulnerabilities of his own country. Following Camille Rougeron's example, he examined the potential effects of aerial attack from geographic and economic points of view, and concluded that increased urbanization magnified a nation's vulnerability.

> Naturally this sensitivity [to attack by air] is greater for cities, and increases with their number. Therefore the number and size of its cities can indicate a country's aerial vulnerability. The degree that a country is endangered depends on the economic significance of the targeted area and its relationship to the entire state. If the country is chiefly agricultural with widely scattered settlements, then the attacks will have very little success and the attackers will fritter away their assets without considerable effect. It is a different situation, however, if a small agricultural country has its entire industrial organization consolidated in a single city (e.g., Budapest). In this case a resounding effect is probable, because the state's entire industrial production could become paralyzed at practically the same time.[65]

After a comparison of the population density of ten European countries (Hungary was the fifth-most densely populated, at ninety-two people per square kilometer), Szentnémedy warned that Germany and Hungary risked "suicide" if they failed to take seriously their need for comprehensive air defense. Breaking with the Douhetian ideal of the sufficiency of the battle-plane, Szentnémedy included fighter aircraft as part of the required tools of air defense. Those fighters would be especially critical to a Hungary deprived of its traditional borders, Szentnémedy argued in his conclusion: "In the end, it can be settled that our rump country has no such point that our neighbors' bombers could not easily reach." This had come about because Hungary, which "lives in a hostile atmosphere," was "disarmed and completely defenseless in the air." Such a condition could not long be maintained, but "fortunately the hearts, thoughts, and intellectual energies cannot be tied down." *Aviation* ended with a strong assertion of its subject's primacy: "We must not forget the basis for the entire world's aerial armament and organization: aviation is the guardian of a modern state's power, the strong pillar of its economy, and is essential to its cultural and commercial needs."[66]

With the exception of a slightly tempered tone in some sections and an implicit rejection of Douhet's conception of the battle-plane as a viable craft for air defense, *Aviation* deviated little from the views Szentnémedy expressed two years earlier in the *MKSz* version of *The War of 19___*. Certainly there was no softening of the core Douhetian belief that air power was a war-winning—not just a war-fighting—instrument. After calling air forces fundamentally offensive and ground forces essentially defensive, Szentnémedy declared that victory could only be achieved through offensive activity and that "the ground forces' role should be restricted to defense of the home territory, while the war is decided in the air."[67]

That same conviction was apparent in Szentnémedy's decision to translate Knauss's work *Air War 1936* for publication in Hungary, first as an abridged serial in the September–November 1934 issues of *MKSz*, and then in a 1935 monograph brought out by the Hadiakadémia press. Elements of Knauss's book read like extracts from Douhet, with Knauss's Air Commodore Brackley standing in for Douhet's General Reuss. Brackley was an air power prophet who realized that the days of chivalrous fighter combat were over, and that a new form of warfare had been born. He formulated its tenets:

> 1. The main purpose of the air arm is to break the enemy's will to war by bombing raids on his country and population.
>
> 2. If large quantities of bombs are to be dropped accurately on targets far from the home aerodrome, very big airplanes will be needed to carry heavy loads over a wide action radius . . .
>
> 3. Such bombing machines can and must defend themselves against attacks by enemy aircraft . . .
>
> 4. Maximum technological achievement can only be attained by apportioning all duties to highly qualified specialists. But such division of labor and specialization is only possible in a large machine carrying numerous crew.
>
> 5. Only large machines of this type, proceeding in close groups, are capable of carrying out aerial tactics which are impossible in a single-seater scouting machine where one man has to do everything simultaneously . . .
>
> 6. Bombing raids must take place in daylight when accurate aim is possible. Only by day, moreover, are squadron flights in close order possible.[68]

Not only were the assumptions of Douhet and Knauss about air warfare strikingly similar, so were their conclusions about how such unrestricted air war would play out. Both believed in the fundamental fragility of a society under attack. In each account the panicked inhabitants of Paris pressed their leaders for peace, although Knauss cast a more jaundiced eye on the French than did Douhet: his Parisians, enraged at the failure of the French air force to stop the British raiders, pulled innocent French aviators from taxis and bludgeoned them to death. "In this night the last vestiges of law and order vanished," Knauss wrote. "Man fought against man, driven by the sheer urge of self-preservation."[69] Knauss also showed a greater appreciation of air power's effectiveness against fielded forces, as he described the complete destruction of the French landing party after a devastating low-altitude attack that cost Brackley his life.[70]

The 1935 publication of Szentnémedy's translation, *Légiháború 1938-ban: Páris szétrombolása,* represented the high-water mark of Szentnémedy's promotion of Douhetism. Through his three major works on the topic he had presented a remarkably consistent view of the role and utility of air power in warfare. That view was fundamentally the one espoused by Giulio Douhet himself, and represented in the United States by Billy Mitchell and in Great Britain by Hugh Trenchard. At its heart was the belief that a large and independent air force equipped with heavy long-range bombers could, with an unrestricted aerial campaign directed at the enemy's center of gravity, bring a war to a quick and decisive end. Szentnémedy had absorbed and incorporated some of the criticism of Douhet, with the result that his own version of strategic bombing theory was less deterministic and his vision of air power more expansive. Without casting off his trust in the ultimate decisiveness of the unrestricted aerial offensive, he broadened his understanding of the offensive to include some of the tactical operations he had previously characterized as "frittering away."

One of these was the idea of *l'aviazone d'assalto* (assault aviation) advanced by Amadeo Mecozzi, Douhet's countryman and critic.[71] Szentnémedy considered Mecozzi's concept, which was a refinement of his earlier *guerra aerea concomitante*, to be one of the three primary strains of air power theory, along with strategic bombing and the French tactic of *l'aviation d'arrêt* (halting aviation).[72] Mecozzi's vision of air force employment was in direct opposition to Douhet's: instead of masses of bombers attacking population centers from high altitude, he advocated multiple formations of fighter-sized airplanes, capable of striking small targets at low altitude in cooperation with ground forces. Szentnémedy first pointed out what he saw as the technological contradictions inherent in assault aviation. Airplanes intended to conduct low-altitude attacks in small formations must be fast, maneuverable, and hardy in order to withstand ground fire, and those characteristics greatly reduced bomb capacity. Overall, Szentnémedy thought its success unlikely. "It is madness to deploy fast machines at low altitudes, where the infantry and artillery fire is concentrated." His second objection was organizational. However much Mecozzi might argue for bureaucratic autonomy, an air force that conducted chiefly tactical missions was at risk of being subsumed by the army. "Although Colonel Mecozzi claims that the attack aviation is not a cooperative arm with other branches, it is to be feared that his idea will lead to the independent air force in large part falling under the ground force command." Some French commentators shared this fear, claiming that assault aviation really represented a return to First World War employment concepts and would make the air service again an auxiliary arm. Unless Mecozzi could prove otherwise, "the entire assault aviation theory can be considered just an extremist idea (*tulzott gondolatnak*)."[73] Szentnémedy was more receptive to Mecozzi's insistence on a fleet composed of a single aircraft type. Douhet had also agitated for a single-type fleet, but his multiplace, multiengine long-range battle-planes would have had little in

common with the single-seat, single-engine low-level attackers
Mecozzi had in mind.

Assault aviation was grounded in Mecozzi's extensive flying
experience. Originally enlisted in the engineer corps, he earned his
wings in 1915, a battlefield commission in 1917, and ended the war
with six air-to-air victories. After the war he served in the Italian
aviation mission in Paris, and in 1929 took command of the 7th
Land Fighter Group.[74] His firsthand knowledge of flight contrasted
with Douhet's limited practical exposure, and it was this, in the
words of RA historians, that "set the fighter pilot against the Regio
Esercito General Staff Colonel."[75] Mecozzi slowly gained support
within the RA, which accelerated the organizing and training of
assault units and the development of the Breda Breda Ba.65, a heavy
attack aircraft conceived along Mecozzian lines. Szentnémedy
sensed the shift in the RA's orientation: "It looks like the Italians have
converted to 'assault aviation' and the new way of employment."[76]

Szentnémedy had not converted, but he had begun to think
more seriously about strategic bombing from the point of view of
the country under attack. When he first considered the topic in
May 1932, Szentnémedy denied the importance of air defense. He
took a Douhetian line in favor of the attack, contradicting Clausewitz's claim that defense was the stronger form of war.[77] Szentnémedy allowed that an "everlasting natural law" provided for
countermeasures to all innovations in the conduct of war, but observed that air defense capability "limped along" behind aircraft
development. "This therefore demonstrates its greatest weakness,
without regard to the fact that air defense naturally, like all defense,
stands from the first at a certain disadvantage against the attack."[78]
Recent air defense exercises in France, Germany, and Czechoslovakia showed some success in areas such as blackout procedures
and military-civilian cooperation, but highlighted shortcomings
in air raid alarm effectiveness. Szentnémedy noted a general lack
of enthusiasm on the part of the cities' inhabitants, a particular
problem in Königsberg. While he dutifully reported the lessons

derived by the various exercise directors, Szentnémedy rendered a larger judgment of his own:

> We can establish as a final conclusion that defense in air warfare is an extremely expensive proposition, and is such a thankless job for the responsible leaders that only negative outcomes can be reached. Air defense is pure defense in a real sense. Either it does not attack the opponent, a lucky outcome for them, or it just moves the war and its victims somewhere else; or in the case that the attack is successful, the fight continues above our heads and stirs anger in the people, because the air defense proved a fiasco. While still in peacetime we have to use all methods (print, radio, film) to quash the formation of mass panic, which, according to experience, can breed revolutionary movements in the cities affected by war, which also must be thwarted.[79]

Szentnémedy here anticipated civilian rage directed at ineffectual air defenders, a fear that was later manifested in its most murderous form in Knauss's *Air War 1936*.

Szentnémedy presented a new perspective in "Is defense against unrestricted air war possible?," published in two parts in the summer 1935 issues of *MKSz*. While Szentnémedy still held "active" air defense (e.g., the attempt to defeat an attacking force with fighters and AAA) was doomed to failure, he had come to believe a program of "passive" air defense could mitigate the worst effects of bombing. The first passive measure was dispersal: "Extensive large cities with their solid mass will always represent favorable and attractive targets. If, however, these targets are divided and dispersed in suitable measures, this immediately offers certain protection."[80] This protection was especially important for rump Hungary, Szentnémedy reasoned, because of the country's vulnerability to the air forces of the Little Entente. A map titled "Hungary's Indefensibility from the Air" tied that vulnerability to Trianon, showing that the entire country lay within range of Czechoslovak, Romanian, and Yugoslav bombers launched from airfields in territory lost under the treaty.[81]

The second passive measure was civil defense. Szentnémedy surveyed civil defense initiatives in other European countries and urged Hungary to emulate them. He judged the Soviet Union to be the most advanced in its preparations, having constructed in Moscow, Leningrad, and Kharkov underground cinemas capable of sheltering masses during an aerial bombardment. In London and Paris the underground railways could perform the same function. The caverns in Kent received particular attention, since the British press had reported a plan to shield up to 100,000 people there in the event of sustained attack. Szentnémedy suggested that the cave system under Buda Castle, which had protected the populace during the Ottoman siege in the seventeenth century, could be used in the same way.[82] Subterranean shelter would provide the most protection against the effects of blast and fire, but it should be avoided in the case of chemical attacks, because the heavier-than-air poison would settle in the tunnels. The best plan in a gas attack, then, would be "to reach the rooftop or highest floor, where the air is clear." This last bit of advice came from a series of drawings in the article's second half, which depicts sixteen "wrong and right" responses to air raids reprinted from the German magazine *Kriegskunst in Wort und Bild*. The pictures reinforce Szentnémedy's earlier point about dispersal, albeit on a human rather than industrial scale. In them, people are instructed to clear the streets, go to cellars, avoid congregating, shelter their horses, seek cover in agricultural ditches and train tunnels, stay away from windows, remain calm, black out lights, move upwind, and wipe chemicals from their clothes with a handkerchief.[83] The specificity of the instructions and the cartoonlike illustrations were unusual for *MKSz*, but presaged the style later adopted by *Riadó!*, the magazine of the Hungarian Air Defense League intended to appeal to the broadest possible audience.

This article elicited a sharp response from *vitéz* Gustáv Hellebronth, a retired Honvéd lieutenant general, who in the August 1935 issue of *MKSz* disputed Szentnémedy's basic premises. Whether from courtesy or contempt, Hellebronth managed to condemn Szentnémedy without ever mentioning his name or even the title of his offending article. Picking up on the editor's penchant for arguing from the authority of international experts, Hellebronth aimed his broadside at "alien ideas":

> There are those who fear that the "unrestricted air war" propagated by foreigners will lead irretrievably to the destruction of civilization. Others, however, trust that the worst danger can be avoided through "civil defense."
>
> Those who believe in "unrestricted air war," on foreign authority, refer in the first place to Marshal Foch, who said, "The civilian population has to be attacked so that the opposing people can be crushed at their root."[84]

But, Hellebronth continued, the First World War had demonstrated just how difficult it was to break down a nation's resistance. It could possibly be done after "years of grinding work," but it is unlikely to occur as the result of a transitory aerial bombardment. "Countless examples show that fleeting destruction, whether caused by nature or enemy forces, can be repaired swiftly." Hellebronth was convinced that "quickly played-out air operations" would not have a lasting or decisive effect on civilian populations, and at the same time he felt sure that emergency programs would make little difference in the event. "Civil air defense is certainly a beautiful and humane thought, but in reality, unfortunately, impractical."[85] Just as no law or measure could prevent mass terror during a terrible natural catastrophe, no preparation could ensure discipline during a surprise air attack. Hellebronth also opposed civil defense on economic grounds, noting Hungary's mounting deficit, and he insisted that the limited military budget be spent on weapons rather than gas masks. He even doubted that many people would mind, suggesting that overtaxed citizens "already bled dry would rather die than pay (especially if death is not too near and not too certain)." Having rejected a key component of Douhetian theory—the essential fragility of modern society—Hellebronth contended that the opposing army was the proper target for aerial bombardment. He wrote, in a passage that echoed Luftwaffe doctrine, "The air force's main mission and concern are not the peaceful citizens, but rather the quick destruction of the opposing air and ground forces and resources. This is the only road leading to victory."[86]

The answer to Hellebronth came in December 1935, but not from Szentnémedy. It was instead a passionate denunciation penned by *vitéz* Lajos Németh, whose use of the first-person plural suggests that he represented corporate convictions. Németh referred to Hellebronth as the "illustrious author" whose article dismissed the efficacy of strategic bombing. "It is possible," Németh conceded, "to have differing opinions about unrestricted air warfare, but it is beyond doubt that the air arm will have a decisive role in a future war."[87] It was less reasonable to question the wisdom of civil air defense, the implementation of which was nearly universal, especially in light of the recent Italian bombing in Abyssinia. Németh countered Hellebronth's assertion that defense against a surprise attack was impossible: "It is indeed possible! We are not defenseless if we prepare conscientiously and thoroughly." He also pointed to a generation gap as a reason for the wide variance in their thinking on the matter: "As old a soldier as he is, he forgets that our military discipline does not in the last instance rest on the results of education and breeding. Laws, propaganda, courses of study, leagues, additional air defense blackouts, and exercises (which unfortunately we still have not held in Hungary) all are necessary so that a broad cross-section of the population can recognize the dangers of aerial attack as well as the possibilities for defense, and at the same time we can train them for air defense discipline!"[88] Although Hellebronth was in fact old—he was three years old when the Dual Monarchy emerged from the Compromise of 1867—ideological orientation may be a better explanation. Németh's confidence in the power of collective action to overcome difficulties was characteristic of a progressive statism that infused political movements on both the right and left at the time, whereas Hellebronth's pessimism in the same matter suggests a conservative turn of mind. Certainly Németh and later Szentnémedy thought him a hidebound reactionary.

Hellebronth considered himself an objective observer who in his earlier article simply endeavored to look at the "boiling-over questions" from a "higher viewpoint and broader scope."[89] He sought a useful general theory of aviation, unlike the "followers of foreign fantasies" who advocated independent air operations. As part of that theory, Hellebronth outlined three areas in which military airplanes had "outstanding advantages" over the traditional branches of the army. Aircraft were much faster than cavalry, which meant they could range farther in reconnaissance, take the place of cavalry in the attack, and better pursue the fleeing enemy after the battle. Bombers rivaled artillery for effect and had a longer reach, and aircraft machine guns could be devastating to opposing infantry. He also acknowledged the growing capability of airborne transport. Against this stood aviation's fatal disadvantage: the utter inability of airplanes to secure and occupy terrain. This deficiency "predestined air forces to the surprise initiation of war," after which they would assist the slower-mobilizing land forces. "Air forces therefore have two roles to fulfill: as an independent force at the opening of the war to conduct raids, and then to fight alongside the army as a separate branch."[90] In tying the air force to the land war, Hellebronth repudiated the basis for strategic bombing. He did so, he claimed, on solid historical grounds. It was well established that in the Great War civilian collapse preceded military defeat. Indeed, the idea of society's breakdown was at the heart of strategic bombing theory. Why then, Hellebronth asked, wasn't bombing the cause of that civilian collapse? In order for unrestricted air war to be a serious strategic theory, its proponents must show that air power is capable of crippling the people's will to resist. In spite of the experience of the First World War, the Japanese bombing of Shanghai, and Italian operations in Abyssinia, there was no proof that aerial attacks could in fact achieve that effect. Hellebronth again compared bombardment to a natural disaster (a theme he would return to in the third installment). "From every example . . . it seems that the passing effects of the danger and destruction—caused by nature

or opposing forces—immediately blow over."[91] Some of Hellebronth's blows must have begun to land, because Szentnémedy
took the extraordinary step of appending an editorial disclaimer to
the end of this article. It was, according to Szentnémedy, "an original thought" and "skillfully presented," but the theory of "restricted
air warfare" was not supported by experience, and this should
therefore be "the end of the argument."[92]

The argument would go two more rounds, however. Szentnémedy published his own lengthy riposte five months later; not, he
claimed, in order to answer directly the previous article or to sustain the dispute, but rather "to show to laymen, on the basis of the
extraordinarily rich foreign literature, the current concepts, conditions, possibilities and functions" of air warfare.[93] These ideas were
"crystal clear" to the experts, and showed the "indisputable influence of air war's possibilities." Predictably, the first expert consulted was Douhet, whose concept Szentnémedy presented in a
500-word précis. It was important to begin with Douhet, he wrote,
because the late Italian general's concept of unrestricted air warfare
was evident in the organization, training, and equipping of the great
powers' air forces. He later offered as concrete evidence the ratio of
"offensive versus defensive" airplanes in a selection of European
countries. In the First World War, according to Szentnémedy, the
proportion of bombers to fighters was roughly 1:9, whereas the current ratio in Britain was 2:1, in France 1:1.5, in Italy 1:2, in Czechoslovakia 1:3.5, and in the Soviet Union 1:4. "These numbers show,
however much it is denied and concealed, that today everywhere
Douhet's ideas are followed."[94] This passage gives further weight to
Szentnémedy's revealing comment earlier in the article concerning
the far-reaching influence of Douhet: "It is no use, however, to
preach 'unrestricted air warfare' everywhere and at all costs, because
it is the fundamental assumption. We now want to examine the current conditions."[95] These statements show that Szentnémedy held
to the central precepts of Douhetism as late as 1937. He had enlarged

his conception of air power beyond the limits set down by Douhet, but he had not abandoned the Italian's core concepts.

This expansive view of air power was displayed when Szent-némedy addressed Hellebronth's objection regarding the inability of air forces to take and hold territory. Szentnémedy admitted that it was not possible at the moment, but he then mentioned the promising developments in airborne infantry, a topic that had been raised in the pages of *MKSz* in March, May, and July 1936, and one that Szentnémedy himself would take up the following year.[96] He pointed to recent maneuvers in which the Soviets delivered by air three infantry battalions behind the opponent's lines, demonstrating the potential of "vertical envelopment." Szentnémedy found the roots for this innovative use of airplanes in Douhet and Clausewitz. "Attaining tactical air superiority, which in time will lead to command of the air, makes the strategic effect felt in the vast majority of cases; and it is possible that with the range, extraordinary speed, and ability to reach quickly the center of gravity, the air force has fashioned such an instrument for the supreme leadership that is worth every other force or enterprise."[97]

Regarding the use of air forces on the battlefield, Szentnémedy offered a partial concession. It was possible, of course, to intervene temporarily in the army's battle, but there would be few targets of value for airmen, and such operations generally meant "foolish sacrifice."[98] He conceded nothing on the bombing of civilians. "If we seek the fastest decision," he wrote, "we have to attack the weakest point." The historical record was clear: "By shattering the people's morale it is indeed possible to reach a decision in war." Abyssinia could not represent a defeat of the Douhetian idea of unrestricted air warfare, because the RA was not tasked with conducting such an operation there. The bulk of Italian airplanes remained in the Mediterranean in case of a European conflict, but air power nonetheless contributed mightily to the Abyssinian campaign. Szent-némedy quoted Italian experts who estimated that the victory achieved there in seven months would have taken two to three years without the RA's contribution.[99]

Hellebronth's reply, the last piece in this long-running exchange, appeared in November 1937. This time the editorial disclaimer, Szentnémedy's final word on the matter, appeared at the beginning: "The editor does not fully agree with this article and publishes it as point of interest, because in contrast to this article, the editor considers the moral and material effects of aerial attacks important."[100] After taking Szentnémedy to task for the condescending tone of his November 1936 item, Hellebronth took up again his earlier comparison of air attacks to natural disasters. He demanded the Douhetians explain why bombardment was fundamentally more destructive of morale than artillery barrages, floods, volcanoes, or earthquakes. He referred once more to the 1923 Great Kantō earthquake that killed more than 100,000 Japanese citizens and devastated the capital Tokyo, but did not result in widespread popular unrest. Then Hellebronth offered another inconvenient example: Madrid, a capital on the front lines of a civil war subjected to both aerial and artillery bombardment, where life went on without a mass exodus. "These real examples testify to the capability of people to resist, and they show that people can bear great danger for short durations, as long as they can get their breath, without suffering societal breakdown." In the First World War, Habsburg civilians were subjected to "propaganda glittering with the hope of dissolution" and suffered "ceaseless torment due to privation," yet nonetheless persevered for years. On what grounds, then, did Douhet expect that just "a few minutes of isolated attacks would lead to the collapse of an entire country?"[101]

Szentnémedy had ignored this line of attack in his November 1936 article, and he never offered a satisfactory answer to Hellebronth's query. The absence of a society-disintegrating mechanism was Douhet's greatest conceptual weakness. He and his disciples simply asserted that large-scale aerial bombardment of population centers would necessarily cause such panic and chaos as to induce near-immediate surrender. That this had never happened did not moderate their conviction; it only strengthened their self-image as visionaries and caused them to regard skeptics as hopelessly backward, like the misguided Franco-Belgian airmen in *The War of 1919* ___. In fact, the lack of historical precedent was critical to survival of the theory: a thing never properly attempted cannot be considered to have failed. In this regard adherents of Douhet are no different from those of Marx. Any supposed flaw in the great man's theory must be properly attributed to insufficiently zealous execution. It was therefore extremely unlikely that a Douhetian would find any argument from history persuasive, but to the open-minded, Hellebronth's approach could be very effective. Technical objections—bombers are too small or slow, aiming is too erratic, explosive yield is too little—could be overcome or swept aside by the promise of future development (which in many cases was fulfilled). Hellebronth, by comparing the supposed effects of aerial attacks to the demonstrated results of long-term shelling or natural disasters, undermined Douhet's theory at its very foundation. When confronted with the central question of how airplanes wrought more emotional damage than artillery or earthquakes, Szentnémedy was silent.

That was rarely the case. For a decade Szentnémedy wrote extensively and well on all aspects of military aviation, and encouraged others to do the same. Under his leadership *MKSz* served as the Honvéd's sounding board for air power doctrine, a place where new ideas could be circulated, debated, amended, or discarded. In spite of his own remarkable productivity and activism on behalf of the independent aerial offensive, there is no sign that Szentnémedy stifled dissent. His editorial liberality and permissiveness make the disclaimers attached to Hellebronth's pieces all the more striking. Because of the importance of the topic and the intensity of the authors' views, that exchange was more spirited than others, but in terms of the seriousness with which it was conducted it was broadly representative. The high participation rate also speaks well of the journal's intellectual integrity. Over 150 authors contributed to the journal, including the esteemed airman István Petróczy and future Arrow Cross (Nyilaskeresztes Párt) leader Ferenc Szálasi.[102] Most authors submitted only a single item, which resulted in a wide range of air power issues being addressed. To take a single example, the July 1935 edition containing the second article on air defense that initiated the Hellebronth-Németh-Szentnémedy imbroglio featured pieces on new Italian fighters, the use of wood in aircraft production, and squadron flight formations. The blend of tactics, technology, and theory was not repeated in every issue, but it was far from uncommon. With nearly 1.5 million words having been expended in *MKSz's* Aviation Bulletin, it seems certain that any deficiencies in the Hungarian air service could not have arisen from a lack of contemplation.

From too much contemplation, perhaps. Or rather, from an unhealthy ratio of contemplation to practical application, caused by external factors largely outside the flying corps' control. One reason Szentnémedy devoted so much ink to covering foreign aviation maneuvers (approximately seventeen pages per year) was that for most of the 1930s Hungary was unable to conduct its own flight exercises. Some military flight activity had been performed even during the period of IMCC oversight, and opportunities expanded after the Allies ended the inspection regime, but they remained strictly limited in scope. In contrast, Italian pilots crossed oceans in mass formations that came to be known in English as Balbos, after the air minister who led them. Eventually the same RA fliers earned combat experience in East Africa and Spain, where they fought alongside Germans and against Soviets. British crews policed the empire from the air, Japanese pilots honed their skills in China, and airmen of the Little Entente were free to observe, participate in, and conduct aerial maneuvers as they wished. Not so the Hungarians. They were free only to read, write, and argue about air power. All else—the hard work of transforming doctrine into capability— had to be done in secret. The next chapter describes the difficulties

Hungarian airmen faced in expanding and modernizing their air arm under adverse political, economic, and legal conditions.

NOTES

1. Quoted in *MKHL, 1938–1945*, pp. 10–11.
2. Szinai and Szűcs, *Confidential Papers of Admiral Horthy*, p. 42. Bethlen's resignation letter was triggered by the outrage in foreign capitals, particularly Paris, following the revelation of government involvement in a scheme to counterfeit large quantities of French francs.
3. Quoted in *MKHL, 1938–1945*, p. 14.
4. Szinai and Szűcs, *Confidential Papers of Admiral Horthy*, pp. 45–49.
5. Hauser: Vesztényi, "A magyar katonai repülés" (HL Tgy 2.787), p. I/24.
6. Madarász, *Légi háború*, p. 51.
7. Ibid., p. 3.
8. Biddle, *Rhetoric and Reality in Air Warfare*, p. 104.
9. Ibid.
10. Quoted in Hippler, "Democracy and War," p. 171.
11. Ibid.
12. Quoted in Meilinger, "Giulio Douhet," pp. 4–5.
13. Ibid.
14. "General Giulio Douhet," *Royal Air Force Quarterly* 7 (1936), p. 148.
15. Meilinger, "Giulio Douhet," p. 8.
16. Gooch, *Mussolini and His Generals*, p. 59.
17. Corum, *Luftwaffe*, p. 89. In "Giulio Douhet and the Origins of Airpower Theory" Meilinger notes that the 1921 version of *Command of the Air* elicited a "muted" response, while the second edition published in 1927, with an even greater emphasis on independent air forces received a "noisy" reception. He attributes the difference to earlier war weariness and the increased militarism of Fascist Italy.
18. MacIsaac, "Voices from the Central Blue," p. 630.
19. Holló, *A Galambtól a Griffmadárig*, p. 55.
20. Willwerth 1896: Szakály, *A magyar katonai felső vezetés*, pp. 128–129; Orsova: 1890 census data from *Wikipedia*, s.v. "Orsova" [in Hungarian], accessed Nov. 14, 2013. http://hu.wikipedia.org/wiki/Orsova. Improbably, Orsova (1890 population: 3,564) produced another prominent military airman: Luftwaffe General der Flieger Stefan Frölich, who served in the Austrian national air service after the dissolution of the empire.
21. Szakály, *A magyar katonai felső vezetés*, pp. 128–129.
22. Kálmán, *A magyar vezérkari tisztek kiképzése*, p. 11.
23. See "Treaty of Trianon, Part V."
24. Szakály, *A magyar katonai felső vezetés*, pp. 128–129.

25. Kálmán, *A magyar vezérkari tisztek kiképzése*, pp. 44, 39.

26. Ibid., pp. 27, 13, 28.

27. See Hazai's "Előszó" (Preface) to Clausewitz, *A Háborúról*, pp. 1–2.

28. See below, pp 18–19. Szentnémedy, *A repülés*, p. 27.

29. Language skill: Szakály, *A magyar katonai felső vezetés*, pp. 128–129; *MKSz* mandatory: Hetés, "Gondolatok a magyar hadtörténet-felfogás alakulásáról," p. 329.

30. Douhet, *Command of the Air*, p. 294.

31. Szentnémedy, "Vélemények és eszmék," p. 102.

32. Szentnémedy, "Az 19.. évi háboru" (no. 3 [1931]), p. 29.

33. Ibid.

34. Cain, "Neither Decadent, nor Stupid, nor Treasonous," p. 1.

35. Douhet, *Command of the Air*, p. 298.

36. Ibid., pp. 305–306.

37. Szentnémedy, "Az 19.. évi háboru" (no. 3 [1931]), p. 33; and (no. 4 [1931]), p. 102.

38. Douhet, *Command of the Air*, p. 309.

39. Szentnémedy, "Vélemények és eszmék," p. 102.

40. Quoted in Corum, "Airpower Thought in Continental Europe," p. 161.

41. Gooch, *Mussolini and His Generals*, p. 105.

42. Knox, *Hitler's Italian Allies*, p. 64; and Corum, "Airpower Thought in Continental Europe," p. 161.

43. 1933 *Royal Air Force Quarterly*: Meilinger, "Giulio Douhet," p. 32; no influence: Higham, *Military Intellectuals in Britain*, p. 258.

44. B. Greenhous, quoted in Meilinger, "Giulio Douhet," p. 40n.

45. Meilinger, "Giulio Douhet," p. 33.

46. Szentnémedy published his translation as *Légiháború 1938-ban: Páris szétrombolása*. He pushed the date of Knauss's war back two years, presumably to account for the lag in translation. The first English translation was published in 1932 under the title *War in the Air* (see note 68).

47. Quoted in Corum and Muller, *Luftwaffe's Way of War*, pp. 118–120.

48. Ibid., pp. 133–142.

49. Corum, "Airpower Thought in Continental Europe," p. 153.

50. Young, "Strategic Dream," p. 59.

51. Szentnémedy, "Vélemények és eszmék," p. 103.

52. Cain, *Forgotten Air Force*, p. 35.

53. Ibid.

54. Szentnémedy, "Vélemények és eszmék," p. 105.

55. Ibid., pp. 106–116.

56. Ibid., p. 109.

57. Ibid., p. 116.

58. Quoted in Holló, *A Galambtól a Griffmadárig*, p. 56.

59. Szentnémedy, *A repülés*, p. 27.

60. Ibid., p. 28.
61. Ibid.
62. Douhet was not alone in this view. B. H. Liddell Hart advanced it in *Paris: or, The Future of War* (1925), and the Russian-American aircraft designer and theorist Alexander de Seversky held it well into the Second World War. See his "Strategy of Air Power More Humane than Blood-Bath of Surface Warfare" in *Pittsburgh Press*, Nov. 13, 1943, p. 1. See also Meilinger, "Alexander P. de Seversky and American Airpower." The geneticist J. B. S. Haldane promoted gas (without regard to its delivery system) as the most humane weapon in his *Callinicus*.
63. Douhet, *Command of the Air*, p. 362.
64. Szentnémedy, *A repülés*, p. 29.
65. Ibid., p. 37.
66. Ibid., pp. 37–40.
67. Ibid., p. 29.
68. Knauss, *War in the Air*, p. 67.
69. Ibid., pp. 85, 171.
70. Ibid., p. 248.
71. Mecozzi popularized the term in his 1933 book *L'Aviazione d'Assalto*.
72. Szentnémedy, "Új hadmüveleti irányelvek a légiháborúra," p. 121.
73. Ibid., p. 122.
74. Sganga et al., "Douhet's Antagonist," p. 6.
75. Botti and Cervelli, quoted in ibid., p. 7.
76. Szentnémedy, "Új hadmüveleti irányelvek," p. 135.
77. Clausewitz, *On War*, pp. 84, 358.
78. Szentnémedy, "A honi légvédelem problémái," p. 108.
79. Ibid., pp. 122–123.
80. Szentnémedy, "Van-e védelem a korlátlan légiháború ellen?," p. 96; passive and active defense: p. 106.
81. Ibid., p. 100.
82. Ibid., pp. 102–103.
83. Ibid., pp. 95–100.
84. Hellebronth, "A légiháború és a védekezés módjai," p. 100.
85. Ibid., p. 101.
86. Ibid.
87. Németh, "Polgári légvédelem," p. 97.
88. Ibid., p. 98.
89. Hellebronth, "A légiháború és a védekezés módjai," p. 117.
90. Ibid., p. 118.
91. Ibid., p. 119.
92. Ibid., p. 122.
93. Szentnémedy, "A légiháború és a védekezés módjai," p. 105.
94. Ibid., p. 115.

95. Ibid., p. 109.

96. Bobok, "Vállalkozás ejtőernyőkkel az ellenség hátában"; Tóth, "Szállitó repülés" and "Csapaszállitások repülőgéppel és ejtőernyős kirakások"; Szentnémedy, "A függőleges átkarolás kérdéséhez" and "Az ejtőernyő ujabb katonai jelentősége."

97. Szentnémedy, "A légiháború és a védekezés módjai," p. 116.

98. Ibid., p. 117.

99. Ibid., p. 118.

100. Hellebronth, "A légiháború és a védekezés módjai," p. 96.

101. Ibid., p. 98.

102. Petróczy, "A lengyel lég és gázvédelmi liga tevékenysége" and "Hogyan szervezte meg németország a polgári légvédelmet"; Szálasy, "A légi erők befolyása a hadászatra." Arrow Cross was the national socialist party aligned with Nazi Germany that held power in Hungary from October 1944 until March 1945.

5

Reality: 1927–1937

FOR JUST OVER A DECADE, HUNGARY'S AERIAL REARMA-
ment proceeded in fits and starts. The environment at the outset of
the program in 1927 seemed promising: political and military leaders agreed on the necessity of an air force, the Italian Friendship
Treaty offered an instrument for acquiring airplanes, and aviation-
minded intellectuals began to provide a theoretical basis for the
service's employment. While these conditions remained relatively
constant through the period, until the late 1930s Hungary did not
see a substantial improvement in its diplomatic and legal standing,
and its economic position deteriorated during the worldwide economic crisis. These problems complicated and slowed the efforts of
Hungarian airmen to expand and modernize their service. Western
aircraft companies were reluctant to trade with Hungary, and for
those so inclined, Budapest's financial difficulties limited payment options. And because Trianon's prohibition against military
aviation remained in force, such improvements they were able to
achieve had to be concealed as commercial or sport aviation. These
factors constrained Hungarian airmen as they sought to organize,
equip, and train a force capable of fulfilling the nation's foreign
policy. Even so, by the end of 1937 the Hungarian air service had
begun to emerge from the shadows, and with the covert assistance
of Italy and Germany, to equip itself with a small number of modern aircraft.

The dynamics of this period illustrate the complex relationship between foreign policy and military power. The role of armed force in bolstering diplomacy was demonstrated repeatedly and persuasively even during those heady years immediately following the foundation of the League of Nations. Hungary's own experience in revolution and intervention, the Italian seizure of Corfu, Japan's conquest of Manchuria, the Italian invasion of Abyssinia, and Germany's reoccupation of the Rhineland all served to buttress Defense Minister Károly Csáky's point to the Crown Council ("In foreign policy it is military strength above all that defines power").[1] An active, and especially a revisionist, foreign policy required a credible armed force. The creation of that force may, as in Hungary's case, depend upon the ability of diplomats to loosen legal restrictions and to negotiate trade agreements, loans, and cooperative training arrangements.

Though the Italian treaty was a victory for Hungarian diplomacy, a symbol of the end of postwar isolation, its immediate results were disappointing. Contrary to the Foreign Ministry's expectations, Italian capital did not pour into the country, and Hungarian finance remained dependent on British investment. Nor did weapons flow freely from Rome to Budapest. On January 1, 1928, one of the early attempts at arms smuggling was foiled when five train cars filled with machine guns and spare parts were intercepted by Austrian customs inspectors at the Szentgotthárd border crossing. This was a repatriation of sorts, since these items were among the materiel surrendered by Austro-Hungarian forces at the end of the First World War.[2] Nevertheless, the Little Entente was irate. The League of Nations investigation that followed concluded that the shipment was indeed a violation of international law, but that it posed little risk to Hungary's neighbors.[3]

The Szentgotthárd scandal epitomized the first year of the Italo-Hungarian relationship: it was a provocation to the region that provided very little increase in the strength of either party. The debut of Italian airplanes in Hungary was similarly inauspicious.

Delivery of a pair of Ansaldo AC.3 advanced trainers was long delayed, and the aircraft arrived in such poor condition that the accompanying Italian pilots refused to fly them. The type had already
suffered twenty-two wing failures, they said, and the undercarriage
was defective.[4] The grounded AC.3s were eventually exchanged for
two airworthy Fiat CR.20s.[5] The relationship did improve after this
rocky start, and Italian factories provided the bulk of the Hungarian
air service's airplanes for the next twelve years. The twin problems
of late delivery and uncertain quality never completely disappeared,
however, and Magyar aviators sometimes had to choose between
an inferior Italian airplane or no airplane at all.

   The Ansaldo/Fiat purchase was a result of a secret Bethlen-
Mussolini meeting in Milan in April 1928. Their main point of discussion was joint support of the right-wing Heimwehr in Austria, whose
ascent to power they believed would shift Vienna away from Paris
and toward Rome-Budapest. Prime Minister Bethlen took the opportunity to press the Duce for a 300-million pengő credit and an
option to buy 400 Italian aircraft.[6] Mussolini agreed, pushed perhaps by the possibility of closer Hungarian-German military relations. Italian diplomats were aware that Bethlen had met in Rome
with General Hans von Seeckt, the recently retired commander of
the Reichswehr and the architect of its resurgence. They also knew
that von Seeckt had visited Hungary in October 1927 at Bethlen's
invitation to consider the prospects for Hungarian rearmament.
Spurred by competition, Italy's military attaché in Budapest offered a number of officer exchange programs. After much delibera-
tion and negotiation, it was decided that Hungarian pilots would
resign their Honvédség commissions and attend Italian flight schools
as civilians. After the Szentgotthárd incident, Mussolini suggested
an additional precaution: the Hungarians should renounce their
citizenship and become, at least temporarily, Italians. Through
these measures it was thought the scheme could avoid breaching
the Paris Air Agreement and Trianon's Article 142.[7] The British Foreign Office learned of this plan and relayed it to Sir Ronald Graham,

London's minister in Rome. In a cable marked "Very secret," White-hall generally agreed with Mussolini's legal analysis while questioning his judgment:

> Our lawyers do not think that Article 142 prevents Hungarians from receiving aeronautical instruction in the air force of a foreign Power, provided they do not 'enlist (s'enrôler)' in it, unless indeed it were possible to maintain that the action taken amounted to sending an 'air or military mission' to Italy. We do not think that such a contention could succeed, especially as the second paragraph of the article makes it plain that the only obligation on Italy is not to employ Hungarians for the purpose of assisting or instructing in military training. . . . It is probably the case that the framers of the article in question did not take into account such a contingency as that which has now arisen, as it seems clear that the object of the article was to prevent the spread of Hungarian military 'kultur'. It was not worded so as to prevent the Hungarians from *receiving* military training. As to whether Mussolini's action is inconsistent with the spirit of the article, there is in any case room for a difference of opinion, and Mussolini may be entitled to 'try it on' openly as he proposes to do.
>
> As regards the first of his proposals, however, there is no getting away from the fact that they reveal the existence of a most discreditable and dangerous intrigue by Mussolini to violate the Treaty of Trianon by collusion between two of its signatories behind the backs of the other signatories, and it is greatly to be feared that the Hungarians will be far too short sighted to resist his overtures.
>
> . . . The feeling here is that the best thing that could happen would be that we should learn of the arrangement by some avowable channel of information and thereupon represent to Mussolini and Bethlen the folly of the whole thing. Otherwise we are afraid that if this scheme succeeds both parties will be encouraged to work out others of a similar nature and to grow increasingly rash in the process until the Yugoslavs discover what is going on and produce a most unpleasant crisis by denouncing both Italy and Hungary to the League.
>
> . . . The whole business shows Mussolini in a bad light and unfortunately is but another sample of his recent policy of giving secret and illegal help to those who in time of trouble would certainly not be friendly to the Serbs. The illicit imports of Italian war material into Hungary and Bulgaria are but other instances of this policy.[8]

This cable shows how much the Foreign Office knew about Hungarian attempts to skirt the air clauses of Trianon, and also how comparatively little it cared. It also demonstrates how easily international law can be dodged when one party is scrupulous to uphold it and the other motivated to subvert it. It seems that no "avowable channel" presented itself, and rather than risk exposing its intelligence source, Great Britain did not confront Mussolini and Bethlen with the evidence of the illegal pilot training.

The plan to change nationalities proved too complex and was never executed. The LÜH instead sent its initial candidates to Italy as private individuals enrolled in a sport-flying course. The program's pioneers were Lajos and Pál Batáry, brothers born in Fiume of an Italian mother. Although ostensibly taking civilian lessons, the Batárys in fact received advanced tactical training from RA instructors, an arrangement much like the faux MALERT training operation established at Szombathely five years earlier. Lajos was sent to a fighter unit, while Pál trained on bombers. Care was taken to keep the brothers out of sight of foreign observers: they were not permitted to participate in the autumn maneuvers, and Pál was moved from the 13th Bomb Regiment at Torino to the 7th at Lonate-Pozzolo for fear of discovery. The exact number of Hungarian pilots trained in Italy before 1938 is uncertain, because those Air Ministry records did not survive the war. Attaché reports and Italian documents refer to other trainees, however, so it is clear that the Batárys were not the only beneficiaries of Italian instruction in this period. Lieutenant Colonel Szilárd Schindler, the Hungarian attaché in Rome, learned to fly Caproni bombers, as did Captain Gyula Tost, who flew combat sorties over Abyssinia with the RA. One of the Hungarian service's chief inspectors, First Lieutenant Elek Ivánkovics, is recorded as attending a four-week course on fighter tactics.[9]

The pilot training program and secret arms exports strengthened the Italo-Hungarian military ties, but the relationship was far from exclusive. Cooperation with Weimar Germany continued through staff visits and licensed manufacturing. In addition to the Udet 12a adopted in 1926, WM had in 1928 purchased for 40,000 marks the license to produce twenty-five Heinkel HD 22 advanced trainers.[10] The HD 22 was used by the MALERT airmail section, which was in reality the air service's bomber squadron. Even as the Italians kept a close eye on German advances toward their new ally, a French flirtation nearly split the Budapest-Rome pairing. In 1928, the French General Staff announced that the following year two Hungarian officers would be seconded to French forces. When questioned by Italian officials, the Defense Ministry suggested that it had simply responded to a French invitation. Upon further investigation by the Italian attaché in Paris, it was discovered that the request was initiated in Budapest. Quiet Italian intervention resulted in the French politely withdrawing their approval, and the Hungarian officers, one of whom was an airman on the clandestine air staff, never went to France. For the next two years, however, a pair of Honvédség officers did attend the French cavalry school at Saumur. Italy again objected, this time more strenuously. Lieutenant Colonel Schindler was summoned to the Italian War Ministry, where he received a dressing down from a senior officer. The war minister, he was told, thought that further Italo-Hungarian cooperation should be suspended, since Hungary, which could not send its officers on courses in Italy due to financial constraints, managed to send them to France. Through a number of miscommunications the disagreement escalated before finally being resolved weeks later. Though no lasting damage was done to relations with Italy, a possible Hungarian connection to France was severed. Budapest declined the next invitation from Paris. This incident, of minor significance in itself, shows the sensitivity of these countries to perceived shifts in power. Italy, fearing a loss of its own prestige and leverage should Hungary move marginally closer to France, forced Hungary to forgo a relationship that could have ameliorated its isolation. Hungary, the junior partner, had little choice, since the small diplomatic advantage that might be gained through exchanges with French forces was far outweighed by the concrete benefits in weapons and training the alliance with Italy offered.

Among the most important benefits of the burgeoning relationship with Italy was access to its aircraft industry. The original LÜH acquisition plan for 1930 included an order for twelve CR.20 fighters in addition to Caproni bombers. Fear that the pace of technological advance would soon make the Fiats obsolete caused LÜH officials to cancel the fighter contract and secure instead the production rights for the Ca.97, a single-engined light transport airplane easily converted to the bombing role.[11] The single prototype from WM suffered from problems with steel-tube soldering as well as splits in the linen covering, and the Ca.97 never entered serial production. Giovanni Caproni sent two Ca.101 aircraft as replacements and trekked to Hungary himself to advise WM on production techniques.[12] With the assistance of Caproni and experts from Fiat, WM engineers finally mastered steel-tube construction, and even pioneered a method of varying tube cross-section and wall thickness to maintain structural stability at reduced weights.[13] In spite of this breakthrough, license production of the Caproni airplanes was not resumed.

The novel technique was put to use in WM's first independently produced trainer. The WM 10 resembled De Havilland's Moth, but was lighter than its British cousin due to the new tube construction, and was powered by a Hungarian-designed four-cylinder air-cooled engine. Unfortunately, it was a demanding machine to fly, and after two of the first ten production models were destroyed in crashes, it was withdrawn from the flight schools. The WM 10 was replaced by the Hungaria, a slightly larger and heavier version of the Udet 12a Flamingó produced by the Székesfehérvár-Sóstó workshop. The Hungaria's extra weight decreased slightly its performance when compared to the Flamingó, but the domestic manufacturing saved 15 per cent of cost without worsening the trade imbalance with Germany.[14]

Trade relations with the Dutch Fokker company remained strong. The LFT had flown Fokker fighters in the First World War, and MALERT's earliest routes had used the five-passenger F.III.

Figure 5.1. Fokker/WM C.V-Ds over Budapest. Photo: Fortepan/Tibor Erky-Nagy.

WM successfully manufactured fifty Fokker C.V-Ds as well as a small number of fifteen-seat Fokker F.VIII passenger planes for MALERT. In 1930, the company ordered four D.XVI "aerobatic airplanes" with an eye toward eventual licensed production. The D. XVI was actually a modern fighter design, and French press coverage of its delivery (Hungary had ordered it with a Gnome-Rhône engine) delayed the fourth airplane's arrival by a year and foreclosed the possibility of WM production.[15]

The Hungarian aircraft industry was proving itself a capable producer of foreign designs. But it had not shown the capacity to move a sophisticated domestic machine from the drawing board to the flight line, nor had it developed an engine strong enough to power more than the most basic training airplane. Many First World War Habsburg aircraft had been propelled by fine Austro-Daimler engines, but the imperial dissolution left no major engine works in Hungary. This was a serious shortfall, because "an engine plant is primarily a precision machine tool shop, while an airframe plant is primarily a sheet-metal fabrication and assembly shop."[16] Metal tube problems could be sorted out with a visit from

more experienced experts; not so with engine fabrication anoma-
lies. Even Germany, to whom Hungary would eventually turn for
engine expertise, was dogged by its own aircraft propulsion deficiencies. Thus the WM-built Gnome-Rhône engines were absolutely critical to Hungary's aviation production. The French engines were themselves derived from the British Bristol Jupiter,
which had its roots in the First World War. The Jupiter had been
refined and improved in the decade that followed, and powered
dozens of postwar aircraft models. From the Jupiter base, Gnome-
Rhône developed a series of radial engines, and sold rights to WM
for the manufacture of three versions: the K-7 Titan Major, a seven-
cylinder plant capable of 370-horsepower; the nine-cylinder, 600-
horsepower K-9 Mistral; and the K-14 Mistral Major, essentially
two K-7s mated front to back, producing up to 1,000 horsepower.[17]
WM engineers introduced a number of small improvements to the
design which were adopted by the Bristol and Gnome-Rhône, including a simpler ignition system, castor oil lubrication, and a cast
cylinder head with more fins and therefore more efficient cooling.
These modifications raised WM's international profile and earned
back a bit of the licensing fee.[18] One of these engines would power
almost every aircraft built in Hungary through the end of the Second World War, with the exception of the Bf 109 and Me 210s.

WM was the parent company of UFAG, Hungary's first aircraft
manufacturing plant and its largest producer of airplanes in the
First World War. The postwar restrictions and convulsions having
made it nearly impossible to sustain a variety of aircraft producers,
the Commerce Ministry decided to maintain WM and MÁG as
viable aviation firms. Other companies were not prohibited from
joining the industry, as when Sóstó moved from repair to production with the Hungaria trainer, but government backing would be
focused on WM and MÁG. The two companies reached an agreement with the Commerce Ministry that WM would handle small
production runs of fifty or fewer aircraft, while MÁG would produce the larger series.[19] The arrangement was apparently reached

amicably, but it proved to be much to WM's advantage: legal and budgetary restrictions in post-Trianon Hungary all but assured that the overwhelming majority of aircraft orders would be for fewer than fifty machines. MÁG, a primary contractor for Fokker and Berg fighters in 1914–1918, was therefore effectively crowded out of the aircraft market, and in fact the company collapsed during the 1931 economic crisis. Airplanes were only a part of MÁG's industrial output, but the firm might have been saved from bankruptcy if contracts had been adjusted to spread work more evenly between WM and MÁG. A possible solution would have been for the companies to specialize in airplane size or purpose (WM, for example, could have concentrated on engines and transport aircraft, MÁG on trainers). Efficiency was served by centralization, but one lesson of the disastrous Knoller program in 1915 was that diversification of product and producer was a strategic strength. This suboptimization of limited aircraft manufacturing capacity was not a serious failure on the part of Commerce Ministry or LÜH planners, but it does underline one area in which the staff officers did not adequately address earlier imperial weaknesses.

The LÜH staff, under the leadership of Colonel Károly Vassel since 1923, generally performed well during its long span underground. From the sanctuary of the Commerce Ministry its officers had seen the air service through the Allied inspections, preserving the seven disguised skeleton squadrons (three training schools, two meteorological, and two airmail sections), stimulating domestic production of training aircraft, and arranging imports from Italy, Germany, Holland, and Britain. They had also established a medical institute devoted to aviation-related maladies, a four-year airplane and engine maintenance school, a legitimate aviation weather service (separate from the clandestine fighter squadrons), and a university course for technical officers. The air service strength in October 1928 stood at 164 officers and civil servants and 719 other ranks. As a result of a Honvédség reorganization it grew nearly 20 per cent within months, to a strength of 1,174 personnel in July 1929.

In December 1929, Colonel Vassel was promoted to lieutenant general and named chief inspector of the air service.[20] His successor at the LÜH was Colonel György Rákosi, whose term included the early phases of cooperation with the RA, the setbacks caused by the worldwide economic crisis, and the intense debates about air power described in the previous chapter.

The effects of the crash of 1929 were just beginning to be felt in Hungary as Vassel and Rákosi took their new posts in December. The next four years would be a "crisis of unparalleled depth" as the economic calamity in the industrialized West led to a precipitous decline in global agricultural prices.[21] The worldwide wholesale price for wheat, for example, Hungary's biggest export, dropped 70 per cent from 1929 to 1933.[22] The market for other agricultural goods also collapsed, leading to increased consumption of domestic produce and the erection of trade barriers. Germany, which increased its own area under cultivation during the crisis, raised its wheat tariff by 300 per cent after the 1930 harvest. Czechoslovakia, Hungary's second best customer (after Austria) in spite of the political tensions between the two countries, declined to renew the trade agreement that expired that year. Thus 1931 exports to Prague amounted to only 4.2 per cent of Hungary's total, compared to 16.8 per cent in 1930.[23] The value of those exports dropped from 45 million in 1931 to 7 million in 1932.[24] Imports from Czechoslovakia also fell, but only to just under half of the previous year.[25] So it went with other trade partners: total trade contracted (as did all other indicators of economic health), but exports shrank more than imports, exacerbating an already poor balance of payments.

In 1931 the crisis hit the Hungarian financial sector. The failure of the Austrian Credit-Anstalt bank in May sent tremors through Budapest, particularly since the Austrian institution was heavily engaged in Hungarian loans through the Magyar Hitelbank. Prime Minister Bethlen, fearing sagging public approval of the government party, dissolved parliament six months early. He was returned with a large majority and for a few weeks his action seemed to have had the desired calming effect. In mid-July, however, Danatbank failed, initiating a run on German banks.[26] "In the wake of one European crash after another, foreign lenders withdrew all credit lines that could be cancelled. Between 1st May and 13th July 1931 the Hungarian National Bank was obliged to pay out gold and foreign currency to a value of some 200 million pengős, which exhausted the country's reserves."[27] Bethlen instituted foreign exchange controls and secured a new international loan, but could not solve the problem of servicing existing foreign debts in the face of reduced foreign earnings.[28] Under pressure from parliament for having failed to anticipate the banking crisis, Bethlen resigned on August 19, 1931, after ten years in office. He was replaced by Count Gyula Károlyi (a cousin of Mihály Károlyi), whom Horthy had suggested to Bethlen as foreign minister in 1930. Károlyi retained nearly all of Bethlen's ministers, and most of his policies. As a condition of further loans, the Financial Committee of the League of Nations insisted on various austerity measures to reduce government expenditures, including heavy cuts in civil service salaries. Standards of living fell across the country; only the very poorest rural laborers were largely unaffected, since they had effectively "dropped *en bloc* out of the economic equation, relapsing into a pre-monetary economy based on self-devised and self-sufficient barter."[29]

The most direct and immediate result of the economic crisis for the Hungarian armed forces was a reduction in the pace of its secret rearmament. The 1929–1930 airplane order from Italy was cut in half, from 11.6 to 5.6 million pengős, and the entire Italian credit line for armament purchases in the 1930–1931 fiscal year declined to 4.7 million pengős.[30] Arms sales around the world took a nosedive during the crisis, dropping over 40 per cent from 1929 to 1933, although that decrease was less than the drop in total exports. The formidable Czechoslovakian arms industry was an exception. It saw a spike in arms exports in 1930, followed by a decline in 1931 to normal levels, a collapse in 1932, a recovery in 1933, and another sharp rise in 1934.[31] The healthy output of its adversary's weapons factories cannot have been comforting to Hungarian military planners.

Two other events occurred as a result of the crisis that would profoundly affect Hungary and the Honvédség. The first was the accession of Gyula Gömbös to the premiership; the second laid the foundation of eventual German economic dominance. Gömbös, who as a captain in 1921 led the anti-Habsburg forces at Budaörs, had in 1928 been appointed secretary of state for defense, charged by Bethlen to cooperate with the retired Lieutenant General Károly Soós in drafting the plan for the expansion of the army. In 1929 he became defense minister following Csáky's sudden resignation. When Gyula Károlyi proved unable to garner significant popular support, the regent in October 1932 asked Lieutenant General Gömbös (the rank had come with his elevation to defense minister) to form a government. In fact, Horthy, with Bethlen's help, formed most of the government, filling the posts with sound and cautious men expected to moderate Gömbös's right radicalism. Horthy's shackling of Gömbös was successful in at least one important area. The secret societies with which Gömbös had been aligned his entire political life, the Hungarian Association of National Defense (Magyar Országos Véderő Egyesülete) and the Etelköz Association (Etelközi Szövetség), as well as his late political party, the Hungarian National Independence (Racial Defense) Party (Magyar Nemzeti Függetlenségi (Fajvédő) Párt) were deeply antisemitic. Gömbös had in the early 1920s written "pamphlets on international Jewry, freemasonry and kindred subjects, which hardly differed in style or content from Hitler's own effusions."[32] Nonetheless, once in power he passed no antisemitic legislation, instead reaching a secret agreement with the leaders of the Jewish Neolog Community, one of Hungary's two Jewish bodies, that would secure their endorsement of his government. In his inaugural address, Gömbös appeared to reject his earlier antisemitism:

To the Jews I declare openly and frankly that I have changed my views. That part of Jewry that acknowledges that it shares a common fate with our People I wish to regard as brethren, just as I do my Magyar brethren. . . . I saw Jewish heroes during the war . . . and I know that they fought courageously. I know prominent Jews who pray for the Magyar fate, and I know that they will be the first to condemn that part of Jewry which could not or would not assimilate with the national community.[33]

Gömbös most certainly had not revised his views on the importance of Italy and Germany to effecting Hungary's revisionist claims, however. Just three days after becoming prime minister, he wrote to Mussolini affirming his admiration for the Fascist system and expressing his desire to continue the foreign policy of Bethlen; that is, one of cooperation with Italy in destabilizing the Little Entente and diminishing French influence in the region. He also requested continued Italian assistance in the matter of importing arms and exporting wheat. A month later, he went to Rome to invigorate the relationship. There was renewed interest in the Italo-Austro-Hungarian customs union, and small arms deliveries intensified. This last development caused all three countries significant embarrassment after a shipment of rifles and machine guns from Italy bound for Hungary was discovered in an Austrian weapons factory awaiting refurbishment. The Hirtenberg incident, so named for the plant in which the arms were found, raised objections from Britain and France, and caused the Little Entente to strengthen their alliance. The weapons eventually were sent back to Italy.[34]

Italo-German relations were at this time quite strained, Mussolini being very concerned to protect Austrian sovereignty lest he share a border with an enlarged German Reich. Austrian officials did not assuage this concern. Vienna's military attaché in Rome warned Mussolini, "If one time the Germans are able to breakfast in Innsbruck, that same day they'll want to lunch in Milan."[35] Gömbös, the originator of the phrase "Rome-Berlin Axis," felt it his mission to bring his patrons together. A letter to Mussolini (whose chest, Gömbös liked to tell confidantes, was the same size as his own) included his belief that "if Rome and Berlin, Budapest and Vienna would form a stronger alliance, they could play an important role in European politics."[36] Gömbös did not live to see the Axis realized (he succumbed to cancer in 1936), but he did more than perhaps any other Hungarian leader to push his country into alliance with Germany.

This push met with little resistance in its early years. The British minister in Budapest reported in 1930 that many Hungarian leaders favored closer economic ties to Germany. "The existing relationship is perfectly harmonious," wrote Viscount Chilton, except for the lack of a commercial treaty, the conclusion of which "is indeed of the highest importance to Hungary."[37] Two years later that desire for a treaty had become desperation for a market. Germany had in 1931 relented temporarily from its refusal to import the Hungarian wheat crop, taking nearly half of its annual surplus, but had not repeated the arrangement in the following two years. In February 1934, the two countries signed a trade agreement that offered near-term relief at the expense of Hungary's long-term economic freedom, although this was not obvious at the time. Through this arrangement, instead of paying their German creditors directly, Hungarian debtors were to purchase Hungarian agricultural products with pengős they owed to German firms. Those goods were then exported to Germany, where the proceeds of their sale could be used to import certain manufactured items back into Hungary. This mechanism substantially increased Hungary's export trade with Germany, which in 1933 totaled 43.7 million pengős and rose the next year to 88.9 million. Imports increased as well, although less dramatically, thereby giving Hungary what appeared to be a small balance of trade advantage (these were official figures that did not include the prohibited trade in arms; the favorable trade balance would disappear if armaments were considered).

It was not only quantitatively that Germany thus came to occupy a domi-
nant position in Hungary's economy. She succeeded in interlocking Hungary's economy with her own in such a fashion than many Hungarian
factories would simply have been unable to carry on production without
the regular supply from Germany of raw materials, or in other cases, of
certain machines, machine tools or spare parts. In other cases the Hungarian factories were only adapted to carry through parts of certain processes
which had to be either begun or finished in Germany. This applied particularly to the armaments industry (the development of which in both countries was one of the objects of the agreements).[38]

Just months before signing this agreement that benefited their
arms industries, both Hungary and Germany had been engaged in
the League of Nations disarmament conference in Geneva. The
defeated countries were already disarmed, and they accordingly
introduced or supported efforts to implement the broad disarmament called for in the imposed peace settlements. Their demobilization had been justified in explicitly universalist terms: "In order
to render possible the initiation of a general limitation of the armaments of all nations."[39] The German foreign minister brought this
to the attention of the League in a September 1931 address, reminding the delegates, "The counterpart of the obligations assumed by
Germany in 1919 is a formal undertaking on the part of the other
states that disarmament by Germany should be simply a prelude to
general disarmament by the other powers."[40] In Budapest in July
1931, the Conference of the International Federation of the League
of Nations Societies affirmed the "principle of equality of disarmament between 'vanquished' and 'victorious' Powers."[41] Of course
"equality of disarmament" was nothing more than a club to be used
by Berlin and Budapest to bludgeon the West for its hypocrisy.
German and Hungarian diplomats wanted to claim the moral high
ground while working for their genuine goal, the recognition of
their equal rights to rearmament. The victorious powers and successor states, however, rejected the accusations of hypocrisy, and
insisted that they must maintain their defensive arms until all revisionist claims had been categorically renounced.

Unable to find an agreeable level of armament, the conference moved from the "quantitative" question to the "qualitative," the prohibition of particular types of weapons, including tanks, submarines, and aircraft. The most extreme example of qualitative disarmament was the proposal put forward in early February 1932 by French war minister André Tardieu, who became the premier later that month. Tardieu's plan called for placing heavy bombers under the control of an international air force, with national governments retaining control only of small defensive aircraft. The revisionist powers objected loudly, claiming that France aimed to perpetuate its military superiority under the authority of the League, and Britain and the United States were cool to the idea of a supranational armed force.[42] American president Herbert Hoover offered his own plan that entailed deeper cuts in arms, but without the ties of collective security arrangements. The plan suited neither of its wartime allies: France insisted on security guarantees, and Hoover's proposed reductions in ships and airplanes were more than Britain's imperial staff could stomach. In the meantime, internal politics caused Germany's position on equality of arms to harden, with the result that Germany threatened not to return to the conference after a scheduled adjournment if its right to rearmament were not recognized. Berlin did not carry the motion, and the conference adjourned after only reaching agreements that banned the use of chemical and incendiary weapons and the bombardment of civilian populations.[43]

Ferenc Szentnémedy, Hungary's most fervent promoter of the unrestricted aerial offensive, framed the debate as one between France and the Little Entente, who tied together disarmament and security for negotiations but truly opposed national equality of arms; and those countries, like Germany, Italy, and Russia, who believed in practical disarmament and demanded real cuts in offensive forces. Arms inequality, Szentnémedy contended, invited trouble because unarmed countries put themselves at the mercy of their neighbors. The problem posed by aerial disarmament was especially acute, because air forces promised to be uniquely destructive. After six months of negotiations in 1932, the details of which he accurately recounted for *MKSz* readers, Szentnémedy observed that the Geneva conference had not produced any substantial positive outcomes. "For this very reason," he concluded, "it is legitimate to claim that the 'devaluation' of the conquered must cease. The disarmed surely must be given the possibility for self-defense, at the same time, however, those who aggressively and falsely are arming, must themselves disarm."[44] Szentnémedy's last sentence perfectly captured Hungary's public position on the question of aerial arms. In *MKSz* and other publications he expounded on Hungary's defenselessness from aerial attack, and the growing strength of the Little Entente's air arms. A chart in his 1933 book *Aviation*, derived from League of Nations numbers and German estimates, showed the combined frontline combat strength of Czechoslovakia, Yugoslavia, and Romania at over 900 airplanes. Hungary, "due to the peace treaty, has nothing" (*A békeszerződés folytán semmi*).[45]

This claim was disingenuous. Not only were the Little Entente's numbers purposely inflated by the reporting countries in order to minimize the effect of any League reductions after Geneva, Hungary had by 1932 managed to acquire a handful of capable combat machines, including the multipurpose two-seat Heinkel HD 22s and Fokker C.V-Ds, Fokker D.XVI and Fiat CR.20 fighters, and Caproni transport bombers. In October 1931, the strength of its secret air force stood at six squadrons: three short-range and one long-range reconnaissance squadrons, and two training squadrons.[46] And further expansion was planned. Even as the distinguished Count Apponyi listened to Tardieu's proposal in Geneva, in Budapest the Supreme Defense Council (Legfelső Honvédelmi Tanács, LHT) issued its blueprint for long-term development of the Honvédség. The LHT planned a 21-division motorized army and a 48-squadron air force. Of the 48 squadrons, 21 were planned as bomber units, 15 as reconnaissance, and 12 as fighter squadrons.

Although it is not possible to trace exactly the intellectual origins of the 1932 plan, it likely was influenced by Szentnémedy's 1931 injection of Douhet into the doctrinal debate. With nearly half of the squadrons dedicated to bombing, it was a decidedly offensive arm, and stood apart from its potential adversaries in the region, in whose forces fighters outnumbered bombers by as much as four to one. Among the first concrete steps to expansion was the 1933 increase of 40 per cent in air service enlisted personnel, from 900 to 1,300 airmen, and a more modest increase in officers and civil servants to 191.[47]

This coincided with a rise in the published annual government subsidy to MALERT from 200,000 to 300,000 pengős. Since MALERT functioned as a legitimate commercial endeavor in addition to its role as a false front for the Hungarian air service, we cannot with confidence completely disentangle the two organizations' sources of funding. The 300,000-pengő subvention acknowledged by Budapest was just a fraction of the total government expenditure laundered through the company's books. MALERT's growth since its establishment in 1922 followed the same pattern as that of the air service, and was dependent to nearly the same degree on diplomatic successes. The airline could also only acquire airplanes and open new lines when negotiations with foreign countries permitted. In the early 1930s its transport fleet consisted of nine Fokker craft (three F.IIIs, two F.VIIs, two F.VIIIs and two F. XIs), and six Capronis (four Ca.97s and two Ca.101s). MALERT's routes expanded in 1930–1931 as the company began domestic service, first to Pécs and Kaposvár, then to Nyíregyháza and Miskolc.[48] The Pécs flight garnered national attention, with photographs in the press of MALERT's president, Prince Ferenc, and the Pécs county high sheriff, Ferenc Keresztes-Fischer (who would soon enter the cabinet as interior minister), emerging from the Fokker.[49] International destinations doubled, with Venice and Klagenfurt added to the schedule.[50] This expansion was short lived, and indeed 1932 saw a precipitous decline in MALERT's operations. In the two

Figure 5.2. One of three fifteen-passenger Fokker F.VIIIs produced by WM for MALERT. Courtesy of the Péter Zámbori Collection.

preceding years, the numbers of flights, passengers, and miles flown had been nearly constant: more than a 1,000 flights each year, carrying around 3,500 passengers 107,000 nautical miles. In 1932 the numbers dropped by almost 40 per cent before climbing slightly the following year.[51] The domestic flights ceased in 1934, as did the service to Venice and Klagenfurt. It is unclear whether the changes were due to softening demand or increasing costs, but the Fokker aircraft were aging, and by 1936 all but the F.VIIIs had been withdrawn from airline service (the F.VIIs and F.XIs were taken over openly by the air force).[52] The HD 22s and C.V-Ds, thinly disguised bomber and reconnaissance machines, continued to carry mail between Budapest and Szombathely.

The failure of MALERT's domestic scheduled flights was not caused by a general apathy toward flying. Sport aviation had an avid following in Hungary during these years and figured prominently in public life. The prewar Hungarian Aero Club (Magyar Aero Szövetség, MASz) had come back to life immediately after the departure of the Allied Aeronautical Commission in 1922. Air shows at regional airfields organized by private groups had tremendous appeal. In September 1924 the War Widows and Orphans Association hosted an air show at Kecskemét. One of MALERT's newly acquired Fokker six-seaters opened the day by scattering advertising leaflets over the city, and in the afternoon treated spectators to a parachutists' display. A similar event in Kecskemét in 1929 "met with huge success." In 1932 the Central Hungarian Automobile and Motor Club organized a larger event there. Seven sport airplanes participated, along with two MALERT Fokkers, in which 133 visitors were able to take a ride (more than a hundred others were in the queue when flying ended for the day). Distinguished guests included István Horthy, the regent's son and an experienced pilot himself, and the director of the LÜH, Dr. György Rákosi. Rákosi arrived in a Fiat BR.3 named *Justice for Hungary*, a gift from Mussolini meant as a replacement for Hungary's most famous airplane that had been lost in a crash earlier in the year.[53]

The original *Justice for Hungary* was flown by György Endresz and Sándor Magyar across the Atlantic in July 1931. The record-setting ocean crossing was the most celebrated feat of Hungarian airmanship in the decades between the wars, and perhaps of all time. The stunt operated as part of Lord Rothermere's campaign to assist Hungary in its quest for rehabilitation and revision. Measured in terms of sympathetic press coverage, particularly in the United States, the flight was a huge success. Christening the aircraft *Justice for Hungary* was a stroke of publicity genius, because it all but ensured that every news item about the flight would print those words in a positive light, and public fascination with aerial exploits meant there was an eager audience. The late 1920s and early 1930s were the golden age of aviation—this was only the fifteenth nonstop transatlantic flight—and it is unlikely that a "Justice for Hungary" polar expedition or round-the-world sail would have garnered the same interest. For the aviators themselves, Lord Rothermere's $10,000 prize offered a tangible monetary benefit in addition to the promise of fame and the admiration of their countrymen.

Magyars living within Hungary contributed very little to the trip ($45, according to one account); it was funded almost entirely by the sizable Hungarian diaspora.[54] The idea originated in the offices of the *Detroit Magyar Hírlap*, and soon gained the support of the American Hungarian Federation. Endresz and Magyar traveled to America to raise funds for their flight. Nearly 8,000 Americans contributed, but the individual gifts were small.[55] After weeks of work, the two had collected just $5,000, and had spent almost $3,000 in the process. Then they met Emil Szalay, a Detroit meat processor who had "a ten-year ambition to do something that would draw the favorable attention of the world to his native Hungary."[56] Szalay's father had served in the Habsburg army after it had crushed the 1848 Hungarian Revolution. He felt a lasting shame, and told his sons, "You must do something good for the Hungarian people to wipe out my disgrace." Szalay mortgaged his salami factory and handed Endresz and Magyar $22,000 to buy an airplane.[57] The aircraft selected by their technical advisor Antal Bánhidi was a Lockheed Sirius 8A, a two-seat, low-wing monoplane powered by a 425-horsepower Pratt and Whitney engine, similar to the K-9 Mistral produced under license at WM. The Sirius was a sleek and modern machine with a smooth plywood skin, designed with input from Charles Lindbergh, who wanted a high-speed, low-drag airplane for his further global adventures.[58] *Justice for Hungary* carried its name and registration letters HA-AAF in stark white against the red fuselage as Endresz and Magyar set out from Roosevelt Field, New York, on July 13, 1931, on the way to Harbour Grace, Newfoundland, from where they would launch the transatlantic flight.

György Endresz was an extremely experienced pilot. He had flown reconnaissance missions over the Balkans before transitioning to single-seat fighters later in the First World War. At war's end, he took command of the Győr squadron of mixed one- and two-seat aircraft and maintained that position through the Károlyi government and the Kun regime.[59] He then flew as a commercial pilot for Aero Express and Junkers, and served as a flight instructor

Figure 5.3. György Endresz (right) with two well-wishers in front of the Lockheed Sirius 8A *Justice for Hungary*. Courtesy of Dénes Bernád.

for the MASz.[60] Sándor Magyar had been an observer in the war and joined the Szeged Whites before taking up a career as an airline pilot in Canada. Born Sándor Wilczek, his choice of adopted surname indicates he was either very enthusiastic about the program of Magyarization, or else possessed of a very dry wit.[61] Magyar was a skilled radio operator and navigator, and his use of radio stations as an aid to navigation was considered by some experts as "only short of Lindbergh's famous exploit for precision."[62] The pair's original plan had called for an arrival in Hungary by August 20, 1930 (a national holiday celebrating St. Stephen), but unusually bad weather across the Atlantic, forecast to extend through the winter, forced a delay.[63] They did move their staging ground nearer the ocean, departing from Flint, Michigan, Szalay's home town, on September 30, 1930, for New York.[64]

During the weather delay, Endresz and Magyar found themselves at odds with Lockheed. The aircraft had been constructed with 650-gallon fuel tanks, but the factory test pilots had not conducted trial flights with full fuel. The Sirius had come off the production line behind schedule, and with Endresz and Magyar waiting to take possession, the full fuel flights were not accomplished. Endresz and Magyar were reluctant to do the test flights themselves, because they knew that two similar airplanes had crashed on takeoff with the same fuel load.[65] Lockheed proved unwilling to share the desired performance data, so Endresz drew on the expertise at the Budapest Technical University. With the university's engineers calculations in hand, he and Magyar were eventually reassured that the airplane could take off safely and, provided fuel consumption were very carefully managed, could make the flight, which Magyar reckoned to take between twenty-six and twenty-eight hours. In the meantime, new radio navigation equipment was installed (paid for at a cost of $4,000 by Lord Rothermere) and stronger landing gear fitted.[66]

With the issues finally resolved and the return of suitable weather, *Justice for Hungary* left Roosevelt Field for a refueling stop in Newfoundland before the July 15, 1931, launch of the nonstop ocean crossing. *Time* magazine described the flight for its American readers:

> Forecast was poor visibility but favorable winds. Unafraid of blind flying, Endresz and Magyar took off. They scarcely saw the ocean during the 16-hour crossing. It was as predicted, a struggle with fog, rain and low clouds the whole way. But Navigator Magyar caught many radio bearings; the monoplane, another Lockheed, hit the coast of France only a trifle off course. They had estimated 26 hours flight to Budapest with two hours fuel to spare. But headwinds over Europe upset that. Just 25 miles short of the goal, at 12 minutes past the 26th hour, the Wasp motor gasped for gas. Endresz landed the plane in a rough field, damaging the undercarriage and propeller.[67]

Flight, the magazine of Britain's Royal Aero Club, recounted the fliers' reception after they arrived in Budapest by way of a twin-engined Fokker sent to their forced landing site near Bicske: "They were accorded a stirring welcome by representatives of the Government and a crowd of about 100,000, and later they were driven through streets of cheering people to the Prime Minister's palace, where they were officially received by Count Bethlen on behalf of the nation. On July 20, Admiral Horthy, Regent of Hungary, received the airmen and decorated them with the Merit Order of the Third Class, and promoted them both to the rank of captain."[68] Emil Szalay was on hand, as were Endresz's wife and son, along with Magyar's mother. Rothermere had wired the $10,000 to Bethlen for presentation to the aviators.[69] The celebrations lasted for a week, and included an intimate brunch (dinner jacket, please) for 500 at Gundel in the St. Gellért hotel.[70] *Pesti Hírlap* published a special nine-page supplement chronicling the flight.[71] The festivities provided a welcome distraction from the worsening economic crisis.

In the months after the successful crossing, Magyar and his new wife moved back to North America, where they were met at the pier by a mayoral welcoming committee, their arrival in New York on a Cunard liner covered by the *New York Times*. Word of a row preceded them, but "Captain Magyar denied that he and Endresz had quarreled and were scheduled to settle their differences with rapiers."[72] Although it did not lead to a duel, Endresz and Magyar had indeed fallen out, and therefore Captain Gyula Bittay replaced Magyar in the *Justice for Hungary* (the damage from the forced landing was repaired at WM) for the May 1932 flight to Rome to attend the first Transoceanic Airmen's Congress.[73] On arrival at the Littorio airfield the Lockheed "appeared to have been caught in an air pocket when only 200 or 300 feet up. It side-slipped and crashed, bursting into flames."[74] Both Endresz and Bittay were killed, and the *Justice for Hungary* completely destroyed. The ensuing investigation could not determine the cause of the crash, but from the descriptions it seems the probable cause was an accelerated stall, the result of attempting to turn too tightly with too little airspeed. A decade later the same error would cost the life of István Horthy, the vice regent and, like Endresz, the nation's most famous airman at the time of his death. A hundred thousand Hungarians viewed the procession from the Southern Railway Station to the funeral at the Millennium Monument, where Admiral Horthy led the official party.[75] Rome grieved with Budapest. Tens of thousands of Italians turned out to see the fliers' flag-draped caskets, and a crowd of similar size gathered at St. Peter's for prayer. Air Minister Balbo, himself a transoceanic airman, was present at Littorio and personally arranged the transportation of the remains, while Foreign Minister Grandi conveyed his condolences to the Hungarian legation.[76] Mussolini expressed sympathy on behalf of the entire Congress in his speech, as did Sir Arthur Brown, the senior airman present and part of the first crew to fly the Atlantic.[77]

The intense Italian reaction to the *Justice for Hungary* is revealing. One Hungarian observer ascribed it to comradely affection. *Huszadik Század* described the Romans "mourning sincerely and truly from the heart," and suggested "anyone who doubted that the Italians felt true sympathy to us Hungarians can now be persuaded just how deep is the love in the Italians for the Hungarians."[78] Another factor may have been the prominent role of aviation in Fascist Italian culture. "The airplane and flight were among the Fascists' most potent symbols."[79] The contributions of Douhet, Caproni, Balbo, and D'Annunzio have been discussed above. Less well known was Mussolini's own close connection to aviation. He had learned to fly in 1919, emerging from the aircraft after one flight in "enthusiastic delirium." His role as "Italy's exemplary aviator was also widely publicized."[80] Like Hitler after him, he traveled widely by airplane while campaigning and ruling, and even had books written about his aerial exploits (e.g., *Mussolini aviatore* and *L'Aviazione negli scritti, nella parola e nell'esempio del Duce*). Not long after coming to power, Mussolini addressed the Italian Aero Club: "Not every Italian can or should fly. But all Italians should envy those who do and should follow with profound feelings the development of Italian wings."[81] And indeed Italian aviation feats were a critical component of Fascist modernism. Italian racers set international speed records in the 1920s and won the Schneider Cup in 1926. Italo Balbo led massive formations on long-range flights intended to build up the regime's prestige as well as prepare RA crews for strategic bombing attacks. The year before the Endresz-Magyar crossing, Balbo led twelve Savoia-Marchetti S.55 flying boats across the South Atlantic to Rio de Janeiro.[82] Italian public life was saturated with the idea of the pilot as an exemplar of Fascism, a noble and pure visionary leading the nation to glory. When viewed in this light, the *Justice for Hungary* crash was an assault on the notion of progress and technology.

In Hungary, even with Gömbös ascending, Fascist modernism did not gain traction in the cultural sphere. The legacy of agrarian aristocrats remained strong, and reaction against the HSR moderated the influence of the avant-garde. Furthermore, *Justice for Hungary* was from the beginning an attempt to garner attention and sympathy for what was already a national tragedy. Endresz and Bittay were mourned as national heroes, but their sacrifice just added to the ledger of catastrophe. The crash did give an extra emotional weight to the Italo-Hungarian relationship. In addition, the flight increased confidence in Hungarian airmanship and encouraged general aviation within the country.

Airmanship and revisionism were also bound together in the country's youth flying organizations. Both the Levente (a post-Trianon institution that offered paramilitary training under the guise of fitness and sport) and the Hungarian Boy Scouts were deeply nationalistic and revisionist, and each had flying wings in their association. Levente's gliding camps were less prominent, but were secretly and directly subsidized by the government.[83] The flying Scout troops had been able to purchase airplanes abroad for training while Hungary was still under Trianon's import restriction.[84] Its "flying subcamp" was a prominent component of Hungarian Scouting's moment in the sun, the 1933 International Jamboree, and its organizational chart used military-type designations and hierarchies, with the regent in overall command.[85] There were flight demonstrations, static displays of airplanes, and aircraft construction seminars. The Jamboree itself was a massive propaganda exercise in soft revisionism. The Scouts were instructed to present Hungary's case for the overthrow of Trianon in compelling but nonthreatening ways, and symbols and rituals served to shore up the Hungarian claim to the Danube basin.[86] Ties between Scouting and revision were not the result of conspiracy or government control, but were rather the natural expression of an organization that explicitly promotes patriotism in all its national movements. That natural tendency was enhanced by the club's adult leaders, men of traditional and conservative outlooks, perhaps typified by Hungary's chief Scout, Count Pál Teleki. Teleki, according to C. A. Macartney, was "at his happiest and best" when surrounded by Scouts, and his role as chief Scout was "the occupation which perhaps lay nearest to his heart of all."[87] Among the Scouts' flying instructors were many LFT veterans, and their "General Staff" included the well-known military and sport fliers *vitéz* Frigyes Hefty, István Hosszú, and Lajos Rotter.[88] The Hungarian Scouts began to take an active role in civil defense exercises from 1934 in cooperation with the National Air Defense Command (Országos Légvédelmi Parancsnokság, OLP), providing first aid and operating alarm systems.[89] Their flight activity was generally confined to constructing and operating gliders, a sport somewhat ignored in the West, but developed to an extremely high level of sophistication in the defeated countries, particularly in Germany.

The exploits of German gliding pilots were already known to István Petróczy in 1921, and he had planned to fly in the Wasserkuppe rally during his study tour. In 1920 a sleek glider designed in part by the self-exiled Hungarian genius Theodor van Kármán flew for more than two minutes—an unofficial world record. If Petróczy had been present in 1921, he would have seen a glider fly for twenty-one minutes, another record. The next year the record was three hours. Wasserkuppe's gliders became a symbol of resistance to the Little Entente, and gliding "a national duty," according to a liberal

Figure 5.4. A Műegyetem Sport Flying Club glider ready for launch in the hills north of Budapest. Photo: Fortepan/Pál Vojnich.

German newspaper. In 1926 the lift properties of thermal updrafts were discovered (by accident; a pilot caught in a thunderstorm climbed to nearly 6,000 feet and glided over 30 nautical miles) and modern soaring was founded.[90] Western experts grasped the significance of the sport, as shown by one report from the *Royal Air Force Quarterly*: "Once again Germany has demonstrated the value of her intense cultivation of motorless flying, her answer to the limitations of the Versailles Treaty . . . The traditions of Richthofen, Boelke, Immelmann, and the rest were handed to the soaring pilots at the Wasserkuppe. . . . Germany is building up a nation of airmen at very low cost—airmen whose knowledge of the air is of a far more intimate nature than anything perhaps dreamed of in aviation history."[91] Hungarian gliding did not develop into a world-leading activity, nor did it attain the status of a center of resistance as in Germany, but it did serve to introduce many young people (mostly, but not entirely, men: István Horthy's wife Ilona, among other women, earned her gliding certificate) to the principles of flight. The clubs were a good vehicle for nurturing air-mindedness, or in Petróczy's words, "the awakening of the interest in aviation in every beautiful and impressionable spirit."[92]

One unheralded member of the *Justice for Hungary* team was also deeply involved in the youth flying movements. Antal Bánhidi was an advisor to flying Scout troops as well as an instructor and aircraft designer at the Budapest Technical University Sport Flying Club. Before joining Endresz and Magyar as technical advisor, Bánhidi was already an accomplished aviator. In 1929 he made a 2,700-nautical-mile journey to Sweden in a light aircraft, and in 1930 he first flew the Gerle, a two-seat biplane trainer of his own design underwritten by a 20,000-pengő grant from the MASz. The Gerle was a capable trainer and tourer, and sixteen were built in the next decade at the Technical University club. In 1933 Bánhidi and Tibor Bisits (the head of the 1933 Jamboree flying camp) were the first aviators to circumnavigate the Mediterranean, completing the 6,000-nautical-mile flight in Gerle No. 13.[93] Later that year, Bánhidi took Gerle 13 from Hungary to Scandinavia and thence to London, where he delivered a medal to Lord Rothermere in appreciation of his support of *Justice for Hungary*. Bánhidi's return to Debrecen in a single 900-nautical-mile, 11-hour hop impressed *Flight* as "a very excellent non-stop flight, not an official record, of course, but certainly something which no one else has done."[94] Gerle 13 was powered by a 100-horsepower Armstrong Siddeley engine, and the Coventry company took out an advertisement in *Flight* that featured Bánhidi's European trip.[95] In 1937 Bánhidi flew with the Archduke Albrecht around South America in Gerles Nos. 15 and 16. Bánhidi also appeared on the margin of Hungary's biggest aeronautical mystery: on June 26, 1941, he tried to intercept the unidentified aircraft that had just bombed Kassa. His CR.42 could not catch the attackers, and he was not able to determine their type or origin.[96]

One year after Bánhidi's visit to the United Kingdom, a group of British pilots made their way to Hungary. Arriving on September 15, 1934, in fourteen privately owned airplanes, the crews spent

Figure 5.5. Antal Bánhidi at Malmo. He flew Gerle 13 from Hungary to Scandinavia and then to Britain. Photo: Fortepan/Tibor Erky-Nagy.

a week on the "Magyar Pilota Pic Nic" organized by the Magyar Touring Club. The event attracted the attention of the highest levels of the Hungarian aviation establishment, with the Archduke Albrecht and LÜH director Dr. Rákosi greeting the arrivals at Mátyásföld. The program was innocuous and included stops at Hungary's best-known tourist locations (baths and czardas at almost every stop), but the group was well-escorted at all times, an indication of the importance accorded the development of aerotourism and Anglo-Hungarian relations. Although traveling as a private citizen, among the British aviators was a senior RAF officer, Group Captain R. Leckie, who presumably took a special professional interest in the current state of Hungarian aviation.[97] The journey was repeated in the next two years in a similar way, with the party landing on the plain at Hortobágy, and at Debrecen, Szeged, and Siófok airfields. Royal participation was provided in 1935 by Duke Francis Hohenlohe and in 1936 again by Albrecht, now flying his own airplane. István Horthy also assumed a large role in the visits, leading the earliest-arriving Britons to landing at Mátyásföld in a

WM trainer. The British contingents each year included RAF officers.[98]

The LÜH recognized the economic, technological, and publicity value of foreign aviators flying private airplanes across Hungary, and it established a special office to encourage aviation tourism. The director of the Foreign Tourism Office was Count Nándor Zichy, a former military pilot and avid sport flier, who worked closely with Dr. Ákos Szentkirályi, a retired colonel of cavalry and lawyer who led the propaganda office of the MASz. Together they sponsored a series of international fly-ins, capitalizing on the natural beauty of Lake Balaton to attract pilots. In 1936, the second annual Balaton Star Tour (so named because of the pattern formed by the sequential out-and-back flights around the country) drew sixty-four airplanes with crews from Austria, Belgium, Czechoslovakia, France, Germany (the best represented), Great Britain, Italy, Poland, and Switzerland. Szentkirályi was indefatigable in his efforts to promote general aviation in Hungary. He had a robust propaganda plan for each year, gave numerous interviews, and spoke at MASz and other club meetings around the country. Outreach to other Hungarian associations was noteworthy: the Magyar Athletikai Club founded a flight section and joined the MASz and LÜH in hosting the Balaton Star Tours, and in 1931 MASz and the Reviziós Liga (Revisionist League) issued joint press releases congratulating the crew of *Justice for Hungary*. Although it was not an overtly revisionist organization, MASz's official letterhead carried the revisionist creed:

Hiszek egy Istenben,	I believe in one God,
Hiszek egy hazában!	I believe in one country!
Hiszek egy isteni örök igazságban,	I believe in God's eternal justice,
Hiszek Magyarország	I believe in Hungary's
feltámadásában!	resurrection![99]

As the 1930s wore on, the veil surrounding secret Hungarian aerial rearmament began to slip. In the early part of the decade, the indiscretions were small. LÜH officers began to wear uniforms and decorations in 1930.[100] Dr. Rákosi wore this uniform and was identified as a general in the photographs that accompanied the "Pic Nic" article in *Flight* magazine. If the incongruity of a uniformed general directing the "Aviation Bureau" of a country denied an air force caused British readers any consternation, it went unrecorded. Likewise, the major English-language papers that covered the *Justice for Hungary* flight referred repeatedly and blithely to the military ranks of Endresz and Magyar. In these minor matters, as in all things related to illegal rearmament, Hungary tended to follow a step or two behind Germany, so that Budapest's transgressions seemed familiar and therefore inconsequential when laid against Berlin's. German attempts to circumvent the proscription of its air force were not accepted, but they were expected, as evidenced by the British air attaché's report that began, "Naturally however the virile, martial-minded, German people have not yielded willingly to such a drastic reduction in their scale of armaments."[101] The British Foreign Office was aware of the secret Luftwaffe base at Lipetsk in the Soviet Union.[102] A memorandum prepared for British negotiators at Geneva concluded, "Although Germany is forbidden to possess any military or naval air forces, there is abundant evidence to show that in fact she possesses at least the nucleus of an efficient military air force camouflaged within the organization of her powerful civil aviation."[103]

That, of course, was precisely the Hungarian aspiration. The difficulty lay in the adjectives. Hungary's camouflaged military air force was not particularly efficient, nor could her civil aviation be described as powerful. Hungary did have a core of notable aviators, its public remained enthusiastic about and engaged in aviation, and its government was able to harness this air-mindedness to further its nationalist and revisionist aims. However, the Hungarian aviation industry could not build itself into a regional air power, and its ability to acquire an air force abroad was restricted by international treaties, by its own financial limitations, and by the scarcity of suitable suppliers.

Certain changes in the European political landscape did seem to favor Hungarian rearmament. The rise of Hitler to the German chancellorship broadened an avenue of support, and Germany's withdrawal from the League of Nations and its subsequent declaration of equality of armaments served to weaken the case for the continued disarmament of the other former Central Powers. Gömbös, the originator of the idea of the Rome-Berlin Axis, was determined to capitalize on these changes. In Gömbös's mind the axis should run through Hungary, whose position in the Danube basin would provide a buffer between the two great powers' spheres of influence.[104] As soon as he was able, Gömbös went to Berlin to pitch his idea to the Führer. His visit in June 1933 was preceded by Count Bethlen's trip in March. Bethlen traveled as a private citizen (as did Gömbös in June), but his task was to prepare the ground for the sitting prime minister. The Hitler-Gömbös meeting was short and informal. Gömbös made a good impression in spite of his impolitic defense of an independent Austria and Hitler's anti-Hungarian prejudice. Hitler promised to buy more Hungarian agricultural products and sell the country more military hardware, and suggested that Hungary could have what it wanted from Czechoslovakia, but he warned Gömbös to leave Romania and Yugoslavia alone. The Führer did not embrace the Axis, and he gave only a limited endorsement of Hungarian revisionism. The encounter did yield important economic agreements and opened the door for more German weapons, the first of which were light howitzers and sport airplanes.[105] Gömbös did not abandon his quest for German-Italian rapprochement, because he saw it as absolutely essential to Hungary's future. If Hungary were successful in playing matchmaker between the two, it would buttress both countries' aid for its territorial claims. If, on the other hand, Berlin and Rome became antagonists, one of them would invariably look for the backing of the Little Entente, which would be fatal to Budapest's ambitions. At the same time, Hungary feared German dominance and was dedicated to keeping Italy and Austria as counterweights.

A slew of diplomatic crises and continuing budgetary shortfalls in 1934 frustrated the hopes of Gömbös and the Defense Ministry regarding increasing the pace of rearmament. Germany felt aggrieved by the Rome Protocol signed in March enhancing political and economic cooperation among Italy, Hungary, and Austria, and neither Gömbös nor Horthy could convince Hitler that the agreement was not directed against the Nazi state. The summer brought an attempted Nazi putsch in Austria, which resulted in the death of the Austrian chancellor Engelbert Dollfuss, and raised fears in Budapest (unfounded, as it turned out) of an Italo-German conflict. The French-Little Entente stance was strengthened by the emergence of the Soviet Union from diplomatic isolation and its admission to the League of Nations. The prospects of a Franco-Soviet alliance as well as the attempted coup in Austria caused Rome to cast its eyes toward Paris, a development naturally resented in Budapest.

The year's second notable political assassination further undermined Hungary's position. King Alexander of Yugoslavia and French foreign minister Louis Barthou were killed by a Macedonian terrorist in Marseilles in October. The assassin had been trained by Croatian Ustaša separatists, who had themselves trained on an estate in southwestern Hungary with the government's knowledge.[106] The Ustaši had been expelled before the Marseilles attack, and there was no evidence that the Hungarian government was involved in the deaths of Alexander and Barthou, but it nonetheless earned Hungary opprobrium in the West and "left her in the position of general scapegoat for sins the worst of which were Mussolini's."[107] Although the League ultimately rejected Yugoslavia's demand for international sanctions against Hungary, the furor had increased international scrutiny and eroded foreign support, both of which made arms purchases from abroad nearly impossible. The feeling of being again alone in the world solidified Gömbös's domestic standing.

The LÜH discarded as unachievable its 1932 plan for forty-eight flying squadrons. According to a 1934 staff study, the maintenance of a force of just eighteen squadrons would cost 16 million pengős, which was more than the budget could bear. Spending constraints, combined with the sour turn in Hungary's diplomatic fortunes and the realization that the CR.20s purchased just three years ago were already outdated, dictated a pause in aircraft acquisition. The Defense Ministry chose to spend its Italian arms credits instead on light tanks from Ansaldo.[108] Perhaps partially in response to this decision, the LÜH submitted a memo in March 1935 to the chief of staff arguing for a larger allocation of the Honvédség budget, noting that it received only 6.5 per cent of defense spending, while the Czechoslovak air service got 10 per cent and the Romanian an astounding 31 per cent. This document also included an assessment of the aerial arm's mission. "The air force command," it read, "directs itself to this ultimate goal: to be able to act as a serious opponent against at least one of the Little Entente states surrounding us" (*minket környező kisentente-államoknak legalább egyikével szemben komoly ellenségként léphessünk fel*).[109] The declaration cast the air force as a distinctly offensive weapon and also defined the range and scope of the expected adversary (one or possibly two Little Entente members, but not all of them at once). The memo urged continued modernization and expansion of the bomber fleet (which at the time consisted of two-seat biplanes and the handful of Capronis), which would function "independently before the initiation of general military operations, then in strict cooperation with the ground forces to contribute to a decisive engagement."[110] This signaled a qualified acceptance of Szentnémedy's Douhetism. The LÜH agreed that bombers should predominate and that they should be used autonomously at the beginning of the war, but it did not suggest that the bomber offensive alone would bring about a decision.

Out of this message came a new plan for the existing six squadrons to grow to fifteen. The three sport clubs would provide the cadres for four night-bombing squadrons, while three light bomber squadrons would be formed from the flight schools and the Sóstó research unit. Kaposvár's existing short-range reconnaissance unit would make two additional light bomber squadrons, with its mission being taken up by new observation squadrons based at Pécs and Miskolc. Pilots from the current fighter squadron ("Meteorological Section") would split into three units. This concept was approved by the Defense Ministry and became part of its "Arpad" rearmament scheme.

In March 1935, the LÜH ordered from Italy twenty-six aircraft, including nine three-engined Ca.101/3m transport bombers (powered by WM-produced K-7 engines) and a pair of Caproni fighters for trials. Three more Ca.101/3ms were ordered in exchange for the Italian production rights to the Hungarian Gebauer motor-driven airplane cannon.[111] In addition, Captain Mihály Nagy was sent to Italy to visit factories and examine aircraft for possible purchase. After numerous test flights and inspections, Nagy recommended taking the CR.32 fighter under contract, with an additional three types—the A.P.1, Br.64, and Ro.37 day bombers—for further trials.[112] The CR.32 order expanded to twenty-six airplanes in 1935 and, with the awarding of a 93-million-lira credit in 1936, grew to fifty-two.[113] Eventually six Hungarian fighter squadrons would be equipped with the CR.32, which served well until the early 1940s, and in which a Hungarian pilot would claim the country's first aerial victory since 1919. The Ca.101/3m was less successful. It was intended to fill the night bomber combat role, but its performance, even with three engines, was less than impressive, although it did look the part of a civilian airliner in MALERT colors.

Delivery of the Fiat and Caproni airplanes slowed in late 1935 when Italy invaded Abyssinia. The importance of the Italian arms trade to Rome's diplomatic efforts was secondary to its role as a supplier of aircraft to the RA, and some of the machines promised to Hungary made their way to Eritrea and Somalia instead. Italian forces there mustered 168 aircraft for the October 3, 1935 assault, and there was no Abyssinian air force to combat them. In the course of the war the RA flew 4,500 combat sorties, dropped nearly 4.5 million pounds of bombs (mostly 5-pound antipersonnel types), and delivered 2 million pounds of supplies, losing only 8 aircraft and 48 airmen in the process.[114] Given the high accident and casualty rates of peacetime and training flights at the time, the RA's low loss rate in Abyssinia was remarkable.

The contribution of Italian air operations to eventual victory and the future implications for air warfare were somewhat less clear. Army leaders and some military commentators highlighted the close cooperation between fast-moving land forces and reconnaissance and attack aircraft in overcoming Abyssinian resistance, while RA leaders (Mecozzi was a notable exception) found validation for Douhet's theories in the RA's ability to attack when ground offensives stalled.[115] Ferenc Szentnémedy agreed with the latter assessment. In his September 1936 analysis of the Abyssinian War, he quoted Douhet's own one-line summary of his theory: "Defend on the land and sea, attack in the air." Szentnémedy continued, "Domination in the air is required—everything else is secondary. Is that the whole of it? Roughly, yes."[116] The Abyssinian army was destroyed and its capital occupied in only seven months, thanks in large part, he contended, to the air force. The victory could not, however, be considered a full vindication of the idea of independent air warfare, because Abyssinia lacked the necessary urban population and industrial centers whose destruction would lead to capitulation. It was for that reason that the Italian army had to engage Abyssinian forces. Because of this, the action was worthy of further reflection: "The Italian war offered a wealth of extraordinarily valuable experience in relation to developing aerial leaders. Douhetism depreciated in value not at all in the course of the Abyssinian war, and the experience of the war must be taken into account in European military doctrine."[117] There were also practical lessons to be learned. In an earlier article Szentnémedy had focused on tactical operations, including sketches of various RA airplanes. His mention of the use of the "eminently tested" three-engined Ca.101 in both bombing and reconnaissance missions would have been particularly interesting to readers aware that this airplane was the backbone of the clandestine Hungarian air service's bomber fleet.[118] He later drew attention to the RA's use of parachute-delivered supplies, detailing the simplicity and reliability of the 5-foot "iron torpedoes" that could deliver up to 450 pounds of goods. According to Szentnémedy, the Italian parachute supply expertise extended to live cows and goats delivered under their own silk canopy. Aerial resupply would make planners revisit the commonly held assumption (affirmed by General Ludendorff) that offensives could advance only 75 miles without a logistical pause.[119]

The importance of aerial resupply also figured in the first *MKSz* article about the Spanish Civil War. Elemér Tóth, who had previously written for the journal about transport and parachute operations, noted that airlifted supplies had allowed Nationalist troops to withstand the Siege of the Alcazar. The majority of Tóth's report, which was based on an account in the French journal *Revue de l'Armée de l'Air*, was concerned with assessments of fighter and bomber employment. As in Abyssinia, the performance of Italian, and increasingly German, airplanes was closely scrutinized. The Fiat CR.32 was judged to be quite vulnerable due to its water-cooled engine and the placement of the fuel tanks in the fuselage, which increased the chance of fire and thereby decreased the possibility of a successful forced landing or escape by parachute. The Junkers Ju 52, which MALERT would soon add to its fleet, was a purpose-designed passenger airplane converted into a bomber for use by the German Condor Legion. Its airliner origins complicated the efforts to retrofit defensive armament, which left it susceptible to enemy fighters. The bombers therefore were given close fighter escort, on occasion at a nearly 1:1 ratio (e.g., a December 1936 raid on Madrid

comprised twenty-five Ju 52s and twenty-three accompanying
Heinkel fighters). One French pilot described a particularly effective Nationalist tactic: ten to twenty fighters would attack a certain
position with machine guns and small bombs while the Nationalist
ground forces prepared to attack. When, after the air strikes, it
seemed that the opposing force's spirit was broken, the infantry
attacked, with continuing support from the air.[120] This tactic would
be used to great effect in Poland, France, and the Soviet Union in
the coming years.

A subsequent piece focused on the size of the forces involved,
especially the tendency toward large air battles consisting of sixty
to eighty airplanes on each side. That meant nearly a third of operational Nationalist aircraft were committed to battle at one time.
MKSz estimated Republican ("Red") air strength by the end of
1937 to be approaching 1,000 aircraft, with the Republican fleet being weighted more heavily toward fighters (approximately a 3:1
fighter-to-bomber ratio) than the Nationalists. Another ratio mentioned was the proportion of Nationalist flying squadrons to infantry divisions, which at roughly 1:1 signaled an insufficient aerial
component (the 1932 plan envisioned forty-eight squadrons for the
Honvéd's twenty-one divisions). To counter the Republicans and
achieve success in the air, the number of Nationalist squadrons
should be tripled to around one hundred, of which almost half should
be bomber squadrons, one-third fighter squadrons, and the remainder reconnaissance. Author András Sólyom listed twelve conclusions that could be drawn from the Spanish war experience
through the middle of 1937. The first was that although both sides
fielded modern machines, much obsolescent equipment was also
in use. This was an important insight that corresponded with Hungarian experience in the First World War, where old models continued to fly productively in the East well after the types had been
withdrawn from service on the Western Front. He also rightly observed that all modern fighters should have retractable landing gear

for greater speeds, that metal skins and air-cooled engines were more rugged than fabric covers and motors requiring radiators. Sólyom's judgment was shakier on a pair of critical points: the expectation that normal fighter armament would not exceed the 8-millimeter caliber, and that superchargers were of limited utility because fighters would rarely fight above 15,000 feet.[121] Both of these conclusions were badly misguided. Because Hungarian aircraft choices were so severely constrained by what its allies made available, however, it cannot be said that the lack of foresight had significant negative effects on acquisition policy. In general, it can be said that Hungarian airmen were well informed regarding contemporary aerial operations, and that they studied the Abyssinian and Spanish wars with a mind toward future air warfare. Journal articles, however faithfully reported and read, were no substitute for actual experience, and the inability to apply practically the lessons derived vicariously was a severe handicap.

Hungarian interest in the German experience in Spain was particularly keen because the door had been opened to increased defense cooperation with Berlin. Prime Minister Gömbös had long wanted to push Italy and Germany to closer relations for Hungary's benefit; events in 1935–1936 brought his dream to fruition. First Hitler unilaterally rejected the military clauses of Versailles, at one blow unleashing Germany's considerable armament production and weakening Trianon's legitimacy. Mussolini then made overtures to Hitler in order to minimize Italian vulnerabilities after the beginning of the Abyssinian campaign. Finally, Italo-German cooperation in Spain clinched the deal. The Rome-Berlin Axis was established in secret protocol of October 25, 1936, pledging the two Fascist countries "to deal with the political and economic problems of the Danubian basin in the spirit of amicable collaboration."[122]

Even before the formalization of the Axis, Gömbös's foreign policy had certainly loosened wallets in Rome and Berlin: the

93-million-lira credit from Italy was followed by a 28-million-mark line from Germany. Using that credit, the LÜH placed an extraordinary order in July 1936 for 190 German aircraft. The order comprised sixty-six Ju 86 bombers and three Ju 52 transports, thirty-six He 46 fighters and eighteen He 70 long-range reconnaissance airplanes, thirty-seven Bücker Bü 131 trainers, eighteen Focke-Wulf FW 56 and six FW 58B advanced trainers, and six Bayerische Flugzeugwerke Bf 108s.[123] The Ju 86s, He 46s, and He 70s were to be powered by WM-produced K-14 engines (the Ju 86s were ordered in spite of an earlier VKF report that found them too heavy for light bombers, and too weakly armed).[124] This order, with the fifty-two CR.32s being delivered from Italy, composed a nearly complete small air force, and would have, if immediately filled, ended the fiction of Hungarian aerial disarmament—the Ju 86 order plainly listed bomb racks and bombsights.[125] It also was more airplanes than Hungary could handle at that time. A complete accounting in 1935 of all qualified pilots in the LÜH, without regard to recency of experience, listed 223 names, including thirteen officers of the VKF, with an additional thirty-eight in various stages of training.[126] Delivery of the primary trainers was to begin immediately, with the entire order to be completed by the end of September 1937. In fact, by the end of 1937, although six fighter squadrons had been formed and equipped with CR.32s, no significant numbers of German combat aircraft had arrived.

But they would. The 1936 order marked the Honvéd's turn to Germany, a move long desired by Gömbös and much of the VKF. German weapons were more sophisticated, and German martial instincts more sure. Hungary would still seek and appreciate Italian military support in a range of areas, but that the resurgent Germany would very soon eclipse Italy as Hungary's primary patron was clear. This of course was welcomed by the officers and men who coveted the newest German aircraft and tanks, but some Hungarian political leaders, including the regent, were wary of growing German power and sought ways to balance it in order to ensure

Hungary's independence. In the next three years Hungary would continue to exploit German aid for its own rearmament and revisionist plans while trying to subtly undermine German designs for domination of Central and Eastern Europe.

For a decade after the end of the IMCC mandate, the Trianon military clauses remained in effect. Hungarian airmen continued the campaign of deception they had initiated in 1920, using civilian aviation to conceal a growing but still clandestine air force. They were exposed to different theories of air power, and developed their own expansive view, informed by but not conforming to Douhetism. But their efforts to build an air force in accordance with their ideas were continually frustrated by treaty, economic crisis, the limit of domestic industry, and lack of foreign suppliers. By 1936, the economic crisis had eased, a few Hungarian aviation factories had proven their ability to build quality (if unoriginal) products, and shrewd diplomacy had secured Italian and German backing. In 1938 the hated Treaty of Trianon would finally begin to crumble, and Hungarian military airmen would be free to operate openly for the first time since 1920.

NOTES

1. See above, ch. 4.
2. Réti, *Hungarian-Italian Relations*, p. 3.
3. Gy. Juhász, *Hungarian Foreign Policy*, pp. 86–87.
4. Csima, "Olaszország szerepe a Horthy-hadsereg fegyverkezésében," p. 294.
5. Sisa, "MKHL olaszországi repülőgép-beszerzései," p. 1051.
6. The pengő replaced the korona in November 1925, at a rate of one pengő to 12,500 koronas. That made the pengő's value approximately equal to the prewar korona. Nötel, "International Credit and Finance," p. 196. The pengő-lira exchange rate in the 1930s was roughly 1:3.2.
7. B. Juhász, "Olasz-Magyar vezénylések," pp. 140–144.
8. *DBFP*, Ser. 1a, Vol. 5, No. 32.
9. B. Juhász, "Olasz-Magyar vezénylések," pp. 146–147, 160–161. Juhász makes extensive use of Italian military and diplomatic archives.
10. Winkler, "A magyar repülés története" (HL Tgy 3.327).
11. B. Juhász, "Olasz-Magyar vezénylések," pp. 153–156.

12. Sisa, "MKHL olaszországi repülőgép-beszerzései," p. 1051.

13. Nagyváradi et al., *Fejezetek a repülés történetéből*, p. 172.

14. Ibid., pp. 170–171.

15. Ibid.

16. Homze, *Arming the Luftwaffe*, p. 82.

17. Gunston, *World Encyclopedia of Aero Engines*, p. 71.

18. Winkler, "A Magyar Királyi Honvéd Légierő harci repülőgépeinek fejlődéséről" (HL Tgy 3.643), p. 5.

19. Nagyváradi et al., *Fejezetek a repülés történetéből*, p. 166.

20. *MKHL, 1938–1945*, p. 11.

21. Berend, "Agriculture," p. 177.

22. Romsics, *Hungary in 20th Century*, p. 139.

23. Macartney, *October Fifteenth*, 1:90.

24. Drabek, "Foreign Trade Performance and Policy," table 7.XI, p. 498.

25. Macartney, *October Fifteenth*, 1:90.

26. Ibid., p. 92.

27. Romsics, *Hungary in 20th Century*, p. 139.

28. Radice, "General Characteristics of the Region," p. 52.

29. Macartney, *October Fifteenth*, 1:93–98.

30. Csima, "Olaszország szerepe a fegyverkezésében," pp. 294, 295n.

31. Hauner, "Military Budgets and the Armaments Industry," pp. 53, 56.

32. Macartney, *October Fifteenth*, 1:34.

33. Quoted in Sakmyster, "Gyula Gömbös and the Hungarian Jews," p. 164.

34. Gy. Juhász, *Hungarian Foreign Policy*, pp. 103–105.

35. Quoted in Fülöp and Sipos, *Magyarország külpolitikája a XX. században*, p. 172.

36. Quoted in Berend, *Decades of Crisis*, p. 310.

37. *DBFP*, Ser. 1a, Vol. 7, No. 225.

38. Macartney, *October Fifteenth*, 1:141–142.

39. See "Treaty of Trianon, Part V."

40. Julius Curtius, quoted in Steiner, *Lights That Failed*, p. 764.

41. Resolution quoted in Wheeler-Bennett, *Disarmament Deadlock*, p. 8.

42. The Round Table, "Disarmament," p. 545.

43. Steiner, *Lights That Failed*, pp. 781–784.

44. Szentnémedy, "A genfi leszerelési tárgyalások légügyi eredményei," pp. 98, 96.

45. Szentnémedy, *A repülés*, p. 74.

46. Winkler, "A magyar repülés története" (HL Tgy 3.327).

47. M. M. Szabó, *A Magyar Királyi Honvéd Légierő a második világháborúban*, pp. 18–19.

48. Mulder, "Magyar Aeroforgalmi Részvény Tarsaság."

49. *Képes Pesti Hírlap*, Apr. 18, 1930, in Winkler, "A magyar repülés története" (HL Tgy 3.327).

50. Mulder, "Magyar Aeroforgalmi Részvény Tarsaság."

51. MALERT forgalmi eredmények, MMKM 1563.

52. Mulder, "Magyar Aeroforgalmi Részvény Tarsaság."

53. Kenyeres, *Kecskeméti katonai repülés története*, pp. 23–24.

54. $45: Zs. Miszlay, "Az első magyar oceanrepülés,"

55. "Aeronautics: For Hungary," *Time*, July 27, 1931.

56. "Budapest Flight Plan to Aid Hungary," *New York Times*, July 8, 1930, p. 8.

57. "Aeronautics: For Hungary" (July 27, 1931).

58. "Lindbergh Picks a Plane," *Popular Mechanics*, Nov. 1930, pp. 803–804.

59. Nagyváradi et al., *Fejezetek a repülés történetéből*, pp. 88, 128.

60. "Endresz György," in *Magyar Életrajzi Lexikon, 1000–1990*.

61. Szeged and Wilczek: Vesztényi, "A magyar katonai repülés" (HL Tgy 2.787), p. I/23; Canada: "Hungarians to Fly Here," *New York Times*, Sept. 5, 1930, p. 12.

62. "Victory for Radio," *Washington Post*, July 17, 1931, p. 3.

63. "Nincs kizárva, hogy tavaszra marad a 'Justice for Hungary' amerikai startja," *Uj Nemzedék*, Aug. 24, 1930, p. 5.

64. "Hungarians to Fly Here," *New York Times*, Sept. 5, 1930, p. 12.

65. "Leszállás nélkül akar Los Angelestől Csikágóig repülni Magyar Sándor és Endresz György," *Uj Nemzedék*, Aug. 28, 1930, p. 10., in Winkler, "A magyar repülés története" (HL Tgy 3.327).

66. Gibás, "A magyar óceánrepülés," p. 4.

67. "Aeronautics: For Hungary" (July 27, 1931).

68. "Hungarian Atlantic Flight Succeeds," *Flight*, July 24, 1931, p. 730.

69. "Aeronautics: For Hungary" (July 27, 1931).

70. Dr. Szentkirályi Ákos hagyatéka (MMKM 108).

71. Gibás, "A magyar óceánrepülés," p. 6.

72. "Captain Magyar Lands as an Immigrant," *New York Times*, Nov. 13, 1931, p. 4.

73. "Aeronautics: For Hungary." *Time*, May 30, 1932.

74. "Oceanic Airmen's Congress: Hungarian Delegates Killed in Crash," *The Times*, May 23, 1932, p. 16.

75. Gibás, "A magyar óceánrepülés," p. 8.

76. "Szerdán délelőtt ¼ 11 órakor érkezik meg Endresz és Bittay koporsója a Délivasuti pályaudvarra," *Huszadik Század*, May 1932.

77. "Oceanic Airmen's Congress."

78. "Szerdán délelőtt ¼ 11 órakor."

79. Gat, *Fascist and Liberal Visions of War*, p. 63.

80. Caprotti, "Technology and Geographical Imaginations," p. 186.

81. Quoted in ibid., p. 64. *Mussolini aviatore* by G. Mattioli; *L'Aviazione negli scritti, nella parola e nell'esempio* (The Air Force in the writings, word and example of the Duce) *del Duce* edited by Adriano Lualdi; both cited in Caprotti.

82. Ibid., pp. 68–69.

83. Winkler, "A magyar repülés története" (HL Tgy 3.327).
84. Weaver, "Revision and Its Modes," pp. 113, 115.
85. Winkler, "A magyar repülés története" (HL Tgy 3.327).
86. Weaver, "Revision and Its Modes," p. 125.
87. Macartney, October Fifteenth, 1:222.
88. Winkler, "A magyar repülés története" (HL Tgy 3.327).
89. Arady, "Magyar cserkészet és légoltalom," p. 28.
90. Fritzsche, Nation of Fliers, pp. 109–115.
91. Scott-Hall, "Sailplane Capabilities at the Wasserkuppe," p. 27.
92. See above, ch. 3.
93. "Bánhidi Antal, Szatmárnémeti szülöttje," Magyar Közlekedési Közművelődésért Alapítvány.
94. "Croydon-Hungary Non-Stop," Flight, Sept. 21, 1933, p. 951.
95. "Advertisement: 1025 Miles Non-stop," Flight, Oct. 26, 1933, p. ix.
96. Bánhidi, "Egy volt vadászpilóta visszaemlékezése 1941. június 26-ára" (HL Tgy 2815).
97. "Magyar Pilota Pic Nic," Flight, Sept. 27, 1934, pp. 1003–1004, 1028.
98. E. Nagy, "Hungarian Holiday," Flight, Aug. 8, 1935; and "Hungarian Interlude," Flight, July 2, 1936.
99. Dr. Szentkirályi Ákos hagyatéka (MMKM 108).
100. Kenyeres, Kecskeméti katonai repülés története, p. 23.
101. DBFP, Ser. Ia, Vol. 7, No. 102 enclosure.
102. Ibid., No. 265.
103. DBFP, Ser. 2, Vol. 3, appendix IV.
104. Gy. Juhász, Hungarian Foreign Policy, p. 108.
105. Macartney, October Fifteenth, 1:138–143; Bethlen's trip: Gy. Juhász, Hungarian Foreign Policy, p. 110.
106. Gy. Juhász, Hungarian Foreign Policy, pp. 115–118.
107. Macartney, October Fifteenth, 1:146.
108. Csima, "Olaszország szerepe a fegyverkezésében," p. 298.
109. MKHL, 1938–1945, p. 19.
110. Ibid.
111. Winkler, "A magyar repülés története" (HL Tgy 3.327).
112. Sisa, "MKHL olaszországi repülőgép-beszerzései," p. 1053.
113. Csima, "Olaszország szerepe a fegyverkezésében," pp. 298–300.
114. Gooch, Mussolini and His Generals, pp. 311, 372; sortie count and bomb type: Szentnémedy, "Az olasz repülőerők müködése Abessziniában," p. 114.
115. Gooch, Mussolini and His Generals, p. 375.
116. Szentnémedy, "Az olasz repülőerők Abessziniában," p. 102.
117. Ibid., p. 116.
118. Szentnémedy, "A repülők szerepe az olasz-abesszin háborúban," p. 107.
119. Szentnémedy, "Az olasz repülőerők Abessziniában," p. 114.
120. Tóth, "Légiháború Spanyolországban," pp. 97–104.

121. Sólyom, "A Spanyol háboru a légierők szempontjából," pp. 120–125.

122. Quoted in Gy. Juhász, *Hungarian Foreign Policy*, p. 124.

123. Winkler, "A magyar repülés története" (HL Tgy 3.327).

124. K-14: Nagyváradi et al., *Fejezetek a repülés történetéből*, p. 179; Ju 86: Vesztényi, "A magyar katonai repülés" (HL Tgy 2.787), p. IV/107.

125. Bomb racks/sights: Vesztényi, "A magyar katonai repulse" (HL Tgy 2.787), p. IV, 106.

126. Winkler, "A magyar repülés története" (HL Tgy 3.327).

6

Independence: 1938–1940

HUNGARIAN NATIONAL LIFE BEGAN TO SPEED UP IN 1938. This year would see the effective end of Trianon, the disintegration of the Little Entente, the recognition of armament rights, and the reoccupation of lands lost to Czechoslovakia. The next two years would bring more prosperity, pride, and population, as a second German mediation resulted in significant territorial gains from Romania. For the Hungarian armed forces, the period was one of growth in both quantity and quality. The air service was officially acknowledged and granted bureaucratic independence from the army, the holy grail of airmen everywhere. There was war in 1939— for Hungary a short border fight with Slovakia—but Budapest managed to remain a noncombatant in the fight that began between Germany and Poland. Even as the government basked in its triumphs, however, there were serious concerns that the alliance with Germany, the mechanism that had produced such wonders in two years, was fatally flawed.

The breakthroughs of 1938 seemed unlikely in early 1937. Although the Defense Ministry had set its cap at Germany, the government's general drift toward Berlin had been checked by Gömbös's death and Horthy's appointment of Kálmán Darányi to be prime minister. Darányi was one of Bethlen's men who had been brought into the cabinet to moderate Gömbös's worst impulses. He was known as a traditional Hungarian conservative, "quite untinged by any radicalism, or even active anti-Semitism," and so his accession to the premiership was seen both inside and outside Hungary as a turn away from Germany.[1] This turn was motivated by the sense that Germany was beginning to dominate Italy in the Axis, and that Gömbös's internal policies threatened dictatorship. Darányi set about strengthening the Italian relationship as well as increasing the power of the regent and the Upper House. He also made public overtures to Britain and France. Germany responded with indirect warnings about excessive revisionism. There was a "perceptible freeze in German-Hungarian relations after Gömbös's death."[2] The Little Entente felt the chill and sought to exploit it. They approached Foreign Minister Kálmán Kánya, an extremely experienced, if high-handed, career diplomat, with proposals to tie rearmament to nonaggression. Kánya declined to sign any agreements, but he played the Little Entente along while trying to entice Germany to greater levels of support for Hungarian claims at the expense of Yugoslavia and Romania. László Bárdossy, Hungary's minister in Bucharest, was invited to the August 1937 Little Entente conference in Sinaia, Romania, where he repeated Kánya's refusal to negotiate with the Little Entente as a whole. Bárdossy instead proposed that each state "voluntarily" recognize Hungary's right to rearm, and then improve the status of their Hungarian minorities, after which Hungary would announce a policy of nonaggression. It was important to Hungary that the Little Entente's concessions come first and that its declaration of nonaggression be seen as a result, and not a condition, of its neighbors' goodwill. The Little Entente ignored the Hungarian proposal for a year, taking it up seriously only the following summer.[3]

In the second half of 1937, relations between Berlin and Budapest began to warm again. Kánya gained little from his feelers toward the West, which seemed determined to grant Hitler's direct demands. Small states survive through their ability to read the changes in the international balance of power, and the sense in Hungary was that German ascendancy would continue. The West was not interested at the moment in a subtle attempt to wean German clients from their patron. And although the Little Entente was trying to do exactly that through its diplomatic initiatives, Hungary realized that more was to be gained through consolidating ties with Germany than in trying to forge new bonds with former enemies. British openness to revision in Central Europe served only to strengthen Hitler's hand in the region, since it was clear that his pen would draft any new borders.

Meanwhile, growing German power was making the Anschluss appear inevitable. Mussolini's earlier fervent opposition had softened considerably. There had been fears of a war with Germany after the abortive Nazi putsch in Vienna in 1934, but by January 1936 Mussolini could tell Hitler's ambassador that he would not object if Austria became a German satellite. He voiced similarly agreeable sentiments to Hungary's military attaché, Colonel László Szabó. In May 1937, Mussolini considered Austria "a German state" and in November he suggested that things should "take their natural course."[4] German foreign minister Joachim von Ribbentrop used similar language with Döme Sztójay, Hungary's minister to Berlin, on March 4, 1938. It was the West that was opposed to a "normal development of the situation," Ribbentrop said, while Germany "was hoping for a peaceful solution."[5] By this time Hungary was resigned to German absorption of Austria, and its leaders were unwilling to risk Berlin's ire by intervening directly to try to save a doomed Vienna. This was also the Italian stance. Baron Villani, Hungary's minister in Rome, reported that Italian foreign minister Count Galeazzo Ciano had confided to him on March 2 that "the *Anschluss* or complete *Gleichschaltung* is unavoidable, and sooner or later must happen. Italy cannot renounce its friendship with Germany; it would, however, provide her some security and permanence if Italy and the states close to her formed a horizontal axis, which would run from Rome through Belgrade and Budapest and lead to Warsaw." Ciano also predicted that "Czechoslovakia as an independent country would soon disappear from the map of

Europe," and that the resulting common border between Hungary and Poland would aid their cooperation.[6] Kánya took up the idea of the "horizontal axis" that same day with Polish foreign minister Joseph Beck, writing, "Italy already takes into account the danger of a shift in the balance of power in Central Europe." Hungary, according to Kánya, "should prefer the maintenance of Austria's independence rather than the neighborhood of an 80-million strong Germany. Being familiar with the related very resolute intentions of the German National Socialist Government, however, we have to be prepared for the event that the union of the two German states will sooner or later be consummated."[7]

Consummation came on March 12, 1938. Austrian troops, in accordance with the last order given by Chancellor Kurt von Schuschnigg, offered no resistance to the German soldiers pouring across the border. Schuschnigg had resigned under intense pressure from Hitler and Hermann Göring, who were infuriated by his having called for a plebiscite to be held on March 13. Hitler convened key generals and pulled from the shelf an old operation plan intended to respond to an attempted Habsburg restoration. He ordered Operation Otto to be put into effect before the plebiscite could be conducted. The Wehrmacht began massing on the frontier on the morning of March 11. Austrian president Wilhelm Miklas initially refused Hitler's demand that Schuschnigg step down in favor of the quisling Arthur Seyss-Inquart.[8] But when Austrian Nazi mobs took to the streets at Berlin's command in the evening, Schuschnigg announced his resignation and the policy of nonresistance over the airwaves. Seyss-Inquart's first duty as chancellor was to request German intervention to restore peace, which gave Hitler a most transparent fig leaf to cover the invasion. Mussolini, to whom Schuschnigg had appealed earlier in the day, declined to help, saying Austria was "immaterial" to him. Hitler was ecstatic over Italian passivity, promising that he would always remember Mussolini's help. "If he should ever need any help or be in any danger," Hitler told Prince Philipp of Hesse, the Führer's personal representative then in Rome, "he can be convinced that I shall stick to him whatever may happen, even if the whole world gangs up on him."[9]

The fact of the Anschluss was no great surprise to Hungarian leaders, although the timing caught some off guard. It did cause a minor uproar among the Hungarian population who heard on radio broadcasts the news that German troops were at the frontier.[10] Many people feared that the Germans would continue east, and some on the extreme right hoped that would be the case. Admiral Horthy attempted to calm the nation via a radio address on April 3, putting the best possible face on the German occupation of Austria, and assuring the country that very little had changed. "It is hard for a sober-minded person to understand exactly what the reason for the unrest and excitement is, for in fact, there is no basis for it whatever," he said. Only the uninformed were agitated:

> For anybody with an open mind and seeing eyes who judges the situation must know that the union of Austria and Germany means only one thing for our country: that an old friend of ours who has been dragged by the peace treaties into an impossible situation has united with another old friend and faithful comrade-in-arms of ours, i.e. with that Germany which in the testimony of history always was a trustworthy ally of her friends, and has kept her pledges for life and death. This is the whole thing. Nothing else happened from our point of view.[11]

Even as he portrayed the Anschluss in anodyne terms, Horthy included a veiled warning to right-wing radicals who sought to take advantage of the situation. "Those who prefer fishing in troubled waters," he said, "have availed themselves of the opportunity to bring about discord to suit their own purposes. Yet this attempt is futile. For by spreading rumors, excitement lasting a few moments may be brought about, yet I can assure everybody that in this country nobody will disturb order and tranquility unpunished." Horthy then issued another warning, less veiled, to restive army officers:

> Although this significance of the Army is recognized by everybody today, they also should know that an army engaged in politics is not only worth-

less but harmful too. To the nation as a whole, and to each citizen. Nevertheless, of late there were some who believed that this body of officers could
be got near to, and this free-of-politics unity broken up.

I feel quite certain that the attempt of these persons will come to
naught. Still I warn those who, although shrouded in the mantle of ideals,
nevertheless, to ensure their self-assertion, are experimenting: hands off
the body of officers! The commissioned officers know that the Army is
above parties and is the nation's own.[12]

Near the end of the speech he returned to the theme of appropriate
spheres of influence: "In this country an end must be put to everybody claiming the right of directing foreign policy and of daring to
disturb the internal peace in whatever manner." Horthy's words
were intended to quell the excessive partisanship growing among
the officer corps led by General Jenő Rátz, the chief of staff. Gömbös had groomed Rátz, who was a friend of Arrow Cross leader
Ferenc Szálasi, although his appointment as chief of staff had come
on Darányi's watch.[13] Rátz had recently circulated a memorandum
in which he advocated an intensification of the furtive rearmament
effort. The government naturally wanted to expand and modernize
the army, but Rátz strayed beyond his area of responsibility in suggesting the country needed "political and moral rearmament,"
along with land reform, income redistribution, and antisemitic
laws.[14] Kánya opposed Rátz, as did the more financially cautious in
the government party. Horthy was approached with these ideas by
Károly Soós, himself a former chief of staff and defense minister.
Horthy rejected Soós's recommendation that he abandon constitu-
tional methods and take the country in a more autocratic direction.

The Rátz-Soós memorandum made its way to Béla Imrédy, a
skilled financier and president of the National Bank. Imrédy embraced the plan, although he had previously shown no illiberal in-
clinations, and took it with Rátz to the prime minister. Darányi
approved the scheme, without the dictatorship, and agreed to put
forward anti-Jewish measures and to embark on an ambitious
rearmament program.[15] Such a buildup could only be considered

after the end of League of Nations financial oversight on January 28, 1938, however.[16] Imrédy drafted the two bills secretly, and on March 5 Darányi floated the ideas in a speech at Győr. The speech went over well in Hungary, and elicited no response from the Little Entente, so Darányi carried on, appointing Imrédy to the cabinet on March 9 as minister of economic cooperation.[17] In April, the Lower House approved the bill that included a five-year expenditure of 1 billion pengős on defense—60 per cent on direct military purchases, the remainder on infrastructure improvements related to defense. The Upper House passed it without change in May, and the following month the "Győr program" became Law XX of 1938.[18] Six hundred million pengős would be raised through a one-time tax on property exceeding 50,000 pengős in value, and the rest would come from an internal loan underwritten by large companies and banks.[19]

Law XX authorized the billion pengős in defense spending, but it did not dictate the Honvéd's organization. That was the responsibility of Defense Minister Vilmos Rőder, who presented a proposal to the Crown Council one month before Darányi's speech in Győr. Rőder's "Huba plan" was based on the 1932 scheme that had gone unrealized, and aimed to maximize Hungary's ability to mobilize its forces at short notice.[20] The army's peacetime strength under Huba would be 107,000 men, growing to 250,000 after mobilization of reserves. It was organized into three armies of seven corps. The corps were composed of twenty-one infantry divisions, two motorized and two cavalry brigades, one air division, plus border guards, artillery, and support forces. According to its designers, only an armed force that could be concentrated quickly would be effective against the "overrunning strategies" (lerohanás hadászatok) of Hungary's neighbors. This dictated that the four motorized and cavalry brigades should receive the highest priority. After the passage of Law XX, the Defense Ministry decided to proceed with Huba in three tranches. Huba-I would consist of the mobile brigades, the core of the infantry divisions (21 two-regiment brigades), some artillery, and a significant increase in the flying corps. Huba-II would add armor and more aircraft, and Huba-III would fill out the infantry divisions' missing brigades. By the end of March the Defense Ministry had worked out the details of the plan, and Rőder instructed the VKF to order the necessary proto-types and acquire production licenses.[21]

At the beginning of 1938, the LÜH was organized into the 1st Aviation Brigade, composed of three air regiments, along with an independent long-range reconnaissance group operating from Má-tyásföld. There were twenty-three understrength squadrons in all. The 1st Flying Regiment was made up of two fighter groups of three squadrons each, based at Börgönd, Veszprém, and Kecskemét.[22] The 2nd Flying Regiment was composed of two bomber squadrons at Szombathely, and the 3rd Flying Regiment consisted of three light bomber squadrons at Tapolca, Veszprém, and Pápa. The short-range reconnaissance squadrons were aligned with and subordinate to the seven mixed brigades, and were based at Budapest, Székes-fehérvár, Kaposvár, Pécs, Szeged, Debrecen, and Miskolc.[23] Until autumn 1938, these designations were for internal reference only; in public the units were still known by their cover names (e.g., 2/I Bomber Group was the "Airmail Company").

Fifty-five million of the Győr program's 600 million pengős were designated for aviation equipment and stores. The first do-mestic beneficiary was WM, which received in July an order for thirty-six WM 21 short-range reconnaissance aircraft. The Defense Ministry insisted on decentralizing airplane production (a tactic advocated by Szentnémedy in 1935), and so ordered an additional twelve WM 21s each from Magyar Állami Vas-, Acél- és Gépgyárak, MÁVAG) and Magyar Waggon- és Gépgyár (MWG).[24] The WM 21 "Sólyom" (Falcon) was an adaptation and improvement of the Fokker C.V-D. A two-seat, open-cockpit biplane, powered by the WM-14 870-horsepower engine, the Sólyom was faster and

Figure 6.1. These WM 21s wear the yellow invasion band and white cross adopted in summer 1942. Courtesy of the Péter Zámbori Collection.

more robust than its German stablemate, Heinkel's He 46, but it was not blessed with easy handling characteristics, and the lower wing restricted the observer's vision.[25] Nevertheless, WM, MÁVAG, and MWG built 128 Sólyoms and they performed satisfactorily until 1942. The WM 21's best attribute was its native origin. Being constructed entirely within Hungary meant no hard currency left the country, and it stimulated MÁVAG and MWG aircraft production at a critical time for the industry.

Despite the air corps' growing preference for German airplanes, the LÜH could not count on Berlin to fill the additional aviation requirements of the Huba plan owing to excessive delays in deliveries. From the 1936 order of 190 aircraft, only the eighteen He 70s had arrived by the end of 1938. In the summer of 1938, the LÜH placed a contract for thirty-six He 112s, a design that had set a world speed record and had narrowly lost the German fighter competition to the Bf 109. A single airplane was delivered in February 1939, followed by two additional prototypes, before the German

Aviation Ministry (Reichsluftfahrtministerium, RLM) canceled the contract.[26] The RLM always prioritized production for domestic needs, and in 1936 Göring had introduced a Four-Year Plan that aimed for self-reliance in the aviation industry. The Four-Year Plan forced manufacturers to fill orders for the Luftwaffe first and to curtail the variety of models produced. This meant that Hungary would take a back seat to the Luftwaffe in delivery of airplane types, like the He 46, that were in use by both services, and that manufacture of models not adopted for series production for the German force, such as the He 112, would be discontinued.[27] Hungary was the single largest customer for German combat aircraft in the period 1936–1938, accounting for over a quarter of all sales in 1937, but the export market represented less than 5 per cent of the 1.3-billion-Reichsmark industry. The rest of the 7,500 aircraft produced in Germany from 1934 to 1939 were dedicated to the Luftwaffe.[28]

Hungarian airmen therefore had to look again to Italy for assistance. Italy had extended another substantial arms credit in 1937, this time of 120 million liras, of which 18 million went for purchases of aviation equipment. The LÜH used this grant to finish paying for the 1936 order of fifty-two CR.32 fighters, all of which had arrived by the end of 1938.[29] The VKF did not support further purchase of the CR.32 because of its approaching obsolescence, but the LÜH persisted.[30] Due to the ready availability of the Fiat, it formed the backbone of the Hungarian fighter force for two years. The CR.32 would have looked at home on a First World War aerodrome, with its open cockpit, fixed landing gear, and fabric wings, although its service ceiling of 25,000 feet and maximum speed of 210 knots far exceeded the performance of 1918 airplanes. The He 112, the other fighter the LÜH ordered in 1938, belonged to the future. It was an all-metal, low-wing monoplane with retractable gear and an enclosed cockpit; it could reach 31,000 feet and 275 knots and was armed with two 20-millimeter cannon in addition to its pair of machine guns. But Heinkel could not deliver the He 112, and Fiat could supply CR.32s, and so Hungarian fighter pilots flew the aging Italian design.

Much the same scenario played out in the acquisition of a suitable light bomber. The LÜH saw the need for a multirole airplane capable of reconnaissance, daytime bombing, and low-level attack. The Ju 86 was known to be "clumsy" and ill-suited to low-level operations, and the RLM did not offer any other models for export.[31] Caproni did make available its new Ca.310, which promised to fulfill the LÜH performance criteria as well as the production requirements: it would accept the WM-14 engine and could be manufactured under license in Hungary. The LÜH therefore ordered thirty-six Ca.310s in late June 1938, with delivery in three batches to be completed by October. The final aircraft did not arrive until June 1939, but given the lengthy delays to which the LÜH had grown accustomed, the Ca.310's tardiness was not a major drawback. Its poor performance was, however, and resulted in the air service returning the entire lot to Italy for replacement by a different model. Although the trial machines had been equipped with a 700-horsepower, 14-cylinder engine, the production airplanes Caproni sent to Hungary came with weaker 7-cylinder engines of only 460 horsepower. The engines tended to overheat at low altitude, and their lower power significantly degraded the airplane's capability. In autumn 1939, the LÜH sent Caproni a list of fifteen flaws to be rectified to keep the type in service. Yugoslavia had reported similar problems with its Ca.311s, and the Italian Air Ministry's inspector validated the Hungarian complaints. With no reasonable prospects of correcting the design's shortcomings, Caproni instead offered to exchange the remaining Ca.310s for a slightly newer and more powerful twin-engined bomber, the Ca.135. The Ca.135 also suffered from a number of deficiencies. Even with the WM-14 engines, it was too slow. Its defensive armament was light in comparison with other similar designs (e.g., Bristol's Blenheim IV, which was exported to Romania and Yugoslavia, sported six machine guns to its three), the hydraulic system was prone to fail-

Figure 6.2. Caproni Ca.135 bomber, 1942. Courtesy of the Péter Zámbori Collection.

ure, and the propeller had a disturbing tendency to fall off. Nevertheless, its payload and bombing accuracy were deemed acceptable, and the Ca.135 served with the Hungarian air service until late 1942.[32]

LÜH officers did not know in 1938 that the Ca.310 order would be such a disaster, but they were aware of the technological challenges facing their service, even with access to German and Italian exports. In the January 1938 *MKSz* roundup of the previous year's aviation developments, Szentnémedy printed a comparative chart that showed one Czechoslovak and four French machines with performance exceeding that of the ordered, but never fielded, He 112, along with a pair of French four-engine heavy bombers far surpassing any planned Hungarian capability.[33] Through the course of the year, material defects and production delays made the situation more bleak. The LÜH staff recommended comprehensive trials be conducted before any orders were placed, but this was ignored, with predictable results. In October, the situation was brought to the attention of Admiral Horthy, through a report by Lieutenant Colonel László Háry, the long-serving fighter pilot appointed in May to head the LÜH. Háry's assessment of the technical state of the air service began with a critique of the procurement process before taking up the problems of particular aircraft. Horthy's extensive handwritten notes on Háry's report reveal the regent's interest in aviation and establish his working knowledge of the air service's challenges, and therefore merit lengthy citation:

> Today *countless ministry* sections share the portfolio for aviation material. Responsibility for motorized and armed airplanes, cannon, and technical parts is established and organized far from the flying. Thus the fliers, without experts and inquiry and in the absence of basic battle-trials, in the recent past spent *27 million* marks on aviation equipment which is not suitable for *combat.*
>
> The procured *bombers* (Junkers Ju 86) are not suited to low-altitude attack.
>
> Our *long-range reconnaissance* machines are bad because the observers cannot *see anything* out of them.
>
> The short-range reconnaissance machines have to be improved at home. (The ailerons break away.)
>
> The heavy bombers are not suitable, because they can carry only a *1000 kg* bomb load 400–450 km distance. We have to carry out a reconstruction on them. *Who is responsible* for the errors? The technical service is not composed of experts. The losses spoil the *corps' spirit* and corrupt confidence in leadership.
>
> This year's order of Italian aircraft also occurred with no connection to battle-trials or expert opinion. For low-level attack we have to use such airplanes which are neither maneuverable nor fast, and are equipped with high-altitude engines. If every tool does not advance the corps' work, then we cannot expect results.[34]

Háry addressed the inability of the air service to take in sufficient numbers of new officers and fresh recruits, and identified one of Hungary's fundamental barriers to becoming a regional air power: its agrarian nature and the attendant obstacles to training suitable young men as mechanics and engineers. He then described the difficulty in conducting combat flight training on a peacetime calendar. Admiral Horthy offered no disagreement with Háry's analysis, and paid particular attention to the recruiting deficits:

It is a mistake that the replacement of active officers (so far) has not been addressed by the flying corps. During academy training it is not possible to recognize the prospective flying corps' officer. If he comes to the flying corps, he is forced into the thankless role of a student for one to two years of training.

In 1935, twenty-one lieutenants were commissioned into the flying corps, and although since 1935 seventeen, and since 1936, twenty-five flying squadrons have been formed, in 1937, thirteen, and in 1938, eight officers have come to the flying corps from Ludovika, when in this year our casualties are already twice that. Thus the present situation, in which there is a shortfall of 60 men from the established officer strength, that is, 1/6 of the officer corps. The officer shortage is temporarily filled with reserve officers, who bring with them to the staff the seed of discontent and agitation, and regard the air service as just a last employment refuge. We fill the gap (as always), but the idea of the unified officer corps suffers (such are the replacements). It is hard to make up for the absence of the nursery [*gyermekszoba*, i.e., cadet training].

The qualification of replacement enlisted men is principally completed—on paper. The new recruit intake is not sufficient to provide our agrarian country with industrial training. It is not possible to train a farmhand to be an *airplane mechanic*, etc., in 2 years. The squadron technical service rests on the shoulders of 5–8 *chief engineers*, together with expensive machinery and security staff. *Flying training* is weak because there is not enough time. Fifty-two Sundays and Saturdays, twenty holidays, Christmas, Easter, harvest holidays, bad weather, guard duty, etc.[35]

Horthy's note about the year's casualties exceeding officer accession was not an exaggeration. From October 1937 until mid-July 1938, the LÜH had suffered sixty-four aircraft accidents at a cost of twenty airmen's lives. The accident rate had so alarmed the Army High Command (Hadsereg főparancsnokság, HFP) that it had commissioned an investigative panel, led by General Elemér Novák-Gorondy. The report was damning. It found the entire structure—organization, equipment, training, material support—unsuitable.[36] Regarding the rash of accidents, the panel observed the increased sophistication of the new aircraft in the inventory and doubted that the pilots had sufficient experience in the recent types.[37] To increase overall effectiveness and efficiency, it recommended the aviation authority be placed directly under the defense minister and have its own budget. The panel also criticized the speed at which the LÜH had attempted to expand, arguing that slower and more methodical growth would lead to better capability. "The Hungarian air force is a young service with immature organizations and equipment," wrote Novák-Gorondy, "which from the beginning has struggled with thousands of difficulties."[38] There is no evidence that Admiral Horthy saw the Novák-Gorondy report himself (Háry made no reference to it in his presentation), but some of its elements were incorporated into Háry's presentation.

A fix for the pilot training shortfall was already underway when Horthy received Háry's report. The Defense Ministry had accepted in June an Italian offer to provide training for 200 Hungarian pilots. The contract was for two years at a total cost of 18 million liras (roughly equivalent to one squadron of Italian airplanes), and would take place at Grottaglie airfield near Taranto. The South Italy Flying Course (Dél-olasz Repülő Tanfolyam, DRT) followed the earlier, small-scale pilot training scheme in which the Batáry brothers took part. It was conceived before the recognition of arms equality, and was expected to be conducted with some discretion, if not complete secrecy. That accounts for the choice of Grottaglie, an isolated outpost and the site of a short-lived secret training program for German pilots in 1933, instead of the established Italian training facilities at Perugia.[39] After the acknowledgment of Hungarian armament rights, the newly hatched training program was able to proceed without the legal complexities required a decade earlier. Instruction began for the first class on October 19, 1938. The eight-month course was conducted under the Italian curriculum, with each student pilot receiving eighty hours of flight time, of which sixty were in a primary trainer and the rest in an operational type. Captain Pál Batáry returned to Italy to command the bomber training squadron; Captain Jenő Forró led the fighter unit.[40] Hungarian officers handled the classroom instruction, while Italians conducted the in-flight training on Breda Br.25s and Romeo

Ro.1s. After their initial solo flights, pilot candidates were sorted into fighter, bomber, and reconnaissance tracks.[41] The DRT was a complete success for Hungary. The program provided instruction for 200 pilots above Hungary's own training capacity and at virtually no cost, since even the 18-million-lira expense came out of an Italian credit line.

Two domestic training programs were established the following year, both of them bearing the regent's name. The first, the Miklós Horthy National Flying Foundation, was an umbrella organization that helped underwrite the university and sport clubs through a public funding scheme. The proceeds of certain cinema tickets and stamps financed civilian gliding and flying training, and promoted aviation through the foundation's magazine, *Magyar Szárnyak*.[42] Horthy was enthusiastic about the foundation because he saw it as a path to "create numerous trained and current young pilots suitable as reservists."[43] The second institution was an aviation academy established on the grounds of a former Habsburg cadet school in the Felvidék town of Kassa. The regent presided over the school's first matriculation on November 9, 1939, and it was known thereafter as the Royal Hungarian Miklós Horthy Military Aviation Academy. Its first class consisted of fifteen cadets, but the number had increased tenfold by 1944. By that time the course had been shortened to meet the wartime demands for air force officers, and no longer granted a diploma equivalent to a civilian college.[44]

The DRT and the indigenous flight schools increased the number of new Hungarian pilots, but they did not address concerns about competence raised by Novák-Gorondy. Lieutenant Colonel Háry recommended the reduction of LÜH pilots' participation with the national airline. Háry acknowledged the role of MALERT in sustaining Hungarian aviation during the period of Allied inspections, but he suggested it no longer performed that critical role, and in fact was a drain on manpower that the country could not afford. "The military vestiges in the air traffic company," Horthy recorded, "which until now have offered a good disguise for the possibility of flying, cannot go any further. . . . It is not possible that when we have a 60-officer shortage, we should attach to the airline (three or four machines) *ten active* officers with the highest flying training, not in their officers' uniforms but in the airline's livery." Both Horthy and Háry looked forward to the time "after the recognition of our military emancipation, when further covering is not necessary," and the air service would be freed from the budgetary and administrative concerns of civilian aviation.[45]

After enumerating the air service's problems, Háry reached the paper's conclusion. "This report shows," he wrote, "that the current situation of aviation is not healthy, and is in need of remedy. For twenty years land forces leaders have experimented with aviation. . . . The outcome of that well-intentioned experimentation is today's sad personnel, material, and training situation." Háry then declared that on November 1 he would "throw out 160 airplanes as worthless rubbish, because for six to ten years they have been mortal dangers." Finally came the proposal, which by this point would have been no surprise: "Under the name Royal Hungarian Aviation Bureau or some other name, an organization should be established that brings independent responsibility for Hungarian aviation under a single individual."[46]

The regent took Háry's report to heart. "Without the knowledge of the theory and application of flight to a minute level of detail," he wrote, "it is not possible to lead, and because of this, in my opinion, we must have aviation experts." Horthy's last page of notes included an organizational sketch that showed a single agency in command of all aspects of military aviation, subordinated to the chief of the VKF, the Defense Ministry, and the HFP) for planning, programming and operational purposes. Under the diagram and above his signature, Horthy described the air service as being "cut out of the Honvédség. . . . It should work autonomously to achieve the organizational and operational goal. To reach independence (Önállósítani)."[47]

The degree of independence that the air service ought to enjoy had been debated throughout 1938. Everyone involved recognized that the growing and barely disguised flying corps needed a more efficient structure, but Hungarians were not immune from the normal administrative affliction that makes bureaucrats eager to accumulate authority and reluctant to relinquish it. Therefore the various proposals from the Defense Ministry and VKF featured new titles and updated reporting requirements, but did little to improve the air service's effectiveness. Since the beginning of the year, responsibility for aviation activities had been shared among three offices within the ministry: a chief of the Aviation Group (Légügyi csoportfőnök), an Aviation Inspectorate (Légügyi szemlélő), and an Air Force Headquarters (Légierő parancsnokság, Lepság). In addition to these was the chief of the air staff post on the VKF. After some shuffling of personnel within the ministries, by May 1938 Major General Waldemár Kenese had been confirmed as the head of the inspectorate, and Colonel Ferenc Feketehalmy-Czeydner appointed chief air officer of the VKF. Ferenc Szentnémedy was promoted to colonel and made chief of the aviation group, while Lieutenant Colonel Háry was given operational control at Lepság. The installation of competent individuals did not resolve the organizational muddle, and after internal attempts failed, the Defense Ministry invited an Italian expert to study the situation. RA lieutenant colonel Gallo arrived in Budapest in August 1938 and submitted his proposal on September 1. He recommended an independent air force composed of six regiments amounting to 309 aircraft, reporting directly to the Defense Ministry. Given Gallo's status as an officer of an independent air force himself (Mussolini had given the RA equal status with the army and navy in 1923) and a representative of the primary supplier of aircraft to Hungary, it would have been surprising indeed for him to have returned a proposal in favor of a small air service that functioned as a branch of the Honvédség. The VKF opposed the Gallo plan on the grounds that it would be too difficult and expensive to create the new organizations and acquire additional airplanes.[48]

General Henrik Werth, previously the commandant of the War College, was by this time the head of the VKF. A change of government in the spring had caused ripples through the defense establishment. Prime Minister Darányi's opponents had succeeded in forcing him out of office because of his secret collaboration with Szálasi's Arrow Cross in connection with the anti-Jewish law. Law XV of 1938, as it became known upon passage, restricted the number of Jews in the professions, and had been introduced as part of the same grand bargain with the radical right that had brought forth the Győr program. Horthy was so strongly opposed to Szálasi at that time that he would have demanded Darányi's resignation for entering into negotiations with him. Faced with exposure, Darányi stepped down on May 13. Béla Imrédy was asked to form a government, and as a sop to the right, he named Jenő Rátz to replace Rőder as defense minister. General Lajos Keresztes-Fischer, the former chief of the regent's military cabinet and brother of the interior minister, filled Rátz's vacated position as chief of the VKF. Keresztes-Fischer held the post only until early October, when Horthy asked him to step aside in favor of Werth.[49]

So it was that Horthy called in Defense Minister Rátz, Chief of Staff Werth, and head of the HFP Hugó Sónyi on October 28 to discuss the future of the air service. The VKF had prepared a memo describing the four competing proposals, arranged on a continuum from Gallo's full independence to a First World War-style field aviation corps. Two days later, Horthy endorsed the Gallo plan. The decision was communicated in a terse note that read, "Supreme decision: the first option [Gallo's] is desirable. This must be implemented immediately!"[50] The evidence suggests it was Háry's paper, delivered on October 26, that galvanized Horthy into opting for an independent air force. But the impetus for an organizational modernization of the service must have been largely provided by the course of events in international affairs, which from August had picked up momentum.

Hitler had scarcely returned from his triumphal tour of Austria when he began to discuss with his generals the details of Operation Green, the planned invasion of Czechoslovakia. He expected that Hungary and Poland would participate in order to reclaim territory lost to the government in Prague, but both countries were determined to avoid active participation in a German attack. They were, however, prepared to insist that any concessions granted to the German minority in Czechoslovakia be extended to ethnic Hungarians and Poles. The Hungarian objection was entirely practical. The saber rattling had begun just weeks after Darányi's speech in Győr, and the Defense and Foreign Ministries knew they would not be in a position to threaten Czechoslovakia militarily for many months, perhaps years. Furthermore, any Hungarian mobilization aimed north would leave it open to Yugoslavian or Romanian attack from the south. Imrédy and Kánya therefore pressed Ciano on the issue of Yugoslavian neutrality at a meeting in Rome in July. Ciano had weeks earlier taken up the matter with the Yugoslav prime minister, Milan Stojadinović, who promised that Yugoslavia would not intervene in a German-Czech conflict if Hungary also abstained. Hungary could benefit afterward from the German action, Stojadinović agreed, as long as it did not take the initiative.[51] Ciano also reported to Villani at the same time that Germany had promised not "to take forceful measures against Czechoslovakia" but rather to "endure Czech provocations, anticipating that in time, the process of internal disintegration will make it easier to reach a solution."[52] The Hungarians were not satisfied with Italy's assurances, and therefore sought guarantees from the Germans themselves, who elected to put off such weighty discussions until the regent's state visit in August.

The official party, consisting of Admiral and Mrs. Horthy, Imrédy and his wife, Kánya, Rátz, and Sztójay, arrived at Kiel on the morning of August 22 for the launching of the new German cruiser, the *Prinz Eugen*. Mrs. Horthy commissioned the ship and the party observed maneuvers and a naval review. The fine atmosphere was spoiled later in the day by reports that Hungary had signed a treaty with the Little Entente. The Germans were furious, seeing the treaty as a renunciation of Hungary's claims toward revision, and therefore weakening Germany's own case. Ribbentrop tore into Imrédy and Kánya the next day. The Bled Agreement, he contended, was a stab in the back, "blocking the road to intervention in Czechoslovakia and making it morally more difficult for the Yugoslavs to leave their Czech allies in the lurch."[53] Hitler was more tactful with Horthy. He detailed Operation Green and asked Horthy if Hungary would participate, implying that it could keep any territory it subsequently occupied. Horthy, by his own account, declined on the grounds that the Honvéd could not mount such an operation. The admiral, a great respecter of British naval power, warned the Führer against an armed invasion that might lead to a world war, in which the Royal Navy would prove decisive. At that point Hitler shouted, "Nonsense! Be quiet!" and Horthy ended the conversation. Another discussion between the two toward the end of the visit was similarly unproductive. Hitler made a little headway with Rátz and Imrédy after he told them "he who wants to sit at the table must at least help in the kitchen."[54] They conceded that Hungary could participate when it was militarily capable and when its southern flank was secured. Kánya also retreated a bit under pressure. He had told Ribbentrop on August 23 that it would take Hungary two years to prepare for conflict, but amended that time on August 25 to less than two months. The officials returned to Hungary somewhat dejected, but their reception at home was enthusiastic. Hungarians were revisionists almost to a man, but they were not eager to follow Hitler into war (yet), and the stories of Horthy and his ministers standing up to the Germans' bluster raised the government's standing considerably.

Regarding the negotiations with the Little Entente, the Hungarian position was that the Bled Agreement was in fact three separate accords, and that the pledge of nonaggression would not become operable until Hungary was satisfied with the condition of its national minority within the other state. The Foreign Ministry emphasized this distinction in a cable to all its embassies on August 23. It had concluded a "gentlemen's agreement" with Romania and Yugoslavia concerning minority rights, but the "finalization of the entire agreement-complex" with Czechoslovakia remained an open question.[55] In any case, the Bled conference left all sides temporarily satisfied. The Little Entente thought it had gained Hungary's pledge of nonaggression in exchange for acknowledging a rearmament that was already under way. Hungary, on the other hand, saw the key enabling feature of Trianon—its forced disarmament—crumble, at the price of a promise not to attack two countries (Romania and Yugoslavia) that its patrons had already placed off limits. All four states were in retrospect hopelessly naive in believing that treaties among them would make any difference at all to the great powers that really controlled their fates. Romania and Yugoslavia were protected because they were useful to Germany and Italy, and Czechoslovakia was doomed because Germany had designs on it.

For Hungary's armed forces, the Bled accords were a welcome relief from the burden of secrecy. Its rearmament program had been increasingly visible in the months since the Győr speech, but the need to cloak the prohibited branches was a drag on efficiency. New orders for airplanes and tanks did not spike in September 1938, because Italy and Germany had long been complicit in Hungary's clandestine rearmament. But recruiting for the air service and armored corps could now begin publicly, and the organizational structures no longer needed to be distorted through disguise.

Among the most visible symbols of Hungary's new status were the red-white-green chevrons that appeared from September 15 on the wings and rudders of airplanes that the day before had been part of an "Airmail Company," "Meteorological Section," or civilian flight school. The same Defense Ministry order that specified the national aircraft markings also adopted for the air force the uniform worn by LÜH officials.[56] That date marked the end of the evasion of Trianon's air clauses that had begun nineteen years earlier, when the Defense Ministry's 37th Section had vowed to abrogate the treaty in order to maintain the nucleus of an air force. The LÜH in September 1938 comprised 196 combat airplanes organized in twenty-five squadrons: ten bomber squadrons, primarily equipped with Ju 86s; six fighter squadrons armed with CR.32s; seven short-range reconnaissance squadrons flying He 46s and WM 21s; and two long-range reconnaissance squadrons operating He 70s.[57] The air service had been officially acknowledged for only three weeks when it received its first mobilization order, in response to the crisis in Czechoslovakia.

The German High Command was prepared to execute Operation Green on October 1, the date that Kánya had told Ribbentrop the Honvédség would be ready for intervention.[58] Hitler's plans were not dependent on Hungarian participation, but he hoped to use a Czecho-Hungarian border skirmish as his reason for abandoning negotiations and initiating military action. The Führer suggested just such an arranged provocation to Imrédy before the second round of talks with British prime minister Neville Chamberlain in late September. Imrédy had gone to Berlin to ask Hitler to endorse the same rights for the Hungarian minority in Czechoslovakia as he extracted for the Sudeten Germans. Hitler was in no mood to coddle Hungarians one month after the "stab in the back" at Bled, and he suggested to Imrédy that, if satisfactory agreement were reached on the Sudeten problem, he "would have no moral title to raise further demands either before the world or himself, and cannot make his standpoint subject to the treatment of other nationalities."[59] A Hungarian invasion that offered Germany a casus belli, however, would be an entirely different matter, and Budapest could then expect to reap substantial rewards. Imrédy was unwilling to

Figure 6.3. Ju 86 and He 70s on the airfield at Kecskemét, 1939. Photo: Fortepan/Zoltán Hídvégi.

risk war alone against Czechoslovakia (and perhaps France and Britain as well), and he did not agree to Hitler's scheme. The Foreign Ministry instead launched a diplomatic offensive against Prague, demanding the return of majority Magyar areas, and autonomy for Slovakia and Ruthenia.[60]

Although Imrédy did not intend open conflict with Czechoslovakia, he did initiate actions to improve Hungary's military readiness. The LHT ordered a limited mobilization of two years' recruiting classes, and Imrédy wrote to Mussolini to ask for the deployment of eight Italian fighter squadrons under Hungarian colors. Action on that request was delayed until German intervention obviated the need, but the remarkable change in circumstances is worth considering: just six weeks earlier a secret Italo-Hungarian aviation deployment would have been arranged so as to hide prohibited Hungarian capability. Now the concern was to reinforce Budapest's air defenses without acknowledging Italian assistance. On September 23, the air service issued its own limited mobilization order for reservists to report for "maneuvers," and three days later a restricted flight zone was established around Budapest. Aircraft that did not comply with published arrival and departure routes risked being shot down.[61] A large air defense exercise was held in the capital on September 26. The Air Defense League simulated mustard gas and incendiary attacks, and firemen responded to a smoke pot on the roof of the stock exchange. Photographs of the event show families scurrying into shelters, decontamination teams trying to contain the spread of the mock gas, and what might have been the first overflights of the capital by airplanes bearing the new national chevrons.[62]

When the terms of the Munich Pact were announced on September 29, Budapest found to its disappointment that its claims had not been settled by the four powers, but were to be reconciled through bilateral negotiations within three months. Imrédy decided to force the issue. The Foreign Ministry demanded plebiscites in Slovakia and Ruthenia, demobilization of Hungarian soldiers in the Czechoslovak army, and the release of Hungarian political prisoners.[63] On October 6, irregular forces known as the Rongyos Gárda (Ragged Guard) began to infiltrate into Slovakia disguised as foresters, with orders to attack targets of military significance such as bridges and railroads, and to prepare ethnic Hungarians to support a possible armed incursion from Budapest.[64] The same day the entire air service, with the exception of the 4th and 5th Short-Range Reconnaissance Squadrons at Pécs and Szeged, was put on alert. Units were to disperse to their combat airfields and be ready for operations from noon on October 7. The squadrons did not meet the October 7 mobilization goal, but a report from October 10 showed the short-range reconnaissance units subordinate to the mixed brigades were in place, along with the four bomber squadrons of the 1st Aviation Brigade. The HFP initially retained control of fighter and long-range reconnaissance squadrons, but on October 24 those were released to the 1st Aviation Brigade.[65]

Diplomatic negotiations continued while Hungary and Czechoslovakia mobilized. When officials from the two states met at Komárom on October 9, Prague was represented by Slovak separatists, who were ill prepared for detailed discussions and disinclined to bargain.[66] The talks made little progress and broke off after four days. Horthy also appealed to Hitler, Mussolini, and Chamberlain. Darányi went to Munich, Csáky to Rome, and Horthy invoked Chamberlain's brother Austen (who had visited Hungary and met with Horthy in 1936) in his letter to the British prime minister.[67] Mussolini was supportive, Chamberlain noncommittal, and Hitler truculent. Darányi, who was no longer in the government but was thought to be well-regarded by Hitler, met the Führer on October 14 to secure German support of a Hungarian attack on Czechoslovakia. Hitler, not surprisingly, opposed this, and denounced Hungary for failing to act earlier at his suggestion. When Darányi showed him a map of the ethnic Hungarian regions that Budapest claimed, Hitler scolded him. "Once I offered you all Slovakia. Why didn't you take it then?"[68] Hitler eventually agreed to consider arbitration, and Darányi, after telephone consultation with Budapest, offered to adhere more closely to the Axis line, and perhaps join the Anti-Comintern Pact. Hitler pushed: Would Hungary leave the League of Nations? Darányi did not commit to that course, but advanced the prospect of economic concessions. The Führer ended Darányi's audience after agreeing that Hungary ought to receive additional German arms.

For three days there were no diplomatic advances, but during this time both sides increased their mobilization. Hungary announced the call-up of five more classes of recruits, bringing its total force to near 300,000, and Czechoslovakia reinforced its position in the east to nineteen divisions. The period October 19–28 was filled with cables and consultations, as the final composition of the arbitration conference was debated (would Poland and Romania be included to help dispense with Ruthenia?) and likely outcomes were mooted. Finally, on the October 29, Hungary and Czechoslovakia officially invited Germany and Italy to resolve the dispute, agreeing ahead of time to accept the Axis decision.[69] That decision was announced on November 2, 1938, in Vienna's Belvedere Palace, and awarded Hungary over 4,500 square miles and roughly a million inhabitants, the majority of whom were Magyars (57 per cent according to Prague's numbers, 86 per cent according to Budapest's). Hungary received the disputed cities of Kassa, Ungvár, and Munkács, but did not gain Pozsony or Nyitra. Critically, Czechoslovakia also retained Ruthenia, disposition of which was not taken up by the arbiters. Hungary and Poland were intent on joint seizure of the area in order to obtain a common border, which would improve each country's strategic position and enhance military and economic cooperation between them.[70]

No major military confrontations erupted between Hungarian and Czechoslovak forces during the time of the First Vienna Award, but along with the activities of the Rongyos Gárda there were a number of minor aerial incidents, including one that resulted in the destruction of a Czech reconnaissance airplane. From the middle of October, aircraft on both sides had committed border incursions, conducting reconnaissance, propaganda leaflet drops, and strafing attacks. On October 25, Lieutenant László Pongrácz of the 1/2 Fighter Squadron was on a routine patrol along the Danube when he and his wingman violated standing orders and crossed into Czechoslovakian airspace in their CR.32s. Approaching the Érsekújvár airfield, they attacked and shot down a Czech Letov Š-328. The Letov crashed and burned, killing the observer.[71] Pongrácz's action was controversial among other Hungarian pilots. According to the memoirs of Mátyás Pirity, a CR.32 pilot in the 1/1 Fighter Squadron, Pongrácz's victim was a trainer in the landing circuit. Because of that, Pirity recalled, "Opinion was divided regarding this feat of arms, but the majority of pilots condemned both the effect of the action and the downing of an unarmed training airplane."[72] Pongrácz was ultimately cleared of wrongdoing by a military tribunal. He was awarded the Bronze Medal for his "energetic and forceful activity that greatly helped to decrease the Czech intrusions" during the period from September 23 to November 25. The actual downing of the Letov was not mentioned in his citation, but no other pilots received decorations for patrols in this time.[73] Despite the award, his fighter group commander, Major János Schwager, regarded the incident as a failure of flight discipline.[74]

This incident, although inconsequential in light of the carnage to come, is nonetheless intriguing. Not only was it the first air-to-air victory in two decades for the newly acknowledged Hungarian air force, but it also parallels Hungary's conduct of foreign policy in the years immediately preceding the Second World War. Like Lieutenant Pongrácz (whose political views are unknown), the radical rightists were aggressive in pursuit of their adversaries, and were willing to overstep the bounds established by higher authorities. Much of Hungary's political center reacted to these tactics as did Mátyás Pirity and his squadron mates: not opposed to the action in principle, but put off by the whiff of dishonor in the particular circumstances. When tried by the tribunal of public opinion, however, the radicals' results (among them the Vienna Awards) won acclaim. The regent nonetheless came to distrust them, and, as Schwager did to Pongrácz, sought to shunt them away as soon as possible.

But first the regent would lead the ceremonial reinvestment of the Felvidék. It was a time of national celebration, capped by the procession into Kassa on November 11. Admiral Horthy entered Kassa astride his white horse, just as he had entered Budapest in 1919. This time he was followed by members of the cabinet and the entire legislature. Thousands turned out to cheer the event, including Lord Rothermere, Hungary's favorite foreign son. Parliament incorporated the awarded areas back into the country the following day.[75] The problem of Ruthenia remained, and Hungary determined to launch an attack, preferably with Polish assistance and Axis approval, as soon as one week hence. Poland, however, declined to offer regular troops for the endeavor, and Italy deemed Ruthenia outside its area of interest. Berlin was strongly opposed, and even warned Budapest that such an act risked invalidating the First Vienna Award. Horthy was unwilling to take the step alone, and so the plan was shelved and troops demobilized. There were, as always, political consequences of the debacle. Imrédy offered his resignation, but Horthy declined to accept it, fearing the dismissal of a prime minister well liked in Berlin would further strain relations with Germany. Instead, he asked Kánya to go, and appointed Kánya's deputy István Csáky, held in higher esteem by the Germans, in his place.[76] The aborted occupation of Ruthenia was a diplomatic disaster for Hungary, and also had unfortunate domestic consequences, weakening the conservative dissidents and pushing Imrédy, formerly thought to have a pro-Western orientation, closer to the Nazis.

The most obvious result of Imrédy's increasing fidelity to the Nazi line was his introduction in parliament of the second anti-Jewish law. This measure drew the definition of a Jew more broadly than the earlier bill, and further reduced the percentages of Jews

permitted in the professions. Ironically, Imrédy's political opponents used his own antisemitic law to force him out, by producing
documents unearthed in Bohemia purporting to show that one of
his great-grandmothers was Jewish. Horthy was therefore able to
secure Imrédy's resignation on grounds that Berlin could not fault.
The regent appointed Count Pál Teleki to the premiership on February 16, 1939.[77]

Teleki was Hungary's fifth prime minister in the eight years
since the end of Bethlen's decade of consolidation. Like Darányi
and Imrédy before him, Teleki owed his appointment in part to
Horthy's hope that he could maintain the country's free hand in
foreign affairs. The esteemed geographer and chief Scout ultimately
fared no better in this regard than did his predecessors, though his
dramatic suicide following Hungary's 1941 decision to assist the
German invasion of Yugoslavia did much to salvage his political
reputation. In early 1939, Teleki left Csáky in place at the Foreign
Ministry, and did not repudiate Imrédy's announcement that Hungary would join the Anti-Comintern Pact. Nor did he dismiss parliament or replace the Imrédyists in the government. Against the
Arrow Cross, however, Teleki took decisive action, dissolving the
party, arresting some of its leaders, and confiscating its records and
assets.[78] He continued to press Hungary's claims on Ruthenia, adding economic and geopolitical rationales to what he considered
flimsy ethnic justifications. As it became more evident that a German invasion of Czechoslovakia was looming, Teleki was determined that Hungary would be the first to occupy Ruthenia. Matters
came to a head one month into his tenure. On March 12, Hitler
informed Hungary's minister to Berlin Sztójay that the operation
was imminent, and that Hungary would have twenty-four hours
after it began to settle its case in Ruthenia. Hungary agreed to provide a pretext for the invasion, which was planned for March 18. The
Slovakian declaration of independence on March 14 rushed events
ahead, and on March 15 Hungarian troops moved north into Ruthenia at the same time as the Wehrmacht headed toward Prague.[79]

The mobilization initiated by Budapest in March 1939 included
a new element: the independent Royal Hungarian Air Force
(Magyar Királyi Honvéd Légierő, MKHL). The MKHL was established on Admiral Horthy's orders as supreme warlord along
the lines agreed in October 1938. Effective January 1, 1939, the Defense Ministry's Aviation Group was disbanded, and its responsi-
bilities assumed by the LÜH and the MKHL headquarters commanded by László Háry, recently promoted to full colonel. This
new Lepság was subordinate only to the Defense Ministry, "operating independently and autonomously" (*függetlenül, önállóan
működik*) of the HFP and VKF.[80] This arrangement meant that the
HFP must seek permission from the Lepság on matters of air-
ground cooperation—a situation that surely would limit the "frittering away" of air power feared by Szentnémedy. The Lepság also
gained its own budget, officer promotion and assignment authority,
and discretion in building airfields. General Károly Bartha, who
replaced Rátz in November as defense minister, retained control
over the deployment of MKHL squadrons, and insisted that Háry
consult the ministry on organizational matters.[81]

Not everyone was pleased by this initiative. The VKF went on
the record with its dissent on January 5. It argued that the HFP
must have a direct relationship to the LÜH director, or else the
office of aviation inspector would be superfluous. Regarding the
LÜH, the VKF also contended that the role of air force commander
was a sufficient challenge in itself, and therefore the direction of
civilian aviation should be separate from the Lepság. Furthermore,
to ensure military readiness, there should be an aviation section
established within the VKF, and a VKF officer should head the
Lepság's mobilization division.[82] These objections of the VKF were
not sufficient to overturn the regent's decision, but they did signal
the its displeasure with the organizational change.

With such short notice, the LHT had to execute the Ruthenian
operation with only the forces already positioned near Upper Hungary. General Ferenc Szombathelyi's Carpathian Group consisted

of VIII Corps (three brigades) and the Rapid Corps (one cavalry, one bicycle, and one motorized brigade). Lepság assembled a provisional Aviation Group under the command of Lieutenant Colonel Sándor Illy, a future commandant of the Kassa aviation academy and MKHL general. Illy's group was composed of Ju 86s from 2/II and 3/II Bomber Groups, and the three CR.32 squadrons of 1/I Fighter Group. He 70s from the 1st Independent Long-Range Reconnaissance Group at Kecskemét and Budaőrs also participated in the action, as did the He 46s from the 6th and 7th Short-Range Reconnaissance Squadrons at Debrecen, Miskolc, and their forward operating base at Ungvár. The Carpathian Group met little organized resistance and advanced quickly. On the March 16, He 46s attacked Czechoslovak troop formations, and the following afternoon, a pair of Ju 86s bombed defensive positions from high altitude. In both cases, Hungarian ground forces reported that the raids were successful. Szombathelyi's troops reached the Polish border on March 17, suffering only 220 casualties in the attack. The northern border secured, Szombathelyi turned his attention to the west. Hungary had recognized the new Slovakian state, but its eastern boundary was not yet agreed, and Budapest was eager to seize as much territory as possible before Berlin intervened. There were compelling strategic reasons as well, since the critical railway link with Poland lay near the frontier claimed by Slovakia and could be subjected to harassing attacks. On March 23, the VKF ordered the Carpathian Group to advance westward up the Ung Valley.[83]

Slovak reconnaissance aircraft spotted the Hungarian advance at midday. Several flights of Letov Š-328s and Avia B.534 fighters were launched from airfields south of Kassa with orders to attack Szombathelyi's force. Two B.534s from 45 Squadron were shot down by the machine gun detachment of the Hungarian 9th Light Artillery Regiment, and seven other Slovak airplanes were damaged in action on March 23. The Slovak attacks killed one Honvéd soldier. MKHL air activity on March 23 was limited to a few reconnaissance sorties. The following day, the Slovaks again sent three-ship formations of Avias and Letovs on low-altitude attack sorties. Three B.534s from 49 Squadron met three CR.32s of the 1/1 Fighter Squadron over the town of Szobránc. The Hungarians from the "Íjász" (Archer) squadron, led by Lieutenant Aladár Negró, had been scrambled from Ungvár airfield after ground observers reported the inbound Slovak aircraft. Negró and one of his wingmen, Sergeant Sándor Szoják, each scored a victory against the Slovak B.534s. Another Avia was downed by Hungarian AAA. Later in the day, the entire Íjász squadron was airborne with its commander, Lieutenant Béla Csekme, in the lead. They spotted and attacked three Š-328s that had just completed an attack against a Hungarian battery. The CR.32 pilots destroyed two of the Letovs in that engagement, and subsequently downed three more Avias. Negró and Szoják claimed their second victories of the day. The Slovak air force lost eight airplanes in combat on March 24, although their attacks were more effective than the day before, resulting in fifteen Honvéd deaths.[84] No MKHL fighters were lost to enemy action, but one CR.32 was shot down by Hungarian AAA. The pilot, Sergeant Árpád Kertész of 1/1 Squadron, bailed out without injury.[85]

The Hungarian bomber force conducted its first raid on March 24. Lepság ordered the 2/II and 3/II Bomber Groups to strike the airfield at Igló (Spišská Nová Ves), from which the Slovak attacks had been launched. The attack was a rushed affair, since the order arrived at 14:55, and the sun would set just three hours later. The MKHL's Ju 86s were not equipped, nor their crews trained, for night-time operations. Major Elemér Kovács, the commander of 3/II Bomber Group, was to lead the attack, and he placed himself in a gunner's position in the fourth bomber. Fourteen Ju 86s, six from 3/4 and eight from 3/5 Squadron, planned to attack in a column of three-ship V formations, each aircraft bearing 1,500 pounds of fragmentation bombs along with sixty-four 2-pound incendiaries. The bombers expected to rally with 2/II's Ju 86s over Miskolc and join the escorting CR.32s before proceeding on to Igló. The plan

Figure 6.4. Fiat's CR.32 (this one in RA colors) was the MKHL's primary fighter during the 1939 war with Slovakia. Photo: Fortepan/Zoltán Hídvégi.

was simple, but adequate for a first large mission against an unsophisticated opponent. Unfortunately, the strike group ran into difficulties on the ground that were compounded by errors in flight. The first flight of Ju 86s took off late from Debrecen due to the heavy bomb load causing the aircraft to sink into the mud. When the lead pilot, Lieutenant Edvin Joubert, caught up with the rest of the force over Miskolc, he could not reach them over the radio. Joubert assumed the formation would follow his flight, and he promptly flew into clouds. The other bombers did not trail the mission commander's section, which was just as well, since Joubert got disoriented in the clouds and exited them heading south instead of north. Finding a huddle of buildings and a clearing, Joubert's crew dropped its load. His wingman, Lieutenant Győző Lévay, recognized the area as being inside Hungary, and did not release his weapons. The flight made its way back to Debrecen and landed. One of the 3/5 Squadron airplanes experienced an engine failure and turned back. Another aircraft accidentally dropped its bombs en route to the target while still over Hungary. Captain Gyula Vághelyi led the remaining ten bombers (including the one with the empty bomb bay) north at 3,000 feet. They reached the target at 16:45 and dropped their bombs without receiving effective AAA fire. The attack damaged twelve Slovak aircraft and killed thirteen—five soldiers and eight civilians. One Avia fighter took off after the attack, but was unable to catch the southbound Ju 86s. None of the aircraft from 2/II Bomber Group participated. Conflicting information about bomb loads had delayed their take off from Szombathely, and on a refueling stop at Mátyásföld they were informed that the mission had been completed. There was little air activity on March 25, and the following day Hungary and Slovakia signed an armistice.[86]

The public response to the MKHL's initial foray into combat operations was enthusiastic. Admiral Horthy authorized a special order on March 25 that included the following:

> On 24 March 1939, elements of our fighter and bomber units were ordered into combat for the first time. Our fighter forces annihilated the enemy air elements; our bombers performed their task—according to reports received so far—with 'horrible' effect. They achieved these results without any personnel or material losses despite the enemy's efforts.
>
> The Regent acknowledges the news of these events with great pride and pleasure, because they confirm to him our young Air Force's outstanding quality.[87]

Magyar Szárnyak carried a full-page in-house advertisement that included the text of the telegraph agency's March 25 report from the front above a poster-style celebration of "the young Hungarian Air Force's glorious feats of arms."[88] The Air Defense League's magazine *Riadó!*, in keeping with its mission, focused on the damage done to Ungvár as a result of the Slovak attacks on March 23.[89] Colonel Szentnémedy called March 24 "Hungarian military aviation's day of triumph," and noted "the military actions attracted the attention of the whole world."

Italian magazines recounted in detail the events on the Hungarian-Slovak border and the success of Hungarian fliers. *Stampa*'s Budapest correspondent declared that the Hungarian aviators' first serious appearance was splendid, and they performed brilliantly.

The *Messagero* and *Corriera della Sera* stated the battle that was played out beside Ungvár showed the Hungarian fliers to great advantage.

Almost all the English papers published the news agencies' reports about the Slovakian fighting. Reuters reported: "It was a time of great jubilation in Hungary because of the striking success of the Hungarian defense fighters." On the editorial pages they write with great appreciation about the performance of the Hungarian fliers. The German papers are the same.

The Hungarian and Slovak battles were covered in detail in *Der Bund* and the *Journal de Genéve*. The *Neue Zürcher Zeitung* stressed the Hungarian pilots' daring fights. According to the article: "Such was the drive with which the Hungarian fliers beat back the Slovak attacks that the Honvédség increased its prestige in the most significant way."

. . . We can see that in the air we are no longer weak, and we can see the Hungarian aviators wing triumphantly in the spring sky, without opposition, with the wonder and acknowledgment of the whole world, accompanying our Honvéd as they take possession of the ancient borders![90]

Szentnémedy viewed the actions as the realization of Horthy's prophecy given a year earlier: "We were a riding nation; we will become a flying nation."[91] Eighteen fighter pilots and ten bomber crews were awarded medals for their deeds. Aladár Negró and Sándor Szoják received the title *vitéz* for their double victories, and in keeping with a time-honored martial tradition, the men changed their surnames to Szobránczy and Szobránci, reflecting the location of their triumphs.[92]

The official assessment of the operation had quite a different tone. The HFP concluded that the Igló attack was characterized by "lax readiness and lack of discipline."[93] Its report noted that the 3/II strike force took off without permission, failed to notice its command airplane's navigational error, and suffered from deficiencies in reading maps and operating radio equipment. The panel recommended the MKHL's training practices be modified to standardize the placement of the mission commander in the formation (Major Kovács, riding in the gunner's compartment with a faulty microphone, could not communicate inside or outside the airplane), and to clarify the definitions of squadron readiness. The MKHL also established more stringent requirements for claiming aerial victories (the Hungarian fighter pilots claimed nine kills, but only seven Slovak fighters were lost in air-to-air combat).[94] Colonel Háry took administrative and judicial action against a trio of MKHL officers. He removed Kovács from command of the 3/II Bomber Group, and confined Lieutenant Joubert and Warrant Officer Elsner, the pilot and navigator who mistakenly bombed the Hungarian hamlet, to garrison custody for fifteen days.[95]

This brief conflict is worthy of extensive consideration because it was, as two authors named their studies, the "baptism of fire" for the MKHL. The existence of the force had only been acknowledged for eight months, and it had been independent from the army for just three months. It was Hungary's first aerial combat, other than Pongrácz's encounter in November 1938, since the Czechoslovak-Romanian interventions in 1919. An entire generation of Hungarian airmen had served without combat experience, and indeed with little sophisticated or large-scale tactical training. These factors give this single day's battle a special significance. In the years that followed, there would be hundreds of days on which the MKHL would be engaged in more numerous and more desperate fights than it experienced on March 24, 1939. But those days would come in a different context, against a different enemy, and with a much higher cost. The short Slovak war was fought in direct support of the country's primary foreign policy objective—regaining territory lost at Trianon—and its air battles, conducted by the arm explicitly proscribed by the treaty, were doubly relished by revisionists.

The defeat of Slovakia cannot, however, be seen as a vindication of the 1935 objective "to be able to act as a serious opponent against at least one of the Little Entente states." The rump Slovak air service, although it retained frontline airplanes with the Czechoslo-

vakia roundels, was patched together hurriedly and suffered particularly from a lack of experienced pilots. Fewer than 5 per cent of
the officers of the Czechoslovakian armed forces were ethnic Slovaks, and hardly any Czech pilots remained to serve in the Slovak
air force.[96] The MKHL faced only two Slovak fighter squadrons;
one-tenth of the number Szentnémedy had attributed to Prague in
1938.[97] It enjoyed a local numerical superiority that would not have
existed in a fight with Czechoslovakia before the German dis-
memberment. On the other hand, Hungarian fighter pilots in Fiat
CR.32s completely dominated the Slovaks flying Avia B.534s, in
spite of the Avia boasting better performance and heavier armament than the Italian machine.

The MKHL's lopsided victory in older and less capable airplanes made Hungarian claims of "glorious feats of arms" seem not
entirely improbable. It must be noted, however, that an air defense
scramble is a relatively simple maneuver that rewards individual
initiative and skill, while a planned multigroup bomber attack
requires a more sophisticated organization. Fighter aircraft are
simpler to maintain and arm (one engine, one type of primary
weapon), and defensive air patrol is essentially reactionary and
requires little premission preparation. Multiengine bombers are
more demanding to prepare for flight (more engines, multiple types
of bombs to load in addition to the defensive armament), and the
mission execution requires more preflight planning.

Satisfaction with the airplanes themselves reflected that dynamic. The MKHL was pleased with the CR.32s' performance, and
looked forward to the impending arrival of the newer Fiat CR.42s
in the summer. It also was happy to take delivery in 1940 of thirty-
six more CR.32s formerly of the Austrian air force for which the
Luftwaffe could find no use. Even the Ju 86, which Háry and Horthy maligned in October 1938, acquitted itself reasonably well. Two
Junkers aborted the mission for mechanical problems, probably
due to malfunctioning spark plugs. The other difficulties encountered by the strike force could be traced to poor procedures and

insufficient training. Captain Dénes Eszenyi, the commander of the squadron to which seven of the nine effective Igló bombers belonged, offered in *MKSz* concrete training techniques for all the duty positions in the Ju 86: gunner, radio operator, navigator, and pilot.[98] The MKHL would wait two years for another test of its own bombing prowess, but in September 1939, Hungarian airmen watched closely the Luftwaffe's devastating air campaign in Poland.

In the spring of 1939, the sine wave of Hungarian foreign policy brought the country closer to Germany. In addition to joining the Anti-Comintern Pact in February and accepting the German-brokered First Vienna Award in March, Hungary left the League of Nations in April. Csáky and Teleki accepted Axis leadership and promised to follow the Axis line, except regarding a possible German action against Poland. They delivered this message in person to Rome in April, and again to both Axis capitals via letter in July. Hungary's refusal to facilitate a German invasion of Poland caused another rift in the Berlin-Budapest relationship. It left the Italians merely "disappointed"; the Germans were furious.[99] They froze armament deliveries and refused to discuss future purchases. Under pressure from Ribbentrop, Csáky relented and asked that the letter renouncing force against Poland be considered withdrawn.[100] Hungarian opinion turned strongly against Germany, as Csáky relayed to Ciano on August 18. "Ninety-five per cent of the Hungarian people hate the Germans," Csáky asserted, before repeating the regent's characterization of them as "buffoons and brigands."[101] Then came word of the German-Soviet Non-Aggression Pact. Nothing could have hardened Hungarian attitudes more. The government was determined to maintain its common border with Poland and offer Germany no assistance. Teleki sent a private message to London to this effect. With the Soviet Union's cooperation assured, Hitler did not feel the need to coerce Hungary in the matter, and therefore Teleki's claim that Hungarian troops would resist German advances went untested.[102]

Riadó! covered in photographs and print the devastating effect of the German combined-arms assault on Poland. The magazine even used the term "lightning war" (*villámháború*) to describe the tactic, following the example of the German press in coining the word *Blitzkrieg*, a word not seen in Luftwaffe doctrine. The pictures showed evidence of indiscriminate city bombing—Wehrmacht troops marching through Polish streets flanked by the charred walls of hollow buildings—as well as the results of highly accurate tactical strikes: an armored train destroyed by a bomb dropped expertly between two rail lines. Its correspondent acknowledged that the Luftwaffe had many advantages, including good weather, accommodating terrain, and a numerical edge. Those were external conditions, he contended, and did not account for the internal factors that contributed to the victory, such as "excellent leadership, a highly offensive-minded air fleet, and carefully produced aviation material, all the result of years of work."

> The fact is, the air superiority quickly established by the German air force . . . made possible the successful realization of the German leaders' numerous large-scale strategic conceptions, and therefore brought the victory. This successful air campaign proved that what the Italian general Douhet and the German field marshal Göring had proclaimed in theory, and what had been demonstrated in the dozens of military and civil-military clashes since the World War, was in fact true: the air force has the capability to decide wars (*a légi haderő a háború eldöntésére képes*).[103]

That Blitzkrieg was offered as an example of Douhet's wisdom shows how the understanding of the Italian's thought had expanded to encompass any operational concept that included a significant role for air power. Douhet himself rejected the close air-ground cooperation that defined German doctrine in Poland. A Douhetian armed force would have had none of the potent German armor, and its air campaign would have seen Warsaw's civilian population as the critical target. The Luftwaffe, in contrast, aimed first to destroy the Polish air force while it was still on the ground, before turning its attention to the rail network and then Polish army forces in the field.[104] Hungarian airmen were drifting away from strict Douhetism without losing any faith in air power's effectiveness. This shift was evident in a March 1940 *MKSz* article by a MKHL fighter pilot who discounted the idea of an independent air war, asserting instead that the air force was "the ground force's most decisive instrument."[105] Although this article did not specifically mention the defeat of Poland, the success of the German combined-arms campaign there was the best example of air power used to decisive effect in conjunction with the land component. The seamless cooperation (as it appeared to observers) between Wehrmacht and Luftwaffe could have made greater operational control of the MKHL by the VKF both more desirable to the VKF officers, and less alarming to Hungarian airmen.

The Polish armed forces in exile after 1939, including the Eagle Squadrons that contributed to victory in the Battle of Britain, owed their existence to the common Hungarian-Polish border established in the spring Ruthenian campaign, and to Hungarian obstinacy in keeping that border open in face of German pressure.[106] From September 17, Hungary allowed Poles into Ruthenia to escape German and Soviet troops. Some 140,000 refugees, nearly all soldiers, entered Hungary in this manner, and by June 1940, over 100,000 had made their way to Britain and France to serve in Western armies.[107]

Once Poland's fate was sealed, Horthy, Teleki, and Csáky tried to patch things up with Hitler. A war with Romania seemed ever more likely, and Budapest was eager for the resumption of German arms deliveries. The MKHL was especially keen to get its hands on the He 111 and Ju 87 bombers ordered earlier in the year. Both had performed very well in Poland, and they would fill a critical need in the Hungarian bomber force. The first examples arrived only in mid-1940.[108] The winter of 1939/1940 was rife with rumors of Soviet plans to invade Bessarabia and German plans to occupy the Romanian oil fields. Neither occurred, but they kept Hungarian states-

men and the VKF busy contemplating different schemes to secure
Hungary's flanks and achieve its revisionist objectives. Following
the rout of France, the long-standing view among Hungarian con-
servatives that Britain would ultimately carry the day began to
wane. Teleki felt that the matter of Transylvania should be settled
before the war ended, and it looked as though the end could be in
sight. So when the Soviet Union demanded in late June 1940 that
Romania cede to it Bessarabia and Bukovina, the LHT ordered a
general mobilization, with the intention of insisting on the satisfaction of Hungary's claims.[109] After the June 27 mobilization, the
Lepság ordered forward deployment on July 2, and by July 6 the
movement was complete. On July 9, the 1st Aviation Brigade's chief
of staff received the task order for attacks against Romania and the
Soviet Union, but last-minute German intervention canceled the
strikes. On July 12, the units received permission to send half of
their enlisted personnel on leave, and three days later the deployed
squadrons were ordered to return to their home bases.[110] The air
force continued to operate and train near the frontiers, however,
which gave a Romanian pilot the opportunity to repeat László Pongrácz's exploit. On August 27, a Ca.135 returning to Debrecen after
a training sortie was attacked by a Romanian He 112 (the RLM
released twenty-four of the type to Bucharest, although only three
preproduction models ever reached Hungary) and forced to land.
The next day, Captain János Gyenes tried to avenge the attack by
bombing the Szatmárnémeti airfield in a WM 21. This incident,
Teleki wrote to Horthy, "attested to the fliers' lack of discipline,"
and was "extraordinarily awkward for the Hungarian government's
promise to keep the peace." Horthy agreed that "a single spark
would have been enough for hostilities to flare up."[111]

Hitler called Teleki and Csáky to Munich, where he warned
them openly not to attack Romania. Instead, he promised to bring
the Romanians to the bargaining table to settle the territorial dispute. The Führer took a renewed interest in resolving the Transylvanian problem after he decided to invade the Soviet Union. To

execute such an attack, Germany needed Hungarian railways and Romanian oil, and it did not want to have to fight either country in order to get them. Therefore a negotiated settlement was in the German interest. After bilateral talks ended in frustration, Ribbentrop and Ciano again dictated the terms in Vienna. On August 30 they were announced. Hungary received 17,000 square miles of territory and 2.5 million inhabitants, of whom nearly a million were Romanian. Almost 400,000 ethnic Hungarians remained in Romania. In return for what Teleki viewed as a poor deal, Hungary granted special recognition to the Volksbund der Deutschen in Ungarn (National Organization of Germans in Hungary), gave Germany additional economic concessions, and promised to pass certain internal measures. Among those measures were the release of Arrow Cross leader Ferenc Szálasi and the introduction of a third anti-Jewish law. Hungary acceded to the Tripartite Pact, which recognized the dominance of Italy and Germany in Europe and of Japan in Asia. It also agreed to the transport of German troops across Hungary into Romania, a concession that expanded until the Hungarian railways were essentially a part of the German military transportation network.[112] These costs were not readily apparent to the Hungarian people (except those Jews directly affected), and they celebrated the Second Vienna Award as they had the First. Admiral Horthy led the parade into Nagyvárad on his charger to the delight of Magyar crowds, armored trains were draped in flowers, and flights of MKHL aircraft turned overhead.[113] It was, according to *Magyar Szárnyak*, "the end of the Trianon captivity."[114]

The mobilization also signaled the end of the Háry era for the MKHL. The VKF had opposed air force independence from the beginning, and László Háry, with his loyal following of MKHL officers and ability to influence Horthy, personified that organizational autonomy. Háry had rightly pointed out to Horthy in 1938 the multitude of problems facing the air service, and had suggested to the regent that airmen, if given the freedom, could solve them. That had not proved to be the case. Recruitment was still too low, airplanes too few, accident rates too high, and combat readiness too shaky. Háry and his staff had not caused any of these problems, to be sure, but neither had they corrected them as decisively as he had led the regent to expect. The VKF seized on the MKHL's shortcomings during the July mobilization to undermine confidence in the organization. Air units had arrived at their wartime bases quickly, but they were not prepared to execute the VKF's plan to reduce Romanian fortresses.[115] The force was still plagued with technical troubles. The newly arrived Ca.135s could fly, but their bomb racks and bombsights were faulty; the short range of the Ju 86s meant they could not reach their intended targets deep in Transylvania; and the CR.42s could not have escorted them that far in any case.[116] The MKHL therefore had no real offensive capability: the only bombers that could get to the VKF's designated targets could not carry, or aim, bombs. In the days that followed this discouraging report, it also seemed that the MKHL had very little defensive capability, since one of its bombers was forced down inside the country, and was ill disciplined as well. With the prospects of the MKHL appearing rather grim, the VKF offered a proposal to bring it back under the control of the army and VKF. The air force, it concluded, was "struggling with an internal crisis that showed its leaders could not handle independence."[117] Chief of Staff Henrik Werth, originally a supporter of the autonomous air force, proposed to combine the MKHL with the air defense and civil defense functions under a reinstituted Defense Ministry Aviation Group. Horthy lost confidence in Háry, and on December 24 the regent removed him from the Lepság. Waldemár Kenese, formerly the inspector general, was brought out of retirement to head the MKHL.[118] Kenese acted straight away to reduce flying accidents—by stopping all training flights.[119] This had the immediate and obvious effect of lowering the loss rate, but it also substantially decreased the proficiency of MKHL pilots, a serious problem but one less apparent and easier to ignore.

As the year 1940 came to a close, Hungarian airmen had cause to worry for their service. In less than two years, it had gone from a clandestine branch of the army to an independent and modernizing force, and had played a dramatic role in a national triumph. But its leaders had been overly zealous in promoting the new arm, and the MKHL's failure to address satisfactorily a range of equipment, training, and operational errors had put independence at risk. Still, there was much to celebrate from a national perspective. Trianon had been overthrown. The Hungarian flag flew over the Felvidék and substantial parts of Transylvania. Czechoslovakia had been dissolved, Romania forced to cede some of its ill-gotten gain, and Yugoslavia neutralized through a treaty signed at year's end. The revisionist goals were almost completely fulfilled. And the price paid for these successes seemed quite low. Casualties in the border skirmishes were minimal, and Hungary had come out far ahead of its neighbors in each arbitration. The country had even maintained its honor by defying German requests for passage in its attack on Poland. This state of affairs was coming very quickly to an end. In the next few months, Hungary would violate its treaty with Yugoslavia, and embark on a disastrous war with the Soviet Union at Hitler's side. The MKHL, like the rest of the nation, would lose many times over. It would lose first its independence as an aerial arm to the Hungarian army, then its national character to the Luftwaffe, and finally its very existence at the hands of the Allies.

NOTES

1. Macartney, *October Fifteenth*, 1:105–106.
2. Gy. Juhász, *Hungarian Foreign Policy*, p. 128.
3. Ibid., pp. 130–131.
4. Quoted in Gooch, *Mussolini and His Generals*, pp. 320–321.
5. *DGFP*, No. 65.
6. *DIMK*, No. 120.
7. Quoted in Gy. Juhász, *Hungarian Foreign Policy*, p. 133.
8. Vidkun Quisling had not yet committed his perfidy in Norway at this time, but the term seems apt.

9. Quoted in Shirer, *Rise and Fall of the Third Reich*, p. 343. Entire paragraph based on Shirer's account (pp. 337–344). Hitler fulfilled his promise to Mussolini on September 12, 1943, when German paratroops rescued the Duce from imprisonment.

10. Cornelius, *Hungary in World War II*, p. 64.

11. Szinai and Szűcs, *Confidential Papers of Admiral Horthy*, pp. 96–100.

12. Ibid.

13. Macartney, *October Fifteenth*, 1:167, 174.

14. Sakmyster, "Army Officers and Foreign Policy in Interwar Hungary," p. 26.

15. Macartney, *October Fifteenth*, 1:214.

16. Gy. Juhász, *Hungarian Foreign Policy*, p. 132.

17. Macartney, *October Fifteenth*, 1:212–216.

18. Dombrády and Tóth, *A Magyar Királyi Honvédség*, p. 112.

19. Ránki and Tomaszewski, "Role of the State," 41–42.

20. Huba was the name of one of legendary seven Magyar chieftains. Earlier plans had been named after Árpád and Előd.

21. Ibid., pp. 111–112.

22. From this point onward, the air service adopted a confusing two-part designation scheme. When discussing a group in relation to its regiment, the designation is given as regiment (Arabic)/group (Roman). Squadrons followed a group/squadron format, but both numbers were Arabic. Thus the 1st Fighter Group of the 1st Flying Regiment would be 1/I, and its second squadron 1/2.

23. Holló, *A Galambtól a Griffmadárig*, p. 60.

24. *MKHL, 1938–1945*, p. 31.

25. Nagyváradi et al., *Fejezetek a repülés történetéből*, p. 183; vision restriction: *MKHL, 1938–1945*, p. 68.

26. *MKHL, 1938–1945*, p. 59.

27. He 112 export orders in the queue ahead of Hungary's did get filled: Spain received 19, Japan 12, and Romania eventually took over 24 former Luftwaffe machines.

28. Homze, *Arming the Luftwaffe*, pp. 148–54, 205–206, 159.

29. Sisa, "MKHL olaszországi beszerzései," p. 1059.

30. Winkler, "Magyar repülés története" (HL Tgy 3.327).

31. Clumsy: *MKHL, 1938–1945*, p. 55.

32. Sisa, "MKHL olaszországi beszerzései," pp. 1068–1074. Bristol armament: *MKHL, 1938–1945*, p. 73.

33. Szentnémedy, "Visszapillantás a légügy mult évi fejlődésére," p. 118.

34. MOL K. 589/8930-12. Emphasis in original.

35. Ibid.

36. *MKHL, 1938–1945*, pp. 82–83.

37. Vesztényi, "A magyar katonai repülés" (HL Tgy 2.787), p. IV/66.

38. Quoted in *MKHL, 1938–1945*, p. 83.

39. B. Juhász, "Olasz-Magyar vezénylések," 163; German program: Eby, *Hungary at War*, p. 153.

40. Vesztényi, "A magyar katonai repülés" (HL Tgy 2.787), p. IV/150.

41. Eby, *Hungary at War*, p. 154.

42. Kistelegdi, "A repülő akadémia története," p. 177.

43. MOL K. 589/8930-12.

44. Rada, *A Magyar Királyi Honvéd Ludovika Akadémia*, pp. 345–354.

45. MOL K. 589/8930-12.

46. Ibid.

47. Ibid.

48. *MKHL, 1938–1945*, pp. 78–84.

49. Macartney, *October Fifteenth*, 1:218–221, 274.

50. Quoted in *MKHL, 1938–1945*, p. 85.

51. Macartney, *October Fifteenth*, 1:234.

52. *DIMK*, No. 240.

53. Quoted in Macartney, *October Fifteenth*, 1:240. This paragraph follows Macartney's account (pp. 238–248), as do most descriptions in later works. In addition to the documentary evidence, Macartney made use of personal statements from many of the Hungarian diplomats involved, including his debrief of Horthy in detention in 1945, and is the most complete narrative of the events.

54. Quoted in Gy. Juhász, *Hungarian Foreign Policy*, p. 140.

55. *DIMK*, No. 298.

56. 40.028/Eln. B.-938 IX. 14, cited in Winkler, "Magyar repülés története" (HL Tgy 3.327).

57. Stenge, *Baptism of Fire*, p. vii.

58. Shirer, *Rise and Fall of the Third Reich*, p. 377.

59. Imrédy, quoted in Gy. Juhász, *Hungarian Foreign Policy*, p. 141.

60. Ibid., pp. 142–143.

61. Vesztényi, "A magyar katonai repülés" (HL Tgy 2.787), pp. IV/159–160.

62. Rakolczai, "Légvédelmi és légoltalmi gyakorlatok Budapesten," pp. 294–298.

63. Ibid., pp. 142–143.

64. Dombrády, *Hadsereg és politika Magyarországon*, pp. 10–11; foresters: Macartney, *October Fifteenth*, 1:279.

65. Vesztényi, "A magyar katonai repülés" (HL Tgy 2.787), pp. IV/160–162.

66. Gy. Juhász, *Hungarian Foreign Policy*, p. 143.

67. Szinai and Szűcs, *Confidential Papers of Admiral Horthy*, pp. 104–110.

68. Quoted in Macartney, *October Fifteenth*, 1:290.

69. Ibid., 1:293–302.

70. Cartledge, *Will to Survive*, p. 374, and Gy. Juhász, *Hungarian Foreign Policy*, p. 144.

71. Stenge, *Baptism of Fire*, p. vii.

72. Pirity, "Visszaemlékezés" (HL Tgy 3.707), p. 100.

73. Stenge, *Baptism of Fire*, p. viii.

74. Pirity, "Visszaemlékezés" (HL Tgy 3.707), p. 100. Pongrácz continued to be an aggressive and unpredictable pilot. One year after the Letov shootdown, during a similar crisis with Romania, he crossed the border in an apparent attempt to confront Romanian fighters. He was subsequently posted to the Aviation Research Institute (Repülő Kísérleti Intézet) as a test pilot, and after further incidents forced to retire in 1943. Stenge, p. 114.

75. Macartney, *October Fifteenth*, 1:305.

76. Gy. Juhász, *Hungarian Foreign Policy*, pp. 147–148.

77. Macartney, *October Fifteenth*, 1:323–328.

78. Ibid., pp. 330–331.

79. Gy. Juhász, *Hungarian Foreign Policy*, pp. 151–154.

80. Order quoted in *MKHL, 1938–1945*, p. 86.

81. Ibid.

82. Vesztényi, "A magyar katonai repülés" (HL Tgy 2.787), pp. V/5–6.

83. Stenge, *Baptism of Fire*, pp. 19–22. Casualty numbers: Macartney, *October Fifteenth*, 1:341.

84. Stenge, *Baptism of Fire*, pp. 40–44.

85. Pirity, "Visszaemlékezés" (HL Tgy 3.707), p. 109.

86. Stenge, *Baptism of Fire*, pp. 60–66; Gaal, "Baptism of Fire," pp. 42–44; Dénes, "Igló bombázása," pp. 5–7.

87. Cited in Stenge, *Baptism of Fire*, p. 84.

88. *Magyar Szárnyak*, no. 4 (1939), p. 25.

89. "Slovák légitámadás Ungvár és környéke ellen," *Riadó!* 3/4 (Apr. 1939), pp. 102–103.

90. Szentnémedy, "A magyar légierő első diadala," pp. 115–117.

91. Ibid., p. 118.

92. Stenge, *Baptism of Fire*, pp. 109, 85.

93. Vesztényi, "A magyar katonai repülés" (HL Tgy 2.787), pp. V/206–207.

94. Ibid.

95. Stenge, *Baptism of Fire*, p. 85.

96. 5%: ibid., p. 23.

97. Two fighter squadrons: ibid., p. 21: Szentnémedy, "Visszapillatás a légügyi múlt évi fejlődésére," p. 124.

98. D. Eszenyi, "Támpontok a bombázó hajózó személyzet kiképzéséhez," pp. 422–431.

99. Ciano, *Ciano's Diary, 1939–1943*, p. 118.

100. Macartney, *October Fifteenth*, 1:360.

101. Ciano, *Ciano's Diary*, p. 129.

102. Macartney, *October Fifteenth*, 1:360–363.

103. "Az első légi hadjárat," *Riado!* 3/12 (Nov. 15, 1939), p. 314.

104. Corum, *Luftwaffe*, pp. 272–273.

105. Csukás, "Az önálló légiháború," p. 706.

106. Kasparek, "Poland's 1938 Covert Operations in Ruthenia," p. 372.

107. Macartney, *October Fifteenth*, 1:368. Gy. Juhász suggests the refugees numbered only half of Macartney's claim.

108. *MKHL, 1938–1945*, p. 59.

109. Gy. Juhász, *Hungarian Foreign Policy*, pp. 172–173.

110. Nagyváradi et al., *Fejezetek a repülés történetéből*, p. 198.

111. Quoted in *MKHL, 1938–1945*, pp. 121–125.

112. Gy. Juhász, *Hungarian Foreign Policy*, pp. 172–176.

113. Photomontage: *Magyar Szárnyak* 3/9 (Sept. 15, 1940), pp. 15–16.

114. Ibid., p. 1.

115. Bonhardt et al., *A Magyar Királyi Honvédség fegyverzete*, p. 248.

116. *MKHL, 1938–1945*, p. 125.

117. Quoted in ibid., p. 96.

118. Nagyváradi et al., *Fejezetek a repülés történetéből*, p. 203; *MKHL, 1938–1945*, p. 96.

119. Bonhardt et al., *A Magyar Királyi Honvédség fegyverzete*, p. 248.

7

War: 1941–1945

IN 1941, HUNGARY WOULD PLACE ITSELF FIRMLY AND, AS it turned out, irrevocably and disastrously, in the Axis camp. Against the wishes of its prime minister, the Honvéd joined the German invasions of Yugoslavia and the Soviet Union. Participation in Hitler's campaigns was advocated by the VKF and embraced by much of the officer corps, who believed in the harmony of German and Hungarian interests, and in the invincibility of German arms. Admiral Horthy recognized the divergence of interests, and believed the Western Allies would prevail. But a combination of gratitude toward Germany for its support of Hungarian revisionism, hope for further territorial gains, fear of the consequences of nonparticipation, and hatred of communism led him to approve Hungary's involvement. The ruling class hoped that Hungary's upward trajectory would continue under Axis patronage. In fact, the country had reached its zenith. The period between the First and Second Vienna Awards represented the apex of Hungary's post-Trianon experience. From 1941, its freedom and prosperity would be curtailed; slowly and almost imperceptibly in the beginning, dramatically and devastatingly at the end.

In many respects, the MKHL was also on the decline by 1941. Although it would achieve its maximum lethality and effectiveness later, flying German airplanes under the Luftwaffe's direction, the institution had already reached its peak of prestige and influence.

The Hungarian air service of 1944 would be twice as large as the 1940 force in both men and machines, but by then its independence was substantially constrained, and Hungarian airmen had abandoned their expectation for the decisiveness of unrestricted air warfare. This diminution of the MKHL, in stature and ambition if not in size, began with the 1941 reorganization that found the air force once again under the control of an infantry general.

The Christmas 1940 replacement of Colonel László Háry by retired Major General Waldemár Kenese was only the opening gambit in the VKF's administrative war against the independent air force. On January 15, 1941, the Defense Ministry forwarded a VKF paper entitled "The unified air forces' guiding organization, and its relation to the Honvédség's centralized transformational arrangement." Behind the bureaucratic jargon was a proposal to strip the MKHL of its autonomy. Since January 1, 1939, the head of the LÜH and commander of the Lepság (Háry) had been subordinate only to the minister of defense, and the MKHL had been charged with "operating independently and autonomously."[1] The VKF proposed to create a Land Chief Department (Földi Főcsoportfőnökség) and an Air Chief Department (Légügyi Főcsoportfőnökség, LF) subordinated to a new position of deputy defense minister.[2] While this in theory would have maintained the air force as a branch equal to, but separate from the army, the reality was quite different. The LF would retain authority only for acquisition, while the VKF would exert administrative and operational control. With Háry out of the picture, and the ailing Kenese unable or unwilling to oppose the VKF, Horthy signed the order instituting this arrangement on February 14, 1941. General Sándor Győrffy-Bengyel, an infantry officer, was appointed deputy defense minister. The head of the LF was András Littay, also, astonishingly, a general of infantry.[3] Kenese himself gave way to Major General Béla Rákosi, an air defense artillery officer, on February 20. The VKF's victory over the MKHL was nearly complete. Not only had the VKF asserted operational command for itself, it had also managed to interpose two infantry officers between the senior Hungarian airman and the defense minister. Further personnel changes remained before the "spring cleaning" was finished. Three MKHL officers were removed from positions on the air staff, and Colonel Rezső Laborczfy was relieved as commander of the 1st Aviation Brigade. Meanwhile, an infantry colonel was appointed as Rákosi's deputy. In a move perhaps intended to end Hungarian Douhetism, Ferenc Szentnémedy was transferred from his position as chief of the air staff to be a department head within the LF. Colonel Géza Vörös, who had sparred with Szentnémedy in the pages of *MKSz* in 1932 and was most recently the chief of staff for the 2nd Infantry Division, became the chief of the air staff. These sweeping changes were characterized, not implausibly, by one historian who experienced them, as a "purge" (*tisztogatás*).[4]

The MKHL seems to have been the only European air service to have been resubjugated to land forces' control. Some air arms, such as the RAF, Armée de l'air, RA, and Luftwaffe, were organizationally independent, while others, as in Poland, had an air inspectorate with no staff or acquisition authority.[5] But the trend was always toward greater autonomy for the air forces. Why did the Hungarian air force alone lose its independence? The VKF's answer was straightforward: the MKHL staff was not capable of managing its own affairs satisfactorily. "The fact is," read one VKF document, "that the Air Force's two years of independence did not bring the expected outcome ... they did not have the necessary organization or material."[6] In fact, the outcome was precisely what the VKF expected, and indeed, what it wanted. The VKF had strongly opposed the creation of the independent air force in 1938, and had worked to undermine its autonomy since that time. It is not possible to determine how much of its opposition was based on a clear-eyed assessment of military effectiveness, and how much was merely defense of its bureaucratic prerogatives. The extent of the 1941 staff purge suggests the second rationale predominated. Even so, Hungarian airmen and senior defense leaders, including Horthy as supreme warlord, must bear most of the blame for the MKHL's organizational failure.

The airmen did not appreciate the degree to which their administrative muscles had atrophied in the two decades of secrecy. Just as István Petróczy had in 1923 underestimated the effect of the production ban on Hungarian airplane manufacturers, Háry and his supporters misjudged the difficulty of simultaneously enlarging, modernizing, and employing an air force. Háry correctly identified most of the air service's problems in his report to Horthy, and he convinced the regent that the solution was a unified service under an airman's command. When the problems persisted, Horthy's confidence in Háry wavered, as did his earlier conviction that only "aviation experts" could lead the air force. The regent did not lose faith in the air force as an operational tool of warfare, nor did he flag in his efforts to increase the MKHL's size and capability. But neither he nor Defense Minister Bartha defended the autonomy of the air force against the VKF's effort to reassert control over the MKHL. A more measured and less disruptive approach might have entailed replacing Háry with a more capable administrator and sprinkling experienced VKF officers throughout the MKHL to bring more coherence to the organization.

The Defense Ministry was not the only organ of Hungarian life facing chaos and intrigue early in 1941. For the Foreign Ministry, at least, most of the disorder was outside its walls. There was a new foreign minister: László Bárdossy, minister to Bucharest, was selected to replace Csáky after the latter died in January. Bárdossy had no natural affinity for Germany, but he believed Great Britain's relationship with the Little Entente to be inviolable, and he therefore did not share Count Teleki's faith that Hungary could reach an agreeable deal with London.[7] The newest article of Teleki's faith was the December 1940 Treaty of Eternal Friendship with Yugoslavia, a pact which he sought in part as a gesture of good will to the British. Ribbentrop approved, seeing the treaty as a way to coerce Belgrade into joining the Tripartite Pact. Teleki had also accepted a Soviet invitation to discuss a nonaggression treaty. Those talks led to a trade agreement and, as a goodwill gesture, the Soviets returned Hungarian battle flags seized by the tsar's armies in 1849. When Admiral Horthy got wind of the negotiations, he ordered them stopped, just as he had in 1925. Horthy did approve a plan in January to establish an émigré government in the event of a German occupation of Hungary. Count Bethlen would head the government in London, and Tibor Eckhardt would be its representative in the United States.[8]

On March 25, 1941, Yugoslavia caved in to German pressure and signed the Tripartite Pact. The following day a military coup overthrew the Cvetković government. The Yugoslav air force general Dušan Simović took his place as premier.[9] Hitler expanded his plan for the invasion of Greece to cover Yugoslavia as well. For this he counted on Hungarian cooperation, and dangled the prospect of territorial gain in front of the regent. Horthy responded gratefully, assuring Hitler that he felt himself "wholly and completely in unity with Germany." Horthy suggested that the new Yugoslav government must be under the influence of the Soviets, and that fact might provide a pretext to escape the terms of the December treaty.[10] The General Staffs immediately began consultations. Horthy briefed the Council of Ministers on March 28, and Teleki registered concern over the matter. Bárdossy tried to gauge possible reactions in London and Washington. On April 1, the LHT approved joining the German attack. Teleki offered the LHT three suitable legal rationales for Hungarian intervention: the requirement to stop anti-Magyar depredations; the disintegration of the Yugoslav state; or the breakdown of governance in territories claimed by Hungary. Reliable reports from the frontiers indicated that none of those conditions was being met. On April 2 came word from György Barcza, minister in London, that Britain would sever relations with Hungary if a German invasion were launched from its territory, and would declare war if Hungarian forces participated. Teleki received the telegram around 21:00, and was deeply distressed. His entire foreign policy had rested on the notion that Great Britain would understand Hungary's impossible situation, and indulge it until Budapest could extricate itself from Germany's grasp. This proved that his hope was an illusion. Sometime in the early morning of April 3, Teleki shot himself.[11] He left a letter addressed to the regent in which he reminded Horthy that the Yugoslav treaty had its origins in the regent's 1926 speech at Mohács.[12] Furthermore, Teleki wrote, "not a word about the trumped up atrocities is true. Not against the Hungarians, and not even against the Germans! We will become corpse robbers! The most foul people. I did not restrain you. I am guilty."[13] Winston Churchill later wrote that Teleki's suicide "was a sacrifice to absolve himself and his people from guilt in the German attack on Yugoslavia."[14] Perhaps so, but it made no discernible difference to Hungarian policy. When Britain's minister to Budapest, Owen O'Malley, called on Horthy to convey his condolences, Horthy informed him of Hungary's intention to reclaim the Délvidék (southern Hungary).[15]

General Werth ordered mobilization on April 4, the same day that German troops began flowing into Hungary. The MKHL's 1st Aviation Brigade was included in the order, as were all AAA elements of General Gorondy-Novák's Third Army. Six Hungarian fighter squadrons were sent to Kecskemét, Pécs, and Szeged, and three bomber squadrons to Hajdúböszörmény and Székesfehérvár.[16] The fighter squadrons flew exclusively Italian airplanes (two units retained their CR.32s; four had received the newer CR.42s), while the bombers were a near-even mix of Ca.135s and Ju 86s.[17] Since squadron strength had been standardized by this time at nine primary airplanes with three unit spares, the MKHL's mobilized striking force amounted to a hundred machines. This was dwarfed by the German air contingent, which numbered over 1,000 airplanes, to which were added almost 700 aircraft from the RA. Against the combined Axis forces, the Royal Yugoslav Air Force (Jugoslovensko Kraljevsko Ratno Vazduhoplovstvo, JKRV) was at an insurmountable disadvantage in quantity and quality. Only half of its 985 aircraft were frontline machines, and just 60 per cent of these were modern designs. With a small number of Hawker Hurricanes and Bf 109s, the JKRV would have outmatched the MKHL on its own, but the Yugoslavs posed no real threat to a German-Italian-Hungarian fleet of over 2,000 airplanes.[18]

German forces invaded Yugoslavia on April 6, while the Honvédség was still recalling personnel and preparing units for deployment. The war immediately made itself felt in Hungary. Yugoslav artillery shells fell inside the border, Luftwaffe fighters departed from southern Hungarian bases, and German bombers made forced landings inside the country. On the morning of April 6, Yugoslav observation airplanes patrolled the frontier. In the afternoon, the JKRV ordered a Blenheim from the 62nd Bomber Group on a long-range reconnaissance mission to the north. Hungarian air defense observers spotted the aircraft as it approached Csepel Island, and initiated Budapest's first actual air raid alert since the First World War. A flight of CR.42s from 1/3 Fighter Squadron scrambled to intercept the Yugoslav bomber, but could not reach its altitude before the Blenheim retreated south. Hungarian air defense officials subsequently put the entire country on a state of high alert against aerial attack. Belgrade had already suffered significant damage from five waves of Luftwaffe attacks, and the JKRV lost over a hundred airplanes to enemy action on the first day.[19]

The JKRV conducted its first raids against Hungarian targets on July 7. Two unescorted Blenheim bombers showed up with no warning (the air raid sirens sounded only as the first bombs hit) over Pécs at 10:30. Six bombs struck the airfield, causing significant damage and wounding some German soldiers and Hungarian civilians. An hour later, another pair of Blenheims attacked Pécs. This time the defense was ready, and both JKRV airplanes were destroyed—one by Hungarian AAA, the other by a Luftwaffe Bf 109. Around the same time, a larger force of eight Blenheims was approaching the Szeged airfield. The leading aircraft, carrying the squadron commander, fell to a German fighter, but the rest proceeded to Szeged. The aircraft were spotted from the ground, but were mistaken for returning Bf 110s, and so no alarm was raised. Bombs fell around the Szeged train station, and a railway bridge was damaged, but at the cost of another Blenheim shot down by Hungarian AAA. The next four days followed a similar pattern. Weak JKRV attacks caused light damage, but resulted in continuing attrition of Yugoslav aircraft to German pilots and Honvéd AAA batteries. Ten of the forty-five Yugoslavian combat losses occurred over Hungary.[20] In addition, one Magyar pilot of the JKRV defected to Hungary, landing his undamaged Blenheim at Érd.[21] MKHL fighters made few forays during the first few days of the conflict, in part because they were still mobilizing, but also because the overwhelming superiority of the Luftwaffe rendered them temporarily superfluous.

The Honvédség began offensive operations only on April 11, when its mobilization was nearly complete and after the declaration of an independent Croatia offered a suitable justification. MKHL fighter squadrons provided air defense and conducted low-level strafing attacks in support of the Third Army, which was advancing quickly against light resistance in the wake of the Wehrmacht. Honvéd casualties were low: only sixty-five Hungarian soldiers were killed in the operation.[22] Hungarian bomber pilots had no opportunity to redeem themselves after the Igló fiasco, as they were used primarily to drop leaflets encouraging cooperation with the Hungarian military administrators following the Honvéd into occupied areas. Although no MKHL aircraft were destroyed by enemy action, six (two CR.32s, two CR.42s, one WM 21, and one SM.75) were written off due to accidents.[23]

The last of these was a catastrophe for the fledgling Hungarian airborne infantry. In the morning of July 12, a Ju 86 from the Aviation Research Institute on a reconnaissance flight discovered an intact bridge spanning the Franz Josef Canal. The HFP decided to seize the bridge with paratroops before Yugoslavian forces could escape across it. *Vitéz* Major Árpád Bertalan's 1st Parachute Battalion received its orders around 16:00, and soon loaded its assault

Figure 7.1. The CR.42 eventually replaced its stablemate CR.32 in the MKHL. Here the 1/3 "Ace of Hearts" Squadron is being refueled. Courtesy of the Péter Zámbori Collection.

force in four Savoia-Marchetti SM.75 transport airplanes.[24] (Five twenty-four passenger SM.75s had been purchased from Italy in 1938, but the installation of the WM-14 engines had not gone smoothly, and MALERT rejected the type for commercial flights. The airplanes were retrofitted by WM for paradrop and air ambulance operations.)[25] The lead aircraft of the 1st Paratroop Transport Squadron took off from Veszprém at 17:40, piloted by the squadron commander, Captain Károly Kelemen. After climbing to 200 feet, the SM.75 lost speed, nosed over, and crashed. Twenty people were killed, including Major Bertalan, Captain Kelemen, and his crew, and fifteen paratroopers. Investigators laid the blame on a hydraulic elevator trim malfunction.[26]

Lieutenant Zoltan Kiss assumed command of the battalion and after some delay the remaining three SM.75s departed Veszprém at 18:50 with sixty soldiers on board. Bertalan had not fully briefed Kiss on the assignment, however, and the only mission map had been burned in the aircraft. In the confusion following the crash, the paratroopers were dropped fifteen miles from the Szenttamás

Figure 7.2. SM. 75 in MALERT livery, Grottaglie, Italy, 1939. This aircraft, converted to carry paratroops and numbered E.101, crashed on July 12, 1941. Photo: Fortepan/Zoltán Hídvégi.

bridge, and arrived there only the following day, transported by the 4th Motorized Battalion.[27] News of the disaster was withheld from the public for two weeks, when acknowledgment came in the form of a death announcement in *Magyar Szárnyak*.[28] Major Bertalan had created the Hungarian parachute battalion, and his paratroopers "loved him to the point of idolatry." The battalion survived his death, but Hungarian airborne infantry withered in his absence. The planned expansion to a regiment never occurred, and the highly motivated and skilled paratroopers were never used in a major airborne operation.[29]

Even with no combat losses and no major operational errors to match the Igló bombing, for the MKHL the Yugoslavian invasion was somewhat dispiriting. There had been little improvement since the previous autumn's mobilization against Romania. Major János Németh, the 1st Aviation Brigade chief of staff, pointed out in the after-action report submitted to General Werth that the VKF needed to give the air force more time to get its units ready for employment, particularly in the spring and fall, when unexpected weather could halt aircraft movements. The report highlighted other shortcomings, such as the poor performance of the ground-based air raid observers and the lack of suitable maps. It also reminded Werth of the problems with the aging CR.32s. On the other hand, according to Németh, Third Army headquarters were very pleased with the level of air support it received: "The Aviation Brigade's frictionless and fast employment (chiefly in the low-level attack role)—which demands close familiarity with, and quick integration into, the ground situation—would have been unimaginable if there had been two commands instead of one."[30] This validation of the MKHL's subordination must have been very pleasing to Werth and the VKF.

Debate about the air force structure continued through April and May 1941. A Lepság paper that made its way to Werth blamed the new arrangement for the "current chaotic situation" within the air force, and suggested that the only cure was a "new, healthy organization."[31] Colonel Géza Vörös, the new chief of the air staff, did not agree with that position, but nevertheless argued the need for unity of air force command. A single agency should be responsible for all aspects of military aviation, he wrote, although he did not insist, as had Háry and Szentnémedy, that the force should have complete operational independence. According to Vörös, the MKHL's earlier problems could be traced to a shortage of resources. A larger and better-trained air staff would provide the necessary oversight of air force training and employment. By the end of May, Werth, aware that an expansion of the German war was imminent and fearing that any more tinkering would only weaken the air force, shut down any further discussion of the topic. He collected the various proposals and scrawled on top of the document stack: "The current organization stays!"[32]

That organization had been fairly stable at the group level and below. The loss of air force independence in March had little effect on the flying squadrons, even if it had induced turbulence in the staff and senior commands. In May 1941, the MKHL comprised 8,500 personnel and 536 aircraft of all types.[33] The 390 combat airplanes were arranged in thirty-one squadrons: ten bomber, eight fighter, ten short-range, and two long-range reconnaissance, and a single parachute transport unit. With only seventy-one Ju 86s and Ca.135s available (roughly even in numbers due to new Caproni arrivals and Junkers attrition), the ten bomber squadrons were well under their programmed size of twelve airplanes per unit. The short-range reconnaissance squadrons had sufficient numbers of aircraft, although the fleet was widely varied. Its single most numerous type was the WM 21, followed by the He 46 and Ro.37. The fighter force was similarly mixed. Fiat CR.32s and CR.42s made up the majority of the 174 fighter aircraft in the operational and training squadrons, but there was also a new Italian addition, the Reggiane Re.2000.[34]

The Re.2000 "Falco" was not in the first rank of European fighter aircraft in 1941, but it was a significant improvement over the Fiat biplanes. The Falco was an all-metal, low-wing monoplane with an enclosed cockpit and retractable gear, and was powered by a 14-cylinder Piaggio engine that was nearly identical to the WM-14. Reggiane, a Caproni subsidiary, had delivered forty-five of its contracted seventy Re.2000s to the MKHL by the end of May 1941. Hungary also purchased the production license, and MÁVAG ultimately manufactured 185 "Héja" (Goshawk) aircraft from October 1942 to October 1944.[35] It was the MKHL's primary fighter in 1942.

On May 31, the day after he squashed the air force organization debates, Henrik Werth sent Prime Minister Bárdossy a memorandum outlining the various security, diplomatic, and economic rationales for joining the coming German invasion of the Soviet Union. It was his second letter to Bárdossy on the matter, and Werth was eager to "take up contact with the appropriate German military authorities, through military channels, with the object of preparing German-Hungarian military cooperation."[36] Werth,

pro-German by background, training, and outlook, was certain
that the Soviet Union would be defeated within weeks, and he
feared that if Hungary abstained, it risked losing its territorial gains
to Slovakia and Romania, both of which were committed to the
offensive. Bárdossy rejected Werth's arguments, and bitterly resented his interference in political matters.[37] Werth continued his
consultations with the German General Staff, whose chief, Franz
Halder, wanted to include Hungarian forces in the invasion in spite
of Hitler's instructions to the contrary. Hitler considered the
Hungarians unreliable troops who had no reason to join the invasion; Halder knew Army Group South's divisions were matched in
number by Red Army divisions, and he craved Romanian, Hungarian, Finnish, and Slovak participation.[38] On June 14, Werth sent
Bárdossy yet another memo. Germany was certain to attack in the
next ten days, Werth wrote, and he requested a general mobilization. Bárdossy called a meeting of the Council of Minsters, which
resolved unanimously to refrain from offering Hungarian participation in an invasion, while at the same time doing nothing to hinder
Germany's own action. The council authorized mobilization of
VIII Corps at Kassa and the frontier brigades, but did not approve
a wider call to the colors.[39]

Operation Barbarossa, to that time the largest military operation in history, commenced at 03:15 on June 22, 1941, with a massive
artillery bombardment followed by armored thrusts and air
strikes.[40] The German minister in Budapest, Otto von Erdmannsdorf, delivered Horthy a letter from Hitler which asked only that
Hungary secure its frontiers. The Ministerial Council decided to
sever diplomatic relations with Moscow in symbolic solidarity with
Berlin. Soviet minister of foreign affairs Vyacheslav Molotov
took the news well, and reminded Hungarian ambassador József
Kristóffy that the Soviet Union had no claims on Hungary, that it
was neutral in Hungary's territorial disputes with Romania, and
that the two countries' commercial relations were improving.
Kristóffy relayed Molotov's message to Bárdossy by telegram on

June 24. Bárdossy also received that day an unofficial request from the German General Staff, via Werth, that Hungary volunteer troops for Barbarossa. "It is essential now that the Hungarian military authorities should bring the political leaders in motion," Halder told his liaison officer, "that these should volunteer by themselves. Germany does not make demands, for which she would be compelled to pay, but she is grateful for any help, especially if given by motorized troops."[41] The Council of Ministers declined to take Halder's bait, and reaffirmed its June 14 position. During the meeting, the prime minister publicly railed against another intrusion of the VKF into political matters. Bárdossy informed Erdmannsdorf of the council's decision on June 25, emphasizing that a declaration of war was a matter for the government and the regent.[42] Bárdossy's moral courage lasted another thirty hours.

Just after 13:00 on June 26, three twin-engine aircraft circled over Kassa for a couple of minutes before dropping twenty-nine bombs on the city center. Thirty-two people were killed and sixty seriously wounded, and there was much material damage.[43] At almost the same time, a lone fighter strafed a passenger train near Rahó. The VKF received a report of the event, and Bartha and Werth immediately informed Horthy that "Soviet aircraft had bombed Kassa." Bárdossy also went to see the regent, and found him outraged. Horthy demanded the MKHL take revenge. Bárdossy convened the Council of Ministers at 14:30—one hour and twenty minutes after the attack. In that time, Bárdossy "made up his mind to a complete reversal of his whole policy": Hungary should enter the war now, on its own terms.[44] The VKF had long agitated for it, and the regent was demanding a reprisal for Kassa. Even the thought that the bombing could be a German provocation did not sway Bárdossy from his new course, because in his estimation such an act simply underscored Germany's determination to have Hungary in the war. Bárdossy announced the Soviet attack, declined to mention Kristóffy's message from Molotov, and polled the council.

All favored retaliation, and only Interior Minister Keresztes-Fischer argued for restraint. The prime minister summarized his points, took silence for assent, and dismissed the council. He then drafted a statement acknowledging that a state of war existed between the Soviet Union and Hungary, and ordered the MKHL to raid the USSR the next day.[45]

The identity of the Kassa bombers was in dispute on June 26, 1941, and remains a mystery. Bartha and Werth told Horthy they were Soviet aircraft, and Bárdossy told the Council of Ministers the same thing. A report to the OLP) around 15:30, however, called them "unknown."[46] Bárdossy himself was apparently not convinced the attackers were Soviets, but it did not alter his conviction that Hungary had to enter the war. "Since the General Staff, which is obviously in agreement with the Germans," he told the chief of the press bureau, "says they were Russian, and since the Regent believes it—*basta!*"[47] Late the following morning, the VFK released a communiqué that tried to reconcile the Soviet line with the German rumor. The bulletin was titled "Soviet airplanes attack Kassa" and read in part:

> Lieutenant Colonel Csejtey, the Kassa area air defense commander, Captain Krudy, and Lieutenant Csirke agreed on the following report:
> Because of adverse weather, the insignia of the attacking aircraft could not be recognized, but in spite of that, a yellow stripe similar to that worn by Hungarian and allied airplanes could be seen. The insignia probably were painted over. Concerning the aircraft type, Lieutenant Csirke reported they had 2–3 engines and strongly swept-back wings, and were in general similar to a Ju 52. In contrast to this, Captain Krudy reported that the attacking airplanes bore a resemblance to our own Savoia heavy bombers.[48]

This dispatch shows that the VKF was aware of the confusion over identification of the bombers, but otherwise is not very helpful. Csejtey first reported "unknown" aircraft, but he later recalled that he saw Soviet markings on the planes. Krudy's recollection also changed, as he later claimed the bombers looked like twin-engine Heinkels. Csirke denied making any report on the matter at all.[49]

The simplest explanation for the Kassa bombing is that it was the result of a Soviet error. But the presence of the yellow stripes points to Axis aircraft, which has given rise to many conspiracy theories. The most widely accepted holds that the bombing was a German provocation intended to get Hungary to enter the war. This theory appealed to surviving Hungarian leaders and communist historians, since it promised to absolve both Horthy and Stalin.[50] The theory relies on two premises: that the Soviet Union had no interest in attacking a Hungary whose neutrality it desired, and that the yellow stripes proved that German bombers executed the attack. The first of these is compelling, if not conclusive; the second is somewhat problematic. Molotov's conversation with Kristóffy indicated that Moscow hoped to keep Budapest out of the war as long as possible, which makes a deliberate decision to bomb a Hungarian city inexplicable. The lack of motive does not rule out a misjudged order from a low-level Red Air Force commander, or, even more probable, a simple mistake by a poorly trained aircrew. Soviet air forces did conduct raids against Germany's ally Romania on June 26, and a small-scale attack against one of its other allies—Slovakia—would not have been an unreasonable use of a flight of bombers.[51] Soviet sources seem to show such attacks were considered on June 25, and captured Soviet maps did not reflect the 1938 change in the border as a result of the First Vienna Award, which means that Red Air Force planners and crews may well have thought Kassa a Slovak town.[52] Against this notion stand the claims of Ádám Krudy, who testified in Bárdossy's trial that he informed the prime minister on the day of the attack the airplanes were German. Krudy, who is often identified as a colonel and the commander of the Kassa airfield, was actually at the time a captain flight instructor at the Horthy Aviation Academy, the only MKHL facility in Kassa's immediate area.[53] His testimony that he could

positively identify the aircraft on the basis of their yellow markings
is almost certainly not true. Other accounts agree that the bombers
attacked between 3,000 and 6,000 feet. The academy's weather report for June 26 indicated that visibility above 3,000 feet was poor
due to humidity.[54] That would have made the yellow stripes very
difficult to discern and, if the summer heat had by 13:00 burned
away the fog, the aircraft would have appeared as silhouettes against
a midday summer sky. The stripes might have been visible if the
airplanes had been lower than witnesses estimated, but even that
identification is less than conclusive. Paint is easily applied and
recovered. Soviet squadrons could have hurriedly applied such
markings in an attempt to avoid enemy fighters and ground fire.
The war diary of Major István Mocsáry, the commander of the 4th
Bomb Group, records seeing yellow stripes on Soviet aircraft.[55]
Krudy also claimed at other times to have identified the bombers
from the air as flying in a distinctly German formation, after he
took off from the academy airfield and chased them down. This is
also extremely unlikely, since the only aircraft on the field were
Bücker Bü 131 and Arado Ar 96 trainers, which were not capable of
overtaking bombers several thousand feet high.[56] Besides these
flaws, this story of German provocation leaves the crucial question
unanswered. Why would the Luftwaffe execute a treacherous attack against an allied country (a member of the Tripartite Pact, if
not a combatant against the Soviets) without bothering to disguise
its aircraft? Krudy's account of the event is not credible.[57]

The physical evidence that the weapons were of Soviet manufacture further undermines Krudy's story. One bomb did not deto-
nate and was exhumed. Photographs confirm that it matched the
size and shape of 220-pound Soviet devices then in use. In addition,
remains of some bomb fuses and suspension straps bearing Cyrillic
letters consistent with a Russian arms manufacturer were found in
the debris.[58] Critics have argued variously that the Soviet equipment was planted, or that the pictures were retouched, or that pro-
vocateurs dropped captured bombs from German airplanes. The

effort required to pull off a conspiracy that would account for un-exploded ordnance buried in a garden in Kassa, or to fake all of the photos that show the Russian origins of the bombs, exceeds other more credible explanations for the event. And József Ormay, a for-mer MKHL Ca.135 pilot and student of the bombing, recalls his own unit making good use of captured Soviet bombs while Ger-man bombers left the vast stock untouched because of the incom-patibility of the suspension equipment.[59] That the bombs landing in Kassa were of Soviet manufacture is all but incontrovertible.

There are other theories. One, advanced by C. A. Macartney, is that the bombing was carried out by defecting Czech or Slovak pilots who dropped their bombs on Kassa before landing in the Soviet Union. *Pesti Hírlap* published a story in July 1942 of a Rus-sian schoolmaster who told the Hungarian officer billeted in his house that his previous boarder had been a Czech pilot who told the Russian that he had led the Kassa attack.[60] The idea of Slovak revenge as a motivation cannot be discounted. In July 1941, after the Hungarians had joined the Axis assault on the Soviet Union, a Slovak fighter pilot deliberately attacked a 1/3 Fighter Squadron CR.42.[61] He failed to do significant damage to the Hungarian ma-chine, but the incident shows the degree of antipathy that some Slovaks felt toward their Hungarian "allies." Another proposition is that the bombers were Heinkels flown from a Romanian airbase, by Romanian crews, at the behest of the German General Staff. This theory takes as its basis the 1984 account of a 2/3 Fighter Squadron pilot whose flight was scrambled from its forward airfield at Bustyaháza, a Transylvanian town 100 miles southeast of Kassa. At around 14:00, the drone of engines could be heard from the northwest, and three CR.42s were ordered aloft. János Balogh was ready first and took off alone to meet the intruders. Balogh got within 1,500–2,000 feet from the bombers, which he described as "similar to He 111s," and exchanged fire with them before they es-caped into a cloud.[62] The well-known Hungarian aviator Antal

Bánhidi, who was also deployed in the east at this time as a reserve CR.42 pilot, cast doubt on Balogh's story. He noted that Balogh's flight leader, who attested to the 1984 statement except for the resemblance of the airplanes to He 111s, had twenty years earlier reported seeing only two aircraft, and had not mentioned Balogh being fired upon. Bánhidi suggested that Balogh had come forward for notoriety after the publishing of a book on the event revived interest.[63]

The most believable of the conspiracy theories is put forward by T. Sakmyster, who lays the blame on Sztójay, Hungary's minister to Berlin, and Colonel Sándor Homlok, its military attaché. Sztójay's pro-German inclination was well established. Homlok shared his outlook and had been implicated in a number of clandestine military operations, including those of the Rongyos Gárda. Most interesting was his visit on September 1, 1938, to Colonel Hellmuth Groscurth, head of an Abwehr section. Groscurth recorded Homlok's statement in his diary: "The Hungarian Chief of Staff requests the creation of a *casus belli* for an attack on Czechoslovakia by the dropping of Czech bombs on Hungarian territory by German aircraft after seizure of the first Czech airports."[64] The incredible similarity between this suggestion and the Kassa bombing led Sakmyster to the conclusion that Homlok and Sztójay arranged the attack with the Abwehr, whose agents carried it out. That the operation existed only at the level of action officers in Berlin solves the problem of motivation, since neither Hitler nor Horthy would have known about it, and it explains the lack of documentation in Budapest. It also answers for the Soviet-made bombs, since Sakmyster suggests that captured Czech aircraft could have been used in the raid. This thesis requires five bombers, not the three almost universally reported, due to the limited bomb capacity of the available Czech bombers. The heaviest bomber and most likely candidate for this mission would have been the Tupolev SB-2, of which fifty-four were delivered to Czechoslovakia in early 1938. The SB-2 (produced under license by Avia as the B.71) had a maximum capacity of six 100-kilogram bombs.[65] There were twenty-nine craters in Kassa, which could not have been caused by three SB-2s.

This writer, naturally skeptical of conspiracy theories and well experienced in the many ways aerial operations can be fouled up, favors the explanation of a Red Air Force navigational error. The Ilyushin Il-4 was a medium twin-engine Soviet bomber widely deployed at the time, and capable of carrying a load of 6,000 pounds. Imagine a wayward flight of three Il-4s circling a large regional town above the haze while the flight leader consults his (outdated) map. The bombers have an unusual paint scheme, perhaps a squadron one-off, which is mistaken for the Axis stripe. The lead pilot correctly locates himself as being over the Slovakian city of Kassa, and decides to expend his flights' weapons on the center of the enemy town. Such a scenario requires no conspiracy and no cover-up, simply a coincidence (paint scheme) and an error (navigation).

It is unlikely that the full truth about the Kassa bombing will ever come to light. Even if they did not engineer it, the event furthered the agenda of the German and Hungarian General Staffs, and no effort would have been expended by those organizations to uncover possibly uncomfortable facts. General Werth is reported to have said in July 1941, "For me, the Kassa bombing really was useful."[66] The political realities then, along with the real necessities of the war, precluded the thorough investigation and reconciliation of conflicting reports that any such event produces. Political pressures did not diminish for long decades, during which time memories grew hazy. By now the documentary collections in central Europe have been thoroughly researched and have yielded no clear answers. Unless a startling new fact emerges from a Russian archive, the bombing will probably remain a matter of contention and speculation.

The record of the next steps is clear, however. In the middle of the morning on June 27, Prime Minister Bárdossy released a press statement and then addressed parliament: "The Royal Hungarian Government concludes that in consequence of these attacks a state of war has come into being between Hungary and the Soviet Union." After being interrupted by cheers, Bárdossy continued, "Only one more sentence. The Hungarian Air Force will take the appropriate measures of reprisal."[67] By the time he spoke, the retaliation raid was complete. Lieutenant Colonel Béla Orosz, 4th Bomber Regiment commander, had received a preparatory order at 16:45 on the June 26, putting his units on alert for action the following day. Approximately sixteen Ju 86s of 4/II Bomber Group at Veszprém were loaded overnight, and they took off at 03:00 for an intermediate stop at Debrecen.[68] They were joined by the crews of eight Ca.135s from 3/5 Bomber Squadron for a final mission briefing. The strike force departed Debrecen around 06:00 and met their escort of nine CR.42s from Aladár Szobránczy's 2/3 Fighter Squadron near its base at Bustyaháza. From there they continued northeast, crossing the Carpathians en route to the target, the Ukrainian town of Stanislau. The air defense was heavy, and the fighters attempted to suppress Soviet AAA batteries while the bombers attacked the airfield and barracks.[69] Records of the VKF show that all of the nineteen participating bombers returned safely, but two CR.42s were shot down. Szobránczy's pilots claimed one Soviet bomber and one fighter destroyed. The 7th and 10th Short-Range Reconnaissance Squadrons also took part in the Stanislau raids, arriving soon after the bombers and reporting heavy resistance, but no losses. At the end of the day, the VKF released the following statement: "This morning, the Hungarian Air Force executed very effective reprisal attacks (*igen eredményes megtorló támadásokat*) against military targets in Soviet Russia. After completing their successful attacks, our aircraft returned to their bases."[70]

The bomber squadrons flew no missions the following day, using the time to complete maintenance and deployment tasks and prepare for an early-morning strike on June 29. That mission followed the pattern of the Stanislau attack, but this time the target was a Soviet supply depot in Strij. Target identification was enhanced by photographs taken on June 28 by He 70s from the Long-Range

Reconnaissance Group. Twenty-five MKHL bombers (seventeen
Ju 86s, eight Ca.135s) took off around 04:00, rendezvoused with
their escorts from 2/3 Fighter Squadron, and proceeded to the target area. Strij was partially obscured by low clouds, so the bomber
formation split up to prosecute their attacks as they were able.[71]
Despite the chaos, the bombers scored hits on the train station and
gasworks, and the gunners from one Ju 86 recorded a confirmed
kill, shooting down a Soviet fighter. One bomber suffered significant damage and made a forced landing.[72] After being refueled and
rearmed, the bombers struck out again in the afternoon, with
orders to attack any targets of military significance except bridges,
which the Wehrmacht intended to use on its march east. When
Lieutenant István Szakonyi passed the bridge over the Pruth near
Kolomea, however, he was shocked to see a mass of khaki uniforms
on the east side. He decided these were Soviet troops about to invade Bukovina and, acting against orders, attacked the bridge. To
his surprise, his first two bombs completely destroyed one span.
Szakonyi returned to Debrecen and reported his action to Lieutenant Colonel Orosz, who advised him to prepare for a court-martial.
During the night, Orosz received a telegram from Lepság advising
that the Red Army had begun a counteroffensive, and bridges were
no longer prohibited targets. There was no court-martial for Szakonyi.[73] Soviet air operations intensified on June 29, and the MKHL
lost a fighter and a WM 21 to enemy aircraft. Bad weather on June 30
limited the effectiveness of bombing and reconnaissance missions,
which were in any case launched in small numbers without specifically briefed targets. For four days, the MKHL had conducted
Hungary's only significant offensive operations, but beginning on
July 1, Honvédség ground units attacked, and the MKHL reverted
to a support role. The reprisal raids were over, and, as the VKF's
daily situation report phrased it, "this concluded the period of air
force strategic employment."

The retaliation attacks against Stanislau and Strij can be considered an independent air campaign, and were directed from the

top levels of government. But they bear little resemblance to strategic attack as envisioned by Douhet and championed by Szentnémedy. The 4th Bomber Regiment did not target civilians with the intention of breaking their national will and instigating widespread societal collapse, as demanded by the theory of the unrestricted aerial offensive. The MKHL was too small to achieve that, even in a single Ukrainian city. Instead, the Hungarian pilots attacked whatever suitable targets they could find in the briefed area, subject to the constraints of weather, enemy resistance, and their own proficiency. The air force carried the weight of Hungary's war effort for a few days while its land forces completed mobilization, and it managed to strike a couple of minor blows while suffering very few casualties of its own. The performance of the bomber squadrons was far from perfect, but it was a major improvement over the embarrassment of the Igló raid—there were no errant strikes on Hungarian territory, for instance. The June campaign could be considered a victory for air power pragmatism. From this point forward, however, the MKHL would conduct offensive operations only in support of Honvéd or Wehrmacht ground campaigns.

The Honvédség had been mobilizing since June 26, and by June 30 Lieutenant General Ferenc Szombathelyi's Carpathian Group, consisting of the Rapid Corps, the 1st Mountain Brigade, and 8th Frontier Brigade, was ready to attack. The Carpathian Group would advance northeast across the mountains with the German 17th Army on its left flank and the Romanian 3rd Army on the right. The combined Axis force aimed to secure the Dniester River crossings.[74] The 1st Aviation Brigade was placed under Szombathelyi, whose order of the day on July 1 included his commander's intent: "The available forces, with bomber force support, attack with weight from the area of Kőrösmező, reaching the line Kolomea-Stanislau as quickly as possible."[75] MKHL units were tasked with battlefield interdiction missions within three miles either side of the rail line to Mikuliczin. Orosz's 4th Bomber Regiment led the attack with escorting CR.42s from 2/3 and 2/4 Fighter

Squadrons. Short-range reconnaissance squadrons responded to the needs of their associated divisions, and the long-range reconnaissance units conducted missions assigned by the VKF.[76] The early days of July continued in this fashion.

In the meantime, MKHL units trickled east. The brigade headquarters moved to Huszt, a small airfield eighty miles northeast of Debrecen, and the 1/I Fighter Group (twenty-three CR.32s) deployed from Szolnok to Miskolc. The Red Army, on the other hand, rushed eastward, ahead of the advancing Axis formations. The pace of the MKHL's movement east was a source of frustration for Lieutenant Colonel Sándor Gyiresy, Hungary's liaison officer with the Luftwaffe's 4th Air Fleet. Gyiresy complained to the VKF: "It is my impression that the Germans would appreciate it if our combat air forces would deploy across the Carpathians and participate in the pursuit of the enemy, in light of the fact that the 4th Air Fleet's range is 1,000 kilometers."[77] On July 5, 1st Aviation Brigade commander Colonel István Bánfalvy informed Gyiresy that the fighter and reconnaissance squadrons were moving forward, and the bomber units would follow in a few days. An additional fighter unit, the 1/3 "Ace of Hearts" squadron, was also being sent east. Both the need for the forward movement and the difficulties the moves caused are evident in the recollection of one 4/I Bomber Group pilot. It had become hard, he remembered, to find Soviet troop concentrations "because they were retreating so fast away from us. . . . There were days when we had to fly 100 kilometers forward, and we still could not find them. Another disadvantage was that the ground details could not keep up with us. We would move forward from one base to the next—no kitchen, no ground personnel—nothing."[78] The race to cross the Dniester ended in disappointment on July 6, when retreating Soviet troops destroyed the last of the remaining bridges. In the first ten days of the war, the MKHL flew 145 combat sorties and dropped 250,000 pounds of bombs. Losses were few, but aircrews struggled with the unpredictable weather above the Carpathians, regularly encountering snow showers and icing conditions for which their Italian airplanes were ill equipped.[79]

During the pause at the Dniester, the Hungarian expeditionary force experienced a number of organizational changes, none of them large, but all having the effect of bringing them under closer German control. Werth agreed to split Szombathelyi's Carpathian Group. The Mountain and Frontier Brigades would remain west of the Dniester as occupation troops, while the 24,000 men of Major General József Németh's Rapid Corps would continue to advance with the German Army Group South.[80] To improve air force coordination with the Honvéd troops, the VKF dissolved the 4th Bomber Regiment and created in its place a temporary Rapid Corps Air Group, consisting of the 2/3 Fighter Squadron, 7th and 10th Short-Range Reconnaissance Squadrons, air defense artillery batteries, two motorized sections, and a mobile field repair unit. Béla Orosz of the 4th Bomber Regiment took command of the group.[81] The bomber squadrons remained engaged, but they were under centralized control from Budapest. Their activities became increasingly restricted because of German concerns about the difficulty of identifying allied troops on the chaotic battlefield. Hungarian bombers were first confined to targets within the Rapid Corps' sector, but by the third week of July they were being used only for long-range reconnaissance. These limitations frustrated Orosz, as did the Rapid Corps' inability to provide adequate supplies for the Air Group, but the VKF rejected his proposal for greater independence.[82] With their capabilities badly underutilized and the airplanes in need of mechanical attention, Lepság withdrew the 4/1 and 4/3 Bomber Squadrons on July 17. The "mixed squadron" composed of six 3/II Ca.135s and nine 4/I Ju 86s remained, and was eventually placed under Orosz's group. [83]

Despite the administrative challenges, Air Group aircrews flew combat sorties nearly every day in support of the Rapid Corps. The WM 21s and He 46s conducted tactical reconnaissance as well as light bombing missions. CR.42s from the 2/3 "Ricsi" squadron provided escorts and also flew fighter sweep and ground attack sorties. July 12 was a banner day for the squadron, as its pilots scored five air-to-air victories. The same day the unit's replacement arrived: the 1/3 Fighter Squadron (twelve CR.42s) and the 1st Short-Range Reconnaissance (nine He 46s) deployed to Kolomea. The 3rd Short-Range Reconnaissance Squadron (nine WM 21s) got into action a week later, and by the end of July the 2/3 Fighter and 7th and 10th Reconnaissance Squadrons returned to Hungary.[84] On August 7, seven Re.2000s from the 1/2 Fighter Squadron at Szolnok landed at the forward base of Sutyska. The VKF was eager for a combat trial of the MKHL's newest fighter before license production began. These Re.2000s saw their first significant combat four days later, when they encountered no Soviet fighters, but lost an airplane and pilot to ground fire.[85]

The August 11 attack on Nikolayev was conducted in support of the Rapid Corps' advance on the city from the north. Sixty thousand Soviet troops of General Zarkov's Ninth Army were established around the city, and the mile-long bridge spanning the Bug River was the best means to escape encirclement. Vitán's mixed bomber squadron received an order late on August 10 directing an early morning attack by the Ca.135s on Nikolayev's bridge, railway station, and marshaling yards. Just after midnight, the Capronis were loaded with captured Soviet 500-pound bombs. Because not all of the unit's ground crews had arrived, the flight crews assisted in preparing the bombers for the mission. All six Ca.135s made the 05.45 take off, but one had an engine problem and turned back right away. One of the six Re.2000s also missed the rendezvous due to a mechanical problem, but all six CR.42s were there, so the MKHL strike force numbered sixteen. Lieutenant Szakonyi, whose lucky bomb had destroyed the Pruth bridge near Kolomea on June 29, led the bombers. Heavy AAA along their approach caused the formation to scatter, and Szakonyi's damaged airplane was the second to turn toward the bridge. This time, it was his wingman who had the luck: Szakonyi could see a span of the bridge lying in the river. He shifted his attack to the city and dropped his weapons on the railway station. The bombers never regained their formation integrity, each one making for home alone. On this mission, MKHL pilots met Soviet I-16 "Rata" fighters for the first time, and, although the I-16s scored hits on most of the bombers, all five landed safely. The Hungarians claimed eight Ratas destroyed—four each from the bombers and the CR.42s. General Löhr, the commander of the Luftwaffe's 4th Air Fleet, personally awarded the Iron Cross to several Hungarian airmen on the Nikolayev raid.[86] This mission, along with others conducted in the following days by the MKHL around Nikolayev, contributed to the success of the Seventeenth Army operation. Nikolayev fell on August 16, its capture forcing Zarkov's Ninth Army farther east and leaving isolated Soviet forces in the critical Black Sea port of Odessa to "fight for their lives."[87]

After the capture of Nikolayev, the Rapid Corps had a period of rest and performed security operations on Seventeenth Army's right flank. As a consequence, MKHL air activity slowed. On August 28, Lieutenant Colonel Orosz was replaced by Sándor Gyiresy. This seems to have been part of a normal personnel rotation and not a removal from command. During the nearly two months Orosz was in command, the Rapid Corps Air Group flew 555 sorties, dropped 85,000 pounds of bombs, and scored twenty-seven aerial victories. This came at the cost of four aircraft and six fliers lost in action. The Air Group continued to fight under Gyiresy, but its strength was slowly whittled away as units returned to Hungary and were not replaced. In early October, the 1st Short-Range Reconnaissance Squadron was withdrawn, followed soon after by the flight of 1/2 Fighter Squadron Re.2000s (two crashed because of bad weather over the Carpathians). The 1/3 Fighter Squadron returned to Mátyásföld in late November, after flying over 800 combat hours and shooting down nineteen Soviet planes at a loss of two CR.42s. By the end of 1941, the Rapid Corps and the entire MKHL expeditionary force were back on Hungarian soil. Fifty-six Hungarian planes had been destroyed or damaged beyond repair, and thirty-six airmen were dead or missing.[88]

This first phase of the war should be considered a success for the MKHL. The performance of its air and ground crews improved steadily. The Nikolayev raid was remarkable not only for the destruction of the bridge and return of all but one airplane, but also because all six Ca.135s were able to get airborne, which was double the usual launch rate. The fighter and reconnaissance units in particular had gained extensive experience in air-ground cooperation and operations in austere environments. MKHL senior leaders must have been very comfortable with the basic unfolding of the 1941 air campaign, because its mission requirements and environmental conditions were so similar to what they remembered from the 1919 interventions—except this time they were moving forward in pursuit, rather than scrambling backward under pressure. The machines were faster and the bombs bigger, to be sure, but the air defense, reconnaissance and interdiction missions flown by the MHKL were essentially the same as those performed by the VR or even the LFT. It must have seemed to Colonel Szentnémedy as if the vigorous and stimulating air power debates of the 1930s had never happened.

The withdrawal of the Rapid Corps from Ukraine in December 1941 was the result of a very different debate between Henrik Werth and Ferenc Szombathelyi. As early as August, Werth had begun to arrange training in Germany for the Rapid Corps' reinforcements that he had promised Halder. He had not consulted or even informed Horthy of this plan, but he sent Bárdossy a long memorandum taking the government to task for its lack of enthusiasm for the war, and suggesting Bárdossy offer the Germans at least four or five additional army corps. Bárdossy immediately passed the substance of Werth's harangue to Horthy in a lengthy memorandum of his own. In closing, Bárdossy politely told the regent to choose between his prime minister and his chief of staff.[89] Shortly after this, General Szombathelyi warned Horthy that the war would be a prolonged affair, and that "Blitzkriegs were over." Horthy recalled Szombathelyi to Budapest so that he and Werth could argue their cases. The regent chose Szombathelyi, and on September 6 named him to replace Werth as chief of the VKF.[90] Szombathelyi's first official duty was to accompany Horthy and Bárdossy to Germany for talks with Hitler, Ribbentrop, and the German General Staff. The regent asked Hitler to release the Honvédség from the Eastern Front. Ribbentrop countered with the suggestion that a withdrawal would "be very alarming from the point of view of morale," and offered instead to reequip the armored brigades of the Rapid Corps. They would then stay engaged against the Soviets through the end of the fighting season, expected to last until mid-October. Further, the Germans asked for replacements for the Mountain and Frontier Brigades, and an additional twelve battalions, with the promise that these units would be used only for occupation and security duties. Since the Hungarians were most eager for the return of their elite Rapid Corps and the offer to refit the brigades seemed reasonable, Bárdossy agreed.[91] He tried to squeeze Ribbentrop for further border revision in the northeast and southwest, but the German was noncommittal. When pressed again on the same issue later, Ribbentrop told Bárdossy, "As long as the war goes on, family quarrels must be suspended."[92]

Germany's attitude toward Hungarian participation in the war changed dramatically after the success of the December 1941 Soviet counteroffensive in the Moscow sector. Hitler replaced all three army group commanders and named himself commander in chief of the German army. Just after Christmas, the Führer wrote to stiffen Horthy's resolve in their shared fight against Bolshevism and to ask for additional Hungarian forces for the summer offensive. Hitler then sent Ribbentrop and Field Marshal Wilhelm Keitel to Budapest in January to work out the details of Hungary's contribution. They were surprisingly straightforward: Hitler wanted the entire Honvédség put at his disposal. Szombathelyi later described the Germans as modifying their view of Hungary's role from "voluntary participation into an obligation."[93] Ribbentrop used his customary tactic of comparing Hungary's commitment unfavorably to that of Romania, and implying that a lack of cooperation on Budapest's part would put the Vienna Awards at risk. Bárdossy conceded in principle to a larger Hungarian contingent than agreed in September, but both he and Szombathelyi were surprised at Keitel's opening demand for twenty-three brigades. Szombathelyi eventually consented to sending nine brigades with supporting armor and air formations, and to allow a 20,000-man Waffen SS division to be formed from among the country's ethnic German population.[94]

Organization of the new formation occupied the VKF through the spring of 1942. During this time, István Horthy was selected vice-regent, and his father pushed Bárdossy out of the premiership. The two events were not unrelated. Miklós Horthy wanted an established successor to avoid an interregnum in the event of his death or incapacitation. As the regent recalled, he "wished the choice to fall on a man of strong character, a man who could make a stand against the ever increasing German pressure."[95] When his advisors put forward his son István as a candidate, Horthy did not object. Béla Imrédy and the radical right did. Ferenc Szálasi called him an "Anglophile traitor" and "a dandy with Jewish morals, wallowing delirious in the delights of depravity."[96] Not to be outdone, Joseph Goebbels wrote in his diary on February 20: "Horthy's older son had been elected Vice Regent in the Hungarian Parliament by acclamation. This is a matter of major political rigging. . . . [He] is a pronounced Jew-lover, an Anglophile to the bones, a man without any profound education and without broad political understanding; in short, a person with whom if he were Regent of Hungary, we would have some difficulties to work out."[97] Miklós Horthy later embraced Goebbels's scorn as proof of István's fitness for the job. About Bárdossy he had grown less sure. The regent felt the prime minister had made too many concessions to Germany, and that his declaration of war against the United States had been a critical error. Bárdossy had to go, and the new prime minister should "regain Hungary's freedom of action and return, if possible, to a state of non-belligerence."[98] This would prove to be an impossible task, although neither Horthy nor his new premier Miklós Kállay understood it at the time.

Between April 11 and July 27, 1942, the Hungarian Second Army moved east in the largest deployment in the country's history.[99] The Second Army was composed of three corps of three light divisions, each of which had only two infantry regiments.[100] At its head was General Gustáv Jány, who had asked to retire after being passed over in favor of Szombathelyi to replace Werth. Horthy had refused his request.[101] The air component was the 2nd Aviation Brigade, commanded by Lieutenant Colonel Sándor András.[102] By the first week of June 1942, the entire brigade had assembled in Ukraine. It consisted of the 1/1 Long-Range Reconnaissance Squadron (four He 111s), the 3/1 Short-Range Reconnaissance Squadron (twelve He 46s), the 1/1 and 2/1 Fighter Squadrons (eleven Héjas each), and the 4/1 Bomber Squadron (fourteen Ca.135s). The brigade also had attached six transport aircraft (three each Ca.101s and converted Ju 86s) and a few Bü 131 and FW 58 trainers for liaison flights.[103] Later in the summer, MALERT's Ju 52s were pressed into service as the 2nd Transport Squadron.[104] In place of the tricolor chevron adopted in September 1938, the Hungarian airplanes now bore a new marking—a bold white cross inside a black square—consistent with other Axis air force insignia. The 2nd Aviation Brigade was the rough equivalent to the Rapid Corps Air Group fielded the previous year. However, at 200,000 men, the Second Army was twice the size of the Carpathian Group, and Jány's force would be spread over an area many times larger than the narrow sector through which Szombathelyi advanced.[105] More worryingly, the Red Air Force was far more capable in June 1942 than it had been the previous year. A large proportion of the 5,300 Soviet airplanes destroyed in 1941 were obsolete designs already scheduled to be replaced, meaning "the Luftwaffe simply completed a job that was already being carried out by the Red Air Force itself."[106] Soviet aircraft factories made up the losses by the end of 1941, producing 5,100 Yak-1, MiG-3 and LaGG-3 fighters, each of which compared favorably with the Héja.[107]

Operation Blue, the German summer offensive designed to seize the Caucasus oil fields, began on June 28. The plan called for the capture of Voronezh, a city on the east side of the Don River. A bridgehead established, Army Group B would follow the Don south, trapping and eventually destroying the Soviet armies on the west side of the river. The Hungarian, Romanian, and Italian contingents would then be left to guard the Don while the Wehrmacht pushed south to the Caucasus.[108] Stalin was convinced the capture of Moscow would be the main German objective in 1942, and the southern attack took the Red Army by surprise. By the end of July, the Hungarian Second Army, exhausted after slogging over 600 miles across Ukraine, took up defensive positions along a 120-mile section of the Don. They soon had orders to take the offensive against three crucial bridges that remained in Soviet hands along the west bank, but due to their lack of heavy weapons, the Red Army units were able to beat back their attacks.[109] Halder did not appreciate the Second Army's efforts, as evidenced by some of his August 1942 diary entries: "The Hungarians are allowing the Russians to come back across the Don! . . . South of Voronezh the Hungarians are running. . . . The Hungarians are making no progress in cleaning up the west bank of the Don. They stop trying and take up defensive positions."[110] This was not an entirely fair assessment of the green Hungarian army's performance. Because Horthy wanted to minimize Hungary's contribution to the German war effort, he had sent the smallest force he could manage. Each division was short an infantry regiment, so that the nine "light" divisions of the Second Army were equal in manpower to only six German divisions. The disparity in weapons was even more striking: the Hungarian formations had half of the light machine guns and antitank guns of their German counterparts, and only 10 per cent of the

trucks and tractors.[111] As in the First World War, when compared
to a German division, the Hungarian unit was "not only smaller, it
was also qualitatively inferior."[112]

The 2nd Aviation Brigade could not compensate for the Second
Army's lack of heavy artillery and antitank weapons. Its reconnaissance units were able to provide useful observation of Soviet movements behind the bridgeheads, but raids by the 4/1 Bomber Squadron
and the Héjas did not break Red Army resistance in the area. To
add to the brigade's firepower, He 46s of the 3/2 Short-Range Reconnaissance Squadron began to conduct armed reconnaissance
from early August. Observation crews were allowed to attack some
targets on their own, if they were weakly defended and outside the
range of Second Army artillery batteries.[113] Giving reconnaissance
crews the freedom to attack the enemy rather than just observe and
photograph probably increased morale in the unit, but it had no
appreciable effect on Soviet strength in the area, because the He
46s were still too few and too lightly armed. The MKHL needed
heavy, rugged airplanes capable of conducting accurate strikes on
small targets and operating with minimal maintenance. This description fitted the Ju 87, for instance, which the MKHL would field
in 1943, and the excellent Red Air Force Il-2, but not the Ca.135 or
the Re.2000. Both were somewhat fragile Italian machines that
required significant mechanical attention. Lack of spare parts and
battlefield attrition gradually reduced the number of mission-ready
airplanes in the group, so that in the middle of August, only twenty-
five aircraft were available for combat.[114] On August 29, the 4/1
Bomber Squadron reported only one of its nine assigned airplanes
was airworthy.[115]

One of the Re.2000s ready for a mission on August 20 bore the
crossed six-guns of the "Sheriff," Lieutenant István Horthy, Hungary's vice-regent. István had been an avid pilot for years before the
war, and was Hungary's best-known aviator. In June 1939, in his role
as president of MÁVAG (which at that time produced mainly locomotives), he had flown solo 4,000 miles to Bombay in his Arado Ar

Figure 7.3. Hungary's vice-regent, Lieutenant István Horthy, at the controls of his Reggiane Re.2000. Courtesy of the Péter Zámbori Collection.

79 sports plane in order to close a deal with the Indian Railways for one hundred locomotives. His competitor had bought all of the seats on the commercial flight to Bombay to keep MÁVAG from competing for the bid, but István beat the airliner to India and had the contract signed when his competitor arrived. This trip was celebrated in the Hungarian press, as was the honeymoon trip István and his bride took in the same Arado around the eastern Mediterranean (they exited the church under an arch of propellers). His wife, the Countess Ilona Gyulai, embraced aviation on her own, earning her glider pilot's license in 1940. István had been the face of his father's Aviation Foundation, and as recently as April 1942 had made a national radio broadcast encouraging Hungarian youth to join the MKHL or flying clubs.[116] A reserve pilot in the 1/1 Fighter Squadron, István had joined the unit in the Soviet Union in July. He had flown twenty-four combat missions and had scored a probable kill against a LaGG-3 fighter on August 6.

Shortly after 05:00 on August 20, István and his wingman took off to escort a 3/2 Reconnaissance Squadron He 46. While joining with the Heinkel at approximately 1,000 feet, István's Re.2000 turned sharply left and fell to the ground. He was killed upon impact.[117] The accident investigation could not determine precisely the cause, but from most descriptions of the accident, it seems that the vice-regent's engine failed, and while turning back to the airfield for an emergency landing, the Re.2000 entered an accelerated stall from which he could not recover in the available altitude. Rumors of German involvement swirled around the country, and were accepted as true by a great many Hungarians. István's death further soured the public against Hitler's war in the east, and the outpouring of grief and condolence for the regent and his family strengthened the admiral's hand politically, even as his resilience wavered. No one else was appointed vice-regent.[118]

In his last letter home, István Horthy praised the Hungarian cavalry, armor, and artillery units, and commended a few senior officers to his father, but the overall tone was negative. István offered the regent his own assessment of the prospects for victory, and recommended a Hungarian withdrawal:

> Our losses have been fairly heavy recently because of a lack of momentum. If I may give you some advice: let's not send reinforcements but rather concentrate our forces. If we constantly replenish our units we will just bleed to death in terms of both men and equipment. The Russians won't by any means be beaten by the end of this year; they are fighting very strongly and are well supplied with munitions and food, so in my opinion they won't be any weaker next year, in fact just the opposite.
>
> I don't know whether this is true, but apparently another two divisions are coming out to act as occupying forces. This news disheartened me greatly because we already have more troops here than we can afford. How reassuring it would be if Bartha were no longer in the minister's seat; I feel he's the evil spirit behind this.
>
> One more sad topic, the Jewish companies: I gather there are twenty or thirty thousand Jews out here who are completely at the mercy of the sadists. It makes my stomach turn it's revolting. It's awful that this could happen even in the twentieth century. . . . I'm afraid we'll have to pay a heavy price for this sometime. Couldn't they be taken home to work there? Otherwise few of them will survive the winter.[119]

István's comments about the Defense Minister and the Jewish labor companies must have struck a chord, since the regent relieved Bartha on September 25.[120] He was replaced by Vilmos Nagy, who had been the military attaché in London.[121]

Szombathelyi remained chief of the VKF, and in early September he paid a visit to the 2nd Army at the front. On September 5 he dined with the 2nd Aviation Brigade commander, Lieutenant Colonel András, and the commander of the 1/1 Fighter Squadron (István Horthy's unit), Major Kálmán Csukás. The men discussed the brigade's future in Ukraine. András relayed to Szombathelyi the opinion of Major General Rákosi, commander of Lepság, that the brigade should stay in the field despite its materiel shortages "to shore up the morale of the ground forces." Szombathelyi agreed, saying "the reputation of the air force demands this."[122] The open-cockpit He 46s and cantankerous Ca.135s were especially ill suited to the brutal winter on the steppes, however, and András pulled them from the line. At the end of October, both the 4/1 Bomber and 3/2 Short-Range Reconnaissance Squadrons were withdrawn from operations over the Don sector. In the course of 1,000 sorties, three Ca.135s had been destroyed in combat and eleven crewmen killed. The dead included the 4/1 commander, Major István Mocsáry, who was killed along with his crew on August 14 while attacking Soviet troops around the bridgehead at Uriv.[123] Only one He 46 was lost, and the squadron's gunners claimed three Red Air Force aircraft shot down. András moved west along with his brigade's airplanes: he was sent back to serve on the Lepság staff, and Colonel Tibor Fráter assumed command of the 2nd Aviation Brigade.[124]

With the departure of the 4/1 and 3/2 squadrons, the brigade's only combat contributions came from the 1/1 Long-Range Reconnaissance Squadron and the 1/1 and 5/2 Fighter Squadrons. The newly arrived 5/2 Fighter Squadron had left its CR.42s in Hungary, and converted to Re.2000s under the instruction of 2/1 Squadron pilots. The reconnaissance squadron, whose He 111s had first been replaced by Dornier Do 215s confiscated from Yugoslavia, received

Figure 7.4. MKHL Bf 109s on the Eastern Front. Courtesy of the Péter Zámbori Collection.

Ju 88s from the Luftwaffe in November. The 1/1 Fighter Squadron had also begun operating German airplanes. Before his departure for the Lepság staff, András had convinced Luftwaffe lieutenant general Korten to supply twelve Bf 109s for operational conversion in the field. Thirteen fighter pilots trained by the Luftwaffe's 52nd Fighter Wing (Jagdgeschwader, JG 52) formed the initial Hungarian Bf 109 cadre, which was led by Lieutenant György Bánlaky. After providing the aircraft and training, JG 52 shared operational control of 1/1 Fighter Squadron with Fráter.[125] MKHL pilots made good use of the Messerschmitt machines. On December 16, Lieutenant Imre Pánzél shot down four Il-2 attack aircraft in two sorties. He soon scored two additional victories, thus becoming the first Hungarian ace of the Second World War. He was killed in combat on January 11, 1943.[126]

The following day, the Soviet counteroffensive that had begun in November around Stalingrad reached the Hungarians on the Don River. The Red Air Force committed two air armies to the Voronezh front: 400 combat aircraft, including 138 fighters and 154 attack airplanes.[127] The assault began when two Red Army divisions, supported by armor, launched a probing attack from the Uriv bridgehead that penetrated 3 miles into the Hungarian sector. A counterattack by the German 700th Armored Group on January 13 failed to dislodge the Soviets. On the January 14, the Soviet Fortieth Army tore a 25-mile-wide gap in the Second Army's lines.[128] General Jány requested permission to retreat the day after, but Army Group B headquarters refused, saying only Hitler could approve such a request. After permission was denied again the next day, he appealed to Szombathelyi, who confirmed the need to follow German orders. With the situation deteriorating quickly, he finally ordered retreat on the morning of January 17.[129]

The 2nd Aviation Brigade's fighter squadrons were based at Ilovskoje, which happened to be the point on which the Soviet pincers were converging. After the Luftwaffe ordered its airplanes there to fall back west, Lieutenant Colonel Fráter asked to follow suit. He was told to wait. With the Red Army approaching on January 18, the evacuation of Ilovskoje was approved. The transport squadron's Ju 52 and Ju 88s from the reconnaissance squadron carried away as many airmen and supplies as possible, and Lieutenant Colonel Csukás was tasked with the airfield's defense. The Re.2000s would not start in the bitter cold (-20 degrees Celsius), and ten Héjas, along with one Ar 96, were blown up lest they fall into Soviet hands. In the battle to defend the airfield on January 19, Csukás and approximately fifty MKHL personnel were killed. The Ilovskoje disaster forced a stand down and reorganization of the 2nd Aviation Brigade. All of the 5/2 Fighter Squadron's Re.2000s had been destroyed, so it was equipped with three Bf 109s from 1/1 when it received eight new Messerschmitts in February. The brigade lost a total of thirty-six airplanes and eighty-two airmen in the January and February fighting. In addition to the Héjas torched at Ilovskoje, seven Bf 109s, five Ar 96s, and two each of the Ju 88s, Ju 86s, and FW 58s were destroyed.[130]

These losses were nothing in comparison to the catastrophe that befell the rest of the Hungarian Second Army. Over the course of Second Army's deployment, it suffered casualties in excess of 50 per cent, the vast majority of these coming in January and February 1943. Of the 250,000 Hungarians (including the approximately 50,000 Jewish laborers) who departed for Ukraine in spring 1942, approximately 50,000 were killed, the same number wounded, and 28,000 taken prisoner.[131] For Hungary's future military capacity, the destruction of equipment was even more devastating. "All of the armor was lost; almost all of the artillery (one regiment saved one gun out of twenty-four); 70 to 80 per cent of the heavier arms of the infantry (machine guns, trench mortars, etc.), about half the horses, practically all the stores, and a high proportion even of the rifles, for many of the exhausted men had jettisoned even these in their flight."[132] Defense Minister Nagy estimated that all of the arms left in Hungary could equip only four and a half light divisions.[133] The 2nd Aviation Brigade on March 1, 1943, had thirty-three airplanes.[134] The Honvédség needed German weapons.

Hitler was not, however, inclined to supply them. He had always favored the Romanians in arms shipments, primarily because Romanian oil was dearer to him than Hungarian grain, but he had also come to doubt the Hungarian fighting spirit, at least when the fighting was done on Germany's behalf. When approached with a request for Bf 109s in 1942, the Führer gave this response: "That would just suit the Hungarian gentlemen! They would not use the single-seaters against the enemy but just for pleasure flights! Aviation fuel is in short supply and I need pilots who attack and not ones who go on pleasure flights. What the Hungarians have achieved in the aviation field to date is more than paltry. If I am going to give some aircraft, then rather to the Croats, who have proved they have an offensive spirit. To date we have only experienced fiascos with the Hungarians."[135] Fortunately for the MKHL, an arrangement had been made that did not rely on Hitler's steadfast goodwill. In

the spring of 1941, negotiations between the two Defense Ministries had resulted in a joint aircraft production program for the
manufacture of Bf 109s, Me 210s, and Daimler-Benz DB-601 engines. Fulfillment of the production quotas would allow the Lepság
to reach its Huba-III airplane targets at the end of 1943: 75 Héjas,
100 Bf 109s, 78 Ju 87s, 250 Ju 88s, and 70 Ju 52s. The arrangement
was not for license production, in which a flat fee is paid for the
right to manufacture, but rather for shared output, at agreed ratios
of 1.5:1 for the Bf 109s and 1:1 for the Me 210s. After ironing out the
inevitable early wrinkles, production rate was expected to reach
fifty airplanes and 200 engines per month by 1943. From the domestic production, the MKHL anticipated obtaining 225 Bf 109s
and 160 Me 210s.[136] The major factories involved were WM, MWG,
and Dunai Repülőgépgyár RT (DR.GY), a new concern formed by
Weiss with German support. Total investment for the German production program was 152 million pengős.[137]

The Hungarian factories spent the entire year of 1942 tooling
up for production. MÁVAG alone made sixty-two WM 21s in 1941,
but output for the entire country the next year was only seven aircraft: four FW 58s, one Bf 109, one Me 210, and one Héja. Engine
production was hardly better, as just ten DB-605s (an improved
version of the 601) and fifty Hirth HM-504s intended for Bü 131s
were completed. The rates increased substantially in 1943: 130 Héjas, the majority of MÁVAG's run of 170 aircraft, rolled off the line
that year, along with all 230 of the WM-14 engines required for the
series. The German-Hungarian program got under way, resulting
in completion of ninety-two Bf 109Gs and fifty-three Me 210s.
Monthly production did not reach the expected rate of fifty per
month until the spring of 1944, after which it decreased dramatically due to the effects of the Allied bombing campaign.[138] The
April 13, 1944, US Fifteenth Air Force raid on Győr caused heavy
damage to the MWG plant and severely restricted subsequent Bf
109 output. After that attack, component manufacturing was distributed throughout thirty-four villages around Győr. Allied bomb-

Table 7.1 Hungarian aircraft and engine production, 1941–1944

Aircraft	1941	1942	1943	1944	Total
WM 21	62				62
Héja		1	130	39	170
FW 58		4	30	38	72
Bf 109		1	92	395	488
Me 211		1	53	216	270
Ju 52			3	27	30
Engines					
WM-14			230		230
DB-605		10	427	615	1052

ing of the WM and DR.GY factories on Csepel Island ended Me 210 and engine construction in October 1944.[139] Table 7.1 shows the production figures for combat aircraft and engines by year. Production of the German aircraft and engines peaked in the first half of 1944, after which it fell precipitously because of the destruction of factories by Allied bombers. Output continued to diminish through the end of the year, when the Red Army's occupation of the factories around Budapest brought it to a final halt.[140]

Reggiane fulfilled its 1939 contract for Re.2000s in 1943, and Caproni delivered thirty-two additional Ca.135s in May 1942. With those exceptions, there were no substantial deliveries of combat aircraft from foreign producers after the invasion of the Soviet Union.[141] The RA and Luftwaffe needed every up-to-date combat airplane that its factories could construct, leaving only trainers and obsolete models for purchase. There were direct transfers of Luftwaffe aircraft to the MKHL, such as the one that gave twelve Bf 109s to the 1/1 Fighter Squadron in early 1943. Between June 1942 and March 1944, at least 170 of MKHL's combat aircraft were passed on directly from Luftwaffe units.[142] It is possible that the number of airplanes moved off the books from German to Hungarian units was substantially higher. At the ratio of 1:1.5 for the Bf 109s produced in Hungary, the MKHL should have received only 158 of the machines in 1944. There are no indications of normal contractual deliveries of Bf 109s to the MKHL from German factories, but the 101st Fighter Regiment reported fielding a total of 400 Bf 109s in that year, of which eighty were serviceable at the end of the year, with another seventy under repair.[143]

The RLM received some compensation for those aircraft in the form of raw materials. Hungarian oil production, especially in the Lispe field southwest of Lake Balaton, increased dramatically during the war, from 42,000 tons in 1938 to 840,000 tons in 1943. Hungary thus became Germany's second-largest oil supplier after Romania. Refining capacity lagged behind crude production, which made the existing refineries on Csepel Island and at Pét especially critical to the Axis war effort. Nearly as important were Hungary's deposits of bauxite, the base ore for aluminum. There was in 1939 a single aluminum plant on Csepel Island that fed the WM works. Its output in 1940 of 3,200 tons was sufficient for domestic needs. With German prodding and capital, an additional plant was built in 1942, and under German direction, Hungarian aluminum production reached 20,000 tons. The majority of that was exported to Germany, along with 90 per cent of its raw bauxite production.[144] The massive export of natural resources did not correct Hungary's balance of payment deficit with Germany. At the end of 1941, Budapest owed Berlin 140 million Reichsmarks; the debt swelled tenfold to 1.5 billion Reichsmarks in December 1944.[145]

The transfer of aircraft in the field were undoubtedly appreciated by the local MKHL commanders, but they were considered favors granted, not contracts fulfilled, and therefore often resulted in the unit receiving the Luftwaffe's cast-offs coming under some measure of German command. That was indeed the situation for Hungarian airmen in the east for most of 1943. The 2nd Aviation Brigade still existed as an organization, but it remained extremely weak. There was little will in Budapest to reinforce it and, until production ramped up late in the year, there were no suitable airplanes to send. Fighter pilots of 1/1 and 5/2 Squadrons flew Bf 109s in Ukraine, mostly conducting ground attack sorties with 500-pound bombs, and occasionally escorting Luftwaffe bombers. They scored twenty aerial victories during the Battle of Kursk, and accounted for 132 Soviet aircraft destroyed by the end of 1943. Through the summer, the Hungarian units retreated west along with the Luftwaffe, passing back along the route they had followed two years earlier.[146] After their autumn 1942 recall from the front, 3/1 and 4/1 Bomber Squadron pilots departed for Istres, France, where they learned to fly Ju 88s, the Luftwaffe's standard light bomber. The 1/1 Long-Range Reconnaissance Squadron had by that time also converted to Ju 88s, although without the benefit of a stay in France. It operated wholly under the command of the Luftwaffe, and in November, when the prospects of ever adding additional squadrons to the reconnaissance group disappeared, its designation was simplified by dropping the "/1."[147]

The November change was a result of a VKF paper that formally abandoned the air force structure of the Huba-III plan. In "Guidance for the air force battle order in the 1943/44 organizational year," the VKF acknowledged that material shortages made it impossible to reach the goals set out three years earlier. Instead, the staff proposed an organization of four groups: an expeditionary formation, an air defense formation, a border defense formation, and a training establishment. This plan was endorsed by Lieutenant General Sándor Magyarosy, the new head of the LF, and approved by the government.[148]

The new MKHL organizational plan took effect on January 1, 1944. On that day, the expeditionary force in the Soviet Union became known as the 102nd Aviation Brigade. The 5/2 Fighter Squadron, composed of twelve Bf 109s, followed the brigade's lead and changed its designation to 102/1 Independent Fighter Squadron. The 3/1 Short-Range Reconnaissance Squadron had twelve FW 189s, but the 1st Long-Range Reconnaissance Squadron was down to six Ju 88s.[149] The MKHL focused on defense of the homeland.

Budapest's air defense formation consisted of the 2/1 and 5/3
Fighter Squadrons (eighteen Héjas until February 15, then Bf 109s)
and the 5/1 Night Fighter Squadron (eighteen Me 210s). The border
defense group comprised thirteen squadrons. Three were short-
range reconnaissance squadrons, two of which were still flying the
He 46s procured in 1937. The Ungvár squadron (4/2) operated Me
210s. The 1/1 Fighter Squadron at Szolnok had been forced back to
Héjas until enough Bf 109s became available in August. The other
fighter squadrons were equipped with Bf 109s. Debrecen's 3/2 Bomber
Squadron flew Ca.135s, but the other four bomber units had Me
210s. The lone transport squadron at Pápa kept MALERT's Ju 52s
in service. Training airplanes were obsolete combat machines:
WM 21s, Héjas, and Ju 86s.[150]

Even as the air force was taking steps to strengthen capital defense, the government was desperate to exit the war. Horthy's determination to secure a separate peace had intensified after the
destruction of the Second Army, and Hungarian peace feelers had
gone out all over Europe. Kállay's emissaries were authorized to
inform British or American officials that Hungary would not resist
an Anglo-American or Polish army, and that the Honvédség was
prepared to act against the Wehrmacht if required. The British were
the most receptive of the Allies to the idea of Hungary leaving the war
on terms other than complete surrender, but even they demanded
some concrete steps from Budapest that Horthy and Kállay judged
would result in a German takeover of the country. Hitler was well
aware of Kállay's pro-Western orientation, and had confronted
Horthy about it in April 1943. Horthy defended his premier, but his
protestations did nothing to assuage German suspicion. Ribbentrop remarked to the German minister in Budapest that Horthy's
support of Kállay only proved "the Regent's full approval of the
Prime Minister's policy of defeatism and detachment from the Axis
Powers."[151] After Italy defected to the Allies in September 1943,
Hitler ordered plans prepared for the occupation of Hungary and
Romania.[152]

Operation Margarethe I was implemented in modified form on March 19, 1944. Two days earlier, Hitler called Horthy to Klessheim Castle to coerce him into agreeing to the German occupation. Hitler demanded the reinstatement of Imrédy and Rátz, and Horthy was to instruct the Hungarian people to welcome the occupying Wehrmacht. The regent refused. After many hours, a compromise emerged. Horthy would appoint an acceptable government, but German troops must thereafter be withdrawn. The regent tried to leave Klessheim right away, but Ribbentrop contrived an air raid alert to delay him. Foreign Minister Jenő Ghyczy sent an encrypted telegram but it, too, was deliberately delayed.[153] The German military attaché informed Kállay that paratroops would occupy airfields around the capital at 04:00, and that eleven German divisions would arrive in Budapest by 06:00. The VKF estimated there were nine or ten German divisions poised on Hungary's borders, along with ten Romanian and one Slovak. The only Honvéd units capable of sustained resistance were in the Carpathians. Furthermore, a telegram from General Szombathelyi had arrived, instructing the army to treat the Germans as friends, and in the absence of a countermanding order, Generals Károly Beregffy and János Vörös advised Kállay that they could not execute an order to resist.[154] The prime minister floated the idea of evacuating the government by air to Transylvania, but Lepság deputy commander Lieutenant General Vilmos Hellebronth demurred, reminding Kállay that the airfields were not equipped for night-time takeoffs.[155] Kállay did order the MKHL to disperse available aircraft to avoid possible internment by German paratroops. Kállay recalled the Wehrmacht's entry: "In the early morning hours the German occupying army marched in in full style, bands playing. Budapest had to be shown the German bayonets. But a great surprise was awaiting the Germans. . . . There was no jubilant crowd in the streets to greet the parading Germans: not one hat was tossed in the air; not one handkerchief was waved; not one cheer was sounded."[156] When Horthy arrived in Budapest on the morning of March 19, his train was met by a German guard of honor. The occupation had been accomplished.[157]

Horthy convened a Crown Council that afternoon. Kállay resigned, with immediate effect; he refused even to sign the minutes of the meeting. The rest of the government also stepped down, and the regent declined to appoint a new one right away, preferring instead to have the seconds in each ministry administer affairs for a few days. The Germans continued to press for Imrédy, whom Horthy refused to appoint. Eventually Horthy convinced Döme Sztójay to accept the premiership. Sztójay was one of Hitler's favorite Hungarians, but Horthy believed that, as a soldier, Sztójay would prove loyal to the regent as head of the armed forces. Rátz was named deputy prime minister. General Lajos Csatay, appointed the previous June after Nagy's philo-Semitism and irregular personal finances had made him vulnerable to the radical right, remained as defense minister. Szombathelyi continued to serve as chief of the VKF until he was replaced by Beregffy in April. Kállay escaped the Gestapo by seeking asylum in the Turkish embassy, where he lived until October. Horthy went into a state of semiexile in the palace.[158]

In the first days of the occupation, the Wehrmacht confined Honvédség troops to the garrisons. Although the operational plan involved disarming the Hungarian soldiers, it was not widely implemented, because Szombathelyi had ordered a friendly reception. The German military commander in the country recorded on March 19: "Only one place where Hungarian troop disarmament took place. And only because my command did not arrive in time. But we took care of it. . . . Nowhere any opposition." And the following day: "The situation is quiet. The Hungarian troops accept us loyally. The population is in general neutral."[159] It would be more accurate to say that the Honvédség was loyal to the regent, who had, through the chief of the VKF, instructed the army to admit German forces to their installations. German actions showed they had no confidence in the Honvéd's loyalty to the Reich. General Greiffenberg, promoted after the occupation from attaché to

"Plenipotentiary General of the Wehrmacht in Hungary" established "operational zones" in eastern parts of the country and put
them under German military control. "Greiffenberg was also given
secret orders that he would have to institute a general purge" of the
officer corps.[160] Besides Szombathelyi, General Náday, commander
of the 1st Army, was also sacked, and the Gestapo arrested two senior
intelligence officers, Major General István Újszászy and Colonel
Gyula Kádár.[161] The purge extended well beyond the army, including several political leaders known to be hostile to Nazism, such as
the Keresztes-Fischer brothers and Endre Bajcsy-Zsilinszky (who
was wounded in a shoot-out with the agents sent to arrest him).[162]

The German occupation had two effects on the MKHL. The
immediate effect was that all units were grounded until the situation had settled. When it was apparent that there would be no defections, normal operations resumed. The definition of normal
operation changed right away, however, because in the aftermath
of the occupation, Allied bombers began striking targets in Hungary. As long as there was the possibility of a separate peace with
Budapest, the B-17s and B-24s of Fifteenth Air Force had passed
over Hungarian airspace with little resistance on their way to targets in Austria and Romania.[163]

That uneasy existence ended on April 3 with a 200-bomber raid
on the Csepel Island aircraft factories. The OLP controllers working in the caves under Gellért Hill scrambled 2/1 Fighter Squadron
at 11:00, and its sister squadron 1/1, a few minutes later. The large
group of American bombers had not made their customary turn to
the northwest over Lake Balaton.[164] The air raid sirens sounding in
Budapest were mostly ignored, because there had not been an aerial
attack on the capital since a pair of ineffectual Soviet raids in September 1942.[165] The 2/1 pilots first tried a tactic based on the specu-
lations of the cadre of the Experimental Squadron in which they
approached under the bomber formation before attacking on the
flank. It was believed that the bomber's wing would shield the
fighter from defensive fire until the last second, but this proved

ineffective. Undeterred, the Hungarians managed to shoot down one bomber and one escorting P-38, at the loss of one Bf 109 and pilot.[166] Over 1,000 people were killed and 500 wounded in the Fifteenth Air Force raid.[167] Through the month of April, the raids were sporadic but destructive. The MKHL responded to each one, but with paltry results, in part due to the deficiencies of the OLP's air defense system. Poor communications and inexperience meant the Gellért Hill controllers sometimes vectored the fighters to an empty piece of sky. On April 13, they compounded the error by directing the fighters to land at Ferihegy to refuel just as bombs started landing on the airfield.[168] The 1/1 and 2/1 Fighter Squadrons flew 114 sorties in April 1944 and accounted for six Allied aircraft. Three Hungarian pilots were killed in action.[169]

Attacks intensified through the spring and early summer. The planners of the Anglo-American Combined Bomber Offensive were instructed to give "top priority to bombing communications in Romania and Hungary and to treat the whole European transport system 'as one' when undermining German mobility."[170] The Allies' concentration from June on destroying the sources of German oil also brought more bombers to Hungary, whose oil fields south of Lake Balaton had grown from almost nothing before the war to an annual production of 840,000 tons per year.[171] Hundreds of Allied bombers attacked in waves, and, despite being reinforced by eighty fighters of the Luftwaffe's 8th Fighter Wing, the defenders were simply overwhelmed. The June 14 attack on the Pét nitrogen plants was a red-letter day for the combined Axis air defense forces: they claimed eighteen American airplanes destroyed (eleven to AAA, five to MKHL fighters, two to the Luftwaffe). That success was followed by the "black day" raids on June 16. Twenty-eight MKHL fighters from the 101st Fighter Group (a new formation created out of existing Budapest squadrons) scrambled to meet the American force of 658 bombers and 290 fighters. Five P-38s fell, but at the astounding cost of thirteen Hungarian fighters.[172] Not all raids were so one-sided, but even when the MKHL defenders exacted a heavy cost from the attackers, as on the June 14 Pét raid, it made no difference to the direction of the battle. The Americans came back the next day, or the next week, with bigger formations, while the Hungarian force just got smaller. By September, fuel shortages kept MKHL fighters on the ground during many US Army Air Force bombing raids. As refined aviation fuel became scarcer, the Luftwaffe retained most of the stock for its own use.[173] With fewer defense fighters challenging the bomber force, American fighter aircraft began low-level attacks on Hungarian airfields. These raids proved effective in further eroding the MKHL's air defense fleet.

That fleet had performed well when compared to its German counterparts. According to Luftwaffe records, from March to November 1944, the height of the Allied bombing raids, its pilots flew 932 daytime air defense sorties over Hungary. Those flights resulted in seventy-three confirmed victories against American attackers, at a loss of eighty-eight Luftwaffe airplanes and forty-three casualties. In the same time, the MKHL flew 649 defensive missions and scored 107 kills, while losing seventy-eight aircraft and thirty pilots.[174] These figures show that the Hungarians destroyed an enemy airplane for every six sorties flown, while the Germans needed thirteen flights on average to achieve a victory. The MKHL suffered a higher rate of airplane losses (one per eight flights) than the Luftwaffe (one every eleven flights), but pilot casualties were identical (one loss per twenty-two sorties). The motivation of defending one's homeland could account for the MKHL's greater lethality, as could the decreasing experience level of German pilots owing to the extremely high casualty rates in other theatres.[175]

Because many MKHL records were destroyed in the war, exact figures for personnel and aircraft losses are difficult to determine. The records of the Horthy Aviation Academy did survive, however, and they show that nearly 700 cadets passed into the air force from Kassa. Through the second class of 1944, the last to face sustained battle, over 20 per cent of the officers from the academy were killed in combat or crashes.[176] Even though primary flight airplanes were imported throughout the war (100 Bü 131s arrived from Germany in 1944), the training schools struggled to replace these airmen.[177]

In early October 1944, the Red Army began its attack on Debrecen, and the weight of the Hungarian defense efforts shifted to the east. The American bombers were not yet left alone: on November 5, four MKHL pilots were shot down by US escort fighters, and four more were killed in the next two days.[178] From November 7, 101st Home Defense Wing only sent its units to attack the Soviet army grinding their way across the plain.[179]

By that date, the MKHL had ceased to exist in any significant way, because Hungary itself had become a true puppet state of Germany. As German losses mounted through the summer of 1944, Admiral Horthy began to reassert himself as the head of state. After forcing an end to the deportation of Hungary's Jews to the death camps, Horthy finally forced Sztójay to resign. In his place he appointed General Géza Lakatos, who had previously commanded both the 1st and 2nd Armies. The change occurred on August 29, just days after Romania had deserted the Axis for the Allies. Finland left the war on September 2, and Bulgaria on September 5. The time was ripe for Hungary to conclude its peace, too. After the Red Army broke through the Hungarian defense line in the Carpathians on September 6, Horthy called a Crown Council. It was reluctant to approve an armistice; days of negotiation and dithering followed. The cabinet was no more resolute. Horthy decided to send General Náday to the West as his personal envoy, accompanied by Colonel Charles Howie, a South African prisoner of war working with the Hungarian underground. The two stole away in a Heinkel flown by a former MALERT pilot named János Majoros. They reached Foggia on September 22, but because Náday did not have written authorisation from Horthy to negotiate on Hungary's behalf, he made no headway with the Allied leaders there.[180]

At the same time, negotiations began with the Soviets through a Hungarian count with freedom to move in Slovakia. The Hungarian mission that was sent to Moscow in the first days of October maintained radio contact directly with the palace. After some delays attributable to the amateur radio operators in Budapest (Horthy's son Nicky, István's widow Ilona, and the regent's aide-de-camp), Lieutenant General László Faragó reached acceptable terms with Molotov on October 10. According to the terms, Hungary would cease operations against the Soviet Union; would within ten days pull its forces out of territory gained after 1937; and would declare war against Germany. The German plenipotentiary in Hungary, Edmund Veesenmayer, had of course learned of Horthy's plan, and was prepared to counter it. The German commando Major Otto Skorzeny (most famous for his rescue of Mussolini) had arrived in Budapest in late September, and Veesenmayer had Szálasi waiting in the wings to take over the government.[181] Feeling mounting pressure from German troops around Budapest and from Soviet leaders in Moscow, Horthy announced the armistice to the cabinet on October 14, five days earlier than he had planned.[182]

The Germans were ready. Skorzeny's team kidnapped Nicky Horthy, rolled him in a carpet and took him to Mauthausen. Ilona told her father-in-law about the kidnapping minutes before the beginning of the Crown Council. All members of the council, including the pro-German stalwarts, approved of the decision to sign the armistice. Horthy's sense of honor required him to inform Veesenmayer of his intentions before broadcasting the proclamation. Lakatos had prevailed on Horthy to strike out a key clause of his address that declared Hungary at war with Germany. The message that went out was therefore somewhat more vague than Horthy realized, and his call for Honvéd soldiers to follow the orders of their commanders allowed room for real mischief. General Vörös approved an order that contradicted the regent's message, and instructed the army to fight on until told otherwise.[183] General Béla Miklós of the First Army went over to the Red Army as Horthy had intended, but his subordinate commanders did not follow. The Second Army's commander, General Lajos Dálnoki-Veress, was arrested by his own chief of staff before he could do the same.[184]

Horthy was convinced that the army would follow the directive of the supreme warlord, and he was stunned when he realized that hardly any large Honvédség formations had changed sides. Through the evening of October 15, German troops in Budapest completed the occupation begun on March 19. Around 04:00, the regent was awakened and encouraged to send his family to the Papal Nuncio for protection. He was prepared to resist to the last, but Lakatos had already agreed an abdication with Veesenmayer. The regent eventually yielded. Horthy twice refused to appoint Szálasi prime minister, but gave in after threats against Nicky, and signed a letter of abdication. The regent told Veesenmayer that he had neither appointed Szálasi nor resigned, but had merely exchanged his signature for his son's life.[185] Horthy and his family left for house arrest in Bavaria on October 17. Nicky was liberated from Dachau (he had been moved from Mauthausen) in May 1945.

The Hungarian army, of whose loyalty Horthy had been confident, failed almost entirely to heed his October 15 order. General Miklós directed his senior subordinate commanders in the First Army to obey the regent and defect. Not a single corps or division commander did so. One regimental commander who attempted to change sides had his own order disobeyed, and was executed by the Germans.[186] Each commander who continued to fight alongside the Wehrmacht would have had his own set of rationales for his actions. A list of those might include an ideological affinity for National Socialism; a strong pro-German ethnic or cultural identity; antipathy toward communism; fear of foreign occupation; desire to retain the Vienna Award territories; feelings of camaraderie for German soldiers; or simple confusion about the validity of the Horthy order when countermanded by Vörös. It is of course possible that all of those notions could be held at once without serious cognitive dissonance, and without feeling oneself a traitor to Hungary. Certainly there were officers who were so committed to the tenets of National Socialism that their loyalty to Hungary came a poor second. Horthy was aware of that contingent and had tried since the days of Gömbös to reduce their numbers and influence. Events suggest that he had underestimated both. The officer corps seems to have had more men like Rátz, Werth, Bartha, Homlok, and Beregffy than those like Szombathelyi and Keresztes-Fischer, or even Horthy himself. But even for those Honvédség officers who were not ideologically motivated to cling to Germany, the idea of swapping sides was distasteful. It must have been nearly impossible for them to see the advancing Red Army as a potential ally, and the Germans they had fought alongside for three years as the enemy. For twenty-five years—or the entire lifetime of a Honvédség company commander—Hungary had mourned its losses in the First World War, and reviled the Russian-inspired communism that had preceded the Romanian intervention. That the order to surrender to the Soviets came from Admiral Horthy, the exemplar of revisionism and anti-Bolshevism, would have seemed too bizarre to credit. The right thing for the nation, they might have reasoned, would be to fight the invading Russians, Romanians, and Slovaks as long as possible. This notion comports with the concept of conditional loyalty proposed earlier. Just as the Hungarian Red Army began defecting to Horthy's Whites when Kun retreated from Czechoslovakia, the Honvédség refused to defect to the Soviets while they had an allied army still willing to fight.

There were no unit defections in the MKHL, either. Hungarian airmen would have felt even closer to their German comrades than did the Honvéds. The relationship between the MKHL and Luftwaffe had been more intimate than that between the Honvédség and Wehrmacht. Hungarian pilots flew German planes, with German training and using German tactics. Although the squadrons themselves remained separate, German and Hungarian pilots often shared the same airfields. They also shared a bond as combat airmen. These factors made it extremely unlikely that a large collection of airmen would have crossed over to the Soviet side.

It is intriguing, however, that the fascistic fervor found in the Luftwaffe and RA was largely absent in the MKHL. Both the

German and Italian air forces were known as the services most penetrated by radicalism, but the Hungarian air force, despite its dependence on those services for equipment and training, appears to have been less affected by extremism than the army. Perhaps the biggest reason lies in the personalities of the leaders. Both Göring and Balbo were devoted to Fascism, and both were larger-than-life, charismatic figures. They deliberately promoted air power in political terms. The interwar Hungarian aviation leaders, namely István Petróczy and László Háry, were well regarded, or even loved, by their airmen, but neither was a political radical, or even especially charismatic. The later prominence of István Horthy in the MKHL, with his liberal pro-Western orientation, suggests the air force was a comfortable place for moderates or the apolitical. The very small size of the clandestine Hungarian air service also made it statistically unlikely that many radicals would be found there. Furthermore, the modest cadre of officers with flight experience made it more difficult for Gömbös and his successors to pack the service with radicals possessed of the necessary technical abilities.

Nevertheless, Hungarian airmen fought on beside the Luftwaffe into 1945. The Szálasi coup made little operational difference to the MKHL, which was by then a force in unalterable decline, unable to exercise initiative. As a sign of its collapse as an airborne force, Ferenc Szálasi appointed Lieutenant General Emil Justy, an air defense artillery officer, to command the MKHL. Through the winter of 1944/1945, Hungarian pilots engaged in hopeless contests against the aircraft supporting the 3rd Ukrainian Front forces besieging Budapest. In December 1944, MKHL pilots shot down twenty-eight Soviet airplanes, but could only muster two Ju 52s to assist the Luftwaffe in aerial resupply missions. During one eleven-day period of the siege, the Hungarians flew 291 sorties and destroyed sixteen Red Air Force aircraft. In the same time, the Soviets flew more than 8,000 sorties.[187] After the capital fell, the remnants of the MKHL conducted a fighting retreat westward toward Austria. Its last aerial victory came on March 27 against an American

P-38. Two days later it suffered its last combat casualty, when Major
János Báthy was killed near the old Habsburg center of aviation,
Wiener Neustadt. As in 1918 and 1919, Hungarian airmen defended
their country until they no longer had airfields from which to operate, and then they attempted to salvage as many aircraft as possible
from the invaders.

NOTES

1. See above, ch. 6.
2. *MKHL, 1938–1945,* p. 96.
3. Vesztényi, "A magyar katonai repülés" (HL Tgy 2.787), pp. V/16, 50.
4. Ibid., pp. V/48–51. János Vesztényi was a wartime MKHL pilot.
5. Poland: Peszke, "Poland's Military Aviation," p. 20.
6. Cited in Vesztényi, "A magyar katonai repülés" (HL Tgy 2.787), p. V/19.
7. Macartney, *October Fifteenth,* 1:466.
8. Gy. Juhász, *Hungarian Foreign Policy,* pp. 181–183. Eckhardt made it to
America later that year, but Bethlen never departed for London. He died in a
Soviet prison camp.
9. Horthy, *Memoirs,* p. 182.
10. Szinai and Szűcs, *Horthy Miklós titkos iratai,* pp. 289–291.
11. Macartney, *October Fifteenth,* 1:487–490.
12. See ch. 3.
13. Szinai and Szűcs, *Horthy Miklós titkos iratai,* p. 292.
14. Quoted in Cartledge, *Will to Survive,* p. 381.
15. Ibid.; and Gy. Juhász, *Hungarian Foreign Policy,* pp. 185–186.
16. *MKHL, 1938–1945,* p. 129.
17. Niehorster, *Royal Hungarian Army,* p. 170.
18. Olasz, "Jugoszláv légitámadások Magyarország ellen 1941 áprilisában,"
pp. 169–171.
19. Ibid., pp. 181–183.
20. Ibid., pp. 183–197.
21. Pagáts, "Légitámadás Pécs és Siklós ellen," p. 11.
22. Macartney, *October Fifteenth,* 2:12.
23. Olasz, "Jugoszláv légitámadások Magyarország ellen," p. 197.
24. Kelemen, "A bombázó iskolától az 1. önálló távol felderítő századig,"
pp. 58–59.
25. Bonhardt et al., *A Magyar Királyi Honvédség fegyverzete,* p. 304.
26. *MKHL, 1938–1945,* p. 132. Károly Kelemen was the older brother of the Ju
86 pilot whose reconnaissance report initiated the paradrop mission.
27. Vesztényi, "A magyar katonai repülés" (HL Tgy 2.787), pp. V/140–142.
28. *MKHL, 1938–1945,* p. 132.

29. Vesztényi, "A magyar katonai repülés" (HL Tgy 2.787), p. V/142.

30. *MKHL, 1938–1945*, p. 133.

31. Quoted in ibid., p. 99.

32. Quoted in ibid., p. 101.

33. Ibid., p. 94, and Neulen, *In the Skies of Europe*, p. 122.

34. Neulen, *In the Skies of Europe*, p. 122.

35. Kováts, *Sólymok, Héják, Nebulók*, pp. 57, 121.

36. Quoted in Macartney, *October Fifteenth*, 2:18.

37. As had Teleki before him, who submitted a resignation letter to Horthy in September 1940 in part to protest Werth's meddling. See Szinai and Szűcs, *Confidential Papers of Admiral Horthy*, pp. 133–148.

38. Stahel, *Operation Barbarossa*, pp. 81–82.

39. Macartney, *October Fifteenth*, 2:18–20.

40. Stahel, *Operation Barbarossa*, p. 153.

41. Quoted in Gy. Juhász, *Hungarian Foreign Policy*, pp. 189.

42. Macartney, *October Fifteenth*, 2:25.

43. Borsányi, "A 1941 június 26-ai kassai bombatámadás," p. 90.

44. Macartney, *October Fifteenth*, 2:26.

45. Ibid., pp. 27–29.

46. *MKHL, 1938–1945*, p. 140.

47. Quoted in Macartney, *October Fifteenth*, 2:29. "Basta!" is Italian for "enough!"

48. Document reproduced in Borsányi, "A 1941 június 26-ai kassai bombatámadás," p. 95. It is unclear if Krudy meant SM.75 transports or Ca.135 bombers, but there were no Savoia bombers in Hungarian service. Neither had a swept leading edge like a Ju 52.

49. Ibid., p. 96.

50. Sakmyster, "Search for a Casus Belli," p. 55.

51. Dreisziger, "New Twist to an Old Riddle," p. 242.

52. Ormay, "Még egyszer a Kassai bombázásról," p. 132.

53. Dreisziger, "New Twist to an Old Riddle," p. 238; Kistelegdi, "A repülő akadémia története," p. 185.

54. Vesztényi, "A magyar katonai repülés" (HL Tgy 2.787), p. V/252.

55. Ormay, "Még egyszer a Kassai bombázásról," p. 132.

56. Pirity, "Visszaemlékezés" (HL Tgy 3.707), p. 150. Pirity also recounts a conversation with Krudy in September 1941 in which Krudy quizzed him about how Pirity, who had earlier fought Soviet bombers in the Finnish War, was able to identify them in flight.

57. Dreisziger, "New Twist to an Old Riddle," pp. 238–239.

58. Ormay, "Kassai bombák," pp. 86–89.

59. Ibid., p. 90.

60. Macartney, "Hungary's Declaration of War on the U.S.S.R. in 1941," pp. 164–165, and *October Fifteenth*, 2:32.

61. Stenge, *Baptism of Fire*, p. 100. The pilot was Ján Režnák, who became Slovakia's highest-scoring fighter pilot.

62. Balogh, "Nyilatkozat az 1941.jún.26.-i Bustyaháza feletti légiincidensről" (HL Tgy 2.979), pp. 1–3.

63. Ormay, "A Bustyaházai incidens," p. 72.

64. Sakmyster, "Search for a Casus Belli," pp. 59–60.

65. Ormay, "Milyen gépek bombázhatták és milyen gépek nem bombázhatták Kassat?," pp. 50–51.

66. Quoted in *MKHL, 1938–1945*, p. 141.

67. Macartney, *October Fifteenth*, 2:29–30.

68. *MKHL, 1938–1945*, pp. 140, 142; and Gaal, "Bombers at Large," p. 83.

69. Gaal, "Bombers at Large," p. 83.

70. Vesztényi, "A magyar katonai repülés" (HL Tgy 2.787), pp. V/255–256.

71. Gaal, "Bombers at Large," p. 84.

72. Vesztényi, "A magyar katonai repülés" (HL Tgy 2.787), p. V/257.

73. Gaal, "Bombers at Large," pp. 85–87.

74. Dombrády and Tóth, *A Magyar Királyi Honvédség*, pp. 195–196.

75. Quoted in *MKHL, 1938–1945*, p. 143.

76. Vesztényi, "A magyar katonai repülés" (HL Tgy 2.787), p. V/262.

77. Quoted in *MKHL, 1938–1945*, p. 144.

78. Quoted in Hangodi, "A M. Kir. Honvéd 4/I-es Nehézbombázó-Osztály története, 1936–1945," p. 158.

79. Punka and Sárhidai, *Magyar sasok*, p. 39; and *MKHL, 1938–1945*, p. 145.

80. Dombrády and Tóth, *A Magyar Királyi Honvédség*, pp. 195–196.

81. *MKHL, 1938–1945*, p. 146.

82. Vesztényi, "A magyar katonai repülés" (HL Tgy 2.787), pp. V/269–274.

83. *MKHL, 1938–1945*, pp. 146–148.

84. Nagyváradi et al., *Fejezetek a repülés történetéből*, p. 245.

85. *MKHL, 1938–1945*, p. 150.

86. Gaal, "Bridge over the River Bug," pp. 80–87.

87. Erickson, *Road to Stalingrad*, p. 204.

88. Punka and Sárhidai, *Magyar sasok*, p. 33.

89. Szinai and Szűcs, *Horthy Miklós titkos iratai*, pp. 307–308.

90. Macartney, *October Fifteenth*, 2:54.

91. Ibid.; Gy. Juhász, *Hungarian Foreign Policy*, pp. 200–201.

92. Quoted in Gy. Juhász, *Hungarian Foreign Policy*, pp. 200–201.

93. Quoted in Cornelius, *Hungary in World War II*, p. 184.

94. Dombrády and Tóth, *A Magyar Királyi Honvédség*, pp. 226–227. The requested contribution is also given as twenty-six divisions (Szabó) and twelve brigades (Cornelius). Waffen SS: Gy. Juhász, *Hungarian Foreign Policy*, p. 207.

95. Horthy, *Memoirs*, p. 182.

96. Quoted in Péntek, "István Horthy's Election as Vice-Regent," p. 76.

97. Quoted in Cornelius, *Hungary in World War II*, p. 197.

98. Horthy, *Memoirs*, p. 193, 203.

99. *MKHL, 1938–1945*, p. 157.

100. Dombrády and Tóth, *A Magyar Királyi Honvédség*, pp. 231–232.

101. Cornelius, *Hungary in World War II*, p. 194.

102. The unit was called the 1st Flying Group until October 15, when it became known as the 2nd Aviation Brigade. I use the later designation for clarity.

103. *MKHL, 1938–1945*, pp. 158–159.

104. Punka and Sárhidai, *Magyar sasok*, p. 40.

105. Cornelius, *Hungary in World War II*, pp. 207–209.

106. Overy, *Air War 1939–1945*, pp. 62–63.

107. Ibid.

108. Weinberg, *World at Arms*, pp. 413–414.

109. Cornelius, *Hungary in World War II*, p. 208.

110. Quoted in Fenyo, *Hitler, Horthy, and Hungary*, p. 42.

111. M. M. Szabó, *A Magyar Királyi Honvéd Légierő a második világ háborúban*, p. 117.

112. Strachan, *To Arms*, p. 284.

113. Horváth, "A Magyar 2. Hadsereg Közelfelderítő Repülőszázadának," p. 117.

114. Ibid., p. 123; and *MKHL, 1938–1945*, p. 187. Twenty-five was the average of seven days serviceability rates, August 11–18, 1942.

115. Punka, *Hungarian Air Force*, p. 10.

116. Gyulai, *Honor and Duty*, pp. 497–498, 441, 438, 493.

117. Punka and Sárhidai, *Magyar sasok*, p. 42.

118. Macartney, *October Fifteenth*, 2:110–112.

119. Reprinted in Gyulai, *Honor and Duty*, p. 499.

120. Ibid., p. 114. Bartha's replacement, Vilmos Nagy, attributed the change to Bartha's tolerance for the mistreatment of Jews in the labor companies.

121. Cornelius, *Hungary in World War II*, p. 214.

122. Quoted in *MKHL, 1938–1945*, p. 201.

123. Nagyváradi et al., *Fejezetek a repülés történetéből*, p. 253.

124. *MKHL, 1938–1945*, p. 206.

125. Nagyváradi et al., *Fejezetek a repülés történetéből*, p. 255–256.

126. Neulen, *In the Skies of Europe*, p. 129.

127. *MKHL, 1938–1945*, p. 214.

128. P. Szabó, "Hungarian Soldiers in World War Two," pp. 452–454.

129. Cornelius, *Hungary in World War II*, pp. 221–222.

130. Punka and Sárhidai, *Magyar sasok*, p. 42.

131. P. Szabó, "Hungarian Soldiers in World War Two," p. 455.

132. Macartney, *October Fifteenth*, 2:135.

133. Ibid.

134. *MKHL, 1938–1945*, p. 223.

135. Quoted in Neulen, *In the Skies of Europe*, p. 131.

136. *MKHL, 1938–1945*, p. 40.

137. Nagyváradi et al., *Fejezetek a repülés történetéből*, p. 214.

138. *MKHL, 1938–1945*, pp. 51–53.

139. Punka, *Hungarian Air Force*, pp. 22, 41.

140. *MKHL, 1938–1945*, pp. 51–53.

141. Ibid., p. 59.

142. Neulen, *In the Skies of Europe*, p. 131.

143. Contract purchases: *MKHL, 1938–1945*, pp. 59–60; 400 Bf 109s: Punka and Sárhidai, *Magyar sasok*, p. 52.

144. Radice, "Development of Industry," 2:436–437; oil tonnage in 1938, 90% bauxite: Romsics, *Hungary in 20th Century*, pp. 142, 207.

145. Romsics, *Hungary in 20th Century*, p. 207.

146. Ibid., p. 132.

147. Punka and Sárhidai, *Magyar sasok*, p. 46.

148. *MKHL, 1938–1945*, pp. 111–112.

149. Neulen, *In the Skies of Europe*, pp. 132–133.

150. *MKHL, 1938–1945*, p. 112.

151. Gy. Juhász, *Hungarian Foreign Policy*, p. 239.

152. Mócsy, "Hungary's Failed Strategic Surrender," p. 99.

153. Cornelius, *Hungary in World War II*, pp. 275–278; Gy. Juhász, *Hungarian Foreign Policy*, pp. 287–291; Macartney, *October Fifteenth*, 2:233–246.

154. Kállay, *Hungarian Premier*, pp. 419–425.

155. Dombrády and Tóth, *A Magyar Királyi Honvédség*, p. 316.

156. Kállay, *Hungarian Premier*, p. 426.

157. Macartney, *October Fifteenth*, 2:245–246.

158. Ibid., pp. 247–253, 255; Kállay, *Hungarian Premier*, p. 427–438. The Crown Council was a broader assembly convoked by the regent in times of crisis. In contrast to the Council of Ministers, the Crown Council included the president of the supreme court, speakers of the houses of parliament, and former prime ministers and foreign ministers.

159. Quoted in Cornelius, *Hungary in World War II*, p. 280.

160. Macartney, *October Fifteenth*, 2:258, 253n.

161. Cornelius, *Hungary in World War II*, p. 287.

162. Macartney, *October Fifteenth*, 2:254. Bajcsy-Zsilinszky was eventually released, but continued to lead the resistance. He was captured again and executed on December 24, 1944.

163. Although the first substantial combat between the MKHL and Fifteenth Air Force occurred on March 17, the intercepted bombers had turned back from a raid on Vienna due to bad weather. Two MKHL Bf 109s were shot down in this inaugural encounter, with a few B-17s possibly damaged. Gaal, "Bombs of April," p. 75.

164. Ibid., p. 76.

165. Soviet raids: Overy, *Bombing War*, p. 231.

166. Gaal, "Bombs of April," p. 76.

167. *MKHL, 1938–1945*, p. 236.

168. Gaal, "Bombs of April," pp. 77–78.

169. *MKHL, 1938–1945*, pp. 236–237.

170. Overy, *Bombing War*, pp. 293–294.

171. Ibid., p. 594; 840,000 tons: Fenyo, *Hitler, Horthy, and Hungary*, p. 241.

172. Nagyváradi et al., *Fejezetek a repülés történetéből*, p. 214; Punka, *Hungarian Air Force*, pp. 14–15.

173. Bernád et al., *A nemzet szárnyai*, p. 47.

174. Cited in ibid.

175. The average Luftwaffe monthly loss rates in all theatres in 1944 was 1,754 (Overy, *Air War*, p. 186.) The loss rate over Hungary for March–November 1944 of five per month equals 0.29% of that total.

176. Rada, *Ludovika Akadémia*, pp. 345–354.

177. *MKHL, 1938–1945*, p. 60.

178. Nagyváradi et al., *Fejezetek a repülés történetéből*, p. 271.

179. Punka, *Hungarian Air Force*, p. 17.

180. Cornelius, *Hungary in World War II*, pp. 312–319; Horthy, *Memoirs*, pp. 222–226.

181. Macartney, *October Fifteenth*, 2:356–359.

182. Horthy, *Memoirs*, pp. 228–229.

183. Macartney, *October Fifteenth*, 2:414–416. Horthy writes that Vörös assured him he had no personal knowledge of the order (pp. 231–232).

184. Cornelius, *Hungary in World War II*, pp. 312–319.

185. Horthy, *Memoirs*, pp. 236–237.

186. Macartney, *October Fifteenth*, 2:445.

187. Neulen, *In the Skies of Europe*, pp. 144–145.

Conclusion

THUS THE SECOND WORLD WAR ENDED FOR HUNGARIAN airmen in a manner very much like the First World War and the 1919 intervention. It was not just the ending that was familiar. In many ways, the experience of the MKHL was remarkably similar to that of the Habsburg LFT. That this would prove to be so might have come as a surprise to readers of *MKSz* in the mid-1930s; it certainly was not the outcome that Ferenc Szentnémedy had led them to expect. Szentnémedy had predicted a Douhetian future of unrestricted air warfare, in which the heart of the enemy was laid open to direct attack by fleets of bombers impervious to air defense, and capable of destroying the adversary's will to resist. As it happened, the closest Hungarian bombers ever came to a strategic attack was the two-day retaliation campaign against Stanislau and Strij. The MKHL, like the LFT and the VR, was a tactical air force whose primary missions were air defense, aerial reconnaissance, and battlefield interdiction. In the chaos that followed the 1918 dissolution of the imperial army, Hungarian airmen had deliberately stressed continuity in creating the first national air service. During the lean years that followed, visionaries among them had argued for something far removed from the First World War field aviation model: an independent air force with the organizational and operational autonomy to pursue a war-winning strategy. The airmen won the argument, for a time, but their inability to fulfill the promise of air power resulted in a service subordinated to its own army, and eventually its patron's air force. This was something of a regression to the mean, yielding continuity in spite of plans to the contrary.

Hungary's failure to develop an air force capable of effective independent operations is entirely predictable, even natural, given its strategic context and economic capabilities.[1] Hungarian foreign policy during the Horthy era had one goal: the reclamation of the territories lost after the First World War. Successive governments agreed that this objective required rearmament and military expansion, including the development of a capable air force. Notions of massive bomber fleets spreading through continental popular culture had begun to take root in Hungary, and the idea of an autonomous air force was not anathema to Hungarian political leaders. Unrestricted air war did not suit Hungary's strategic context, however, and, if attempted, could have been counterproductive. Hungarian revisionism, even in its maximalist form, had fairly limited aims—it required only the reoccupation of contiguous territories sliced away at Trianon. Aerial destruction of Prague or Bucharest might have been satisfying to consider, but it would have been a strategic disaster, inviting certain Western retaliation. That an air force was expressly prohibited by treaty did not dissuade Hungary from trying to protect and expand its air service, but it did place sizable obstacles in its path by severely limiting its ability to purchase, produce, or operate military airplanes.

The creation and sustainment of an air force that could conduct strategic bombing campaigns was also beyond Hungary's economic capability. The worldwide economic crisis of the early 1930s had hit Hungary late, but hard, erasing the financial gains realized in the late 1920s. Lack of capital and collapsing commodity prices left Hungary unable to finance further large weapons purchases. Only Mussolini's willingness to extend arms credits to Horthy's regime allowed Hungary to slowly modernize and expand its clandestine air service. It was not until the institution in 1938 of Imrédy's Győr program that Hungary's rearmament was domestically funded, and its billion pengős were raised from internal loans and a one-time wealth tax—hardly a formula for a sustainable defense buildup. Hungary possessed large deposits of bauxite and some oil, but these industries were underdeveloped until German wartime investment financed their expansion.

Hungary also lacked the scientific and technical mobilization required to create a strategic air force. Habsburg factories had not been able to provide sufficient airplanes for the LFT in the First World War, and the situation had not improved for an independent Hungary in the intervening years. The country had neither the established aircraft manufacturing capacity nor the raw economic strength required to create one from scratch. It did have a few industrial concerns, such as WM and MÁVAG, that could produce foreign designs and make incremental improvements, but even those production lines, subsidized by foreign credits, could not sustain the MKHL losses in combat. Air power, perhaps more than any other form of military strength, requires a strong industrial base. No country, with the possible exception of present-day Israel, has been able to become even a regional air power without manufacturing its own combat airplanes in substantial numbers. As Hungary's experience with both Italy and Germany shows, reliance on foreign producers can lead to inopportune interruptions in the supply (as when Berlin held up deliveries of He 112s to Budapest, but fulfilled Bucharest's order) or to on-time delivery of inadequate machines (the returned Ca.310s). Kálmán Csukás, who later commanded 1/1 Fighter Squadron and was killed at Ilovskoje, recognized in March 1940 the difficulties that a small country would face in trying to conduct an independent air war. He suggested that in the future, small countries would probably fight as part of a larger alliance. Further, he wrote, "small countries normally do not possess their own independent aviation industry, but rather purchase particular types from large powers. They have to be familiar with the large power's strategic concept, because only then can one judge whether the material is suitable for its objective."[2]

The strategic context and economic and industrial deficiencies should not have caused Hungarian airmen to abandon the idea of a strong, and even independent, air force, but perhaps more consideration should have been given them when planning the air service's force structure. Having no vital interests outside the Danube basin, Hungary had no immediate need for long-range bombers. An all-fighter force based on the WM-14 engine and the CR.42 and Re.2000 could have fulfilled the critical missions of Hungarian aviation: defending the country's exposed industrial center, supporting the Honvéd in limited ground incursions, and blunting an armored invasion. A tactical air fleet of comparatively few varieties of single-engine airplanes would have simplified production and repair, as well as aircrew training, and it would have permitted the MKHL to build deeper stocks of spare parts. Increased pilot proficiency and a concentration on tactical operations would have encouraged the development of more sophisticated tactics, and could have led to innovations in fields such as aerial communications and close air support.

This approach (very similar to the one championed by Mecozzi) would have been no less dependent on political and social receptiveness than was the one followed by the LÜH. The *Justice for Hungary* flight and the later crash, Bánhidi's Gerle 13 successes, and the glamour of international travel increased air-mindedness among the Hungarian public. Support for air power among the Hungarian political and military elites turned out to be broad but shallow. The enthusiasm created for the air arm in the 1930s was fleeting, and could have been intensified by its very prohibition by Trianon. Once the service was able to operate in the open, criticism of its performance increased, and the organizational weaknesses were exposed. After the regent withdrew his protection of the MKHL, the VKF was able to reassert control of the air arm. Had the airmen inclined toward independence pressed their case with less vehemence in the 1930s, it is possible that the service would have gained its autonomy somewhat later, but maintained it much longer. That is by no means certain, however, for a more restrained campaign could have resulted only in a force of short-range reconnaissance squadrons, one of the options proposed by the VKF in 1938.

Ultimately, this study of the Hungarian air service demonstrates the degree to which circumstances constrain action. Examinations of the American, British, Japanese, and German air forces often turn on principles declared, decisions taken, and opportunities missed. Those are of critical importance indeed, and the intellectual history of the Hungarian air force as depicted in its professional journal occupies a central part of this book. But the great powers were free to follow their strategic and operational concepts in a way that was completely unknown to the smaller combatants. The composition and employment of the large air forces, at least in the first years of the war, reflected their airmen's conceptions of aerial warfare. In marked contrast, the Hungarian airman operated from the beginning at a severe disadvantage. The years of aerial disarmament deprived him of realistic training and experience in large-force operations, and the lack of adequate domestic aircraft production meant that he flew too little, and in out-of-date machines. Unlike his German comrade, he found that equality of arms was merely a legal status, not a tactical reality.

NOTES

1. Strategic context, economic capability, scientific and technical mobilization, and political and social reception are the factors identified by R. J. Overy as conditioning the evolution of air forces. See Overy, "Air Power in the Second World War."

2. Csukás, "Önálló légiháború," p. 45.

Bibliography

MANUSCRIPTS AND ARCHIVAL STUDIES

Hadtörténelmi Levéltár (HL–Military History Archives, Budapest)
HL Honvédelmi Minisztérium Elnöki (HM Eln.)
    HL HM Eln. 5141/37.-1919.
    HL HM Eln. 16059/37.-1919.
    HL HM Eln. 16385/37.-1919.
    HL HM Eln. 21626a/37.-1919.
    HL HM Eln. 21688/37.-1920.
    HL HM Eln. 16606/6.k-1927
Balogh, J. "Nyilatkozat az 1941.jún.26.-i Bustyaháza feletti légiincidensről." HL
    Tanulmánygyűjtemény (Tgy–Study Collections) 2.979, pp. 1–3.
Bánhidi, "Egy volt vadászpilóta visszaemlékezése 1941. június 26-ára", HL Tgy
    2815.
Horváth, M. "Visszaemlékezés (repülő élményei 1915-től 1918-ig és 1919-es tábori
    pilóta élményei)" (1973), HL Tgy 3.643.
Pirity, M. "Visszaemlékezés." HL Tgy 3.707.
Vesztényi, J. "A magyar katonai repülés, 1920–1945" (1978), HL Tgy 2.787.
Winkler, L. "A magyar repülés története 1927–1945" (1992), HL Tgy 3.327.
————. "A Magyar Királyi Honvéd Légierő harci repülőgépeinek fejlődéséről"
    (1994), HL Tgy 3.643.
Hadtörténelmi Intézet Könyvtára (HIK–Military History Archives, Budapest)
Petróczy, I. "A legyőzött Németország aviatikája: Tanulságok és teendők" (1921),
    HIK 5271.
Magyar Műszaki és Közlekedési Múzeum Levéltára (MMKM–Hungarian Tech-
    nical and Transportation Museum Archives, Budapest)
Fehér, A. "Berepülő pilóta naplója, 1915–1927." MMKM 988.
MALERT forgalmi eredmények, MKKM 1563
Dr. Szentkirályi Ákos hagyatéka, MMKM 108.

Magyar Országos Levéltár (MOL–Hungarian National Archives, Budapest)
K. 589/8930-12 (Regent's Official Documents, 1919-1944)

PRINTED PRIMARY SOURCES

"2 More Airplanes Poised for Sea Hop." *Washington Post,* June 25, 1931, p. 1.
"354 Aero Club de France Pilot Aviators." *Flight,* Feb. 4, 1910, p. 88.
"Accidents to Flyers." *Flight,* Dec. 3, 1911, p. 997.
"Advertisement: 1025 Miles Non-stop." *Flight,* Oct 26, 1933, p. ix.
"Aeronautics: For Hungary." *Time* magazine, July 27, 1931.
"Aeronautics: For Hungary." *Time* magazine, May 30, 1932.
"Aircraft and the War." *Flight,* March 26, 1915, p. 298.
"Aircraft and the War." *Flight,* February 17, 1916, p. 144.
A Magyar Tanácsköztársaság röplapjai: bibliográfia és dokumentumgyüjtemény (Budapest, 1959).
A Magyar Vörös Hadsereg 1919, válogatott dokumentumok (Budapest, 1959).
Arady, I. "Magyar cserkészet és légoltalom." *Riadó!* 1/1 (Oct. 1937): 28.
"Armistice Convention with Austria-Hungary . . . November 3, 1918." Accessed Apr. 23, 2016. http://www.forost.ungarisches-institut.de/pdf/19181103-1.pdf.
"Ascension Captive" broadsheet advertisement. Accessed May 20, 2016 https:// www.loc.gov/item/2002724879/.
"Austria Stunned." *The Times,* June 7, 1919, p. 11.
"Austrian Military Dirigible." *Flight,* Dec. 11, 1909, p. 801.
"Aviators' Certificates." *Flight,* Jan. 7, 1911, p. 11.
"Az első légi hadjárat." *Riadó!* 3/12 (Nov. 15, 1939): 314–316.
"Ballon Captif Godard" poster (1896). Navtech Aviation Poster Collection. Accessed Apr. 23, 2016. http://posters.navtech.aero/pages/00192.html.
"Balloon Park" poster (1893). Navtech Aviation Poster Collection. Accessed Apr. 23, 2016. http://posters.navtech.aero/pages/00213.html.
Bobok, M. "Vállalkozás ejtőernyőkkel az ellenség hátában." *MKSz,* no. 3 (1936): 132–135.
"Budapest Flight Plan to Aid Hungary." *New York Times,* July 8, 1930, p. 8.
"Captain Magyar Lands as an Immigrant." *New York Times,* Nov. 13, 1931, p. 4.
"Chateau Aerien" broadside advertisement (1894). Accessed May 20, 2016. https:// www.loc.gov/resource/cph.3g10460/.
Ciano, G. *Ciano's Diary, 1939–1943.* Edited by M. Muggeridge (London, 1947).
"City Intelligence," *The Times,* July 1, 1910, p . 19, col. 2
Clausewitz, C. von. *On War.* Translated by M. Howard and P. Paret (Princeton, NJ, 1976).
———. *A haborúról.* Translated by S. Hazai (Budapest, 1917).
"Croydon-Hungary Non-Stop." *Flight,* Sept. 21, 1933, p. 951.
Csukás, K. "Az önálló légiháború." *MKSz,* no. 3 (1940): 700–706.

Diplomáciai iratok Magyarország külpolitikájához 1936–1945 (DIMK), Vol. 2. Edited by L. Zsigmond and M. Ádám (Budapest, 1965).

Documents on British Foreign Policy, 1919–1939 (DBFP). First Ser., Vol. 12. Edited by R. Butler and J. P. T. Bury (London, 1962).

———. First Ser., Vol. 16. Edited by R. Butler and J. P. T. Bury (London, 1986).

———. First Ser., Vol. 22. Edited by W. N. Medlicott and D. Dakin (London, 1986).

———. First Ser., Vol. 24. Edited by W. N. Medlicott and D. Dakin (London, 1986).

———. First Ser., Vol. 26. Edited by W. N. Medlicott and D. Dakin (London, 1985).

———. First Ser., Vol. 27. Edited by W. N. Medlicott and D. Dakin (London, 1986).

———. Ser. 1a, Vol. 5. Edited by W. N. Medlicott and D. Dakin (London, 1973).

———. Ser. 1a, Vol. 7. Edited by W. N. Medlicott, D. Dakin, and M. E. Lambert (London, 1975).

———. Ser. 2, Vol. 3. Edited by E. L. Woodward and R. Butler (London, 1948).

Documents on German Foreign Policy, 1918–1945 (DGFP). Ser. D, Vol. 2. Edited by J. Wheeler-Bennett et al. (London, 1949).

Douhet, G. *The Command of the Air*. Translated by D. Ferrari (New York, 1942; repr. Washington, DC, 1983).

Eszenyi, D. "Támpontok a bombázó hajózó személyzet kiképzéséhez," *MKSz*, no. 2 (1940): 422–431.

"Federation Aeronautique Internationale." *Flight*, Apr. 5, 1913, p. 387.

"The Fokker F III Commercial Monoplane." *Flight*, May 26, 1921, p. 56.

"Foreign Aviation News." *Flight*, July 9, 1910, p. 530.

"Forty-Seven Lives Lost in Airship Accidents." *New York Times*, July 14, 1910.

"German Pilot Aviators." *Flight*, Mar. 18, 1910, p. 230.

"The Great Powers and Aviation," *Flight*, Apr. 24, 1909, p. 232.

Haldane, J. B. S. *Callinicus: A Defense of Chemical Weapons* (London, 1925).

Hellebronth, G. "A légiháború és a védekezés módjai." *MKSz*, no. 8 (1935): 100–103.

———. "A légiháború és a védekezés módjai." *MKSz*, no. 6 (1936): 117–122.

———. "A légiháború és a védekezés módjai." *MKSz*, no. 11 (1937): 96–105.

Horthy, N. *Memoirs* (New York, 1957).

"How Hungary Received the Treaty." *The Times*, Jan. 19, 1920, p. 11.

"Hungarian Atlantic Flight Succeeds." *Flight*, July 24, 1931, p. 730.

"Hungarians to Fly Here." *New York Times*, Sept. 5, 1930, p. 12.

Imperial and Royal General Staff. *Die Armeemanöver in Nordungarn* (Vienna, 1912).

"India and Ceylon Exhibition of 1896" advertisement. *The Times*, Apr. 18, 1896. Also available at http://www.victorianlondon.org/entertainment/indiaandceylon.htm.

Italian General Staff. *The Italo-Turkish War (1911–12)*. Translated by R. Tittoni (Kansas City, MO, 1914).

Kállay, N. *Hungarian Premier: A Personal Account of a Nation's Struggle in the Second World War* (New York, 1954).

Károlyi, M. *Memoirs of Michael Karolyi: Faith without Illusion*. Translated by C. Károlyi (Oxford, 1956).

Knauss, R. *War in the Air*. Translated by C. Sykes (London, 1932).

"Leszállás nélkül akar Los Angelestől Csikágóig repülni Magyar Sándor és Endresz György." *Uj Nemzedék*, Aug. 28, 1930, p. 10.

"Lindbergh Picks a Plane." *Popular Mechanics*, Nov. 1930, pp. 803–805.

Madarász, L. *Légi háború: A repülők harcászata* (Budapest, 1928).

"Magyar Pilota Pic Nic." *Flight*, Sept. 27, 1934, pp. 1003–1004, 1028.

Mecozzi, A. *L'Aviazione d'assalto* (Rome, 1933)."More Continental Aviators." *Flight*, May 7, 1911, p. 402.

Nagy, E. "Hungarian Holiday," *Flight*, Aug. 8, 1935.

———. "Hungarian Interlude," *Flight*, July 2, 1936.

Németh, L. "Polgári légvédelem." *MKSz*, no. 12 (1935): 97–100.

"Nincs kizárva, hogy tavaszra marad a "Justice for Hungary" amerikai startja." *Uj Nemzedék*, Aug. 24, 1930, p. 5.

"Oceanic Airmen's Congress: Hungarian Delegates Killed in Crash." *The Times*, May 23, 1932, p. 16.

Petróczy, "A lengyel lég és gázvédelmi liga tevékenysége." *MKSz*, no. 7 (1932): 121–127.

———. "Hogyan szervezte meg németország a polgári légvédelmet." *MKSz*, no. 1 (1933): 126–132.

"Przemysl leltára." *Huszadik Század*, Apr. 1915. Accessed Apr. 23, 2016. http://www.huszadikszazad.hu/1915-aprilis/politika/przemysl-leltara.

Rakolczai, S. "Légvédelmi és légoltalmi gyakorlatok Budapesten." *Riadó!* 2/10 (Oct. 1938): 294–298.

The Round Table. "Disarmament." *Commonwealth Journal of International Affairs*, 22/87 (1932): 532–551.

Seversky, A. de. "Strategy of Air Power More Humane Than Blood-Bath of Surface Warfare." *Pittsburgh Press*, Nov. 13, 1943, p. 1.

"Slovák légitámadás Ungvár és környéke ellen," *Riadó!* 3/4 (Apr. 1939): 102–103.

Sólyom, A. "A Spanyol háboru a légierők szempontjából." *MKSz*, no. 3 (1938): 119–129.

Szálasy, F. "A légi erők befolyása a hadászatra." *MKSz*, no. 5 (1932): 123–130.

Szentnémedy, F. "Az 19.. évi háboru." *MKSz*, no. 3 (1931): 29–39.

———. "Az 19.. évi háboru." *MKSz*, no. 4 (1931): 90–102.

———. "Az 19.. évi háboru." *MKSz*, no. 5 (1931): 93–107.

———. "Az 19.. évi háboru." *MKSz*, no. 6 (1931): 102–115.

———. "Vélemények és eszmék Douhet 'Az 19.. évi háboru' cimű tanulmánya kapcsán." *MKSz*, no. 7 (1931): 102–117.

———. "A honi légvédelem problémái és korszerű légvédelmi gyakorlatok." *MKSz*, no. 5 (1932): 108–123.

———. "A genfi leszerelési tárgyalások légügyi eredményei." *MKSz*, no. 11 (1932): 96–118.

———. *A repülés* (Budapest, 1933).

———. *Légiháború 1938-ban: Páris szétrombolása* (Budapest, 1935).

———. "Van-e védelem a korlátlan légiháború ellen?" *MKSz*, no. 6 (1935): 96–110.

———. "Új hadmüveleti irányelvek a légiháborúra." *MKSz*, no. 10 (1935): 121–135.

———. "A repülők szerepe az olasz-abesszin háborúban." *MKSz*, no. 4 (1936): 102–116.

———. "Az olasz repülőerők müködése Abessziniában." *MKSz*, no. 9 (1936): 102–116.

———. "A légiháború és a védekezés módjai." *MKSz*, no. 11 (1936): 105–120.

———. "A függőleges átkarolás kérdéséhez." *MKSz*, no. 2 (1937): 97–111.

———. "Az ejtőernyő ujabb katonai jelentősége." *MKSz*, no. 4 (1937): 115–131.

———. "Visszapillantás a légügy mult évi fejlődésére." *MKSz*, no. 1 (1938): 113–139.

———. "A magyar légierő első diadala." *MKSz*, no. 6 (1939): 108–118.

"Szerdán délelőtt ¼ 11 órakor érkezik meg Endresz és Bittay koporsója a Délivasuti pályaudvarra." *Huszadik Század*, May 1932.

Szinai, M., and Szűcs, L. (eds.). *Horthy Miklós titkos iratai* (Budapest, 1965).

Szinai, M., and Szűcs, L. (eds.). *The Confidential Papers of Admiral Horthy* (Budapest, 1968).

Tóth, E. "Szállitások repülés." *MKSz*, no. 5 (1936): 91–96.

———. "Csapaszállitások repülőgéppel és ejtőernyős kirakások." *MKSz*, no. 7 (1936): 116–118.

———. "Légiháboru Spanyolországban." *MKSz*, no. 6 (1937): 97–104.

"Treaty of Friendship, Conciliation and Arbitration between Hungary and Italy, Signed at Rome, April 5, 1927." Accessed July 13, 2013. http://ungarisches -institut.de/dokumente/pdf/19270405-1.pdf.

"Treaty of Peace between the Allied and Associated Powers and Hungary and Protocol and Declaration, Signed at Trianon June 4, 1920, Part V. Military, Naval and Air Clauses." HyperWar Foundation. Accessed Apr. 23, 2016. http:// www.ibiblio.org/hyperwar/////ETO/Dip/Trianon.html.

"Victory for Radio." *Washington Post*, July 17, 1931, p. 3.

PRINTED SECONDARY SOURCES

Balogh, E. S. "Nationality Problems of the Hungarian Soviet Republic." In I. Völgyes (ed.), *Hungary in Revolution, 1919: Nine Essays* (Lincoln, NE, 1971), pp. 89–120.

"Bánhidi Antal, Szatmárnémeti szülöttje," Magyar Közlekedési Közművelődésért Alapítvány. Accessed Mar. 24, 2014. http://mkka.hu/historia/hiressegek /banhidiantal.

Barczy, Z., and Sárhidai, Gy. *A Magyar Királyi Honvédség légvédelme, 1920–1945* (Budapest, 2010).

Berend, I. T. *Decades of Crisis: Central and Eastern Europe before World War II* (Berkeley, CA, 1998).

———. "Agriculture." In M. C. Kaser and E. A. Radice (eds.), *The Economic History of Eastern Europe 1919–1975.* Vol. 1 (Oxford, 1985), pp. 148–209.

Bernád, D. "A Román Királyi Légierő első magyarországi hadjárata." *Aero Historia* (Aug. 1991): 32–46.

———. Magó, K., and Punka, Gy. *A nemzet szárnyai: a magyar katonai repülés évszázados története* (Budapest, 2013).

Biddle, T. D. *Rhetoric and Reality in Air Warfare: The Evolution of British and American Ideas about Strategic Bombing, 1914–1945* (Princeton, NJ, 2002).

Bödők, Z. *Magyar feltalálók a repülés történetében* (Dunaszerdahely, 2002).

Bonhardt, A., Sárhidai, Gy., and Winkler, L. *A Magyar Királyi Honvédség fegyverzete* (Budapest, 2002).

Borsányi, J. "A 1941 június 26-ai kassai bombatámdás 'fehér foltjai.'" *HK* 104/2 (June 1991): 88–122.

Botting, D. *The Giant Airships* (Alexandria, VA, 1981).

Cain, A. C. *The Forgotten Air Force* (Washington, DC, 2002).

Caprotti, F. "Technology and Geographical Imaginations: Representing Aviation in 1930s Italy." *Journal of Cultural Geography*, 25/2: 181–205.

Cartledge, B. *The Will to Survive: A History of Hungary* (London, 2006).

Chadwick, H. M. *The Nationalities of Europe and the Growth of National Ideologies* (Cambridge, UK, 1945).

Chant, C. *Austro-Hungarian Aces of World War 1* (Oxford, 2002).

Cole, L., and Unowsky, D. (eds.). *The Limits of Loyalty: Imperial Symbolism, Popular Allegiances, and State Patriotism in the Late Habsburg Monarchy* (Oxford, 2007).

Cornelius, D. *Hungary in World War II: Caught in the Cauldron* (New York, 2011).

Cornwall, M. *The Undermining of Austria-Hungary: The Battle for Hearts and Minds* (London, 2000).

Corum, J. S. *The Luftwaffe: Creating the Operational Air War, 1918–1940* (Lawrence, KS, 1997).

———. "Airpower Thought in Continental Europe between the Wars." In P. S. Meilinger (ed.), *The Paths of Heaven: The Evolution of Airpower Theory* (Maxwell Air Force Base, AL, 1997), pp. 151–182.

Corum, J. S., and Muller, R. R. *The Luftwaffe's Way of War: German Air Force Doctrine, 1911–1945* (Baltimore, 1998).

Csima, J. "Olaszország szerepe a Horthy-hadsereg fegyverkezésében (1920–1941)." *HK* 16/1 (1969): 289–312.

Csizmarik, V. I. "A Magyar Tanácsköztársaság Légiereje." *HK* 16/2 (1969): 350–387.

Csonkaréti, K., and Sárhidai, G. *Az Osztrák-Magyar Monarchia tengerészeti repülői, 1911–1918* (Budapest, 2010).

Czirók, Z. "A magyar repülőcsapatok 1918–1919. évi történetéhez." *HK* 122/3 (2009): 603–644.

———. "Az első légiháború Magyarország fellett-1919." *HK* 124/2 (2011): 335–361.

Davies, R. E. G. *A History of the World's Airlines* (London, 1964).

Deák, I. *Beyond Nationalism: A Social and Political History of the Habsburg Officer Corps, 1848–1918* (Oxford, 1990).

Dénes, E. "Igló bombázása." *Magyar Szárnyak* (1986): 5–7.

Denzel, M. A. *Handbook of World Exchange Rates, 1590–1914* (Farnham, Surrey, 2010).

Dienes, I. *A honfoglaló Magyarok* (Budapest, 1978).

Dombrády, L. *Hadsereg és politika Magyarországon, 1938–1944* (Budapest, 1986).

Dombrády, L., and Tóth, S. *A Magyar Királyi Honvédség, 1919–1945* (Budapest, 1987).

Drabek, Z. "Foreign Trade Performance and Policy." In M. C. Kaser and E. A. Radice (eds.), *The Economic History of Eastern Europe 1919–1975*. Vol. 1 (Oxford, 1985), pp. 379–531.

Dreisziger, N. F. "New Twist to an Old Riddle: The Bombing of Kassa (Košice), June 26, 1941." *Journal of Modern History* 44/2 (June 1972): 232–242.

Eby, C. D. *Hungary at War: Civilians and Soldiers in World War II* (University Park, PA, 1998).

Ellis, J., and Cox, M. *The World War I Databook: The Essential Facts and Figures for All the Combatants* (London, 2001).

"Endresz György." In *Magyar életrajzi lexikon, 1000–1990*, edited by Kenyeres Ágnes. Accessed Apr. 23, 2016. http://mek.oszk.hu/00300/00355/html.

Erickson, J. *The Road to Stalingrad* (London, 1975).

Farkas, M. "The Military Collapse of the Austro-Hungarian Monarchy, October 24 to November 3, 1918." In P. Pastor (ed.), *Revolutions and Interventions in Hungary and Its Neighbor States, 1918–1919* (Boulder, CO, 1988), pp. 11–23.

Fenyo, M. D. *Hitler, Horthy, and Hungary: German-Hungarian Relations, 1941–1944* (London, 1972).

Fritzsche, P. *A Nation of Fliers: German Aviation and the Popular Imagination* (Boston, 1992).

Fülöp, M., and Sipos, P. *Magyarország külpolitikája a XX. században* (Budapest, 1998).

Gaal, J. R. "Austro-Hungarian Air Corps, 1918–1920." *Air Classics* 14/9 (Sept. 1978): 75–81.

———. "Baptism of Fire." *Aero Album* (Winter 1972): 42–44.

———. "Bombers at Large." *Air Combat* 5/6 (Nov. 1977): 83–89.

———. "The Bombs of April." *Air Combat* 7/5 (Sept. 1979): 74–82.

———. "The Bridge over the River Bug." *Air Combat* 6/2 (Mar. 1978): 80–87.

Gellért, T. "Adalékok a magyar Polgári Demokratikus Forradalom és a Tanácsköztársaság Légierejének történetéhez." *HK* 12/3 (1965): 502–523.

"General Giulio Douhet: An Italian Apostle of Air Power." *Royal Air Force Quarterly* 7/1 (1936): 148.

Gibás, A. "A magyar óceánrepülés." *Aero Historia* (Aug. 1991): 2–8.

Gooch, J. *Mussolini and His Generals: The Armed Forces and Fascist Foreign Policy, 1922–1940* (Cambridge, UK, 2007).

Gosztony, P. "The Collapse of the Hungarian Red Army." In P. Pastor (ed.), *Revolutions and Interventions in Hungary and Its Neighbor States, 1918–1919* (Boulder, CO, 1988), pp. 69–79.

Grosz, P. M., Haddow, G., and Schiemer, P. *Austro-Hungarian Army Aircraft of World War One* (Mountain View, CA, 1993).

Gunston, B. *World Encyclopedia of Aero Engines* (Cambridge, UK, 1989).

Gyulai, I. E. *Honor and Duty: The Memoirs of Countess Ilona Edelsheim Gyulai, Widow of Vice-Regent Stephen Horthy of Hungary* (Lewes, East Sussex, 2005).

Hajdu, T. *The Hungarian Soviet Republic* (Budapest, 1979).

Hallion, R. P. *Taking Flight: Inventing the Aerial Age from Antiquity through the First World War* (New York, 2003).

Hangodi, L. "A M. Kir. Honvéd 4/I-es Nehézbombázó-Osztály története, 1936–1945." *HK* 116/1 (Mar. 2003): 144–163.

Harvey, A. D. "Bombing and the Air War on the Italian Front, 1915–1918." *Air Power History* 47/3 (Fall 2000): 34.

Hauner, M. "Military Budgets and the Armaments Industry." In M. C. Kaser and E. A. Radice (eds.), *The Economic History of Eastern Europe 1919–1975*. Vol. 2 (Oxford, 1985), pp. 49–116.

Hetés, T. "Gondolatok a magyar hadtörténet-felfogás alakulásáról." *HK* 16/2 (1969): 314–337.

Higham, R. *The Military Intellectuals in Britain, 1918–1939* (New Brunswick, NJ, 1966).

Hippler, T. "Democracy and War in the Strategic Thought of Giulio Douhet." In H. Strachan and S. Scheipers (eds.), *The Changing Character of War* (Oxford, 2011), pp. 167–183.

Holló, J. F. *A Galambtól a Griffmadárig: a magyar katonai repülés 100 éve* (Budapest, 2010).

Horváth, Cs. "A Magyar 2. Hadsereg Közelfelderítő Repülőszázadának működési rendszere a szabályzatok tükrében 1942 június-október." *HK* 107/2 (June 1994): 101–127.

Huntington, Samuel. *The Soldier and the State* (Cambridge, MA, 1957).

Jeszenszky, G. "Hungary through World War I and the End of the Dual Monarchy." In P. F. Sugar, P. Hanák, and T. Frank (eds.), *A History of Hungary* (Bloomington, IN, 1990), pp. 267–294.

Juhász, B. "The Inter-Allied Military Commission of Control and the Military

Control of Hungary between 1921 and 1927." *Hadtudományi Szemle* 5/1 (2012): 47–72.

———. "Olasz-Magyar vezénylések és tanulmányutak a két világháború között." *HK* 125/1 (2012): 133–174.

Juhász, Gy. *Hungarian Foreign Policy 1919–1945*. Translated by S. Simon and M. Kovács (Budapest, 1979).

Kálmán, K. *A magyar vezérkari tisztek kiképzése és továbbképzése az 1920–1944 közötti években* (Budapest, 1992).

Kasparek, J. "Poland's 1938 Covert Operations in Ruthenia." *East European Quarterly* 23/3 (Sept. 1989): 365–373.

Kelemen, A. "A bombázó iskolától az 1. önálló távol felderítő századig." *Magyar Szárnyak* (1981): 57–59.

Kennett, L. *The First Air War, 1914–1918* (New York, 1991).

Kenyeres, D. *Kecskeméti katonai repülés története kezdetektől a Gripenig* (Kecskemét, 2006).

Kerr III, J. L. "Against All Comers: Operations of the K.u.K. Luftfahrtruppen." *Cross and Cockade Journal* 15/4 (1974): 291–356.

Kertesz, S. D. *Diplomacy in a Whirlpool: Hungary between Nazi Germany and Soviet Russia* (Notre Dame, IN, 1953).

Kistelegdi, E. "A repülő akadémia története." In T. Rada (ed.), *A Magyar Királyi Honvéd Ludovika Akadémia és a testvérintézetek összefoglalt története*. Vol. 2. (Budapest, 2001), pp. 176–183.

Knox, M. *Hitler's Italian Allies: Royal Armed Forces, Fascist Regime, and the War of 1940–1943* (Cambridge, UK, 2000).

Kováts, L. *Sólymok, Héják, Nebulók: A Magyar Kir. Állami Vas-, Acél-, és Gépgyárak Repülőgépgyárának tevékenysége 1936–1944* (Budapest, 1990).

Kupiec-Weglinski, J. W. "The Siege of Przemysl, 1914–1915." *American Philatelist* (June 2012): 544–555. Also available at http://stamps.org/userfiles/file/AP /feature/Feature_06_12.pdf.

Macartney, C. A. *October Fifteenth: A History of Modern Hungary, 1929–1945*. 2 vols. (Edinburgh, 1957).

———. "Hungary's Declaration of War on the U.S.S.R. in 1941." In A. O. Sarkissian (ed.), *Studies in Diplomatic History and Historiography* (London, 1961), pp. 153–165.

MacIsaac, D. "Voices from the Central Blue: Theorists of Air Power." In P. Paret (ed.), *Makers of Modern Strategy from Machiavelli to the Nuclear Age* (Princeton, NJ, 1986), pp. 624–647.

Meilinger, P. S. "Alexander P. de Seversky and American Airpower." In P. S. Meilinger (ed.), *The Paths of Heaven: The Evolution of Airpower Theory* (Maxwell Air Force Base, AL, 1997), pp. 239–278.

———. "Giulio Douhet and the Origins of Airpower Theory." In P. S. Meilinger (ed.), *The Paths of Heaven: The Evolution of Airpower Theory* (Maxwell Air Force Base, AL, 1997), pp. 1–40.

Miszlay, Zs. "Az első magyar oceanrepülés," http://www.historia.hu/archivum /2002/0207miszlay.htm

Mócsy, I. "Hungary's Failed Strategic Surrender: Secret Wartime Negotiations with Britain." In N. Dreisziger (ed.) *Hungary in the Age of Total War (1938–1948)* (New York, 1998), pp. 85–106.

Morrow, J. H. *German Air Power in World War I* (Lincoln, NE, 1982).

———. "Defeat of the German and Austro-Hungarian Air Forces in the Great War, 1909–1918." In R. Higham and S. J. Harris (eds.), *Why Air Forces Fail: The Anatomy of Defeat* (Lexington, KY, 2006), pp. 99–134.

Moys, P. "Légiforgalmi irányításunk története (1920–1945)." Accessed Aug. 6, 2013. http://www.hungarocontrol.hu/download/81c2a8af5cc857a6b156789bbo 4fd059.pdf.

Mulder, R. "Magyar Aeroforgalmi Részvény Tarsaság—MAEFORT (1920–1921) and Magyar Légiforgalmi Részvény Tarsaság—MALERT (1922–1945)." European Airlines. Accessed Sept. 12, 2013. http://www.europeanairlines.no/wp -content/uploads/2010/06/A_Maefort_Malert_020209.pdf.

Nagy, V. "A 3. Hadsereg átkelés a Dunán és Belgrád elfoglalása 1915 október 6–10." *HK* 27/3 (1926): 310–322.

Nagyváradi, S., Szabó M. M., and Winkler, L. *Fejezetek a magyar katonai repülés történetéből* (Budapest, 1986).

Neulen, H. W. *In the Skies of Europe: Air Forces Allied to the Luftwaffe 1939–1945.* Translated by A. Vanags-Baginskis (Norfolk, 2005).

Niehorster, L. W. G. *The Royal Hungarian Army, 1920–1945* (Bayside, NY, 1998).

Nötel, R. "International Credit and Finance." In M. C. Kaser and E. A. Radice (eds.), *The Economic History of Eastern Europe 1919–1975.* Vol. 2 (Oxford, 1986), pp. 170–295.

Olasz, L. "Jugoszláv légitámadások Magyarország ellen 1941 áprilisában." *HK* 117/1 (Mar. 2004): 167–203.

———. "Lépések a honi légvédelem kiépítésére Magyarországon az 1920-as években." *HK* 122/3 (Sept. 2009): 635–676.

Ormay, J. "Kassai bombák: Tárgyi bizonyítékok szemtanúk." *Magyar Szárnyak* (1982): 86–90.

———. "Milyen gépek bombázhatták és milyen gépek nem bombázhatták Kassat?" *Magyar Szárnyak* (1984): 46–58.

———. "A Bustyaházai incidens." *Magyar Szárnyak* (1984): 68–72.

———. "Még egyszer a Kassai bombázásról." *HK* 105/3 (Sep. 1992), pp. 131–134.

Overy, R. J. *The Air War 1939–1945* (New York, 1981).

———. *The Bombing War: Europe 1939–1945* (London, 2013).

———. "Air Power in the Second World War: Historical Themes and Theories." In H. Boog (ed.), *The Conduct of the Air War in the Second World War* (Oxford, 1992), pp. 7–28.

Pagáts, P. "Légitámadás Pécs és Siklós ellen." *Aero Historia* (Aug. 1991): 9–13.

Palmer, S. W. *The Dictatorship of the Air: Aviation Culture and the Fate of Modern Russia* (Cambridge, UK, 2006).

Pastor, P. *Hungary between Wilson and Lenin: The Hungarian Revolution of 1918–1919 and the Big Three* (New York, 1976).

Péntek, R. "István Horthy's Election as Vice-Regent." In N. Dreisziger (ed.), *Hungary in the Age of Total War* (New York, 1998), pp. 73–84.

Peszke, M. A. "Poland's Military Aviation, September 1939: It Never Had a Chance." In R. Higham and S. J. Harris (eds.), *Why Air Forces Fail: The Anatomy of Defeat* (Lexington, KY, 2006), pp. 13–40.

Punka, G. *Hungarian Air Force* (Carrollton, TX, 1994).

———. and Sárhidai, Gy. *Magyar sasok: A Magyar Királyi Honvéd Légierő 1920–1945* (Budapest, 2006).

Radice, E. A. "General Characteristics of the Region between the Wars." In M. C. Kaser and E. A. Radice (eds.), *The Economic History of Eastern Europe 1919–1975*. Vol. 1 (Oxford, 1985), pp. 23–65.

———. "The Development of Industry." In M. C. Kaser and E. A. Radice (eds.), *The Economic History of Eastern Europe 1919–1975*. Vol. 2 (Oxford, 1986), pp. 416–451.

Ránki, Gy., and Tomaszewski, J. "The Role of the State in Industry, Banking and Trade." In M. C. Kaser and E. A. Radice (eds.), *The Economic History of Eastern Europe 1919–1975*. Vol. 2 (Oxford, 1986), pp. 3–48.

Réti, Gy. *Hungarian-Italian Relations in the Shadow of Hitler's Germany, 1933–40* (Boulder, CO, 2003).

Révész, T. *Repülőtér az Alpokalján: A szombathelyi katonai repülőtér története* (Budapest, 2009).

Romsics, I. *Hungary in the Twentieth Century*. Translated by T. Wilkinson (Budapest, 1999).

———. "The Social Basis of the Communist Revolution and of the Counterrevolutions in Hungary." In P. Pastor (ed.), *Revolutions and Interventions in Hungary and Its Neighbor States, 1918–1919* (Boulder, Col., 1988), pp. 157–168.

Rothenberg G. E. "Military Aviation in Austria-Hungary, 1893–1918." *Aerospace Historian*, Vol. 16 (1972), pp. 77–82.

———. *The Army of Franz Josef* (West Lafayette, IN, 1976).

———. "The Habsburg Army in the First World War: 1914–1918." In R. A. Kann, B. K. Király, and P. S. Fichtner (eds.), *The Habsburg Empire in World War I* (Boulder, CO, 1977), pp. 73–86.

Sakmyster, T. "Army Officers and Foreign Policy in Interwar Hungary, 1918–41." *Journal of Contemporary History* 10/1 (Jan. 1975): 19–40.

———. "The Search for a Casus Belli and the Origins of the Kassa Bombing." *Hungarian Studies Review* 10/1 (Spring 1983): 53–65.

———. *Hungary's Admiral on Horseback* (Boulder, CO, 1994).

———. "Gyula Gömbös and the Hungarian Jews, 1918–1936." *Hungarian Studies Review* 33/1–2 (2006): 157–168.

Scott-Hall, S. "The Sailplane Capabilities at the Wasserkuppe, 1935." *Royal Air Force Quarterly* 7/1 (Jan. 1936): 24–28.

Sganga, R., Tripodi, P. G., and Johnson, W. "Douhet's Antagonist: Amadeo Mecozzi's Alternative View of Air Power." *Air Power History* 58/2 (Summer 2011): 4–15.

Shirer, W. L. *The Rise and Fall of the Third Reich: A History of Nazi Germany* (New York, 1960).

Sisa, A. "A Magyar Királyi Honvéd Légierő olaszországi repülőgép-beszerzései." *HK* 115/4 (2002): 1050–1083.

Sondhaus, L. *Franz Conrad von Hötzendorf: Architect of the Apocalypse* (Boston, 2000).

Stahel, D. *Operation Barbarossa and Germany's Defeat in the East* (Cambridge, 2009).

Steiner, Z. *The Lights That Failed: European International History, 1919–1933* (Oxford, 2005).

Stenge, Cs. *Baptism of Fire: The First Combat Experiences of the Royal Hungarian Air Force and Slovak Air Force, March 1939* (Solihull, West Midlands, 2013).

Stone, N. "Army and Society in the Habsburg Monarchy, 1900–1914." *Past and Present* 33 (Apr. 1966): 95–111.

Strachan, H. *The First World War.* Vol. 1: *To Arms* (Oxford, 2001).

Sullivan, B. R. "Downfall of the Regia Aeronautica." In R. Higham and S. J. Harris (eds.), *Why Air Forces Fail: The Anatomy of Defeat* (Lexington, KY, 2006), pp. 135–176.

Szabó, M. M., *A Magyar Királyi Honvéd Légierő a második világháborúban* (Budapest, 1987).

———. *A Magyar Királyi Honvéd Légierő, 1938–1945: elméleti-technikai-szervezeti fejlődése és háborús alkalmazása* (Budapest, 1999).

Szabó, P. "Hungarian Soldiers in World War Two: 1941–1945." In L. Veszprémy and B. K. Királyi (eds.), *A Millennium of Hungarian Military History.* Translated by E. Arató (New York, 2002), pp. 441–484.

Szakály, S. "The Officer Corps of the Red Army." In P. Pastor (ed.), *Revolutions and Interventions in Hungary and Its Neighbor States, 1918–1919* (Boulder, CO, 1988), pp. 169–178.

———. *A magyar katonai felső vezetés, 1938–1945* (Budapest, 2001).

Thompson, M. *The White War: Life and Death on the Italian Front, 1915–1919* (New York, 2008).

Tőkés, R. *Béla Kun and the Hungarian Soviet Republic* (London, 1967).

Várdy, S. B. "The Impact of Trianon upon the Hungarian Mind." In N. Dreisziger (ed.), *Hungary in the Age of Total War (1938–1948)* (New York, 1998), pp. 27–48.

Vas, Z. *Horthy* (Budapest, 1981).

Vermes, G. "The October Revolution in Hungary: From Károlyi to Kun." In I. Völgyes (ed.), *Hungary in Revolution, 1919: Nine Essays* (Lincoln, NE, 1971), pp. 31–60.

Vesztényi, J. "A Magyar katonai repülés 1920–45." *Magyar Szárnyak*, 4/22 (1993): 205–224.

Young, R. J. "The Strategic Dream: French Air Doctrine in the Inter-War Period, 1919–39." *Journal of Contemporary History* 9/4 (Oct. 1974): 57–76.

Weinberg, G. L. *A World at Arms: A Global History of World War II* (Cambridge, 1994).

Wheeler-Bennett, J. W. *The Disarmament Deadlock* (London, 1934).

Woodhouse, J. R. *Gabriele D'Annunzio: Defiant Archangel* (Oxford, 1998).

Zeidler, M. *Ideas on Territorial Revision in Hungary, 1920–1945*. Translated by T .J. and H. DeKornfeld (Boulder, CO, 2007).

UNPUBLISHED THESES

Cain, A. C. "Neither Decadent, nor Stupid, nor Treasonous." PhD diss., Ohio State University, 2000.

Weaver, E. "Revision and Its Modes." DPhil thesis, Oxford University, 2008.

Index

Szentnémedy, Ferenc, 110–111, 119, 127;
    influenced by Clausewitz, 112–113,
    122; apostle of Douhet, 111, 113–114;
    translates *The War of 19__*, 114–118;
    translates *Air War 1936*, 118, 125–126;
    authors *Aviation*, 122–125; on active
    and passive defense, 128–130;
    extended debate with Gen
    Hellebronth, 130–137; and *MKSz*'s
    reach, 137–138
Szoják, Sándor, 222, 225
Szombathelyi, Ferenc, 220–221, 261,
    263, 266–267, 268, 269, 274, 276,
    283–285, 291
Sztójay, Döme, 192, 209, 219, 257, 284, 288

Tardieu, André, 159–160
Teleki, Pál, 76, 79, 170, 228, 230; appointed
    prime minister, 219; and Second
    Vienna Award, 231–232; opposition
    to invasion of Yugoslavia and suicide,
    242–244
37th Section, Aviation Department
    (Légügyi osztály), 44–45, 47, 67,
    74, 75, 212
Tisza, István, 17, 39n91
Trans-Europa Union, 90
Transoceanic Airmen's Congress, 167
Transylvania, 31, 47, 48, 92, 99–100, 231,
    233, 234, 256, 283
Trenchard, Sir Hugh, 117, 126
Trianon, Treaty of, 43, 45, 66, 68, 73, 87,
    92, 95, 102n20, 104n79, 106–107, 122,
    129, 152, 169–170, 183, 190, 211, 239; air
    clauses, 76, 81, 98, 143, 185, 212, 302;
    territorial losses, 77, 226, 300; public
    reaction to, 77–78: Articles 131
    and 132, 84; Article 111, 111; Article
    142, 145–146; effective end, 232, 234
Tusnád raid, 48

Újvidék, 25, 49
Ungarische Flugzeugfabrik AG (UFAG),
    20, 40n98, 46, 60, 65, 93, 151
unrestricted air warfare (korlátlan légi
    háború), 109, 117, 119, 123, 126, 129,
    131–135, 159, 240, 261, 299, 300
Uzelac, Emil, 15–16, 18–19, 21, 23, 24,
    34, 36

Vassel, Károly, 94, 152–153
Veesenmayer, Edmund, 289–290
Venice, 2, 32, 161–162
Versailles, Treaty of, 73, 82, 92, 171, 183
Vezérkarfőnökség (VKF). *See* General
    Staff
Vienna, 2, 3, 4, 5, 10, 13, 18, 22, 33, 44, 54, 56,
    63, 67, 89–90, 104n74, 192, 216,
    297n163
Vix, Fernand, 55–56, 71n48
Vörös, Géza, 122, 241, 249, 283
Vörös, János, 283, 289–290, 298n183
Vörös Repülőcsapat (VR), 53, 56, 58,
    61–68, 73, 75, 80, 111, 266, 299

War College. *See* Hadiakadémia
War Ministry: Austro-Hungarian, 11,
    18–19, 21, 35, 40n98; Italian, 109, 148;
    Prussian, 4
War of 19__, The, 110, 113–119, 125, 137
Wasserkuppe gliding rallies, 170–171
Wells, H. G., 109
Werth, Henrik, 107, 112, 208, 233, 244,
    248–253, 258, 263, 266–267, 269, 291,
    294n37
Wiener-Neustadt, 11, 33
Wollemann, István, 43, 58
world aviation records, 11

Zeppelin, Ferdinand Graf von, 3, 5,
    38n55

COLONEL STEPHEN RENNER is Professor of Strategy and Security Studies at the United States Air Force School of Advanced Air and Space Studies. He is a career A-10 pilot who commanded the 25th Fighter Squadron at Osan Air Base, Republic of Korea, and has deployed to Bosnia, Kuwait, Iraq, and Afghanistan. He holds a DPhil from Oxford, a Master of International Public Policy from Johns Hopkins SAIS, and studied at the Budapest Institute for Graduate International and Diplomatic Studies.

www.ingramcontent.com/pod-product-compliance
Lightning Source LLC
Chambersburg PA
CBHW070402100426
42812CB00005B/1609